ONE MAN, ONE MEDICINE, ONE HEALTH: THE JAMES H. STEELE STORY

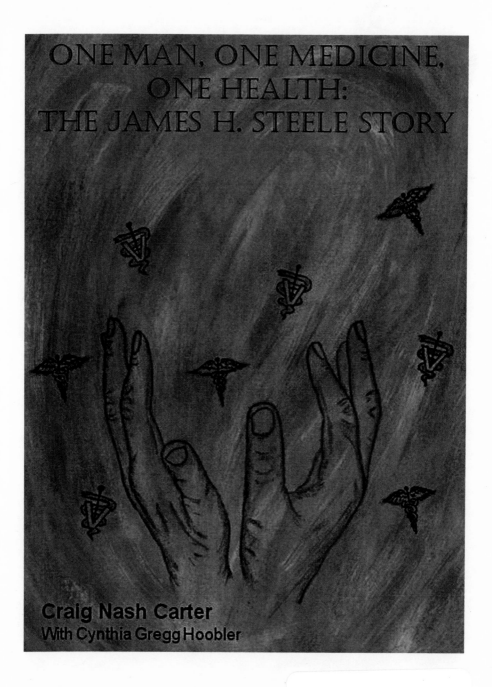

Craig Nash Carter
With Cynthia Gregg Hoobler

7-11-09

Russ Currier,

Thanks for your
contributions to vet
public health!!!

ONE MAN, ONE MEDICINE,
ONE HEALTH:

The James H. Steele Story

*Thanks for 40 years
of VPH progress,*

Jim Steele

by CRAIG NASH CARTER

with Cynthia Gregg Hoobler

Best wishes & thanks!

Cynthia Carter

ISBN: 1-4392-4004-3

EAN13: 9781439240045

DEDICATION

To veterinary medicine–the greatest profession in the world.

TABLE OF CONTENTS

FOREWORDS

Dr. Jim Steele: Leader, Teacher, Mentor, Colleague, Friend

James H. Steele was the leader in envisioning and participating in the establishing of Veterinary Public Health. He graduated from Michigan State University with a DVM in 1941 and a MPH from Harvard University in 1942. In, 1950 he was one of the participants in the First Expert Committee on Zoonoses meeting of the World Health Organization that defined Veterinary Public Health as 'the application of the veterinary medical arts to the resolution of community and public health problems'.

As we read this diary of Dr. James Steele, we learn that he became intrigued during his student days with diseases which invaded both animals and humans. Three years later, Jim asked the dean of his college whether he should go on in studies in human medicine; then listened to the response, "dedicate your career to public health under your own colors as a veterinarian, not under two flags". Those words became Jim's guiding light. During the almost seventy years of that career, Dr. Steele became known as the founder of Veterinary Public Health, more recently as the father of One Medicine, and currently as a founder of and advocate of 'One World, One Health, One Medicine.

Dr. Steele's professional years have joined him to health entities throughout the United States and the world. He established the Veterinary Public Health Division of the Centers for Disease Control and Prevention, served as its Chief Veterinary Officer, as Assistant Surgeon General of the US Public Health Service, and as Professor in the University of Texas School of Public Health. He has served as a consultant and advisor to essentially all agencies with ties to public health: CDC, WHO, PAHO, OIE, and congresses worldwide. He has been a member and in most cases a founder of associations in Veterinary Public Health and Epidemiology. Very important among these are the American College of Veterinary Preventive Medicine allied to the American Veterinary Medical Association, and the American Veterinary Epidemiology Society which presented him the very prestigious historic Gold Headed Cane award.

The entities and associations through which he has worked have integrated a veterinary medical focus into essentially all of health, a focus which is becoming ever more beneficial as world interactions enhance the knowledge of the inter-transmission of zoonotic and emerging diseases. Through publications, speeches, and organizing specialty associations and through reports of accomplishments, Dr. Steele has influenced developing veterinary education curricula. His passion has been pivotal in preparing, recruiting, motivating and assisting veterinarians in the development of veterinary public health.

Dr. Steele is a knowledgeable professional speaker and scientific writer. He is a competent and exciting teacher, developing his lectures, clinical laboratories and guidance applying his practical knowledge and experience. In his CDC days, the veterinarians he recruited into the US Public Health Service Epidemiologic Intelligence Service brought Veterinary Public Health into State Public Health Departments, enhanced it in CDC and practiced it in clinical services. Many of these EIS officers became teachers of veterinary public health in colleges of veterinary medicine.

Dr. Steele's career has centered around developing veterinary public health. He has been the pivotal leader in developing the cadre of public health veterinarians. His extensive knowledge and investigation of zoonotic and vector borne diseases, environmental diseases, food borne diseases, and as world experience continued, of emerging diseases have formed the base for his action. Through partnership with the human health professions and professional team development, he has enhanced knowledge of animal and human disease epidemiology, prevention, and control, and laid foundations for their eradication. His prodigious knowledge and professional team participation has led to health promotion at human, animal, avian and environmental levels and to most efficient and effective application of control measures. Recognizing societal, animal population and ecological differences, he has emphasized studies and development of community based approaches in prevention and control. Laboratory findings and support, and scientific evaluations of measures and outcomes have been critical to control.

As one of the eight young veterinarians in the first Epidemic Intelligence Service training program at CDC in 1954, we early recruits were mentored by Dr. Steele. For me, this has extended into a career-long participation in veterinary public health, first in years of Christian mission at Silliman University in the southern Philippines, in many countries with World Health Organization and other international associations, and in developing a veterinary public health academic and research program at Iowa State University.

As a principal EIS trainer; Dr. Steele led me into laboratory applications, and stimulated me to take advanced studies in epidemiology of infectious diseases. Dr. Steele's principles guided me to work with the university and hospital, and governmental entities in the Philippines in the development of a comprehensive public health laboratory for diagnosis and surveillance of animal and human diseases, and for licensure for vaccine production. That early EIS training under Dr. Steele helped prepare me for efforts in halting human cholera through diagnosis, environmental measures and vaccine development in the Philippines, in an extensive program of rabies control in dogs adapted to the local tropical environments in Southeast Asia and Latin America, and in a comprehensive southern Philippine area dengue control through environmental action against vector mosquitoes. At Iowa State University, his example led me to develop an academic Veterinary Public Health teaching, research and food safety program. This progressed through our collaborative textbook writing, interaction at professional meetings, consultation and occasional guest lectures Dr. Steele continued to influence my teaching and research, and WHO and USDA consultancies, implementing programs that ring familiar with many of Dr. Steele's emphases.

Today, as One World, One Health, One Medicine becomes a comprehensive concept binding all of public health together, we continue to press forward with Dr. James H. Steele.

George W. Beran, DVM, PhD, LHD
President, American Veterinary Epidemiology Society

Standing on the Shoulders of a Giant

The renown scientist, Sir Isaac Newton, wrote in a letter to Robert Hooke in 1675 that "If I have seen further, then it is by standing on the shoulders of giants." In other words, we often develop our future intellectual pursuits and gain great insights by understanding the works and ideas created by notable and special thinkers who have preceded us.

Those of us who have had the good fortune of knowing Dr. Jim Steele and who have interacted with him over the years are initially taken by his physical presence (Jim stands about 6' 6" with an infectious and booming laugh) but then are quickly impressed and spellbound with being in the presence of a true intellectual giant. Through his vision, genius and lifetime of exceptional experiences and work, we have truly been able to see further and expand our horizons and possibilities in veterinary public health because of this giant among our peers.

Dr. Steele's life is replete with accomplishment, transformational leadership, and exceptional public service that have helped to define contemporary public health and the role of veterinarians working across all segments of the health sciences. Jim's ground-breaking work and tireless advocacy of veterinary public health has enabled all of us who have followed him to view public health with greater scope, clarity, and sense of possibilities.

As a past dean of the College of Veterinary Medicine at Michigan State University, I was always especially pleased to acknowledge that Jim was a graduate of the college and member of the class of 1941. The experiences and encouragement that he received at Michigan State was influential and helped shape Jim's career and his life's work in public health and his interest in zoonoses. Both the college and university have given Jim distinguished alumni awards and I have fond memories of walking across campus with Jim, listening to his stories about the brucellosis lab and reliving his life during these special years.

I have engaged in many other enjoyable and insightful conversations with Dr. Steele over the years and like so many others have been inspired by his work, challenged by his ideas and probing questions and dazzled by his exceptional mind that, somehow, is just as sharp and probing in this tenth decade of life as it was many decades earlier. To some, Jim's presence might seem to be overwhelming or even intimidating; however, actually the opposite is true. This gregarious and larger-than-life personality has been a mentor for a countless number of people, including myself, and an exceptional visionary always working to create new opportunities and a special future for all of us who have followed his lead.

Jim Steele's illustrious career has sown seeds for so many of us; I have intently watched the seeds grow, spread, and then seed themselves anew. Today, we are enjoying a renaissance in One Health and are thankful for Jim's leadership and helping to sow the seeds of the concept many decades ago. I am indebted to Dr. Craig Carter for his passion and skill in giving us this superb biography and hope that, through his efforts and this book, others will now get to know and admire Jim like I have, and will be inspired toward a career in public health. To do so, will lead to a life of significance and meaning for the next generation of followers and will also honor the man on whose shoulders we have all been able to see further and improve public health for so many.

Lonnie King, DVM PhD

Director, National Center for Zoonotic,
Vector-Borne and Enteric Diseases

CDC, Atlanta, GA

Jim Steele: As I Have Known Him

My longtime friendship with Jim Steele began with our first meeting at the Officer's Club, Fort Amadar, Panama Canal Zone in 1957. In that era, Panama seemed to be a crossroad for many international medical science celebrities as was and is, Dr. Steele fifty-two years later. He was accompanied by Dr. Robert G. Matheney, Director of Veterinary Services for the Panama Canal government. Dr. Matheney had recently received his Master's of Public Health from Michigan State University, Jim's alma mater. These two raconteurs provided for a lively and informative evening. I was then a Major in the U.S. Army Veterinary Corps assigned to the U.S. Army mission to the Republic of Panama.

One of Jim's earlier investigations had been with Dr. Karl Habel of Rockefeller fame, into the 1946 outbreak of Eastern Equine Encephalitis (EEE) in Panama. Jim recounted for us the excitement and difficulties of overseas investigative studies. I was able to capitalize on this information a year later when I became involved in the laboratory diagnosis and studies of a recurrence of EEE in Panama. This began my direct and indirect professional relationship with Dr. Steele. During my service in Panama, colleagues from the U.S. Public Health Service (USPHS) Middle America Research Unit, Canal Zone and I identified encephalomyocarditis (EMC) virus infection in a Panama swine herd, the first such evidence of the natural infection of domesticated animals with this organism. Dr. Steele, ever alert to new development in zoonotic diseases, invited me to write a chapter on EMC for the CRC Handbook Series in Zoonoses for which he was the Editor-In-Chief.

In May, 1966, I called on Dr. Steele at his home in Atlanta, Georgia. I was assigned to the 9th Medical Laboratory which was staging at Fort McPherson, Georgia prior to our departure for the Republic of Vietnam (RVN). It was a Sunday afternoon and I was among several guests. Jim's home was a Mecca for distinguished and aspiring public health investigators visiting the CDC laboratories in Atlanta. Mrs. Steele, Brigitte, was a generous and accommodating hostess who catered to Jim's vast array of friends. Again, Dr. Steele provided me firsthand knowledge of rabies, plague, and other zoonotic diseases in Southeast Asia. He is a walking, talking encyclopedic resource of national and international zoonotic disease issues. Amazingly, too, he is a personal acquaintance of so many American and foreign authorities in the field. His recollection of events and people is remarkable to this day. Following my return from Vietnam, we met occasionally at national meetings and conferences. These were always pleasant and enlightening reunions. We share humbly our membership in that unique club of veterinary generals and admirals. Given Jim's impressive stature, he wears the uniform well.

I am so very honored to have been selected a Diplomate of the American Veterinary Epidemiology Society, a distinguished organization founded by K.F.

Meyer and James H. Steele. Later, I became a recipient of the Meyer-Steele Gold-Headed Cane Award which honors these two icons of veterinary public health. I treasure this award as I have known both men.

For many years, Jim and I have been regular correspondents, engaging in spirited telephone conversations. I always enjoy these interludes as occasions of professional relaxation. Jim's phenomenal memory assisted me in preparing the history of the first fifty years of the American College of Veterinary Preventive Medicine of which he was a charter member. The College, then the American Board of Veterinary Public Health, was approved by the AVMA in 1951 along with the American College of Veterinary Pathologists as the first officially recognized veterinary specialties. Jim, as the first secretary, and one of two charter members yet alive recalled for me with great precision dates, places, discussions and personalities associated with those seminal years of the College. He imparted life to the script and we colleagues are forever grateful for his distinctive input to our early history.

The history and ascendancy of veterinary public health in the U.S. and internationally over the last half of the 20th century and the early 21st century closely parallels the extensive professional career of Dr. Steele. He is a "man of many seasons" having worked and played in the very best sense of these words longer than any peer or other distinguished veterinary public health specialist entering the new millennium.

I, among many, have benefited from our alliance, his numerous publications, remarkable memory, wisdom and guidance. Like the battery-operated Energizer rabbit, he just keeps going and going. If not speaking, he is writing. He is the everlasting advocate for improved measures in food safety—many thanks Jim!

Tom Murnane, DVM, Brigadier General, U.S. Army, Retired

Jim Steele: A Father of Veterinary Public Health

Veterinary public health has emerged as a discipline of great significance in protecting the food supply of the world and zoonoses control. Dr. James Steele, widely known and recognized as the father of veterinary public health has been instrumental in promoting work in this area for more than half a century. Information presented in this book appropriately outlines the evolution of important advances to which Dr. Steele has made major contributions. Each year there is an increase in the number of publications on diseases of zoonotic importance. Therefore, scientists and allied health professionals must rely on specialists to keep pace with the value of new information. This text serves a very important purpose as it presents relevant knowledge in the field of veterinary public health in a manner that will serve as a reference in the future for investigators in research and administrators of regulatory programs as well as students in academic programs.

Literature reviews of a subject are of limited value except when a trained specialist can critically analyze the worth of each contribution based on his own experience. Dr. Steele was highly qualified to conduct such reviews as he made numerous original contributions and has been involved as a consultant to national and international agencies, including the World Health Organization, United Nations, Organization International of Epizootics and Pan American Health Organization. He was responsible for early epidemiological investigations on brucellosis, tuberculosis, rabies and trichinosis. Dr. Steele has been involved in policy making and in the promulgation of regulations designed to prevent, control and eradicate diseases of humans and animals. Early in his career, he was responsible for establishing the Veterinary Medical Corp of the United States Public Health Service. It should be emphasized that information presented herein has been critically summarized and organized by Dr. Craig Carter so that it will be useful to physicians, veterinarians and allied health professionals in developing and industrialized countries around the globe. This contribution will be a highly regarded reference for scientists for many future generations.

Charles O. Thoen, DVM, PhD
Professor of Microbiology and Preventive Medicine
College of Veterinary Medicine
Iowa State University, Ames, Iowa

PREFACE

Thanks to Dr. Konrad Eugster, I met Dr. Jim Steele a few months after I received my veterinary degree at Texas A&M University in 1981. He delivered a fascinating lecture on his current activities around the world to a large audience of professors and scientists. Now I can truly say that I enjoyed my classes in veterinary public health and epidemiology immensely during veterinary school. But that night, Dr. Steele opened my eyes to the sheer enormity of it all. Later, Jim graciously agreed to serve on my PhD committee. This was quite a blessing as I not only had a living, veterinary legend to guide and mentor me on my committee; it also provided me with many more opportunities to visit with and to learn about this amazing man.

Jim and I attended the World Veterinary Congress in Rio de Janeiro in August 1991. By that time, I was totally in awe of Jim's career and accomplishments. One morning we were out on the hotel veranda eating breakfast and I asked him if his life story had been written. He informed me that although he had put down some summary papers about his career, he had not written an autobiography, and no one had yet offered to write his biography. I made a commitment right there that I would find a way to make this happen. Somehow, someway, some day, Jim Steele's life history had to be captured for present and future generations.

I immediately questioned if I was personally qualified to take this on. I had done a lot of technical and other writing and considered myself a decent essayist. But I have never written a biography or anything close to it. Not being sure how to proceed, I decided to begin interviewing Jim to get things moving. At the same time, I made a pact with myself that if a professional writer materialized during the project who wanted to finish the job, I would stand down. One did appear about ten years ago but, unfortunately, he expected a large sum of money to do the job. That strengthened my resolve to finish the book. I felt that I needed to give something back to the profession that has been so good to me. Jim and I agreed that if the biography ever made it into print, any funds generated by sales would go direct to his endowment at the University of Texas, School of Public Health.

That said, I want to apologize to you up front, Jim. I am certain that your story could have been told much more eloquently if done by someone with the right skill set and experience. There is no question that you deserve the best. All I can say is I consider it the highest honor to have had this opportunity. I promise you that I have given you my very best effort in this undertaking. And I sincerely hope that you are pleased with the outcome.

I need to state what this biography is *not*. First, it is not an exhaustive compendium of Jim's life, career and accomplishments. Capturing that would have taken three times the effort and would have resulted in a three or four volume book set. Secondly, I can't state that everything in this biography is absolutely correct. While I worked hard to verify all the facts, I know that I didn't get them all. Most of the people Jim interacted with early in his career are gone. The details surrounding some of the situations described in the biography were never documented. Finally, this biography does not identify every significant person he has interacted with by name over the years. The same thing goes for the pictures in the middle of the book. There are simply too many of you! Please accept my heartfelt apologies to those who are not mentioned or seen in the book.

Now I want to say what the biography *is*. It is the result of eighteen years of personal interviews with Jim, over two hundred of them. These occurred in his home in Houston, my homes in Texas and Kentucky, hotel rooms all over the country, and even driving down the road to meetings. The majority of the biography is Jim's story in his own words. I have tried to interleave his tale with information about his family, the environment he grew up, studied and worked in, and the relevant history that predated Jim and which accumulated along the path of his career. I have tried to communicate his dreams, aspirations, major challenges, successes, and adventures from birth up to the time of his retirement from CDC, and a little beyond. The biography is also the result of the careful study of Jim's personal files and correspondence, meeting reports, and favorite books in his extensive library. Lastly, it is the product of scanning through hundreds of photographs to decide which ones would be included in the book.

For those who know Jim quite well, I hope that this will reveal a few novel facts and stories that you were not aware of. For those who have little or no knowledge of Jim Steele's life and career, I hope that his story provides you with the same level of awe and inspiration as it has for me.

ACKNOWLEDGEMENTS

This project all began with my being afforded the profound opportunity to attend the Texas A&M College of Veterinary Medicine. I thank Drs. Richard Nelson and Ralph Brock for letting me ride with them on farm calls in Texas to get prepared for veterinary school. Much gratitude to Dr. Roger Feldman for being my first mentor and advisor, Dr. George Shelton, Dean of the College at the time, for his guidance and leadership, for Dr. Bill McCulloch, Chair of my Master's degree Committee, Dr. Leon Russell for Chairing my PhD Committee and Dr. Robert Crandell for his encouragement and assistance toward becoming board certified in veterinary preventive medicine (ACVPM). Thanks to Dr. Tommy Thomas for encouraging me to take a commission in the US Air Force Reserves and for Dr. Murle Bailey's mentoring toward my commissioning and transfer over to the US Army Reserves. I also want to thank Dr. Konrad Eugster for believing in me and launching my career in veterinary diagnostic medicine in Texas and Deans Scott Smith, Nancy Cox and Dr. Lenn Harrison for bringing me to the University of Kentucky where I now have the dream job of my career.

So many individuals contributed to the successful completion of this project. Much credit goes to Margaret "Peggy" Coleman, Jim's past administrative assistant at the University of Texas, School of Public Health for her careful transcription of dozens of tapes of the early interviews. I want to thank Ms. S. L. Dickerson of Texas A&M University for her beautiful artwork on the cover of the book, painstakingly drawn from pictures of Jim's hands, and for her careful editing, review and transcribing. I offer much appreciation to Drs. Robert Dunlop and David Williams for producing *Veterinary Medicine, an Illustrated History*. This wonderful volume gave me rich historical material for chapter one, which sets the stage for Jim's life and career. Thanks to Dr. Russ Currier for providing reprints of hard-to-find articles and for helping to coordinate Jim's book-signing activities. My appreciation goes out to Dr. Leon Russell who assisted me in locating early literature on rabies and locating some of Dr. Steele's papers that were donated to Texas A&M University. I also want to thank the many skilled staff at Amazon.com Book Surge department who worked so diligently to help me get this book in print in time for Jim's book-signing at the ACVPM booth in Seattle at the AVMA meeting, July, 2009.

My heartfelt gratitude goes to Dr. George Beran, BG (Ret.) Tom Murnane and Dr. Edward Arvizo, for their extensive review and editing of the manuscript. Their collective cultural and historical knowledge was invaluable in this effort. I also want to express my appreciation to Dr. George Beran, Dr. Lonnie King, Dr. Charlie Thoen, and BG (Ret.) Tom Murnane for their forewords. These add a wonderful dimension to Jim's biography. I also wish to say thanks to the many donors which made it possible for us to publish this book and to have it available on Amazon.com for sale anywhere in the world. The generous donations came from the ACVPM Board of Directors under the leadership of Dr. John Herbold; various ACVPM Diplomates; the EIS Alumni Association and one very special individual who wished to remain anonymous. Please know that your investment in this worthwhile project will live on. The full royalty from every book sale will go to Dr. Steele's endowment at the University of Texas, School of Public Health.

Very special thanks go to Dr. Cynthia Hoobler for her tireless efforts to assist with interviewing, writing, editing, gathering photos and every other detail imaginable. I simply could not have completed this project without her. Loving thanks to my wife, Ronda, for her unswerving support, patience, and understanding during the course of this long and demanding project. I also thank her for driving the car during our rolling interviews of Dr. Steele!

I extend exceptionally warm thanks to Jim's wife, Brigitte Meyer Steele, for dictating and editing the moving story of her youth and of her rich life experiences and adventures with Jim. Lastly, I thank you, Jim, for your outstanding leadership, inspiration, and bountiful contributions which have resulted in saving countless lives and improving the quality of life for people and animals throughout the world. Thank you also for donating your personal time and effort to help record this amazing story for future generations.

One Man, One Medicine, One Health

CHAPTER 1:
EVERYTHING BEFORE JIM STEELE

Depending on whom we listen to, our solar system, including planet Earth, was formed as a result of some remarkable galactic events some 4.5 billion years ago. It all began as a hot, rotating, gaseous mass, slowly cooling into a mixed solid and liquid state. As temperatures dropped the rains began, lasting tens of thousands of years. Contemporary evolutionary theories generally agree that free-ranging chemicals on our newly birthed planet combined to form the so-called pre-biotic, primordial soup, which included simple inorganic—and later, organic—molecular structures. Amino acids were formed with the help of the energy of lightning and fell to the sea. Scientists postulate that some of the early moieties may have been of extra-terrestrial origin. These structures and others led to the formation of proto-cellular units. Simple molecules began to form structures which combined to form cells protected by a cell membrane.

What kind of world led to RNA, a molecule capable of coding for its own creation? We may never know exactly. Molecular and cellular systems learned to evolve. This probably occurred in warm ponds and deep-sea hydrothermal vents. The earliest evidence of life may be found in Australia. There, sedimentary structures can be found that resemble blue-green algae. Did photosynthesis exist that far back? Early life was likely a mass of microbes living in sulfur-charged bodies of water. Five hundred million years later, algae and bacteria were well developed. They were the precursors of all plant and animal life.

By around 1.5 billion years BC, the collective activity of these processes began to make the planet habitable. Multi-cellular organisms appeared 1.2 billion years ago, followed by sea and land plants about 450 million years back, and finally, the invasion of animals on land at around 350 million years in the past. Amphibians were the first to roam, followed by reptiles, bugs and beetles. The dinosaurs appeared 325 million years ago, represented by the brontosaurus, the stegosaurus, and tyrannosaurus rex. The skies saw pterodactyls with wing spans of twenty-five feet. Suddenly, about 70 million years ago, they disappeared. Scientists are still debating the cause.

At the same time, the continents were in flux. Ice ages came and went. Soon, reptiles produced their successful descendants, the birds. Mammals developed relatively quickly from that time up to 20 million years ago, yielding the first live young. The origin of primates is a little fuzzier, with few fossils to be found and studied. Primitive monkeys probably rose about 20 million years ago, leading to the human-like Ramapithecus at about 14 million years back and then Australopithecus about 5 million years ago, cradled in Africa. As temperatures fluctuated, hippos swam in the Thames and lions lived as far north as Yorkshire, England. About 500,000 years ago, *Homo erectus* became widespread in Asia, Africa and Europe followed by *Homo sapiens* 250,000 years later. The Neanderthal man, a variant of *Homo sapiens*, disappeared about 70,000 years ago. Around 35,000 years ago, modern humans emerged as *Homo sapiens sapiens*. Roughly 10,000 years ago, the ice finally retreated for the last time, making planet Earth much friendlier for animals and humans.

Man's link to animals began with hunting for food. Prehistoric art depicting many species of animals was found in 1994 in a cavern known as Chauvet Cave in southern France. The artwork there is estimated to be 20,000 years old. There are drawings of rhinoceros, lions, hyenas, leopards, panthers, bison, elephants, deer, horses, bears and owls. Cro-Magnon man, an early *Homo sapiens* specimen, was a hunter-gatherer. He made tools and crude weapons, especially spears that could be used for hunting large animals. Paleolithic art illustrating hunting scenes has also been found in Spain, Africa, and other parts of the world. In the New World, large projectiles have been found between the ribs of an Ice Age mammoth near Clovis, New Mexico. The Clovis hunters are thought to have hunted at watering holes. Their descendants became avid bison hunters.

What appear to be "butcher marks" on bones of horses and reindeer are evidence of early meat processing in the Paleolithic era leading up to roughly 15,000 years ago. One might question when man began to suspect food-borne illness and zoonoses. Paleopathologists have found evidence of animal disease by studying skeletal remains. Lesions seen include fractures and healed fractures, luxations, mandibular abscesses, periodontitis, osteomyelitis, dental injuries and anomalies. Periosteal exostosis, a signature of infection with *Treponema* organisms, was observed in the skeleton of a short-faced bear discovered in Indiana. The skeletal remains of a Columbian mammoth in Utah dated back 10,000 years. The mammoth was estimated to be about sixty-five years old at the time of death and had lesions of osteoporosis and arthritis.

Early domestication of animals probably began about 10,000 years ago. But animal agriculture had its true beginnings at the end of the Mesolithic era, about 6,000 years ago. People began a transition from hunting to farming. Travel with herds of cattle, sheep and goats minimized the uncertainty of the availability of food. At about the same time, the domestication of the horse in Russia and China yielded a powerful tool of warfare. Around 1000 BC, the Chinese invented aquaculture and were soon stocking ponds with carp. In 300 BC in south and southwest Asia, ruminants and donkeys were domesticated and raised for food and beasts of burden near the great river regions including the Indus, Nile, Tigris and Euphrates. Hindus thought that cows were sacred and should not be killed and eaten. Elephants and camels were trained for battle. Early Greek civilizations learned to use the oxen to plow the ground. Ruminants and pigs were ceremonially sacrificed.

The Mesopotamian literature of around 2300 BC describes an early cattle doctor or *azuanshe*. The presumed cause of disease was spiritual demons, and healing was thought to be accomplished through a combination of exorcism, medication and meditation. The Kahun papyrus of Egypt, dated 1900 BC, lists large and small animal diseases along with some systematic veterinary procedures and treatments. Early Egyptians could have had a crude understanding of vector-borne diseases as there is evidence that they used nets to prevent mosquito bites. Or possibly they just didn't like to get bit. Egyptians also pioneered the concept of pet dogs and cats. Some were even mummified.

Famous Greek philosophers and scientists and their students helped to form the beginnings of investigative science and the art of medicine. Aristotle, a student of Plato, worked diligently to categorize the animal kingdom. Scientists began to perform animal and human dissections to better understand the secrets of life. Aristotle was one of the first to compare the anatomy and physiology of people and animals, forming the basis for comparative medicine. Galen would later expand on his work. Hippocrates' work fashioned the basis of modern human and veterinary medicine around 400 B.C.

The Romans were enamored with horses and cattle. They developed spectator sports and circuses through the use of animals, including chariot racing. Pelagonius of Rome may have been the world's first racetrack veterinarian. Marcus Terentius Varro of Rome studied and wrote about "invisible organisms" that he suspected were the cause of animal diseases. Much later, after the Roman Empire was divided and reunited by Constantine in the third century AD, the threat of war catalyzed the need for veterinarians like Apsyrtos who could help maintain the health of horses. He described conditions such as volvulus, colic, and stomach rupture in the horse. He even linked laminitis with overeating.

The unforgiving desert environment of early, nomadic Arab cultures created a natural symbiosis between animals and people for transportation and food. Over time, horses and camels came to be worshiped. Much of the early veterinary care was focused on these animals. To be sure, their expert horsemanship and veterinary abilities enabled the Arabs to make many successful conquests. The Dark Ages saw a series of invasions on horseback by the Britons, Normans, Turks and Arabs. Horseshoes were invented. The late medieval Europeans made great advances in agriculture, medicine, and science. One great example is the comparative studies of the pig conducted at Salerno in the twelfth century AD Soon, veterinary care for birds of prey and hunting dogs became a priority. The fields of veterinary pharmacology and surgery were born.

By the sixteenth century, the art and science of anatomy of domestic animals made great strides with the contributions of Leonardo da Vinci, Albrecht Dürer and others. John Fitzherbert published his famous *Boke of Husbandry* in 1523, covering diseases of the horse, cattle and sheep. Hieronymus Fracastorius of Verona defined the idea of "contagium" to explain how disease is transmitted using the fundamentals of epidemiology, also in the sixteenth century. William Harvey postulated his explanation of cardiovascular circulation of blood in the seventeenth century. Veterinary scientists of the time such as Michael Harward of Ireland characterized many infectious diseases of animals. Francesco Redi's work at the University of Pisa helped to birth veterinary parasitology. In 1662, John Graunt, an English haberdasher, published a book entitled *The Nature and Political Observations Made Upon the Bills of Mortality*. This work is one of the first to utilize systematically collected medical data to calculate disease incidence, helping to launch the field of modern epidemiology.

Moving into the eighteenth century, James Clark of Edinburgh, Scotland made great contributions on the shoeing of horses, disease prevention, veterinary physiology and pathology. In addition, he may have been one of the first veterinarians concerned about the welfare of animals. At this time, epizootics were ravaging Europe. Diseases such as rinderpest were decimating animal agriculture, leading to a plethora of public health issues. Governments and educated people of the time decided that effective measures must be developed to prevent and manage such disease outbreaks. This stimulated more interest and work in comparative medicine and experimental physiology, pathology, and anatomy and led to a whole new approach to the concept of diseases in both people and animals during the Enlightenment or Age of Reason. The first recorded rabies epidemic occurred in Virginia in 1753 followed by yellow fever in Philadelphia tied to Haitian immigrants. This led to the first nationally supported quarantine programs.

Through a complex political process, the first veterinary school in the world was established in Lyon, France in 1791. It was later named the Royal Veterinary School. Formalized veterinary education was born. This was followed by the development of other veterinary schools and colleges around the globe. These events also stimulated great advances in animal agriculture, not the least of which was livestock advancement through selective breeding. The famous breeds of domestic food animals came into being. This underscored the need for veterinary care to assure adequate nutrition, care and management of the animals to keep them healthy until they reached market age.

The war against animal diseases was underway. Veterinary historians estimate that rinderpest was responsible for the death of 200 million head of cattle during the eighteenth century. These outbreaks continued into the nineteenth century. When rinderpest entered Europe from Russia in the 1850s, J.B. Simonds of the London Veterinary College was asked to investigate. He wanted to stop the movement of animals, but many still did not believe in the theory of contagion. This outbreak stimulated the Britons to reexamine the miasma theory of disease. In the nineteenth century, the field of microbiology emerged with the leadership of Pasteur and Koch along with many other medical and veterinary scientists like Daniel Salmon and his brilliant research assistant, Theobald Smith. Their early work with anthrax, tuberculosis, salmonellosis and clostridial organisms paved the way toward the full understanding of the etiology of infectious diseases.

The causative agents of typhoid, streptococcal, staphylococcal and pneumococcal infections and many others were identified before the end of the nineteenth century. The science of disinfection and aseptic surgery evolved quickly. In 1887, David Bruce identified *Brucella melitensis* as the cause of brucellosis in human patients who had died of the disease. Subsequently, Bernard Bang discovered the causative agent of bovine brucellosis. In 1896, this bacterium was named *Brucella abortus*. Next came the realization that all infectious diseases were not of bacterial origin. Further research by Chamberland and others identified smaller "filterable" infectious agents such as viruses and mycoplasma.

The rational next step was to facilitate disease prevention. The Chinese had experimented successfully with smallpox vaccination of young children in the sixteenth century. Edward Jenner's work in the late eighteenth century demonstrated that the agent of cowpox could be used to protect people from smallpox infection. Pasteur learned to attenuate the *Pasteurella* agent of fowl cholera by serial passage of in vitro cultures. Similarly, he learned to attenuate the rabies virus to successfully vaccinate people and dogs. Cellular and humoral mechanisms of immune defense were elucidated in the late nineteenth and early twentieth centuries. Paul Ehrlich recognized that antigens generated specific antibody responses from white cells. At this time, research was being conducted around the world to better understand the role of vectors in the transmission of disease and in the understanding of blood parasites to include diseases like trypanosomiasis, Tyzzer's disease, theileriasis, and piroplasmosis.

The first documented transmission of a disease from animals to man, trichinosis, was made by Friedrich Zenker, a pathologist, in 1860. In 1862, Dr. John Gamgee, a veterinarian in the United Kingdom, was appointed to look into the livestock industries. He found that up to 20% of animals consumed by humans were not healthy. These findings and others stimulated global interest in food safety and meat inspection. In 1891, he and Dr. James Law, a veterinary graduate of Edinburgh Veterinary College in Scotland, compiled the *General and Descriptive Anatomy of the Domestic Animals*. Dr. Law later became a professor of veterinary medicine at Cornell University. His work on bovine tuberculosis and foot and mouth disease made him a legendary leader in the field of veterinary public health.

As a result of the outstanding work of these leaders and others, rudimentary laboratories began appearing in slaughter facilities in the 1880s. Veterinarians soon became recognized as the subject matter experts in the field of food safety through pre-mortem and post-mortem inspection. Robert von Ostertag, a German veterinarian, wrote the early seminal textbooks on animal hygiene in the 1890s. In his books, he challenged veterinarians to embrace their new role in public health through animal hygiene. *The Jungle* written by socialist Upton Sinclair uncovered deplorable conditions for workers and totally unacceptable hygienic conditions in Chicago packing houses. This book compelled President Theodore Roosevelt to work with Congress to pass the Pure Food and Drug Act of 1906, further stimulating the field of food safety and hygiene.

Swiss veterinarian, Dr. Karl Friedrich Meyer, was a true pioneer in the field of zoonotic disease research. After he completed a PhD in microbiology at the University of Zurich and the curriculum at the veterinary school in Bern, he worked with Dr. Arnold Theiler in South Africa to work on hemoprotozoal diseases such as theileriosis, a tick-transmitted disease of cattle also known as East Coast Fever. During his research of malaria, he contracted the disease but was successfully treated. After a three-year stint at the University of Pennsylvania, he joined the Hooper Foundation for Medical Research at the University of California in 1915. He stayed on the faculty there for forty years studying zoonotic diseases almost exclusively. Dr. Meyer elucidated the risk of botulism to humans, identified the etiology of western equine encephalitis, and became an expert on diseases such as plague, typhoid, and brucellosis. He discovered the cause of psittacosis and helped develop a treatment for treating turkeys and pet birds utilizing tetracycline impregnated feed. His veterinarian assistant from CDC, Dr. Don Mason, contracted psittacosis in the laboratory twice during this project. As you will learn in this biography, Dr. Meyer became exceedingly influential in Jim Steele's career.

And so throughout history human and veterinary medicine continued to develop, sometimes in concert, sometimes on parallel, separate tracks. At the beginning of Jim Steele's veterinary career the stage was set for James Watson and Francis Crick to announce their double helix model of DNA in 1953, launching the field of molecular biology. Much had been learned about human and animal diseases throughout the centuries by thousands of insatiably curious scientists. This rich legacy set the stage for Jim's career, enabling him to bring the fledgling field of veterinary public health to full fruition.

Jim hopes that his story will serve to inspire the young and the old, students and seasoned professionals, and those inside and outside of the allied medical professions. His exceptional contributions as a lifelong public servant and as an incredibly focused and passionate human being have helped make the world to a better place for all.

"Big Swede" James Harlan was delivered at the Steele residence by the family physician, Dr. Buswell, on Thursday, April 3, 1913. It was a bone-chilling early spring Chicago day that only Windy City residents can appreciate. The Steeles' home was at 1829 Berenice Avenue on Chicago's north side. The home was given to Jim's parents as a wedding gift by his paternal grandmother, Nancy Hahn Steele, the family matriarch. James weighed in at over nine pounds. One of his cousins supposedly remarked, "That's the biggest baby I've ever seen!" To be sure, this baby was destined to do big things. Chicago was a scrappy city to grow up in, but James Harlan Steele would succeed there and in the far corners of the globe.

Jim's father, James Hahn Steele, was born in 1876. He was the youngest of six siblings. The name Steele was originally *Stahl*. It was changed to Steele during the American Revolution when Hessian troops, essentially mercenaries, arrived and began mistreating German settlers. The middle name *Hahn* came from the maiden name of his paternal grandmother, whose family came from the Pennsylvania Dutch country. James Hahn Steele was big and handsome, six feet, two inches tall and weighing in at 240 pounds. He was a jokester and a storyteller among family and friends. Jim can recall the smile on his dad's face in the early days. Unfortunately, his smile and the smiles of many of the family members were destined to be erased by alcohol and hard times.

Jim's mother was statuesque and elegant. She was Lydia Catherin Nordquist, born in Stockholm, Sweden in 1888. She was an impeccable dresser and a spotless housekeeper who had worked as a postal telegraph clerk after high school prior to marrying. Her own mother frequently chided her that she was too fussy about the men who came courting. Lydia was twelve years younger than James Hahn when they were married; she was twenty-four and he was thirty-six. They married in a chapel in Waukegan, Illinois rather than have a church wedding, even though she was a member of St. James Episcopal Church. Jim's father was not a church-going man. James Harlan was born one year later.

Lydia surrounded herself with books and often read to Jim– works such as Robert Gordon Anderson's *Seven O'clock Stories* and Robert Louis Stevenson's *Child's Garden of Verses*. She planted the seeds of his insatiable curiosity and penchant for knowledge. He remembers a large, attractive bookcase that was home to his mother's library. When Jim was a teenager, she told him that at age four, he would beg her to explain what the pages said. Jim's mother eventually divorced James Hahn Steele for abuse and drunkenness in 1924 and then returned to work as a postal telegraph clerk in 1925 when he was twelve.

Augusta Nordquist, Lydia's mother and Jim's beloved grandmother, was named after the German empress Augusta. Her maiden name was Forsberg. Directly translated, "Forsberg" means "strong force." Her name is traceable back to mid-eighteenth century Sweden through church records. *Mormor* (grandmother) Nordquist had a tremendous influence on James Harlan.

When Jim's mother went back to work in 1925, Mormor was the only one at home after school to greet him. He recalled the splendid aroma of her fine cooking and baking. He also remembers her warm manner. She was a dignified Swedish lady who was, in Jim's mind, more nurturing to him than his own mother was. He remembers her putting hot mentholate on his chest and fetching cough syrup whenever he had a cold. His mother seldom nursed him like that, possibly because Mormor managed to get to Jim's side first.

Born in Sweden, she came to America in 1893 with Lydia one year after her husband, Axel Nordquist, arrived. A self-taught mechanical engineer, Axel worked for DeLaval, a company that produced milk separators and milking machines. Axel traveled to the United States in 1892 to the Chicago World's Fair to display their machines and later to help build the first factory in Elgin, Illinois for DeLaval. Axel died in 1915 of pneumonia. Slender and petite at 5' 2", Augusta yearned to be an opera singer or an actress. Folks who dealt with her at the stores and elsewhere all spoke of her wonderful sense of humor.

Mormor Nordquist spoke mostly Swedish. She anxiously anticipated her copy of a Swedish newspaper each week. She held precious the news from her home country. One of her favorite places was the movie theater. She loved to tell Jim stories about the dark interior of the theater. This was probably one of the ways she kept the stars and entertainers of her youth alive in her mind. She had dreamt of joining them onstage one day.

Mormor Nordquist taught Jim to appreciate the ethnic diversity of their neighbors and the melting pot that was Chicago. Little did she know that she was helping Jim prepare for a career that would lead him to circumnavigate the globe many times and to be respected and loved by people at the four corners of the earth. Speaking in her broken English, she made dozens of Jewish, Irish, and Italian friends effortlessly up and down Berenice Avenue. They all seemed to love her cheery demeanor. Her diplomatic and cordial ways undoubtedly rubbed off on Jim. These skills would become the hallmark of his persona and would pay off for him immensely in his career.

One day during a walk with Jim down Berenice, Mormor struck up some light conversation with friends. They were conferring about the topic of Norway separating from Sweden in 1905 and she quipped, "Those Norwegians didn't appreciate what the Swedes did for them!" causing the ladies to erupt into waves of laughter. She always knew how to put a smile on everyone's face, especially Jim's.

Tragically, Mormor Nordquist was killed by a car after stepping off a streetcar in her home neighborhood in May of 1929. She was clipped on the head by the mirror of the vehicle and died a few days later. Jim, sixteen years old at the time, remembers how empty the house was after the horrible accident. This was Jim's first experience with a death of someone he loved very much.

Jim did not get to know Henry Steele, his paternal grandfather. Henry was born in Pennsylvania in 1833. His parents were from eastern Pennsylvania and were of German origin. Henry met and married Nancy Hahn and gave birth to Alice. Henry traveled through the Pennsylvania Dutch country and later to the Midwest. In 1876, he attended the US Independence Centennial celebration in Philadelphia and learned of opportunities for land and work in Kansas. He decided to move his family west to Kansas shortly thereafter. He eventually became a respected farmer and mechanic in Junction City, Kansas. He died in 1888 of the "galloping consumption," a lay term for tuberculosis, before Jim was born.

Jim also never met Nancy Hahn Steele, his paternal grandmother. She was born in Pennsylvania in the 1830s. The family matriarch in the truest sense, she sent all of her children through college. Her family was related to the famous General "Mad" Anthony Wayne of the Revolutionary Army. His seizure of Stony Point, a British defense post, in 1779, demonstrated the wild tactics that gave rise to his nickname. Her father was a veteran of the War of 1812 and was married to an Irish woman by the name of Elizabeth Simpson who lived beyond one hundred years of age. Nancy Hahn Steele died of heart failure in 1915 when Jim was only two.

Grandma Nancy Steele gave James Hahn and Lydia an impressive wedding present—their own house—in 1912. It was a typical North Side Chicago residential home of the period. The houses in the neighborhood were built close together on narrow, thirty-to forty-five-foot lots. There were cottonwoods up and down the street that softened the landscape. In addition, there were elm trees and fragrant lilac bushes in the backyard along with an old cherry tree. Jim also remembers a Chinese "tree of heaven" (Ailantus glandulosa) that the kids would make whips out of sticks to chase and swat each other with. They were common trees in Chicago as they, like the residents, were tough and could resist cold, pollution, disease, and insects.

After the wedding, Grandpa and Grandma Nordquist moved downstairs and James Hahn and Lydia set up residence upstairs. The house was of solid wood frame construction painted green with porches on the front and back, upstairs and down. The occupancy arrangement worked out nicely as it did for many families of the era before nursing homes became an accepted place to outsource aging parents. There were gas jets on the wall for lighting. The house also had some electricity and even a phone. There was a living room, dining room, a kitchen, one bathroom, a pantry, and three bedrooms. The rooms were small but the house was comfortable. Jim recalled nice views of neighboring homes and trees through the many windows. To the west there was a single dwelling and to the east a two-flat residence.

About three houses down, a train trestle formed the underpinning of tracks that continued on to new residential areas throughout the city. The "L," as the train was called, could be heard clacking by periodically, taking passengers on their way to work or home. The "L" dates back to 1892 and is operated to this day by the Chicago Transit Authority. The clip-clop of hooves often provided percussive background sounds as horse-drawn wagons were still in operation delivering groceries, milk, ice, coal, vegetables and fruit. The trash man gathered old papers, junk and scrap, also by horse-drawn, and even man-drawn carts. Jim recalled the excitement when a fire engine would breeze by, pulled by powerful draught horses. "Kids ran with their dogs to try to keep pace with the engines. Even the police department paddy wagons were horse-drawn. My favorite horses were the Morgans that pulled the funeral carriages," said Jim. He also enjoyed visiting the stables nearby, being impressed with the skill of the "smithies" that fastened metal shoes to the hooves. He also remembers the smell of burning hoof tissue and how dogs would chew on the nipped hoof remains.

The upstairs rooms of the house were screened. On hot, humid summer evenings Jim's father would sometimes sleep out on the porch to enjoy the cooler air and the breezes from Lake Michigan. "One technique for keeping cool at night was to moisten the sheets to benefit from evaporative cooling," Jim said. Jim's mother had a piano that she played quite well. He remembers her filling the house with soothing music.

The basement provided copius storage space and a workbench for Jim's father. Two old World War I veterans, Mike and Joe, lived in a room at the back of the basement. Jim's mother passed them off as drunks. He recalled that they were quite friendly and got along well with his father. Jim talked to them about the war. "They showed me souvenirs brought back from the battles in France and other countries." Jim said. Jim learned later that the old men were never charged any rent for staying in the room. They disappeared one day after Jim's dad became ill.

After Grandpa died in 1915 of pneumonia, Mormor Nordquist decided to move up to the attic bedroom, possibly to help bring closure to her loss. On the walls were pictures and posters of presidents and heroes of World War I. She was very patriotic and had an intense interest in world affairs. Later the same attic would become a refuge for the whole family when James Hahn would come home in a drunken rage. Mother and Mormor were concerned for Jim's and brother John's safety during these episodes. "I remember seeing bruises on Mother and Mormor, it was very disturbing," said Jim.

One thing that still puzzles Jim is that, with the exception of his grandmother, he received little affection at home. Why didn't his family hug and engage in warm, loving behaviors like other families? The "big Swede" found out early in life that he had a big heart, a heart that yearned to love and to be loved–a heart that wanted to help people wherever and whenever he could.

"I was blessed to have aunts and uncles that helped guide me and even encourage me to become educated," Jim said. There was Uncle Ira Steele, the dentist, who had a son, William Taylor Steele. After Uncle Ira died from alcoholism, Cousin William was adopted and raised by Aunt Letha Steele Thorp, a schoolteacher, and Herbert Thorp, a dentist. Jim remembers the sad tale told about Uncle Ira, who was found one winter day in 1915 frozen to death, lying on the grave of his beloved wife, Laura, who perished during childbirth.

The Thorps were good to Jim as well. He spent many summers at their farm working with the cows and riding horses. This experience undoubtedly stimulated his interest in animals.

Aunt Letha contracted tuberculosis and was forced to give up teaching in Chicago. She and her husband moved to Michigan to help her recover from the horrible disease that would haunt Jim later in his own life. Cousin William Taylor attended the Michigan State College of Veterinary Medicine and eventually became the dean of the College of Veterinary Medicine at the University of Minnesota. In addition, he was the first to establish laboratory animal medicine at the National Institutes of Health (NIH). Earlier, he encouraged Jim to consider veterinary medicine as a career after his mother died in 1937.

Uncle Nelson Steele was the first veterinarian in the Steele family. He attended the old Indianapolis Veterinary School and established a practice and livery stable in Muskegon, Michigan in 1900. He got into politics and eventually became a state legislator in Michigan. He was a successful veterinarian, achieving some status researching parasites on fox farms. Scientific papers written by him can still be found in the Bureau of Animal Industries (BAI) citation index. Nelson and his wife, Grace, had twin daughters Myrle and Myrna, in 1910. The colorful twins would later travel with Jim to Europe in the fifties and sixties.

Pioneering Aunt Alice Steele-Schneider was the first in the Steele family to attend dental college. She attended Kansas City Dental School, graduating in 1888. "She was a tough one. She packed a pistol walking to school to assure her safety," Jim reported. She married a dentist, Cory Schneider, and established a practice in Paris, Texas.

Aunt Sarah Catherine Steele-Norman also became a dentist. She attended Northwestern University in Chicago in the early 1900s. Thanks to Aunt Sarah, Jim grew up with most of his teeth. Aunt Sarah had one daughter, Ruth, who became a modern classical dancer, and a son, Dale, who remained in Kansas on the farm. He wanted to study electrical engineering but was discouraged by his rural friends. The story was that Dale passionately wanted to attend high school but didn't live close enough to one. However, his father bought him a horse so that he could travel to and from school and he went on to earn his high school diploma. He became fluent in Latin and could remember poems from high school into his nineties. He died nearing one hundred years old. Ruth nursed Jim's dad and Aunt Luella in later years.

Aunt Luella Steele was a shining star for Jim. She was a schoolteacher who put her niece Nanine Steele, Ira's daughter, through the University of Chicago, where Nanine majored in history and graduated with honors in 1924. She encouraged Jim to attend there as a working student. Her constant encouragement sent Jim's mind reeling about the possibilities of acquiring a good education. He dreamed about studying political science and history and possibly becoming a lawyer. "I didn't get a lot of encouragement from my family, but when I learned about Nanine's success it fueled my desire to go to college," Jim said. Luella died of "dropsy" (severe edema due to kidney, liver and heart failure) in 1927. Jim remembers the gangrenous odors at her house in the years prior to her death.

When Jim was about five years old, his mother took him to a barber shop near his dad's dental clinic at the corner of Roscoe and Robey. There he got a "pageboy" haircut by his father's barber. "I didn't like it when the barber cut my bangs!" In later years when Jim's hair grew long, his mother would say, "You look like a Kansas haystack!" After haircuts, they usually stopped by his father's dental clinic. Jim has memories of the clinical odors of clove and isopropyl alcohol. Often his father would give his teeth a good examination in the dental chair. When Jim was a little older, his mother sent him to the clinic to ask his father for grocery money. The most his dad would ever give him was a little silver. In later years, Jim wondered if his father was bringing any income home from his practice. Money always seemed to be tight.

At age six, Jim was off to Hamilton School. At first, his mother walked the mile with him. He soon began making the trek alone. Weather permitting, Jim wore knickers until junior high school. There were forty-three students in his class. By age ten Jim was selling the *Saturday Evening Post, Ladies' Home Journal* and other magazines on the street corner or outside grocery stores. It is no surprise that his first job kept him close to the printed word that he had already learned to love. "The money that I made with this little business helped me to buy more dime novels and books to read!"

Jim went directly from first grade to third because of his reading skills. He vividly remembers Mary Elizabeth Farson, the principal. She was an old-fashioned dresser, wearing long velvet skirts with a purse attached. She recited poems from *Snowbound* by John

Greenleaf Whittier, a well known poet of the nineteenth century. She nurtured Jim's lifelong penchant for literature. She also gave lectures on astronomy and chemistry, including long discourses on the elements in the periodic table. He remembers learning from her that uranium, atomic weight 92, was the heaviest element. This was Jim's first introduction to science. "I remember thinking, this is exciting. I wanted to be a part of this!" Ms. Farson also lectured on Greek mythology, which fascinated young Jim. In the eighth grade, she made Jim chief of the student patrol officers around the school. "She evidently thought that I was big, strong, reliable, had good judgment and was up to the job." When Jim graduated, she told him, "I hope you remember me."

Jim loved books from a very early age; he read just about everything he could get his hands on. At the age of nine, he began reading the Buffalo Bill series and moved on to dime novels featuring heroes like Frank Merriwell by Gilbert Patten, and Nick Carter, the detective who was invented by John Coryell. The following excerpt provides a glimpse into Nick Carter's character:

> What a long strange trip it's been for Nick Carter. He first appeared as a 19th century detective and adventurer, in Street and Smith's New York Weekly dime novel, on September 18, 1886. He was young, strong, dedicated to clean living (no cigarettes or booze!) confident, a master of disguise, and possessor of a keen mind, filled with more trivia than anyone would ever need to know (except, of course, for dime novel master sleuths!) and was usually accompanied by his loyal (and manly) partners-in-arms Patsy and Scrubby.
>
> Contributed by Stewart Wright, Dec 1998

Nick Carter was a hero and a positive role model for Jim. He emulated his character to a certain degree. Jim liked the way Nick Carter would overcome adversaries and make things right. Jim believed that his exposure to Frank Merriwell's characters helped him to build the motivation and strength to attend college.

Jim has many fond memories of the Steele household and growing up. Most cold mornings he would rise to the aroma of fresh-baked sweet rolls, sweetbreads, and hot oatmeal. There was always a pot of hot coffee on the stove, and Jim learned to drink it as a young boy with lots of milk. Mormor Nordquist drank her coffee through a lump of sugar she called "succa bitte" which she held between her teeth. Jim walked home for most of his school lunch breaks. "I remember seeing the maple trees turning their beautiful colors in the fall, and I wanted to understand the science behind it all." Jim recalled the fun of running and sliding on the ice and snow in the winter. "When the trees and other plants came back to life in the spring I found it so very amazing. Nature and biology intrigued me, and my thirst for knowledge was almost painful at times!"

Lunch was simple yet always satisfying. There was usually homemade German or Swedish rye or fresh rolls for sandwiches. Mormor or his mother often made cakes with mocha frosting. Jim wasn't too fond of the frosting but he would always have a piece because he loved the cake. The conversation around the table was always light, much of it in Swedish. After a quick lunch and a few soothing minutes with Mormor, it was time to hustle back to school to learn and study. Unlike many students, Jim Steele truly enjoyed going to school and playing games at recess.

After school, Jim hurried home for supper. "I was growing quickly and always seemed to be hungry!" said Jim. Supper was always a large meal that included meat cutlets, ham, herring, and Lake Superior whitefish. Sometimes they would prepare Lake Michigan perch, a real delicacy. There were always plenty of side dishes of potatoes, vegetables and lots of fresh bread. His father would often bring home a candy bar for Jim and his little brother John. Every now and then after supper, Jim would play ball in the backyard with his father. "My childhood was good until Prohibition in 1922. This is when alcohol really began to ruin my father and our family life," Jim reported.

John Axel Steele, Jim's only sibling, was two years younger. Jim was very protective of his brother. They shared a bed for at least ten years growing up. John got pleurisy in 1922, when he was seven, and nearly died. The illness only served to bring them closer. However, Jim recalled that in spite of their bonding, they truly didn't have much in common. "John didn't seem to be interested in sports or school as I recall," said Jim. In many ways, they were opposites. However, John did finish high school. He became a streetcar conductor, married and served in France and Germany under General Patton in World War II. One of John's favorite stories was how his platoon captured a German train roundhouse.

After the war, John and his wife, Dorothy, had a son who later contracted polio and became paralyzed from the neck down. John eventually became a master carpenter and earned a comfortable living. He enjoyed a long retirement and succumbed to cancer in February 2001 at age eighty-five. John's son, Jack, survives his parents. He still lives at 1829 Berenice Avenue in Chicago where he was born and is attended to by friends.

There was always rich, cultural conversation in the Steele household. Jim remembers discussions of opera singers like Geraldine Farrar of the Metropolitan Opera in New York. Her career spanned from 1906 to 1922 and was noted for her roles in the operas *Carmen* and *Madame Butterfly*. Jim's elders also chatted about musicians like Fredric Stock, the famous conductor of the Chicago Symphony, and the celebrated pianist Paderewski, who later became the Prime Minister and Secretary of Foreign Affairs of Poland. In addition, they would talk about famous dancers, symphonies and movie stars like Douglas Fairbanks, the American actor known for his swashbuckling roles in silent films such as *Robin Hood;* or Gloria Swanson, who appeared in numerous silent films and later made a heralded comeback in *Sunset Boulevard* in 1950. She was said to be from the North Side of Chicago.

War and politics were also commonly discussed. Current events, such as the establishment of Woodrow Wilson's League of Nations in 1920 to promote international cooperation and peace, were lively topics of discussion. Jim can recall the elders after Sunday school talking about World War I as the "war to end all wars," with some disagreeing, stating that there would always be war. The simple fact that Jim can remember these conversations is strong evidence that his mind was a veritable sponge, even at a very young age, and he wished to assimilate and understand everything in the world that he was exposed to, a trait that he still possesses today.

Jim remembers tales of war and disease, hushed conversations about neighbors who died in the war of the Spanish flu pandemic of 1918. He could grasp the reality of the war deaths. But what was the Spanish flu? How could it spread throughout the world? He wanted understand this phenomenon. He learned that germs are the cause of diseases like the flu. At the same time, the Germans were being characterized as monsters in the news and in adult conversations that he would overhear. He was trying to put it all together in his mind. "Interestingly, I began thinking that maybe the *Germans* were somehow responsible for the *germs* that were causing all the diseases. It couldn't be a coincidence that the war and the epidemic were ending at about the same time without a direct association with the Germans!" Jim recalled.

Were the Spaniards responsible for the Spanish flu? Much later he learned that Spain became associated with the epidemic because the country had not imposed war censorship. The allies and the Germans did not want to admit that the influenza outbreak was adversely affecting their war effort. For Jim it was all very confusing, but at the same time fascinating. Jim "Nick" Steele had discovered yet something else he wanted to investigate.

Of course, Jim realized later that he made the error of drawing a cause-and-effect relationship between two events that are only temporally connected. In the meantime, he couldn't get the Germans or the Spaniards out of his head. Although the Germans had nothing to do with the flu epidemic, it is somewhat interesting that young Jim was thinking that biological warfare might be part of the German war strategy. Of course, after World War II he became heavily involved in biowarfare defense.

"Of course, war and disease go hand-in-hand. It surprises students of military history to learn that in every recorded war in history, significantly more injuries and fatalities are caused by disease than by bullets or other weapons. Today, this is referred to as DNBI or disease and non-battle injuries. In fact, history tells us that in the late spring of 1918, the Spanish influenza took a heavy toll on both German and Allied forces. The Germans launched their last big attack in April 1918, but could not prevail as, among other things, they were too debilitated by the flu," Jim explained. Much later, Professor Jim Steele would lecture to his students, "The tides of war flow on disease patterns that affect the troops."

Many years later, Ralph McGill, publisher of the *Atlanta Constitution* and one of Jim's neighbors and friends, told him about his experience as a young marine on his way to France in 1918 on a ship. Many men died helplessly of influenza in their berths. One of Jim's cousins, Dale Norman, who died at the age of ninety-nine, told him that he was at Fort Riley, Kansas when the first case of the Spanish flu was reported at the camp in February of 1918. Interestingly, Jim spent much of his career trying to better characterize the epidemiology of influenza.

Jim had many early experiences with life and death in his neighborhood. He remembers warning signs posted by the Chicago Department of Health for diphtheria, measles, and whooping cough. He can also recall how shocked he was when he learned that a little girl that he played with four houses down had died of diphtheria. Later, one of his baseball playmates died of juvenile diabetes. Pneumonia was a common disease among adults with frequent fatalities in and around the neighborhood, including Jim's grandfather. These events may have stimulated Jim's interest in public health. They were surely locked into his memory, and he would relive them often during his career.

Jim's mother could do just about anything, it seemed. She could play the piano, make her own clothes, cook excellent meals, and participate actively in any conversation. She was slender, attractive, and five feet, eight inches tall. Jim can remember her looking in the mirror on her thirty-fifth birthday, exclaiming, with a beautiful smile on her face, "Look at me, I am a perfect thirty-five!" She wore hats wherever she went and always wanted to look her best.

But by 1919, Jim's father had become a hard-drinking man. Jim recalled the near-constant smell of booze on his father's breath. His family was never what you would call well-to-do, but until that time they had always seemed to be able to find money for most things. Jim's father had inherited some funds when his mother died in 1915, but much of it was spent on stockpiling cases of whiskey when the Eighteenth Amendment was ratified commencing prohibition on January 16, 1919.

Lydia began locking herself in the bedroom when James Hahn would come home late at night in a drunken rage. During these occasions, Jim's father would try to force Lydia to have sex with him and would get quite violent. "I was about six years old. I climbed in between them and tried to stop my father, only to be thrown to the floor." Jim recalled. There was no Alcoholics Anonymous and no Al-Anon at this time. Treatment centers for alcoholism simply did not exist. Inebriates might be held overnight in jail, but that was about the extent of it. "Alcoholism was like a cancer with no cure at the time," said Jim. The paddy wagon made frequent trips to the Steele home to collect Jim's father when things got too brutal. "I can recall the strong feelings of relief after the police took him away." Jim remembered his dad and a neighbor, Charlie O'Connor, throwing bricks at each other in the yard in a drunken rage. In the midst of the Prohibition era in 1925, Jim's mother divorced James Hahn and went back to work at the postal telegraph office to support the family.

The story of Jim's dad didn't end there. After the divorce, James Hahn was a totally broken man. He lost his dental practice and all respect in the community with it. In a courtroom hearing, the judge said to him, "How could you possibly do this to your life and your wonderful family?" In 1928, Jim's father was diagnosed with a brain tumor. He was living with his sister Luella and her daughter Ruth at the time. Luella was caring for James Hahn as well as she could. Jim remembered visiting his father from time to time, but he had lost almost all feeling for him. "I was forced to face the painful and undisputable truth. On occasion, my father had beaten and sexually abused my mother and had even beaten Mormor Nordquist during his drunken outrages."

At this point, Jim began losing himself in books. He fantasized about what a normal household could be like. He escaped into the plots of the mystery novels and immersed himself in the knowledge that surrounded him at school.   Instead of turning to the streets for trouble like many young boys, he found asylum and catharsis within the confines of his mind. He learned to fully experience the exciting and adventurous world of the written word, a world that he has cherished and that has served him so well throughout his life.

James Hahn wasn't the only Steele family member ravaged by alcohol.   Ira Steele, Nelson Steele and William Taylor Steele Thorp also suffered from various forms of alcoholism until their deaths.

Because of the significant presence of alcoholism in their family, the Steele sisters, Alice, Luella, Sarah and Letha, all became members of the Women's Christian Temperance Union (WCTU). They were concerned about the how alcohol was affecting their families and society. Members chose total abstinence from all alcohol as their lifestyle and protection of the home as their watchword. The WCTU was founded in 1874 and is still active today. The organization's definition of temperance came from the Greek philosopher Xenophon:

> **Temperance** may be defined as:
> **moderation** in all things healthful;
> **total abstinence** from all things harmful.
>
> Xenophon (Greek philosopher), 400 bc

In spite of it all, Jim was a strong, industrious young man, anything but passive. He joined the Boy Scouts at age eleven and played basketball in his freshman year in high school and at church. He was invited to join the regular team but he decided that a part-time job after school was more important. He held many jobs as a boy, including working at a fruit store making two dollars a week in addition to the fringe benefit of a sack of fruit to take home daily for the family. He worked as a soda fountain clerk in a drugstore for almost two years. During his last year in high school, he became a Western Union clerk. All of these jobs made it impossible for Jim to participate actively in sports. But his highest priority was to help out his family by bringing home some needed cash.

After completing the ninth grade at Horace Greeley Pre-High School, Jim moved on to Lakeview High School. The school building was of Germanic architecture. "It was almost castle-like in appearance," he recalled. Jim lived for his mind-expanding classroom experiences. Jim remembered Mrs. Brown, his English literature teacher, telling her class, "You're fifteen now, but you won't appreciate Shakespeare until you are fifty." It was about this time that Jim realized he was severely nearsighted. This was impeding his progress in geometry and other classes that used illustrations. He was soon outfitted for glasses.

Ms. Coyne, his history teacher, gave a closing lecture to her class that he will never forget. She was discussing several technological advances such as flight, the reciprocating engine, the railroad and steamships and contrasted those with sociological changes over time. She issued this challenge to her students: "Industry and technology have come a long way, but our social advances have been fewer for the last hundred years, with the exception of the freedom of slaves. The most important thing for your generation is to contribute to social advances—housing, health and nutrition." In 1930, Jim graduated from Lakeview High.

After high school, Jim became an insurance clerk for Fireman's Insurance Comkpany in Chicago for sixty-five dollars per month. To Jim it looked like a company with pride and a future. It was just not the future he had envisioned for himself. However, Jim had a strong sense of responsibility to help his mother and his brother in the midst of the Great Depression. For now, he needed to continue to help the family financially.

If it hadn't been for William Taylor Steele Thorp, Jim might never have pursued a career in veterinary medicine. Instead, he might have climbed the corporate ladder, perhaps to become the president of an insurance company.

CHAPTER 3:
AN INSURANCE CLERK GOES TO VETERINARY SCHOOL

The Great Depression was, let's say, depressing. Jim described it as its own cosmos, a cocoon that quietly wrapped itself around people, slowly smothering their lives. It was difficult to think optimistically and to believe that you would be able to have a successful career and a happy, fulfilling life. He met young lawyers and other graduates from good schools who could only find jobs at a grocery store or a filling station, and even those jobs were rare. When FDR's New Deal was implemented in the thirties, jobs became available cleaning and fixing up the towns and cities around the country. But the lines were long even for this kind of employment. Newly organized programs like the Civilian Conservation Corps (CCC) and the Works Progress Administration (WPA) provided some opportunities for those in need of work. It was a full-fledged depression, in which banks collapsed and people lost just about everything, including their self-confidence.

Jim had his job as a clerk with the Fireman's Insurance Company, making roughly fifteen dollars per week. He was thankful for that, but it just wasn't enough for him and his mother to get by on. To supplement his income, he sold pipes, kitchen knives, ladies' dresser sets, anything that would bring him and his mom an extra dollar or two. Jim finally got a raise to seventy-dollars per month, only to be cut back to sixty dollars when the insurance industry began to experience more problems related to the slumping economy. *Three years in this business and I'm not getting ahead,* Jim said to himself over and over.

In 1933, Jim met Aina Oberg at an office party. They bonded promptly and began spending a lot of time together. "Early in our courtship, I could feel that Aina truly believed in me. She was an optimist and encouraged me to move ahead with my plans for getting an education," Jim said. In 1934, Jim began to think that his mother could get along without him and he started thinking seriously about going back to school.

Cousin William Taylor Steele Thorp came down from Michigan State College for the Chicago World's Fair in 1933-34. The theme of the international exposition was *The Century of Progress;* it was designed to highlight the industrial marvels of the twentieth century. Jim's own transition from the past to the future seemed to begin with this visit. Cousin Bill was soon to graduate as a doctor of veterinary medicine in 1935 and was full of all kinds of exciting information for young Jim.

"Jim, you have no idea all the things going on in veterinary medicine right now. There is plenty of interesting work for everybody!" Cousin William was correct in his assessment. FDR's federal programs included plans to eradicate bovine tuberculosis and to improve market prices of agricultural animals. There was a strong, growing demand for veterinary services. "Jim, now is the time for you to come to Michigan State College and get back in school before it is too late," he strongly encouraged him.

During late summer of 1935, Jim, Aina and his mother traveled to visit Uncle Nelson, a veterinarian practicing in Muskegon, Michigan, to discuss his aspirations to attend veterinary college. Surprisingly, Uncle Nelson gave Jim no encouragement whatsoever. "What in the hell would you want to do that for?" he blasted. "You'd be better off painting houses!" Jim interpreted this as meaning his uncle didn't think he had the intelligence or the fortitude to make it through the grueling veterinary curriculum.

On their way back home, they stopped in to visit with Aunt Letha, Uncle Herb and Cousin William again at their farm near Allegan, Michigan. This time Bill was emphatic: "Jim, you need to seriously consider Michigan State College."

When they returned to Chicago, Aina was insistent: "Jim, it is time to do what you want, get your education!"

His mom echoed Aina: "James, do what you want to do!"

At first, he was unsure. He had Aina, a roof over his head and a decent job. You could buy a cold beer anywhere for ten cents. Maybe life in Chicago wasn't all that bad.

When Aina heard Jim talking this way, she decided that it was time for him to get some old-fashioned counseling from the minister at the nondenominational North Side church where they attended services. She made an appointment and Jim went to see Reverend Bradley. "James, you are a bright young man and you definitely need to finish your education," the minister told him. It was then that Jim learned that the preacher was an armchair environmentalist. Reverend Bradley began speaking with great conviction about the emerging environmental issues of the time. "The lumber barons are raping the country of its trees, stripping the land greedily and avoiding taxes and land use fees. We need young men like you to save the forests and the land from ruin!" Jim was so impressed that he decided to enroll in the Michigan State College School of Forestry. There were no schools offering degrees in environmental sciences at the time. Jim thought, *I'm twenty three years old and I'm never going to make anything of myself hanging around Chicago.*

Jim had taken some evening courses at the YMCA College but he was pretty certain that they wouldn't transfer to Michigan State College. He had also attended some night courses in literature at Northwestern University. Late in the summer of 1936, Jim signed out on "vacation" from his job without any intention of coming back. With the grand sum of sixty dollars in his pocket, he hitch-hiked to East Lansing, Michigan to start classes. He linked up with Cousin Bill Thorp, who was completing a master's degree in pathology.

But Jim's university dream wasn't in the cards just yet. As he was about to enroll, a distressing telephone call came from Chicago. Jim's mother had taken seriously ill and was in St. Elizabeth's hospital. She was diagnosed with a perforated stomach ulcer. "Of course I felt responsible," Jim said. In the span of two short weeks, Jim had left his job as an insurance clerk, made a bold decision with Aina to leave Chicago behind, traveled to East Lansing, immersed himself in the excitement of Michigan State College and the realization of his dreams, only to be called abruptly back to Chicago. "I went home immediately. Aina and I didn't talk much about what had happened," he said.

Jim's mother was very ill that entire year and underwent further surgery. The technique for the correction of peptic ulcer was very crude at the time. Often, the ulcerating tissue that was removed from the stomach would leave a scar and cause a constriction at the junction of the stomach and the duodenum. This is exactly what happened to Lydia. The following July she deteriorated to the extent that another surgeon wanted to try to correct the constriction. The surgery was performed but this would be her last. After the procedure, she died of an embolism without ever regaining consciousness. This was July 21, 1937. Ironically, it was Aina's birthday.

By September of 1937, Jim had regained his strength and determination. He registered as a freshman forestry major at Michigan State College. *Nothing will stop me now,* he recalled thinking.

In 1937, at the time of Lydia's death, some of Jim and Aina's young and friends were talking about joining the Abraham Lincoln Brigade to take up arms in defense of the Spanish Republic against a military rebellion led by General Franco, aided by Hitler and Mussolini. This ultimately turned into the Spanish Civil War, which lasted from 1936 until 1939. But Jim ignored his idealistic buddies and chose to get an education instead, hoping to make more substantial contributions to the world. "We never heard from any of our Spanish Civil War volunteers again. Sometimes I wonder what happened to them," Jim said.

The changing of the seasons and the smell of the leaves in East Lansing warmed Jim's heart as he walked roughly one mile from one end of the campus to the other. At twenty-four, Jim was older than most of the other students, but he didn't care about that. He proudly wore his traditional green cap with the rest of the freshmen. *I am finally realizing my dream!* he repeated to himself. Most of his first semester classes such as English, algebra, military science, botany, forestry, agriculture and physical education were held in the inner campus. The veterinary school buildings where he would later spend countless hours were several hundred yards away.

Jim rented a room in an old white clapboard house from a Mrs. Olin on 124 Bailey Street in East Lansing. She was an elderly lady, probably in her sixties or seventies. Her husband, a World War I veteran, was a maintenance man and a janitor at the college. The room was comfortable and cost Jim only $2.50 per week. His flat was in the front of the house. This required him to walk through a fellow student's living area, Robert Webster's, to enter or exit his own room. Erwin Massa and Frank Molinari resided at the other end of the house. Erwin was a civil engineering student who spent a lot of his time visiting his girlfriend downtown. Frank was an Italian from the Upper Peninsula who was working on an agricultural degree. He worked part-time as a barber to pay for his education. He went on to become a county agent. There were other students who rotated through the house during Jim's time at Michigan State College. Jim kept up with many of them through the years. Aina stayed back in Chicago working for the Fireman's Insurance Company. They corresponded frequently.

Jim squeezed a lot into his freshman year. He enrolled in the ROTC cavalry, but they had no boots to accommodate his size fourteen feet. So he had to settle for an artillery unit. The length of his stride made marching difficult, and he got a lot of attention because of this. One day during a ceremony, he was called out of the ranks to join the reviewing party. "Everyone was confused about the special treatment I was getting. But in actuality all they were doing was to keep me from marching!" Jim said with a grin.

He joined the track team for a while, but boxing was his sport of choice. Jim had boxed as a boy at the Catholic Youth Organization in Chicago so he knew how to keep his chin down and his arms up, leading with his left and following with his right. These self-defense skills had often come in handy as he grew up in the tough city.

Jim listened to his boxing coach carefully. "The coach told me to be aggressive and to always maintain a good defense and be able to take a hard blow and come back," Jim said.

During the final examination for the class, Jim was matched up with the biggest boys. The first match was with a burly farm kid who was every bit as big as Jim was. "I really went after him, like we were in a street fight. I put him away in short order," Jim reported. He can remember his coach saying, "Hey, Steele, take it easy!" causing him to wonder what all the lectures about aggressiveness were about. He took out his second opponent with similar ease. By the time he got to his third opponent, Jim was getting tired, so he just hit him once, hard, in the stomach, then the ribs, and gave him a good punch to the head. The coach then stopped the fight. The next thing Jim knew the coach asked him to join the boxing team.

Jim weighed in at 180 pounds, which put him at the bottom of the heavyweight class. Most of the fighters in this class weighed 190 or more. His first few matches were similar to his earlier contests, as no one seemed to be able to give Jim a really tough time. "But there was this kid I boxed on Lincoln's birthday, February 12, 1938. Don't ask me why I remember the holiday. I found myself matched up with a blockhouse of a guy," he said. Jim went after him immediately, but the punches just seemed to bounce off. He couldn't seem to hurt the kid even with his strongest punches. "Soon, the big brute came after me and began pummeling my ribs. I could protect my head but couldn't seem to block the incoming rib jabs," Jim recalled. Jim won the first round but it was downhill from there and he lost the match. He did finish all three rounds, however.

"After the fight, I went to the hospital for an examination and ended up staying there aching all night. I can remember being happy to be in a safe bed drinking a glass of warm milk," he said. The next day, he was discharged with his pride injured more than anything else. On Valentine's Day he decided that his boxing career was over, thinking that maybe he should be more of a lover than a fighter. But he forgot to send Aina a card and received a scathing letter from her a few days later. She complained that Jim was now an important college student and had forgotten about his sweetheart back in Chicago. Now he was not only beaten up in the ring but in the heart as well. He then made a strong commitment to focus all of his energy on Aina and his career. With the exception of a little participation in track the next spring, Jim stayed true to his pledge.

Jim learned a hard lesson in the spring of 1938. During his botany final exam, he let a fellow student look at his bluebook. The professor saw this, took his exam away from him and told Jim he would receive a "D" in the class. Jim swallowed hard and decided that he would never do that again.

Moving on to other pursuits, Jim ran for freshman class president against Bill Knox, a congressman's son, and lost. "Bill went on to excel in dairy science journalism in Wisconsin. He used me later as a consultant for lobbying on milk issues," Jim stated. They stayed good friends and colleagues for many years. Bill Thorp's wife Cecelia earlier had helped Jim get a job at the student union washing dishes to help cover expenses. The position also included free meals. He landed a second job washing walls at the Union Building on the weekends for thirty-five cents per hour.

Jim's interest in environmental issues continued, and he attended every possible lecture on the subject. He was getting good grades, but was losing interest in his forestry studies. He quickly learned that foresters weren't really environmentalists but were in school to learn how to harvest and market lumber.

Bill Thorp gave Jim periodic recruiting sessions: "Why not veterinary medicine, Jim?"

Jim would respond, "I'm not sure I could adapt to a rural community Bill; there's got to be more to life than that."

Bill replied, "If not practice, what about the growing field of public health–milk and meat inspection?"

The dairy science teacher, Dr. Gould, also counseled Jim: "Maybe you should take a degree in the liberal arts school? After all, you love art and literature!" These words echoed in his head, and finally he decided to visit the dean of the School of Veterinary Medicine to get his advice.

"How did you get interested in veterinary medicine, Jim?" Dean Ward Giltner asked gruffly.

Jim replied, "I have a great interest in healthcare for animals, but I also understand one can make a good living."

"I suppose you'd take home economics if you thought you could make a good living?" he snapped back.

"Yes, sir. When you grow up in Chicago like I did, you do whatever it takes. I admit that I have very little experience with animals."

"What would you do with a sick calf found out in the field?" the Dean asked.

"I would carry it back to the barn so I could examine it!" Jim replied with sincerity.

After the impromptu interview with Dean Giltner, he proclaimed, "Well, I think you'll do just fine!" Jim went back to Dr. Gould and told him that he had been accepted into the pre-veterinary curriculum.

Jim enrolled in the pre-vet curriculum in the winter quarter, January of 1938. After completing courses in all the basic science subjects, including embryology and histology, Jim was accepted into the School of Veterinary Medicine at Michigan State College in the fall of 1938. He would be a member of the graduating class of 1942. Ten years later, Michigan State became a full-fledged university and the veterinary school converted to a college of veterinary medicine.

After Jim started his formal veterinary medical studies, Dean Giltner would quiz him on politics, government, the New Deal reform and more. Jim was well read in history and literature, and Dean Giltner obviously enjoyed his company. "Jim, why does the South turn out so many good writers?" he asked one day.

"A good writer must have tragedy in his or her past. There's no shortage of that in the South!" was Jim's response.

Soon after Jim started veterinary school, cousin Bill helped him to obtain a new job working in the state *Brucella* laboratory under Dr. Hans Ruhland, cleaning glassware. Jim can remember mixing up solutions of trisodium hydroxide and soaking the various vessels and plates. By the next year, he was learning how to make antigen and media. "I was well aware of the dangerous nature of the Brucella organism. I used a bichloride of mercury disinfectant to decontaminate my cubicle work areas," he said. He remembered that some of his coworkers came down with dull headaches, sweats and other symptoms of the disease after they had become infected in the laboratory. Jim still believes that good laboratory techniques saved him from that fate.

In his freshman year, in the fall of 1938, anatomy classes were held in the same building as the *Brucella* laboratory. The horse was the principal species for anatomic study, but later he also studied dog, cat, pig, and ox anatomy. The smell of formalin was pungent and exciting at the same time. This was the aroma of medical success to Jim, and it constantly reminded him that he would be an animal doctor one day. However, the study of anatomy for Jim was tedious. Working with three other students in a group on one horse was not productive, as they spent a lot of time talking and not paying attention to their dissection. Near the middle of the semester, Jim began doing his own private dissections at night and on Saturday mornings so as to make the best use of his limited time. He wanted to learn everything he could while in school, and he avoided any activity that didn't lead him toward a higher plane of knowledge.

After the fall semester of 1938, Jim went home to see Aina for Christmas. He then returned to East Lansing before the New Year to earn some money and to gain experience performing necropsies on otters, muskrats and other sea animals. This work was done in the pathology laboratory, which was in the same building as the anatomy facility. "The fishy smell was so strong and tenacious that it was impossible to shower it away," he said. On New Year's Eve, Jim hitchhiked to Detroit and found he had trouble making friends at the parties due to his unique laboratory-derived aroma. "After the celebrations, I returned to my room in East Lansing and read Mark Twain stories all day. That was New Year's Day, 1939," said Jim.

In the spring of 1939, Jim became involved with the Junior American Veterinary Medical Association, now known as the Student Chapter of the AVMA. The seniors accepted Jim and invited him to the large animal clinics where he was able to get some valuable hands-on time with the animals. One of his senior mentors was Ray Bankowski, a Chicago native, who went on to become a prominent veterinary virologist. Jim was also elected to the honorary veterinary fraternity Alpha Psi that spring. The fraternity was first established at Ohio State in 1907 and is still active today. Eventually, Jim was elected president of the Junior AVMA in his senior year of veterinary school. This office provided him with excellent visibility and greater access to Dean Giltner. They were good friends, and they continued their rich discussions on medical and political issues in the dean's office. During these sessions, he learned that Dean Giltner possessed a graduate degree in public health from the University of Michigan.

Dean Giltner's bacteriology classes were stimulating. Jim began to understand the inner workings of normal animals. However, Jim found the laboratory portion a blur of catheters and needles to measure responses such as blood pressure and heart rates. He knew that physiology would not become his chosen specialty. "There was something too predictable about drugs and their physiological effects; I just couldn't get excited about it!" Jim recalled.

There were no courses in toxicology in those days, only classes in poisonous plants. Because of good coaching by his mother and by a great art teacher in high school, Jim could draw quite well. Jim drew many of the toxic plants as he studied them. His professor noticed the drawings and asked Jim if he had done them. When he stated that he had, the professor rolled his eyes as if in disbelief and walked away. "I guess they were so good he thought I was lying!" Jim used his knowledge of botany in this class as he learned about the toxic properties of locoweed and other dangerous plants that animals consume.

Jim was a unique student. He took few notes in class so that he could pay total attention to the lecture. He then went back to his dorm room and summarized the lecture on paper from memory. However, he couldn't seem to do this for his parasitology class. The complex taxonomy of the parasites was overwhelming. His parasitology professor, Dr. William Chandler, had earned the title "Whiskey Willie." An alcoholic, he would drink cod liver oil to cover up the alcohol on his breath. When he leaned over to help the students to identify what they were looking at through the microscope, the smell of his breath was extremely offensive. One day, Jim couldn't take any more and simply told Professor Chandler what he thought about his habit of coming to class under the influence. This incident resulted in a failing grade for Jim in parasitology. Dean Giltner came to the rescue by administering his own exam to Jim, which resulted in a passing grade. Professor Chandler was subsequently fired but ended up as a professor at Middlesex University in London. On one occasion, he visited the Harvard School of Public Health where Jim was working on his MPH degree. "He looked me up and told me that I was his best student!" Jim said with a laugh.

In Jim's sophomore year of veterinary school, Dean Giltner was teaching basic bacteriology and public health classes. These courses were offered not only to the veterinary class but also to students pursuing degrees in other fields. A part of one of Dr. Giltner's lectures stayed with Jim throughout his career: "There is one thing that I can assure you: There is constant change in all living organisms. Nothing in nature is static. All bacteria you will see and work with are constantly changing biologically. There are all degrees of virulence and invasiveness."

In the fall of 1939, Dr. Henrik J. Stafseth, also a professor of bacteriology, spoke about participating in a delegation from Michigan State to Harvard University's three hundredth anniversary celebration in 1936. During one of Jim's classes, Dr. Stafseth announced that the Harvard School of Public Health would accept applications from veterinarians for fellowships leading to a graduate degree in public health. *Imagine that, a veterinarian going to Harvard!* Jim thought. The announcement set his imagination on fire. He began signing up for any course that covered public health topics and attended any special lectures he could on the subject. The idea of a new scientific field that would bring public health and veterinary medicine together was exciting to him.

In November 1939 there was an accident in the bacteriology building where Professor I. Forest Huddleston had his laboratory in the basement. This event would help shape Jim's entire career.

CHAPTER 4:
MORE THAN A LABORATORY ACCIDENT

In 1939, Jim Steele was employed on the fourth floor attic of what is now Giltner Hall at Michigan State College as a sophomore veterinary medical student. His job was to make *Brucella abortus* antigen for use by the Michigan State diagnostic laboratory. The first floor of the building was reserved for gross anatomy classes, histology and embryology classes were held on the second floor, while the pathology department was located on the third floor. "Wildlife pathology was also on the third floor," Jim said. About four hundred yards away, in the building where Jim was taking introductory bacteriology classes, a bizarre saga was unfolding.

The bacteriology building was a grand Victorian structure that was built in the 1890s. "It had a magnificent wooden staircase and four spacious floors. The first floor was mostly office space for the professors and a lecture room where I was taking a course on introductory bacteriology from Dean Ward Giltner. The second floor was reserved for graduate student offices and the third had more classrooms where the junior class was taking the course in pathogenic bacteriology taught by Dr. Stafseth," Jim recalled.

Dr. I. Forest Huddleston's laboratory was in the basement of the bacteriology building. He was researching a highly pathogenic strain of *Brucella melitensis*. He had collected his isolates from the Isle of Malta during one of his visits there. Sir David Bruce, a British bacteriologist, discovered the cause of Malta fever in 1886. There had been some discussion among the college administrators about whether he should have been allowed to bring the organisms on campus in the first place. However, he had done so, and Dr. Huddleston's work on the zoonotic pathogen continued. "I can still remember muffled conversations in the hallway about how Huddleston's basement laboratory was not the place for working with a bacterium that possessed such profound public health risks," said Jim.

Professor Huddleston is ranked as one of the top brucellosis researchers in the world for the period from 1920 through 1950. He focused on developing vaccines for many species of *Brucella* organisms. "Dean Giltner staunchly defended Huddleston's work, even in the wake of a student vaccination experiment he conducted in 1936 that left all participants quite ill and resulted in chronic health problems for many," Jim said. Some members of the study group experienced anamnestic immune reactions upon exposure to live or dead *Brucella* organisms later in their careers. Because of Dr. Huddleston's special expertise, Jim consulted him on the problems he was having in growing *Brucella* in the diagnostic laboratory where he worked. "Sometimes the rough strains of *Brucella* would appear that were useless for diagnostic testing. Dr. Huddleston would provide me with tips for properly culturing the organisms. He gave me invaluable guidance in my work at the diagnostic lab," Jim said.

Just before the college shut down for Christmas, a student in the pathogenic bacteria class was diagnosed with brucellosis. He became the index case in the outbreak that was to follow. Jim was working in his lab in the anatomy building when he learned of the case. By holiday break, several students had been hospitalized, with many too weak to walk. Some came down with severe fever and chills and were picked up by the campus police to be transported to the hospital. There was no campus ambulance service at the time.

Jim came home one day and visited his roommate, Joe Strong. "Joe was having such powerful chills that his whole bed was shaking. Joe wasn't a veterinary student but was taking one of the other courses in the same building," he said. Jim felt that Joe needed medical attention and called the campus police to take him to the clinic. "The next thing you know, our landlady is accusing me of disgracing her boarding house by reporting a sick student living there! Joe remained out of school for the rest of the year," Jim recalled.

Jim went home to Chicago over the Christmas holiday. Upon returning he learned that another student and friend, Arthur Goldberg, had come down with the brucellosis. "He later died of pericarditis. Somehow, I ended up with all of Arthur's books. In January of 1940, almost the entire veterinary class that was to graduate in 1941 came down with brucellosis," Jim remembered. As the new semester began, many students were unable to report for class. Others returned from their holiday only to become ill within a week. The campus infirmary was soon occupied by about fifty students. Most of them were enrolled in the pathogenic bacteriology class. A few of the students were attending other classes in the same building. Interestingly, some of the patients had only visited the building to make pickups and deliveries.

As expected, the Michigan State Health Department came in to investigate. In addition, an epidemiologist and some sanitary engineers from the US Public Health Service were brought in. The college soon learned that the team was convinced that the outbreak was waterborne. They suspected that live *Brucella melitensis* organisms were entering sink drains, the contents of which were somehow back-siphoned into the water supply. Dr. Huddleston strongly disputed this theory, pointing out that all of the plates and glassware were being autoclaved.

Curiously, none of the professors came down with the disease. However, a couple of salesmen who made deliveries to the building contracted brucellosis. The state investigators summarily incriminated the drinking fountains in the building and even published their findings. Once again, Professor Huddleston disputed their theory in his own rebuttal article in the *Journal of the American Public Health Association,* 1942. "There is no way that the water can be implicated here!" he told Jim. A few years later, Professor Ken Maxcy of John Hopkins University presented a convincing hypothesis for an airborne dissemination of the organism in this outbreak in an article. His theory was ultimately accepted by the scientific community as the correct epidemiological assessment of the event.

Jim's fellow students voiced concern for their safety in future classes. However, Jim was not worried, as he worked with *Brucella* almost every day in the laboratory. "I never did develop a titer to the organism then or at any time in the future. I guess my laboratory technique was pretty good. However, the fact remains that

I was not taking a class in the building when this occurred. If I had, I likely would have been infected too," he said.

When Arthur Goldberg died in February, newspapers from coast to coast put Michigan State College in the limelight. Many years later in his role at CDC, Jim learned that the incident drew renewed attention to *Brucella* as a possible agent of biological warfare by the U. S. Army. "I was already pretty sure that I wanted to pursue a career in public health. However, this event likely erased any doubt that remained in my mind."

He continued to meet with Dean Giltner on a regular basis. Without Jim's knowledge, Dean Giltner then approached the Michigan State Health Department about creating a special, unprecedented internship that Jim could complete in lieu of some of his clinical rotations in his senior year. A Dr. C. C. Young was director of the Michigan State Health Department laboratories at the time. He met with Jim in to discuss the position. Dr. Young and Jim got along famously and both agreed to the terms of the internship. "This activity started a rumor that I was quitting veterinary college to take a job with the health department."

"The internship was a perfect idea," commented Jim. It provided him with valuable experiences that he would not have had otherwise. He learned how to make antiserum using rabbits for the treatment of bacterial pneumonia in people. "The need for the antiserum was later eliminated by the development of sulfa drugs. This demonstrated to me how a new product could quickly change the public health landscape," he said. He also learned how to make tetanus antiserum, grow bacteria to be used in pertussis vaccine, harvest vaccinia virus from infected calves for production of smallpox vaccine and inject mice to confirm rabies cases. In addition, he was involved in a water purification study that was tied to dairy and meat inspection. "To this day, I thank Dean Giltner for his vision and guidance. The extra attention he gave me made the big difference!"

Jim was a candidate for program director of the Junior American Veterinary Medical Association and was elected. In July of 1940, Jim and classmate Al Fahlund traveled to Washington, DC to attend the annual AVMA convention. There they attended the Michigan State College alumni meeting. Jim made a presentation about the *Michigan State College Veterinarian,* a new journal that Jim and Al started. This publication stayed in production for the next thirty years. They ran into Dr. Huddleston at the meeting; he congratulated them both on their work with the journal. During the trip, Jim was treated to a tour of the Bureau of Animal Industries (BAI), the forerunner of the Animal Plant Health Inspection Service (APHIS) of the USDA. This provided Jim and Al with the opportunity to meet many of the early leaders of veterinary science. Most notably, Jim met Dr. John R. Mohler who was the chief of the BAI at the time. He invited Dr. Mohler to Michigan State College to speak at a meeting of the Junior AVMA.

After the AVMA meeting, Jim traveled to a community near Baltimore with classmate Henry Keane to attend the World's Fair in New York City. Next, it was off to Boston to see Harvard and Massachusetts Institute of Technology (MIT) campuses with his friend and classmate Harrison Siegle. "I took a swim in the MIT pool. Harrison was a lightweight boxer at Michigan State College. We had a lot in common and were good friends," Jim said.

At Harvard Jim met with a Ms. Burnside in the administration office to ask about admission forms for the graduate program in public health. On the same day, Jim wanted to meet Hans Zinsser, a Harvard professor and the author of *Rats, Lice and History.* " Dr. Zinsser's goal in *Rats, Lice and History* was to bring science, philosophy, and literature together to establish the importance of disease, and especially epidemic infectious disease, as a major force in human affairs," said Jim. Dr. Zinsser was a bacteriologist and a pioneering immunologist who had led the development of vaccine and control programs to help manage typhus fever.

Unfortunately, Dr. Zinsser was very ill at the time and died a few months later. Jim did meet with Dr. Ed Huber, an Associate Dean of the Harvard School of Public Health who later mentored him during his year at Harvard. From there, Jim went on to Ithaca, New York to experience the grandeur of the Cornell University campus. He stopped en route at Holy Cross College to see his old friend Moose Krause, who had played football at Lakeview High

School back in Chicago. Moose later coached at Notre Dame. Next, Jim hitchhiked across Canada and returned to East Lansing, Michigan at the end of August, just in time for his senior year.

Jim was anxious to fill out his application to attend Harvard. Dean Giltner provided much guidance and support in this effort. During their meetings in the dean's comfortable office, the conversation would often stray back to politics. They discussed world events, attacks on free society and the imminent World War. Dr. Giltner was impressed with Jim's maturity and enjoyed talking global politics with him. Jim believes to this day that Dean Giltner really looked forward to their meetings. Jim looked forward to them as well.

Jim's veterinary medical education fell squarely in the middle of Franklin Delano Roosevelt's twelve-year presidency. FDR, much like Herbert Hoover, wanted to help eliminate poverty in the US. At the same time, Secretary of Labor Frances Perkins was drafting what ultimately became Social Security. Harry Lloyd Hopkins, a social scientist and close FDR advisor on the New Deal, recognized that the prevention and elimination of bovine tuberculosis was an important goal and helped to set the stage for funding the these efforts. This, coupled with the Department of Agriculture's desire to cut back on grain and livestock surpluses, meshed well with the tuberculosis eradication program. The unique set of conditions during the Great Depression provided veterinarians with many opportunities for work. To this day, Jim has admired FDR and for his leadership and support of public health.

During Jim's final year in veterinary medical school, Aina began making plans for their wedding. His proposal to her in the summer of 1937 now seemed a long time ago. In the meantime, Jim was struggling with a course in genetics and ended up with a "D." "I simply didn't pay enough attention!" Jim said. But he also knew that he was overextended. Most of Jim's senior year involved classes and clinics in small and large animal medicine in the mornings followed by his work and studies at the Michigan Health Department in the afternoons.

Jim's last invited Junior AVMA speaker was physician and wildlife biologist Dr. Robert G. Green from the University of Minnesota. He had recently differentiated fox encephalitis from canine distemper and later developed a vaccine that prevented encephalitis in foxes. He had also developed revolutionary theories on how cancer spreads in the body. With such a world renowned guest, Jim was concerned that the campus auditorium wouldn't be large enough for the attendees. He asked Dean Giltner about the feasibility of using the college music hall instead. Dean Giltner joked, "I suppose you want to give him my office too! Where do you plan to put me?" Jim got the hall and the seminar was well attended.

About this time, Dean Giltner began probing Jim about the veterinary curriculum and what should be changed to improve it. "There should be more exposure to the environmental aspects of farming. Also, veterinary students should be required to have better writing skills," Jim told him. Dean Giltner replied, "Writing skills? That's why you need a good secretary, Jim!" This was the only thing that Jim and Dean Giltner ever disagreed on.

The war was not going very well in Europe in the spring of 1941. Jim listened to the news reports on the radio every night. The Nazis had fully occupied Czechoslovakia, Poland, Norway, Denmark and France. Jim can remember being very concerned about Hitler and the possible negative outcomes of the war.

Jim remembered Mr. Krause, an undertaker in his neighborhood in Chicago. He was a German sympathizer who espoused Hitler's mission to stomp out communism and to build a new society. He encouraged Jim to join the movement, and promised to would get the German American *Bund*, a pro-Nazi organization, to support him. There was a lot of antiwar sentiment in the United States at the time but Jim did not buy into the *Bund* philosophy. The draft was imminent, and Jim could see his career plans possibly taking a sharp detour. In 1941, the United States abandoned its strict neutral position and began the historic "Lend-Lease" program with a $7 billion cap to help out Britain and its allies with weapons and equipment. Jim would soon receive his draft number, six in Lansing, Michigan.

In the midst of all this turmoil there were carefree nights at a pub. "It was ironic to guzzle German beer and to listen to their classical music for recreation," Jim said. Jim remembers one night

at the pub when it was announced that the Germans had just invaded Holland. He was out that night with a Dutch friend and
classmate, Ronny Steensma, who decided to join the Free Dutch
Air Force on the spot. Ronny returned to Michigan one month
prior to graduation, went off to war and was killed while serving
in Indonesia. He was awarded a Doctorate of Veterinary Medicine
degree posthumously in 1948. Jim would soon receive the same
degree. But he couldn't help thinking that he might one day meet
the same fate as his good friend Ronny.

CHAPTER 5:
A NEW DOCTOR, MARRIAGE
AND A PRACTICE IN PETOSKEY

Many of Jim's friends, and his brother John Axel, arrived the day before his graduation from the Michigan State Veterinary College. Jim was elated to see "Little Swede" John and close buddies whom he had played football and baseball with in high school. Jim's Uncle Art Nordquist came in from Milwaukee, and a cousin, Ruth Norman, flew from Modesto, California for the occasion. Aina's coworkers at the Chicago insurance office gave her a wedding shower before she left to join Jim in East Lansing. That evening, after all the guests had arrived, Jim and Aina threw a party on the front lawn of the house to set the mood for the next day. The guests were unaware how stressed Jim was at this time. He still hadn't heard back from Harvard regarding his application for graduate school. "I couldn't understand what was taking so long, and I was beginning to think that my dream to attend Harvard would not materialize," Jim recalled. Regardless, he kept his worries to himself and tried to focus on the joy of the immediate occasion.

The next day was a whirlwind. Jim received his Doctor of Veterinary Medicine diploma on Saturday, June 14, 1941 at 5:00 p.m. The youngest student in his class was twenty years old. Jim felt somewhat geriatric at twenty-eight. At 7:00 p.m. the same day, Jim said, "I do" to Aina. He invited his entire graduating class to the wedding. About fifty guests attended the ceremony at the non-denominational church on Grand River Street at the Michigan State College campus. His best man was Robert "Boone" Webster, one of his favorite housemates during veterinary school. He immediately went off to war. Dean Giltner sat in the front row of the church during the ceremony. Jim remembers choking up a little during his wedding vows. "I couldn't seem to pronounce the words!" he recalled. Dean Giltner told him later that he had trouble hearing Jim speak.

Since Jim had started out majoring in forestry, "I thought it somewhat paradoxical that the last event I would attend on the Michigan State College campus was my wedding reception at the Forestry Cabin!" Jim exclaimed. The reception was a grand affair; a great time was had with numerous toasts and predictions made by Jim and the guests. Alcoholic beverages weren't allowed on campus, but someone brought a sack of beer and stashed it in the attic of the cabin. "We made lots of trips to the attic that night!" Jim said with a grin. After the party, Jim learned that Al Fahlund, one of his classmates, spent much of the evening telling friends and family what an amazing person he thought Jim was and that he knew that Jim would be very successful in life and in his career. "This really stuck with me. At one point I worried that I wasn't even worthy of attending college. Yet on this day, Al was bragging on me. I never got this out of my mind and I tried to live up to what he said about me throughout my career. This is one of my more unusual memories from that time. We never know who or what will end up having a great influence on our lives," Jim said.

There was no time for continued celebration or rest the day after the wedding. Jim spent all of that Sunday studying for the state board exams which he would take on Monday and Tuesday of that week. There was still no word from Harvard, and he had not even considered an alternative pathway for his career. "In the meantime, I needed to find an internship or some kind of gainful employment," said Jim.

Dr. Chris Jensen was a Dane who came to the US and earned his veterinary degree at Ohio State. After veterinary school, he became a private practitioner in Petoskey, Michigan. He settled there during the Great Depression to serve the Scandinavian population living in that region. Dr. Jensen had lost an associate to the war and was working to find a replacement. He had recently hired another graduate, who had found a better opportunity in Missouri. Jim heard about the opening, applied and was hired. Clinical practice was not part of Jim's master plan, but he saw this job as something that would provide some valuable experience.

Dr. Jensen was quite involved in his community. He was a Rotary and Lions Club member and volunteered in other worthwhile organizations. These activities took a lot of time away from the practice, and he expected Jim to fill the gaps. The practice was about equally split between large animal and small animal medicine. When working, Dr. Jensen did most of the surgery and the country calls, leaving Jim with the balance of the work. "When Doc Jensen was gone, I was it. The caseload wasn't too heavy, so I could take a reasonable amount of time to work up each case and try to arrive at a solid diagnosis for each patient," he said. The practice provided Jim with numerous interesting experiences with his furry patients and their owners. This bolstered his confidence and became a long-term source of pride for him. Aina stayed with Jim in Petosky until the end of June and then went back to work in Chicago. Money was tight and she wanted to help save for their future home.

"One day a wirehaired fox terrier named Peter was brought in that was very depressed. He wouldn't eat and was quickly deteriorating," Jim recalled. Dr. Jensen examined the dog and couldn't find anything specifically wrong. He asked Jim to work up the case to see if he could come up with a diagnosis. The clinic was equipped with a fluoroscope. Jim put on the lead gloves and apron and went to work. "I still wonder about the radiation exposure that veterinarians were receiving in those days," Jim reflects.

During the fluoroscopic exam, he found a suspicious shadow in the dog's gut. He then palpated the dog's abdomen and felt what might be a steak bone lodged in the small intestine. "I reported this to Doc Jensen, and he was impressed," Jim said. Dr. Jensen recommended emergency surgery to remove the bone. Once they had opened the dog up, they found considerable necrosis in the small bowel. Dr. Jensen removed the bone and what he thought was all of the necrotic tissue and joined the gut back together via an end-to-end anastomosis. Unfortunately, the day after the surgery, the dog died.

Dr. Jensen was shaken up, as the clients were wealthy people who had traveled from New York to Petoskey for their summer vacation. "Jim, I want you to break the news to our clients. This is one of the tough parts of this job, and you need the experience," he directed. Dr. Jensen was confident that Jim could patch up this situation, as he had seen him deal expertly with clients in the past.

"This is a rare and tragic outcome, and we are very sorry." Jim said with gravity. He went on to say, "Unfortunately, in spite of the best surgeon's skills, animals can go into shock and sometimes this condition cannot be turned around. These things can and do happen in the veterinary world as they do in human medicine." The conversation then strayed on to how to handle Peter's remains. "I suggested cremation but the owners immediately went silent. As an alternate I proposed to have Peter embalmed and have him placed into a wooden coffin for burial," Jim said. The wife exclaimed, "Oh, Doctor, that would be so wonderful!" Jim was thinking to himself, *Embalming a dog? We didn't learn that in veterinary school!* He then called a local funeral home and arranged for them to embalm the dog.

But first, Jim was curious as to why the dog had died and performed a necropsy. He discovered that the sutures holding the gut together had failed. "Intestinal contents had flowed into the abdominal cavity resulting in a toxic septicemia and death," Jim recounted.

The bill included the surgery for $75, hospitalization $75 and another $75 for the services of the funeral home, totaling $225. This was quite a large fee by 1941 standards. Jim prepared the billing statement and presented it to Dr. Jensen, who exclaimed, "Isn't this too much?"

Jim replied, "These are important people with means who want the best care for their pet, and they expect to be billed accordingly!" Jim had learned this lesson in the insurance business and from his days of selling on the streets of Chicago. The clients took their embalmed dog back to New York with a coffin built by the local lumberyard for a proper burial in their yard. Before they left for their trip home, they stopped by the clinic and paid the bill in full.

Jim suggested many sound business practices that Dr. Jensen adopted. When animals came in with lacerations or abscesses, he pointed out how bad the teeth and nails were and would do a parasite exam. Jim remembers one well-to-do fellow from Chicago who said, "Well, I have never had all these things done to my dog."

Jim replied calmly, "This is all a part of our comprehensive service; we try to cover everything to be sure your pet is healthy." The man then paid his bill. From then on, Dr. Jensen gave Jim all the tough cases. "He loved to let me have the dogs with a muzzle full of porcupine quills!" Jim said.

In 1991, Jim went back to Michigan for his fiftieth class reunion. He was scheduled to speak at the Michigan Veterinary Medical Society meeting. On that trip and at least one time earlier, he went back to Petoskey to visit Dr. Jensen's hospital. Jim was amazed at the way the practice had expanded. The house where the original practice was located and where Jim and Aina lived in the attic was gone. "The new clinic was large, with five veterinarians, each with their own exam room." Jim learned that Dr. Jensen died in 1989.

Near the end of that summer, Jim finally received his acceptance to Harvard. Dr. Jensen was visibly upset when Jim gave him the news and urged him to stay. "I have to pursue my dream, Doc!" Jim told him. Jim rode the train back to Chicago with his things in preparation for the trip to Boston with Aina.

On returning to Chicago, Jim couldn't resist hitchhiking up to Mayo Clinic in Rochester, Minnesota to learn about the encephalitis in horses that seemed to be spilling over into people. In 1941 there was a major epidemic of Western equine encephalomyelitis, also known as Kansas horse disease, and also an outbreak of Eastern equine encephalomyelitis. While at Mayo, Jim met with a Dr. Feldman, who was studying drugs to treat tuberculosis, Dr. Al Carlson who was investigating bovine leukosis, and a prominent bacteriologist who was researching the equine encephalitides. "He had a theory that viruses were an alternate form of bacteria at the time," Jim said. Afterwards, Jim hitchhiked back to Chicago through Wisconsin.

After the short but sweet stint in practice, Jim and Aina were off to Boston, Massachusetts for a new adventure. The freshly minted Michigan State College veterinarian was determined to get a Master of Public Health degree at Harvard. Jim was only the second veterinarian to ever make the attempt. Jim and Aina bid farewell to family and friends and boarded the Grand Trunk Railroad bound for Boston.

CHAPTER 6:
GRAND TRUNK RAILROAD TO BOSTON

A strong feeling of adventure came over the newlyweds as they bought two tickets on the Grand Trunk Railroad that September morning in 1941. Starting from the Chicago station, they would travel back through East Lansing to say good-bye to some friends, then to Toronto, Montreal, down through Vermont, New Hampshire, and on into Boston, Massachusetts. They packed no household items, only luggage filled with clothes, books and personal mementos.

The trip gave them quality time to reflect, talk and dream. The train car they were in was coach class with side-by-side seating. They ate romantic meals in the dining car and talked about their future along the way. Aina was so happy that they had stayed together through it all. At one point she quizzed Jim, "Why did you want me? You could have had any girl!"

They talked of having a big family. "I thought of trying for nine boys so we could have our own baseball team!" Jim said with a smile. Jim was thinking at the time that he might still end up in practice or be a public health officer in a quiet, small town. He even thought about returning to Michigan State to teach.

Jim had visited Boston once before. He described to Aina what a grand city it was. However, as exciting as the big cities were, Aina and Jim made a pact to never return to Chicago or any similar big city to live. "We thought that living in a suburb of Chicago like Elgin or of some other large city would be ideal. We could easily come into the town to enjoy the musicals, operas and art galleries and then slip back into the bliss of suburbia," Jim reflected.

Aina dreamed of a sprawling one-story ranch home with lots of animals around. She loved all animals, especially horses. In the wake of the Great Depression and the war, international travel wasn't high on their list of priorities. "There is so much to explore right here in the United States!" Aina told Jim. The magic of the train and the dreams of a perfect future led to a lot of snuggling, nothing more. Even though they were technically on their honeymoon, they both decided that intimacy should be postponed until they had their total privacy.

Upon arriving in Ottawa, the capital of Canada in the southeast at the junction of the Ottawa River and the Rideau Canal, they decided to take a long walk in the cool air to take in the beauty of the town. They strolled by the old Dominion and the Parliament Buildings. "We were thinking that we might never be this way again and it was a beautiful day," said Jim. They apparently lost track of the time, because when they returned to the station their train had already departed. All of their bags were checked through to Boston, and Jim was carrying only a small briefcase. Jim thought to himself, *Heck, I can afford a decent hotel for my new bride; we'll just spend the night and get on the next train tomorrow.*

They walked on to the Chateau Laurie, the grand hotel of the Canadian National Railway system and went directly to the registration desk. The rate was a little high at five to six dollars per night, but they were on their honeymoon, after all. The stay would be well worth the price.

To their surprise, not only did the desk clerk refuse to give them a room, they were asked to leave. They had no luggage. The management apparently decided that the couple was attempting to arrange a sordid one-night stand. "We explained the whole story to them, but their minds were made up," said Jim. The one thing the couple needed to settle the dispute was their marriage license, but they didn't have it in their possession. Aina was wearing only a small gold band with no engagement ring. The whole presentation was not very convincing to the hotel staff. They left feeling embarrassed and a little confused. From there they walked on to a less expensive hotel near the railroad station and obtained a room for $2.50 per night. Jim can still hear Aina exclaiming, "I told you not to check all of our baggage to Boston!"

The next morning they boarded another train bound for Montreal, Quebec, a scenic island city at the confluence of the St. Lawrence and Ottawa Rivers. The town was named after Mount Royal, a hill that is located in the center of town. It is one of Canada's largest cities, a major port and a busy industrial complex. Originally founded by the French in 1642, the town was a stopping-off point for western exploration in the early days. For the Steeles, the exploration would be to the east. "As we rolled into Montreal, we noticed a significant military presence. There were soldiers and sailors in uniform and military vehicles everywhere," Jim recalled.

They decided to stay the night at the Dominion Hotel. "This was an old hotel with long corridors near the railroad station. I remember the difficulty we had communicating to the maid about wanting to take a bath as there was none in our room," said Jim. The only bath was a good distance down the hall, and the use of the room had to be arranged with the floor clerk. They finally found the clerk and were able to schedule some overdue bath time. "It was an amusing exercise with all the maids and hotel help speaking French and the Steeles hopelessly locked into the English language," Jim recalled.

The maids led Aina to the bathroom. She soon returned to their room to tell Jim that there was no way to lock the door. He was then enlisted to stand watch in the hallway while Aina bathed. It all worked out, and they chalked this up as their first experience taking a bath in a foreign country. It was all part of their first real adventure together.

Their next experience in Montreal would become a bittersweet memory on the trip and throughout their lives. Mount Royal provided a nice opportunity to take an invigorating walk and to see scenic Montreal from the top. After walking about a mile to the top of the hill, Aina was visibly worn out and breathing hard. She told Jim, "You know, I am really tired; why don't we take a cab down the hill?" Jim remembers getting a little upset with this request. *Why would anyone need a cab to go down a hill?* he thought to himself. After they returned to the hotel, Aina was able to rest. Later, Jim learned to regret the way he had acted that day. Aina's lack of stamina was the first sign of what would later be diagnosed as tuberculosis. Jim relived these memories when he was in Montreal in 1987 for the World Veterinary Congress. He looked for the Dominion Hotel but it had been torn down by that time.

The next day they boarded a train that took them through Vermont, White River Junction, New Hampshire and on in to the

Boston North Station. That night they stayed in a hotel that was eventually torn down to make room for a basketball arena for the Boston Celtics. Once in Boston, they immediately noticed that war news reporting was more spirited than in Chicago. The US was still somewhat neutral, with many in the streets saying things like, "If Germany takes over, so what?" and "Don't give the Brits any aid until they pay all their old war debts."

For Aina, Boston was everything that Jim had told her and more. "Aina was enthralled with the awesome architecture and cultural sites like the Paul Revere House, the Old North Church, and the Old State House. They provided a rich cultural ambience similar to what she enjoyed in Chicago," Jim remembered. She especially loved the breathtaking Cambridge campus of Harvard University, the oldest institution of higher learning in the United States. Founded in 1636, Harvard began holding classes in 1638 and was named in 1639 for the English clergyman John Harvard, the school's first benefactor. An arboretum, observatory, and museums are all associated with the main campus. "There was so much to do and so much to learn!" Jim said.

Jim and Aina attended a reception for new students at 55 Shadduck Street, where they served beer and snacks to the incoming students. "Gosh, this is a liberal place!" Jim whispered to Aina, contrasting Harvard with Michigan State College, where the serving of beer was not permitted even in town. Jim remembers speaking with one nice old lady with a proper Boston accent who was openly espousing the advantages of being a Harvard student and being immersed in the culture of wealth. Jim was thinking to himself how great it was just to be there. "I immediately wished I was better versed in American history!" Jim recalled. Jim and Aina were both totally captivated by the collective culture of Harvard. At one of the receptions, a local grand dame proclaimed, "Harvard has a great respect for breeding!" Jim quickly responded to her observation by announcing that he was a man of agriculture and added for fun, "Yes, we certainly have a great respect for breeding!" pawing the ground with his foot.

Harvard was going to be an adventure!

CHAPTER 7:
THE HARVARD EXPERIENCE

It was difficult for it to all sink in: *I am actually here in Cambridge registering to attend Harvard!* Jim and Aina were also excited about the adventure of setting up their first real home together. Only one other veterinarian had ever made it through the MPH program at Harvard, Phillip Carter, an Army officer who completed the program in 1937. Jim always wondered what Dr. Carter's career was like. For some reason, he never did meet him face to face. However, toward the end of his career at CDC, Dr. Carter wrote to Jim to compliment him on his fine work in public health and to congratulate him on his upcoming retirement. "I can still recall how nice it felt to hear that from him. We never worked together but yet we had this connection," Jim said.

With a little time on their hands before the fall semester started, Jim and Aina looked up Harrison Siegle, an old friend from Michigan State who had attended their wedding, and his mother. The Siegles invited Jim and Aina to stay with them at their house in Brookline while they hunted for their own place. The first weekend they all went on a clam-dig outing on the Atlantic shore. Afterwards, they had a traditional clambake and made clam stew. Unfortunately, Aina became nauseated. Ms. Siegle felt for sure that it was morning sickness. "I can remember worrying about that a little bit," Jim said. Soon they both broke with diarrhea. It was probably all related to too much activity and seafood they weren't used to. Aina recovered quickly, but Jim's diarrhea persisted for several days. He went to Harvard Medical School to see if he could receive treatment. He wasn't officially in the health system yet, so he ended up treating himself with whatever was available at the local pharmacy over the counter. "I began my stint at Harvard in rare style," Jim said.

It was difficult for Jim to contain his excitement while registering for the fall semester courses. He and Aina were still apartment hunting. The Siegles suggested some flats near their home. They finally rented a place at 372 Longwood Drive on the edge of

Brookline, Massachusetts. It was a nice first-floor studio apartment with a view of Plymouth Court. The flat included a kitchen and a private bath. There was no furniture other than a bed that folded out from the wall. They ended up renting the balance of the furnishings they needed. There was storage for suitcases and trunks in the basement. Jim recalled getting attacked by fleas from the cats that resided down there. This resulted in a strong allergic reaction, something he would experience again many years later in South America. They paid rent of fifty dollars per month and had to watch their budget closely to make the payments on time.

Aina was a great cook. She made many tasty meals that they both enjoyed in the warmth of their first domicile together. Sometimes they would go out to a restaurant for dinner. One of their favorite places was the Howard Johnson's on Huntington Avenue in Boston. Eventually, this location became the seed for the national chain known to most Americans.

One day an elderly couple stopped Jim and Aina on the street and exclaimed, "You two look like the new generation of Americans and the leaders of the future!" They both beamed and Jim thought to himself, *Right on, we will make our contributions!* Jim's self-confidence was growing by the day.

It seemed as soon as they arrived in Boston that classes were starting. One of Jim's first courses was statistics in public health taught by Professor Wilson, an aeronautical engineer in World War I. In those days, they solved complex mathematical problems with a hand-crank calculator. Some of Jim's favorite courses included public health administration with Dr. Edward Huber, a retired US Army Colonel in the Medical Corps, and public health epidemiology with Dr. John Gordon, who was a well known epidemiologist at the time. Dr. Gordon was editor of the *Handbook of Communicable Disease Control*, a tome first published in 1915 by the American Public Health Association. It is now available in at least seven languages and has become one of the most widely used infectious disease references in the world.

Public health microbiology was to be taught by the famous Dr. Hans Zinsser. As has been mentioned earlier, he was an

American bacteriologist and pioneer of modern immunology who facilitated the development of a vaccine against several varieties of typhus fever and who also authored *Rats, Lice and History*. Unfortunately, Dr. Zinsser had died a year earlier. Jim remembers being profoundly disappointed. However, Dr. John Enders, another leading bacteriologist at Harvard, taught the course. He later shared the Nobel Prize in 1954 for his work on culturing the polio virus. "He was a real friend of veterinary medicine, possibly because he had acquired brucellosis by exposure to animals on his own farm," Jim said. He remembered Dr. Enders's exciting introductory lecture on the Corynebacteria species, the bacterial cause of diphtheria. He also recalled the stories about some Harvard students from Japan who isolated leptospires from a pond near Cambridge sometime in the 1930s. Interestingly, they came to believe that the pathogen may be the cause of yellow fever.

Next there was a course in immunology taught by a Dr. Smith. Public health policy was taught by a Dr. Huber. Dr. Huber talked Jim into taking a course in advanced statistics in the spring semester. Jim somewhat regretted this as the homework took up a great deal of his time. He also took courses in nutrition, sanitary engineering and the ecology of disease. A course in venereal diseases became the only class Jim ever got a "D" in.

Dr. James Bryant Conant was a world-renowned chemist and president of Harvard from 1933 to 1953. He delivered a memorable lecture that Jim recalled vividly. "There will be many significant changes occurring in the world during your time here!" he stated in a serious tone.

"We didn't know if he was referencing the fall of Britain or possibly events even more terrible and unforeseen," Jim said.

The global nature of the public health movement was becoming very apparent to Jim as he met his new Harvard classmates at a reception. There were physicians from Colombia, China, Mexico, the Philippines and other countries whose students came to Harvard for their graduate work in public health. Being surrounded by fine minds from all over the world was exhilarating to Jim. Many top scientists were fleeing Europe and joining the faculty at Harvard. "These experiences planted the seeds of my dream of globalizing the concept of veterinary public health," he said.

Jim quickly realized that the privilege of obtaining his Master's in Public Health at Harvard came with a big price. "Graduates of this prestigious program were expected to advance the field of public health to benefit all the peoples of the world. The thought was a little daunting, but I knew I was up to the challenge," Jim said. He can remember realizing that he had not previously thought of himself as a global health worker or that global activities would have any significant role in his future career.

Dr. Thomas J. Parran, the sixth surgeon general of the US (1936-48) under President Roosevelt, visited Harvard during the fall semester of 1941. He delivered a brilliant lecture on sexually transmitted diseases. "He was pushing society to bring these problems out into the open so that solutions could be found. Furthermore, he was adamant that it was wrong to call them *social* diseases, as he believed that this classification had the effect of suppressing the general knowledge of the diseases," Jim said. Attending lectures like this one was stimulating for Jim. "I always seemed to come away with ideas that I might apply in the realm of veterinary medicine and public health," Jim recalled.

Aina was invited to join the staff of the British-American Ambulance Corps to raise money to buy ambulances for England in support of the war. Aina also got a job as a salesclerk with the Harvard Co-op, a bookstore on campus. Many of the young Harvard men would flirt with her and ask her to go out on dates. Jim remembered that she enjoyed all the attention. Jim recalled buying a typewriter from the store at a great discount; the machine is still in his possession today. Aina loved her work on and around the campus and enjoyed her intellectual interaction with the students.

With Thanksgiving holiday arriving soon, a group of students arranged for a weekend of camping. Jim and Aina drove up on Wednesday and stayed on through Sunday with six other couples. They had a fun time, but unfortunately, this was to be their last such outing together.

War news was pervasive at this time. German General Erwin Rommel's forces had recently been turned back by the British in North Africa. This was one of the first positive things Jim can remember hearing about the war. Later in 1944, Rommel would be implicated in the failed defense of France and even in a plot to assassinate Hitler. He later committed suicide. Jim was concerned about Hitler's plan to dominate the world and oppress, even eliminate, minorities, especially the Jews. Jim was so very proud to be an American. "The United States is one country that sees there are two sides to a story" Jim said.

Back in Chicago the news media had adopted an antiwar stance. But in Boston it was entirely different. There, America was presented by the press as the savior of the new free world. "This was the Woodrow Wilson view," Jim pointed out. On December 7, 1941, Jim was listening to the Chicago Bears and the Washington Redskins game at about noon when a reporter broke in with the news that there had been large explosions at Pearl Harbor. By around 3:00 p.m. it was confirmed that the Japanese had executed a successful surprise air attack against the United States. Jim remembers pacing the room with anger. "The yellow peril is coming true!" he muttered to himself. This referred to the perceived threat of the expansion of Asian populations into the Western world. Jim told Aina, "Somehow I need to be a part of this!" Aina worried about him going off to war.

Jim visited the Navy recruiter the next day to see how he might be able to contribute to the war effort. "I can't recall why I picked the Navy over the Army or some other branch of the military," Jim said. The recruiter told him that the bulk of the war would likely be in the Pacific theater. However, the Germans declared war on the United States later that week, on December 11, making it a global conflict. "At first, my anger at the Japanese exceeded that at the Germans, but that was before any knowledge of the Holocaust and of Hitler's views on Christianity," Jim recalled. He felt very close to the British and finally decided that Europe needed to be saved before worrying about the Far East. A year earlier, the peacetime draft had passed by only one vote in Congress. The Navy advised Jim to wait until he finished his degree before considering entering the military.

Harvard soon assembled a medical team that deployed to England to help in caring for the war wounded. This spurred Jim's first thoughts regarding the health aspects of the war effort. He learned later that many universities were assembling health teams. There was one public health expert on the Harvard team by the name of John Gordon. He and Jim became good friends after the war. Dr. Gordon did some pioneering work on controlling scarlet fever in children and was recruited to head the Harvard Department of Epidemiology. Jim remembers being very disappointed that Dr. Gordon wouldn't be available to teach his epidemiology class while he was at Harvard. In 1960, Dr. Gordon asked Jim to join the editorial staff for the *Handbook of Communicable Disease Control* as a consultant on zoonotic diseases. He continued in that role for the next forty years. Jim later recommended A.B. Benenson to succeed Dr. Gordon as editor in 1975.

One day in December 1941, shortly after the bombing of Pearl Harbor, Aina came home nearly delirious with fever and chest aches. Jim thought she might have pleurisy. After all the diagnostics were performed, he went by the hospital and spoke to a resident, who explained what they had found. Her radiographs clearly showed lesions of tuberculosis in Aina's lungs. "I was devastated. I began crying as I left the hospital and literally cried all the way back to our apartment," Jim recalled.

The cruel facts began to sink in one by one. There were no effective medications to treat tuberculosis at the time. Penicillin was still a military secret. Dr. William Feldman was working with sulfa drugs. They were available but unfortunately were not showing promise against tuberculosis. Since 1914, Selman A. Waksman had been experimenting with soil bacteria and fungi and in 1939 had discovered the inhibitory effect of actinomycetes on bacterial growth. In 1940, he and his team members isolated the first antibiotic effective against the tuberculosis organism, called actinomycin. Unfortunately, this version of the drug was found to be too toxic for use in humans.

The code was finally cracked in 1943 by Waksman and his team at Rutgers University. In experimental animals, streptomycin, purified from the fungus Streptomyces griseus, a soil-derived organism, proved to inhibit the tuberculosis bacteria with some minimal side effects to the inner ear. In November 1944, strep- tomycin was given for the first time to a severely ill tuberculosis patient; it had an almost immediate positive effect. The disease was arrested and the bacteria could not be found in his sputum. A wonder drug had been born. But this discovery would oc- cur two years after Aina began showing serious symptoms of the disease.

After much consultation with medical specialists, Jim decided to put Aina into the Channing Home. This institution was origi- nally the Channing Street Home for Sick and Destitute Women, which admitted its first patient on May 1, 1857. The home started in the vestry room of the Federal Street Church. Most of the pa- tients had tuberculosis or what was then known as consumption. The home moved four times and finally ended up in a building in the Longwood area of Boston on the corner of Francis Street and Pilgrim Road. This was close to where the Harvard Medical School was relocating and is where Aina was hospitalized. With the advent of successful drugs, fewer patients were taken in over time. The Channing Home was closed in 1958.

The cost of Aina's residence at Channing Home was high at five dollars per day. "This was a lot of money for an unemployed graduate student," Jim stated.

However, Dean Drinker offered to help Jim to pay for her stay at Channing with his own personal funds. "You don't need any unnecessary distractions from your studies, Jim!" Dean Drinker told him. The famed Angell Memorial Animal Hospital offered to let Jim work some evening and weekend hours as a clinician, but he never took them up on the opportunity. He wanted to focus as much as he could on his studies. His Public Health Ser- vice fellowship was bringing in $125 per month, but he still had to pay for rent, food, utilities, books and other incidental expenses.

To make a little extra money, Jim shared a room with military engineering, and medical officers who attended short courses at Harvard. "Somehow, it all worked out financially, but it definitely wasn't easy. Dean Drinker was a thoughtful and generous man," Jim said.

There were some happy moments along the way. Aina was allowed to come home for the Christmas holidays that year. Unfortunately, final exams for the fall semester were after Christmas, so Jim had to keep studying through the break. Aina and Jim had guests during this holiday season. But reality set back in on January 2. Aina had to return to Channing Home. Fortunately, her fever seemed to be under control and she was in good spirits overall.

In the spring of 1942, Dr. Carl Brandley, a veterinarian, came to Harvard to establish a laboratory on Huntington Avenue to study the Newcastle disease virus. Caused by a paramyxovirus, the agent was listed by the department of defense as a potential biowarfare weapon. Dr. Brandley knew Jim from Michigan State, where he had done some work on avian leukosis. "We would go out to dinner on occasion and talk shop," said Jim.

During spring break, Jim and some friends went to New York City to visit the Rockefeller Foundation. Today, this is the Rockefeller Laboratories of Rockefeller University. He met with some of the scientists there, especially the laboratory staff, whose members asked Jim to consider coming there to take care of the animal colonies. Jim learned abut Theobold Smith, MD, the famous epidemiologist and physician who had spent time at Rockefeller University. Even though he was a physician, Dr. Smith became was appointed Inspector for the Bureau of Animal Industry (BAI) in 1884 and was directed to investigate a number of livestock diseases. He did some outstanding work on diseases like Texas Fever, Glanders and others.

From there they went on to Princeton University in New Jersey. Jim got to meet Richard Shope, MD, an internationally recognized physician and virologist of the time. His son, Robert Shope, also became famous as a physician and an arbovirologist. He finished his distinguished career at the University of Texas Medical Branch in Galveston, Texas, near Houston, where Jim would eventually join the faculty of the University of Texas, School of Public Health and later retire. Jim told Dr. Shope various stories about the Harvard Veterinary School, which was in operation from 1879 to 1910, and how misguided the school was. "The faculty was apparently more interested in lameness in horses than it was basic veterinary research," Jim said. He was surprised to see how well the students lived at Princeton. "Fraternities weren't enough for these guys. They had their own supper clubs!" Jim recalled.

Jim's experiences at Harvard linked him to some of the world's greatest scientists of the time. He became friends with Dr. John Enders, who established an infectious disease laboratory at Boston Children's Hospital in 1946. Dr. Enders isolated the polio virus for the first time in 1949 with the assistance of Thomas Weller and Frederick Robbins. This made it possible for Sabin and Salk to develop a vaccine that eradicated polio from the world. "Dr. Enders had tremendous respect for veterinarians. He encouraged me to become a part of the public health team. I was thrilled when they were recognized for their work on polio," Jim stated. Dr. Thomas Weller later did some laboratory work for Jim when he was working with the Public Health Service in Puerto Rico. Dr. Alex Langmuir of CDC introduced Jim to Dr. Frederick Robbins many years later.

Back at Harvard, graduation was imminent. The message boards around campus were full of job offerings for health officers and epidemiologists. But Jim was hearing that a veterinarian would not be competitive for a position as a health officer or an epidemiologist, even with a graduate degree. This had Jim concerned. He turned to Dean Drinker and his wife for advice. "Do I need an MD degree to be taken seriously in the public health field?" Jim asked. "Dr. Drinker had not yet embraced the term *zoonosis*, but spoke of the importance of animals in the ecology of disease," Jim recalled. Jim's experience with the brucellosis outbreak at Michigan State College had intensified his resolve to pursue a career in the veterinary aspects of public health. Dr. Drinker responded to Jim's concerns by stating firmly "If you want to make your point that animal diseases are important as they relate to human health, fly under one flag, young man!"

Jim's passion was to integrate veterinary medicine with human medicine and public health—to help bring the concept of *One*

Medicine to fruition. "Veterinarians would protect the public by maintaining animal health," said Jim.

Dean Giltner, back at Michigan State College, wrote letters to Jim that supported Drinker's guidance. Dr. Giltner encouraged him over and over, "Stay the course, Jim!" And, thankfully, that's exactly what he did.

CHAPTER 8:
THE OHIO HEALTH DEPARTMENT–BEGINNINGS

Dr. K. F. Meyer came to lecture toward the end of Jim's last spring term at Harvard. "He was looking for what he termed a 'bright young man' to come to San Francisco to work with him on military research projects," Jim said. After the lecture, Jim asked Dr. Meyer a question about the pathogenesis and epidemiology of brucellosis. Dr. Meyer responded with a long, detailed discourse on the disease. "He was absolutely brilliant," Jim said. The feeling was apparently mutual; after the lecture Dr. Meyer inquired about Jim's plans. "He offered me full status as a research associate in his lab. He also would support me in pursuing a PhD or MD degree if I wished," Jim recalled. The opportunity excited Jim very much. That night, he told Aina the details, and she was equally inspired. Furthermore, he knew that Aina would receive the very best of medical care at the University California Medical School in the Bay area. Jim told Dr. Meyer that he was indeed interested and asked him to keep him in mind for the position.

It was time to leave Boston and make their way to Chicago. Jim got tickets at the Brookline rail station and arranged to have Aina picked up by taxi at the Channing Home. He had their household goods shipped directly to Chicago. Jim remembers that he was dressed warmly for the trip and was wearing a blue Homburg hat. After linking up with Aina, he had the taxi driver take them on a nostalgic tour of Boston and Cambridge to pass time until their departure time from the train station.

Five years later, Jim learned the taxi driver in Boston turned Jim in to the federal authorities. He reported that he had driven a suspicious couple with Germanic accents and clothing. In addition, they were taking a lot of pictures and were discussing details of the war efforts. This prompted an investigation that led back to the School of Public Health at Harvard. The FBI was initially ordered to arrest the Steeles in New York City, their first scheduled train stop. Fortunately, this did not happen. "Once my records were checked out at Harvard, the investigation was closed. We were dumbfounded when we learned about all of this!" Jim said smiling.

Jim and Aina changed trains in New York City to travel to State College, Pennsylvania to visit Cousin Bill Thorp. Most of their two day stay was spent discussing Jim's career plans. "Bill was very impressed with the possibility for me to work with K. F. Meyer," Jim said. Next, they traveled to Chicago by train, where they spent a month with Aina's family. Jim also spent some time with his brother John. The future looked bright, and optimism regarding Aina's health remained high as they planned their move to California. At this time, her fever was gone and she was feeling well and gaining weight.

In July, Jim received a disappointing wire from K. F. Meyer. Unfortunately, the Army contracts did not materialize and the job offer had to be withdrawn. He learned later that Dr. Meyer was denied full participation in war-related research because of his Germanic lineage. Jim was at a loss to know what to do next. "Aina kept her positive attitude and worked hard to cheer and encourage me," Jim recalled. For the time being, Jim stayed with his brother and Aina stayed with her folks.

With no other promising opportunities on the horizon, Jim contacted the Michigan Health Department to inquire about job openings. He thought about going back to Lansing to continue his work there, but somehow it didn't make sense. "I was thinking, maybe I should go back to the University of Chicago to pursue an MD degree?" Jim said. He shuddered to think of this, as it would be like starting over with all the qualifying exams and prerequisites for medical school.

Jim decided to visit the US Public Health Service (USPHS) office in Chicago to see what opportunities might exist. "I wasn't sure how I would be received. But they supported me in school. What did I have to lose? In some ways I felt indebted to them. Maybe this could be an opportunity for me to give something back," Jim said.

On the day of his interview, Jim told the receptionist his career goals. "She looked at me like I was from Mars!" Jim recalled.

A young physician named Henry Holle was walking through the office and asked Jim, "Can I help you?" Jim began telling him about animal diseases of public health interest. "He invited me to meet with Dr. Mark Ziegler," Jim said. Dr. Ziegler was the Chief of the USPHS regional office at the time. "They were both big, tall guys. I told them my dream of integrating veterinary medicine and public health. They listened carefully," said Jim. Dr. Ziegler called the Washington office and learned that there were openings for sanitarians in Indiana and Ohio. "Jim, you should take a close look at these positions," Dr. Ziegler stated.

Jim traveled to Columbus, Ohio by train to check out the open position there. He was interviewed by the chief of the Sanitary Division on his first day in town. Jim remembered that the staff was quite impressed with his MPH from Harvard. "In those days, we had a simple rule of thumb for calculating a decent wage. This involved taking your age and multiplying by one hundred. I was twenty-nine and so I asked for $2,900 a year for a starting salary. They responded that the average starting pay for the position was $2,400 but that they could offer me $2,800. I guess that was the Harvard factor, regardless, I was ecstatic!" Jim said with a grin.

Jim returned to where Aina was staying with her cousin on the North Side of Chicago. He told her about the Ohio opportunity. "I would be paid by USPHS funds but would be working under the State Department of Health," he told her. This kind of arrangement is still common today. Aina was thrilled with the news. Jim liked the people in Ohio and the offer was more than fair. "We decided to not even bother exploring the Indiana position," he said.

In August of 1942, Jim and Aina purchased a 1941 light-green Mercury two-door sedan from a friend who was going into the military. Jim drove to Columbus, Ohio and rented a small furnished room with just the basic amenities. He met a retired Ohio businessman who helped him to get settled in Columbus. "Throughout my career, I have had so many people that have gone out of their way for me. I have been very lucky in this regard!" Jim said. Later, Jim came back to Chicago to get Aina. Back in Columbus, they found a three-room apartment within walking distance of the Ohio State campus.

"It felt great to be employed and to have some direction," Jim stated. He was enjoying his work and felt assured that it was a good start toward realizing his career goals. "One of my duties was to inspect dairies. Their goal was to be upgraded to 'Grade A' status so that milk products could be sold to the military," he said. Colonel Greenlee, the chief veterinary officer at Fort Hayes, was Jim's liaison at the Army post. He schooled Jim on the role of military physicians. "Fungal mycelia were discovered in some butter products. Colonel Greenlee asked me if this was something to be concerned about. From my training, I knew that this was a harmless contaminant that did not constitute a public health problem and I told him as much," Jim said.

Colonel Greenlee reported this back to Washington, DC, and the information was relayed to Frank Merriwether, MD, the medical liaison officer with the military. In turn, he reported back to the Chicago office. Some months later, Jim went to a luncheon where Dr. Merriwether was speaking. "He said some really nice things about me in front of the group, something about me being part of a new generation of public health sanitarians," Jim said. Dr. Merriwether was transferred to Chicago and became a regional director for the Midwest. "He was a staunch supporter of veterinarians in public health," Jim stated.

An outbreak was reported at Fort Campbell, Kentucky that was suspected to be food-borne. The investigation by a local Army medical officer pointed to milk as a possible source. However, it appeared that the milk had been properly pasteurized. Jim read the report and suggested that staphylococcus toxins might be involved, as they would survive pasteurization. He traveled to Fort Campbell with Dr. Haskell, the senior veterinary sanitarian. There they confirmed that staph toxin was the etiology. "It was their practice to pool raw milk in containers that were not chilled all night prior to pasteurization, allowing for the formation of toxin," Jim reported.

Later, Dr. Haskell asked Jim to come to Chicago for a short assignment at the regional office. He wanted Jim to inspect some of the large constant flow pasteurization operations. This was considered a new technology at the time. "This was when I realized that we were chasing engineering problems, not veterinary issues.

I wanted to concentrate on veterinary public health problems that originated at the farm level," Jim said.

During his stint with the Ohio Health Department, Jim attended the American Public Health Association (APHA) meeting in St. Louis in November 1942 and the American Veterinary Medical Association (AVMA) meeting in Chicago in July 1943. All of the annual AVMA meetings were held in Chicago during World War II. Jim delivered a presentation of an outbreak of swimmer's itch as his first of many contributions at AVMA meetings. Swimmer's itch is caused by an avian parasite that passes through snails during its life cycle. The snail releases schistosome larvae in the water that burrow into the skin of swimmers, as well as animals, resulting in the itching symptoms. Swimmer's itch was a disease he had researched while at Harvard. Dean Ward Giltner sat in the front row during his presentation and listened intently.

Within two months after moving into their new apartment in Columbus, Aina's fever began spiking again. Jim and Aina drove to Chicago for Thanksgiving in 1942. After the holiday they went to Ann Arbor to see a Dr. Alexander at the University of Michigan. He came highly recommended by the medical faculty at Harvard. Dr. Alexander performed an intensive examination including radiographic studies. Jim remembers Aina coughing up pus at this stage, sometimes uncontrollably. After the laboratory results were in, Dr. Alexander reported callously, "Young man, don't waste your time trying to save her; she will be dead in two years or less." Jim couldn't believe his ears. "He was so heartless. I didn't know how to respond. I learned later that Dr. Alexander came down with tuberculosis himself and died a few years after he had examined Aina," said Jim.

They went from there to the Ingham County Sanitarium in Lansing in for a second opinion. There they met with a Dr. Stringer. Jim was so distressed that he introduced himself as a dentist. He can remember Aina reacting, "What did you say, 'dentist'?"

Dr. Stringer told Jim, "I think we can give you a little more hope than Dr. Alexander did." Aina was admitted to the Ingham County facility and ended up spending seven years there. During that time, the medical staff would try several therapies and surgeries to improve her condition.

During the time Aina was hospitalized, Jim continued on with his job in Ohio, gaining valuable field knowledge and experience. One day he was called to investigate a patient, a county agent, who lived near Lima, Ohio. Jim traveled there and gathered a complete history. He learned that the man was well liked in the community. He became ill and visited a chiropractor to try to find out what his problem was. Soon, the man experienced severe neurological signs, was hospitalized and died. The case was confirmed by the public health laboratory as rabies.

"The thing that stood out in my mind was that there was no history of animal contact as far as I could tell," Jim related. Little was known about the role of skunks, raccoons or bats with respect to rabies at that time. In 1970, Jim read a report of a six-year-old boy named Matthew Winkler from Lima, Ohio who had been bitten by a bat while sleeping and later developed rabies but miraculously survived. Jim would always wonder if the patient he investigated in 1943 had been bitten by a bat.

A case of smallpox was reported in East Liverpool, Ohio. "I had an intense interest in the disease. I had worked with vaccinia at the Michigan State Health Department while a student in veterinary school," Jim said. An extensive investigation was conducted. Being a veterinarian, Jim wasn't asked to examine the patient, an elderly woman. The question that Jim was trying to answer for his superiors was whether there could be an animal source of smallpox. "I advised everyone involved that there was no known animal reservoir of the disease. I suddenly became an expert on the topic," Jim said with a smile.

Jim enjoyed learning about the rich Ohio culture and history. One time while on a road trip, he visited a yellow fever monument in the town square of Ironton, Ohio. The memorial documented an outbreak of the mosquito-borne viral disease that had traveled up the Mississippi River from New Orleans in the 1870s. "A resident told me an interesting story about how they used to smear lard on flooring to keep the wood from warping after the floods. I made many trips between Columbus and Lansing. On one cold winter Sunday evening I fell asleep at the wheel, ran off the road, tore through a fence and careened helplessly across a farm field. I managed to wake up and stop the car just before slamming into a huge tree. I often think about how everything could have been cut short right there!"

Jim stayed in Columbus until September 1943, when the draft board notified him that he would be called up before the end of the year. At the time, Jim's number in the Michigan draft board was seven. He spent many nights at Fort Hayes in Columbus dining at the mess hall and making friends. In September 1943, he was offered a commission as a first lieutenant in the Army by Brigadier General Kelser, chief of the US Army Veterinary Corps. Back in Chicago, Dr. Merriweather learned about the Army offer. "Jim, why not take a commission in the Public Health Service as a lieutenant junior grade, the same rank as a first lieutenant in the Army?" he asked. Jim decided to go for the USPHS commissioned corps. "My commission was delayed because the prerequisite was a total of six years of school and job experience. I had just attained this with five years of school and one year Public Health Service field work," said Jim. The commission was approved at the end of October 1943 and the Michigan draft board was notified. "I called Brigadier General Kelser to say that I wouldn't be coming into the Army after all. I felt that I had made the right decision," Jim stated.

Jim was soon notified that he would be assigned to Puerto Rico. His duties would be to investigate food-borne illness and animal disease problems. "I remember packing my green Public Health Service fatigue uniforms for the trip," said Jim. In January 1944, Jim traveled to Washington, DC and received his orders for duty in Puerto Rico from Slim Atkins, a senior officer in the Sanitary Engineering Division. Before leaving the United States, Jim was offered a brief mission at the regional office in Chicago so he could spend some time with Aina. "Unfortunately, Aina was not healthy enough to accompany me to Puerto Rico. She was, of course, upset. But I assured her that I would stay close in touch by phone and visit as often as I could. But overall, she encouraged me to tackle my new assignment with a passion and to pursue my dreams!"

CHAPTER 9:
USPHS COMMISSION: PUERTO RICO, WEST INDIES AND BEYOND

With orders in hand for his assignment to the Caribbean, Jim stopped back in Washington, DC to visit the USPHS office in January 1944 for final processing. There he met Mr. Abe Fuchs, another sanitary engineer, who was in charge of the Milk and Food section, and several others. "I immediately came away with the feeling that the Public Health Service was a very close-knit organization that cared about its members. I was really impressed with the way people greeted and accepted me," Jim recalled.

He also met with Colonel Lawrence B. Bixby, who was married to Jim's cousin Nanine Steele. Nanine was the daughter of his Uncle Ira Steele. Colonel Bixby took Jim to dinner one evening. "He said he was really proud of me. It felt really good. Unfortunately, Nanine was an alcoholic. Colonel Bixby divorced her in 1950," Jim recalled. As discussed earlier, many of the Steeles suffered with alcoholism, including Jim's father and Uncles Ira and Nelson. Interestingly, Nanine became a member of the Women's Army Corps. She was well educated, with a degree in history from the University of Chicago and later a master of arts in literature. She taught in Colorado for a while but later died of cirrhosis.

Soon it was time for Jim began the long trip to his new assignment. The first leg was by train to Miami. "I had a sleeping berth on the coach and the trip was pretty comfortable as I recall. I would make this trip many more times," Jim said. Along the way, Jim met a man who was traveling to Miami to stay for the winter. "He was a bookie from Steubenville, Ohio, who loved horse racing. We talked about how veterinarians support the racing industry," he said. Jim knew Steubenville from his work in milk sanitation. "I had a flight delay in Miami, so my new found friend invited me to the horse races. We had a great time. But I remembered feeling almost guilty, enjoying the Florida sun while the war was raging on around the world," Jim recalled.

Jim's departure was finally confirmed for 6:00 a.m. on his third day in Miami. "I reported to the airport in my green fatigue uniform. This was only my second time in an airplane. We flew on a twin-engine Douglas DC3, one of the most recognizable and reliable aircraft in the world at the time. I would log many hours in the DC3," he said. The first stop was Camaguey, Cuba, a city located almost dead center in the island with sandy red soil quite different than the black dirt of Illinois that Jim was used to. After a brief layover he flew on to Port-au-Prince, Haiti. "There I was greeted by beautiful, light-brown-skinned girls speaking in English with French accents," said Jim. Soon he was off to Trujillo City, Dominican Republic, a city that was named after Rafael Leónidas Trujillo Molina, dictator of the country from 1930 to1961. The last leg of the journey flew him direct from the Dominican Republic to San Juan, Puerto Rico. "I remember the spectacular view of the pristine blue coral reefs as we approached from the north end of the island," he said.

"Elmer Herringer was the senior sanitarian on the island. He was the one who requested that a veterinary sanitarian be assigned to Puerto Rico. Mr. Herringer greeted me with a *rum salute* when I arrived at about 4:00 p.m. We chatted while I waited for my luggage. I was tired from the trip. The rum made me even sleepier. I felt like I might be coming down with something," he said. Jim was taken to the Normandy Hotel and checked into a room with three US Army officers, one lieutenant and two captains. The hotel was equipped with a large mess hall to provide meals for the resident military officers.

The next day, they traveled to the customs building at the port near the Coast Guard headquarters and also to the offices of federal inspectors in the Old San Juan area of the base. "I loved the sprawling banyan trees, a tropical fig, in the square and the beautiful pre-peeled oranges that were being peddled in the streets," said Jim. Jim was soon assigned to an office that he would share with a sanitary engineer.

The first day, Jim met Dr. Raymond Vonderlehr, a physician who was in charge of the USPHS medical mission for Puerto Rico. He welcomed Jim with his soft Virginia drawl. Dr. Vonderlehr's chief of staff was Commander Joe Dean. Under Dr. Dean was Dr. Jack Haldeman, who led the sexually transmitted disease program. Jim was formally introduced to all the staff.

Within forty-eight hours after arriving, Jim developed a severe cold and was admitted into the hospital. "I really didn't think this was necessary but I went along with my doctor's recommendations. It was a bit embarrassing for me as a new arrival. I remember the Puerto Rican nurses telling me that I was like most Americans–big, blond and loud!" he said. Jim had many visitors. Dr. Tom Shinnick, the director of the hospital, even came by to see him. Many years later, Jim would collaborate with him on a project at a hospital in Galveston, Texas.

"Amy Dean, the wife of Executive Officer Joe Dean, brought some baked goods to my room. I really appreciated this gesture, and it was the beginning of a long relationship with the Deans. Once they learned about Aina's illness they really took me under their wings. Joe arranged for me to use the phone in the FBI office so that I could stay in close touch with Aina," said Jim. Upon being discharged from the hospital, Jim was introduced to the chief sanitary public health officer in Puerto Rico, Nelson Biaggi. He was also recently commissioned and would be working closely with Jim.

After about six months in the Normandy Hotel, Mr. Herringer moved Jim over to the Navy billets. Jim's roommate was a pilot who flew submarine patrol planes each morning. He left early in the morning and returned at lunchtime. Soon, the Caribbean was declared free of German submarines, and food shortage problems began to subside. Jim's next roommate, Francis McMannis, was the navy ship store director. A real jokester, Francis was a Notre Dame graduate and a bachelor. Jim can recall many enjoyable evenings drinking "Fajardo river water," a rum drink, with Francis at the Navy club on Saturday nights where there were evening fiestas. "After the late Saturday nights, it was sometimes difficult to get up for church services the next morning," Jim said with a grin. The beautiful Fajardo River comes out of the El Yunque Mountains, cool and clean, in eastern Puerto Rico. The area is the focus of many projects to protect the delicate environment of the coastline today.

Jim's assignment to Puerto Rico kindled strong relationships with the US Army and the United States Department of Agriculture (USDA). The USDA was established in 1862. The Bureau of Animal Industries (BAI) was created by President Chester Arthur in 1884 to provide a much needed animal health and food inspection service for the United States at the demand of European bankers and food importers. The BAI was the predecessor of the Food Safety Quality Service (FSQS) that was created in 1977, later to be renamed the Food Safety Inspection Service (FSIS) in 1981. Today, the FSIS is a vibrant, high-tech organization that exists almost solely to protect our meat supply. The strong relationships that Jim built while in Puerto Rico became very valuable in his future activities.

"Lowell Barnes was with the Bureau of Animal Industries (BAI) in Puerto Rico at the time. Oxen were valuable beasts of burden on the island for centuries during the sugar cane harvest. But my primary mission on Puerto Rico was to assure adequate hygiene for dairy products used by the military. Our strategy was to lower bacterial counts in the milk. We were also responsible for finding wholesome water sources for the dairies," Jim said. This became a joint project involving the Puerto Rico Department of Public Health, the USPHS and the BAI. Many decades later, Lowell Barnes spoke at Jim's ninetieth birthday dinner.

The ice cream plants on the island were also inspected, although the problems there were simple hygiene issues. "One of my other missions was to salvage meat from herds of cattle that tested positive for tuberculosis but, upon slaughter, showed no lesions of TB," Jim recalled. The local health department and medical community wanted the animals destroyed and disposed of. Jim advised them that these animals were safe for consumption. The BAI was pleased with Jim's judgment and backed up his recommendations. His guidance conserved agricultural assets, especially quality protein food resources for the military.

Jim was sent on a mission to the Virgin Islands to review the US Navy hygiene practices for reconstituting powdered milk. This was a new practice that introduced some novel hygiene problems. Dr. Norman Thetford was a medical officer on St. Croix in charge of the main hospital and worked closely with Jim while he was there. Dr. Thetford and Jim became lifelong friends. "For many years, he was the last survivor from my duty in the Caribbean. He died in November, 2005. We planted a tree in Houston in his honor," said Jim.

Jim was also asked to investigate a high incidence of animal bites that were occurring on the islands. "All of the brain specimens that I collected in the Virgin Islands and Puerto Rico were examined for Negri bodies by Dr. Tom Weller at the US Army laboratory. No positive results were ever found. I came to the conclusion that there was little or no rabies in Puerto Rico or the Virgin Islands at the time. I reported this up the Public Health Service chain of command," he said.

Soon, Jim was strongly urging his superiors to establish a formal veterinary public health program in Puerto Rico. Dr. Joe Dean and senior medical officer Jack Haldeman often invited Jim over for cocktails in the evenings. This was an opportunity for rich discussion. "One night, they asked me what contributions veterinarians could make to public health. These sessions helped me to build confidence in my ideas. Joe Dean took a great interest in me and always spoke highly of me to other officers," said Jim.

Jim fondly recalls the tropical khaki uniforms that were issued for USPHS officers in the Caribbean. It was common for his uniform to get dirty while collecting milk and fecal specimens for testing. One day, Joe Dean asked, "Is that manure on your trousers Jim?" Rarely did the medical officers get their uniforms soiled. Jim savored the uniqueness of his chosen profession. The dairy work was hard and grimy, but Jim made progress. "During my tenure on the islands, we demonstrated that sulfa drugs were useful for the treatment of streptococcal mastitis, but *Staphylococcus* remained a significant problem in the dairies," Jim explained.

In Trinidad, a group of sailors exhibited severe neurological symptoms. The Navy doctors thought it might be polio. At the same time, an Army veterinarian on the island was investigating a neurological illness in donkeys. The Army vet suspected that the sailors were suffering from Venezuelan equine encephalitis or VEE, a disease that infects all of the equine species. The outbreak raised concern about the potential for the disease to move up the chain of islands to Puerto Rico and eventually into the United States by insect vectors.

Jim suggested that mosquito control should be implemented as a control measure. DDT was invented in 1939 and was very effective for controlling mosquitoes. "I recall thinking how amazing it was that a simple chemical had the potential of saving so many lives. Through my experience as a consultant on VEE, I learned that the medical officers on the island had no knowledge of the zoonotic encephalitides," Jim said. This helped to solidify Jim's resolve to promote the understanding of zoonotic diseases in the allied health professions.

In May 1944, Dr. Joe Dean was transferred to Washington, DC to become Dr. Joe Mountin's deputy. Dr. Mountin was the assistant surgeon general for states' relations. Dr. Mountin visited Puerto Rico soon after Dr. Dean's departure. "I had a rare opportunity to take him on a tour of the island. We went to some dairy farms and I explained about the progress we made in helping to eliminate mastitis."

Dr. Mountin was impressed with Jim's work and complimented him by saying, "You've got a promising future in the public health service, Steele!"

Jim was a fan of Surgeon General Tom Parran. "He was the first to have the courage to use the phrase 'venereal diseases' in place of the archaic expression 'social diseases.' He lobbied to sway public sentiment away from moral condemnation of sexually transmitted diseases. He believed that diseases like syphilis were a common medical condition and should be treated like other communicable diseases," Jim recalled. Dr. Parran was raised on a farm and was tuned in to rural health issues. He spent much of his early career promoting rural health.

On one of Dr. Parran's trips to Puerto Rico, Jim hoped he might be able to meet with him. As chance would have it, one day Jim was walking in from the Naval Air Station on the Atlantic shore enjoying the fresh ocean air when a car pulled up, "Hey, Jim, hop in and meet Dr. Parran!" Dr. Vonderlehr, the driver, yelled out to him. The threesome drove around the island together. "Dr. Parran asked a lot of questions. He was especially interested in rabies, mosquito-borne disease and issues related to the dairies," Jim stated. During this encounter, Dr. Parran revealed a planned realignment of USPHS officers relating to the challenges of the next stage of the war in Japan and the South Pacific.

That morning was the only time Jim got to spend with Dr. Parran. "I felt very lucky to have had any time at all. I couldn't believe that the surgeon general of the US had shown so much interest in my work!" Jim exclaimed.

Jim was sent back to Washington, DC on official business often. These trips provided him with opportunities to visit Aina at the Ingham Sanatorium in Lansing, Michigan. "I can remember the contrast of my tanned body next to Aina's pale skin. These visits were bittersweet but always memorable."

Transportation in and out of the Caribbean was often in a PBY-4, a twin engine "flying boat." It was a workhorse of the Navy at the time. "On one trip, the pilots were having some fun flying right on the surface of the water and tipping the wings. This was a little more excitement than I needed, but I assume the pilots were just trying to break the boredom," Jim said.

Rexford G. Tugwell was the governor of Puerto Rico during Jim's tenure on the island. Governor Tugwell was chosen by President Franklin D. Roosevelt and served from 1941 to 1946. One evening Dr. Vonderlehr was talking with the governor's chief of staff, Mason Barr. Mr. reported that his dog, a West Highland White terrier, seemed to be bleeding from the vaginal area. "Dr. Vonderlehr told Mason about the young veterinarian on the island, Dr. Jim Steele, who could be dispatched to assist," Jim said.

La Fortelaza, the governor's executive mansion, overlooked San Juan Bay high above the city. Jim was taken there to examine Mason Barr's dog. "Upon physical examination, the dog was definitely a female and there was a bloody discharge from the vagina. I decided it was probably bladder stones. Surgery was indicated," Jim stated. The Army had a veterinary clinic on Fort Buchanan. Jim obtained permission to use the operating room and garnered the assistance of a veterinary corpsman. "We used IV Nembutal to induce anesthesia. I irrigated some sand-like crystals from the bladder. The mucosa was inflamed but I knew that would resolve. The procedure went well," Jim said. The dog began to awaken during the final suturing so some additional anesthetic was administered. Jim brought the dog back to Mason Barr and told him that the dog should awaken in a few hours.

Later in the evening, Jim called to check the status of his patient and learned that he was still unconscious. He called again at 11:00 p.m. and once more at midnight—the dog was still sound asleep. At this point Jim began to worry and consulted with the physicians at the hospital. "They suggested that I use caffeine to help reverse the effect of the Nembutal but I really didn't have any faith in that advice," Jim stated. He came back to his quarters and fell asleep totally exhausted from the activities of the day. Jim awakened with a start to the ringing of the phone at 6:00 a.m. Thankfully, the dog was awake and doing fine.

Now that he had gained recognition on the island as an expert veterinary surgeon, Jim began receiving invitations to the governor's mansion for elaborate Sunday night soirees. "At each event, the chief of staff's wife, Mary Barr, introduced me to the group like a hero," said Jim. This generated a bit of interest, and maybe jealously, on the part of the other young USPHS staff. Jim was told he could bring a guest to the parties and often asked his roommate Francis to come along. As far as Jim knows, he was the only USPHS veterinarian who was ever invited to the governor's mansion.

FDR ran for reelection in the fall of 1944. Jim was invited to a get-together at the governor's mansion on election eve. Governor Tugwell was pointing out to everyone which states would likely select FDR. Jim chimed in with the comment that if he carried the coal miners' vote, FDR should have the election in the bag. Tugwell was impressed and asked, "Are you a politician, too?" FDR swept the election easily.

Toward the end of 1944, Jim was promoted to O-3, equivalent to a US Army Captain. "I wanted to celebrate this milestone and arranged for a party at the Navy Club for my friends and colleagues,"

Jim said. Earlier, Jim had met some Navy officers at the Naval Air Station and invited them to his celebration. The officers had recently been on patrol with the cruiser USS Chicago in the South Atlantic. "They became inebriated and began pawing the wives of the guests. I had to physically remove some of them from the room!" Jim stated. He was counseled by Dr. Vonderlehr the next day, "Please don't invite the entire US Navy to your next promotion party!"

One night in the winter of 1944-45, Jim was driving Commander Jack Holleman from Ponce, on the south side of the island, to San Juan when a big military truck pulled right in from of him. Jim had been traveling at about fifty miles per hour. "I immediately swerved to avoid an accident and ran into a ditch. Neither of us experienced any major injuries, but I can remember my buttocks being sore for a long time," Jim reported. After this incident, on long flights his feet would get numb and his heels would ache. "An Irish USPHS physician examined me and wrote a letter stating that I should be allowed to fly first class when traveling on official business. The letter worked. I flew first class for the next twenty years!"

Dr. Dave Kairy was with the Coast Guard at Ponce, Puerto Rico. Jim and Dave became good friends. One night they were having supper at the Officers' Club and learned that Paris had been liberated from the Nazis. The date was August 25, 1944. Dave and Jim stayed at the club late that night drinking rum to celebrate. The world was changing and Jim would have to keep pace. "Puerto Rico had been a great experience. I now felt prepared for more difficult challenges!" Jim Steele left Puerto Rico at the end of April 1945.

CHAPTER 10:
PUBLIC HEALTH ADVENTURES IN HAITI AND THE DOMINICAN REPUBLIC

A special request came in to the USPHS in March 1945. The Pan American Health Organization (PAHO) wanted an officer to conduct field investigations in the Dominican Republic (DR) and Haiti. The two countries had a variety of veterinary public health concerns, including rabies and milk and meat sanitation. This was Jim's first interaction with PAHO which would lead to a lifelong professional relationship with the organization. Sixty-one years later, in 2006, at the age of 93, he received the Abraham Horwitz award from PAHO for a career that spanned seven decades, across the Americas and the globe.

PAHO is an international public health agency founded in 1902. It has been in existence almost twice as long as the World Health Organization (WHO). The PAHO mission is to improve health and living standards in the countries of the Americas. Since 1946, it has served as a regional office for WHO, an agency of the United Nations.

As Jim read the reports about rabies in the DR, he became very curious about why the disease seemed to have spared Puerto Rico. The Mona Passage is only about 100 miles of open sea between the two islands. There was ship commerce between the countries that frequently transported dogs. The Coast Guard patrolled the area with sailors based in Puerto Rico, and many of them reported being bitten by dogs. "The epidemiology wasn't adding up!" Jim recalled.

Dr. David Kairys, the USPHS physician working with the Coast Guard doctor in Ponce, questioned the need to treat sailors bitten by dogs while in Puerto Rico. He often asked Jim if vaccination was necessary. "I explained to him that the human rabies vaccine wasn't to be used unless rabies was confirmed in the animal causing the exposure," Jim said. He also told him he had researched the possibility of rabies in Puerto Rico and was convinced there was none on the island. Unless the sailors had been traveling on another island or a neighboring country with history of a dog bite, he didn't see any reason to vaccinate the sailors. Along with the PAHO inquiry, Jim was interested in determining the rabies risk to Puerto Rico from the Dominican Republic. "Five years later, rabies did appear in Puerto Rico," Jim stated.

This was Jim's first visit to a true foreign country. Puerto Rico and the Virgin Islands were both protectorates of the United States. The secretary of health of the DR, a physician, was Jim's host. His mission was threefold. He was to evaluate milk hygiene and the meat processing plants and to investigate and make recommendations on rabies. The secretary inquired about diseases in dairy cows such as brucellosis and tuberculosis and how the diseases may affect the wholesomeness of milk. What was interesting to Jim was that there were no practicing veterinarians in the DR at the time. There was no way to know for sure if brucellosis or tuberculosis was endemic. "The lesions of bovine tuberculosis had reportedly never been seen in a packing plant," Jim said.

The local sanitarians' responsibilities were strictly hygienic. They controlled insects and rodents that might mechanically contaminate the carcasses. Jim recommended that the dairy farms maintain a source of clean water to wash the milking equipment. "But the locals thought that a better use of clean water would be to extend the milk. This is a common practice in many poor countries to improve dairy profits," Jim said.

"The work I was doing was really interesting and enjoyable," Jim said. One evening as he was preparing to have dinner with a missionary friend from Illinois, the bellman brought him an important message. There were two guests waiting for him in the restaurant on the veranda. To Jim's surprise, they were the Dominican commissioner of health and the commissioner of agriculture. *What do these guys want from me?* Jim thought as he walked toward their table.

"The president and dictator of the country was the famous Rafael Trujillo, a man with an enormous ego. He changed the name of the capital from Santo Domingo to Ciudad Trujillo and had even named the country's highest mountain after himself," Jim reported. Jim hoped he hadn't somehow offended the president. "My trip report was going to be strongly worded, but I hadn't even finished writing it yet! As I shook their hands, I noticed they were both packing guns. They were evil-looking, little square ones hanging neatly on their pants belts. *What are officials doing with pistols?*" Jim thought to himself with a sick feeling. He was smoking in those days and immediately reached for a cigarette, only to realize that his pack was empty. The agricultural commissioner offered him a smoke and even asked the waitress to bring him another pack. Then one of the commissioners reached across the table and lit his cigarette. The waitress brought a tray of Cuba Libres, rum drinks, for the group. "I was thinking that these guys had something on their minds!"

"Good evening Dr. Steele; we will get right to the point," stated the agricultural commissioner. "President Trujillo has a stable of horses that are ill. These animals were imported from the US in 1938, before the war. The president is aware you are here and he wants you to examine them and perform any necessary surgery. Will you please be help?" Apparently they had no veterinarian of their own or were convinced that Jim, as a qualified American veterinarian, would be versed in equine medicine and surgery.

"Gentleman, please understand that I am a public health veterinarian and I don't feel qualified to treat horses." The debate continued for several minutes, but Jim continued to hold his ground. "They left me with a definite coolness but I thought that they understood," Jim said.

Jim learned later that it was common practice to ship second-rate racehorses from Florida to Central America and the West Indies. Horses that weren't marketable in the United States found buyers in these countries to the south. "During the war there was no commerce in horses, so they had become a cherished commodity in some areas," Jim said. There was no horse racing in Puerto Rico, but President Trujillo had established races every Sunday in DR. "He had a group of old racehorses that he enthusiastically raced each week. Many of these animals had all kinds of problems as they aged, including lameness," Jim reported.

Early the next morning, Jim was in his hotel room, finishing his trip report for the commissioners. His next stop was Port-au-Prince, Haiti. Jim's phone startled him with an obnoxious ring. "Is this Dr. Jim Steele?" barked a person on the other end of the line. "Are you a member of the United States Public Health Service?" the caller asked. Jim finally realized that the call was from an officer at the US embassy. The voice continued on, "You have been abusive and insulting to the highest officials of this country. If you don't respond to their needs immediately, we will report your actions directly to Washington DC. I can assure you that you will be persona non grata!"

Jim's response to this fell on deaf ears. "I am not a practicing veterinary surgeon; I am a public health officer!" he pleaded. He could see the headlines in major newspapers of the world and his career going down the tubes:

US Public Health Service Veterinarian Refuses To Treat President Trujillo's Sick Horses

Why couldn't you just be polite and tell them that you could do the things you can't do? he asked himself. He guessed now that if he refused to go to the farm, police would follow him to the airport and execute him as he got out of his vehicle at the terminal. Jim had heard stories about unusual killings in the area. The embassy would file their report that Dr. Steele had been uncooperative with the Dominican government and was attempting to flee the country. As a result, he had been killed at the airport by unknown gunmen. Reluctantly, he told the voice on the other end, "Have them send a car for me."

Jim ate his breakfast, thinking anxiously about what his best strategy should be. In veterinary school, he had only watched equine surgery. What anesthetic would he use? He thought about Dr. Hutton, his surgery professor, saying, "You have got to have confidence to do surgery. Once you have the experience, you can do it. And you must have a good man on the twitch!" Jim didn't have the experience and he didn't even know if there was a twitch in the country. *So much for Dr. Hutton's formula for confidence!* Jim thought.

Soon, a car arrived to pick him up. The driver said, "We have made an appointment for you at the president's stable to see his horses. Get into the car, please."

As usual, Jim was looking official in his khakis with a necktie. In one last-ditch effort to sidestep the situation, he stated, with a huge smile in the most cooperative tone he could muster, "Hi, I'm Dr. Jim Steele with the US Public Health Service; please take me to your officials." The driver countered with, "No, señor; caballeriza, caballeriza [horse stable]!"

Upon arriving at the stable, Jim tried to explain his dilemma to the American horse trainer who was on staff at the mansion. The trainer told Jim that there was a foreign veterinarian on the island who might be able to assist with the surgery. *Maybe he is an experienced large animal vet; the day may be saved!* Jim thought. Later, he learned that the veterinarian was a Spanish political refugee hiding from Generalissimo Francisco Franco. To make things worse, he arrived at the farm with a German anatomy book and couldn't speak any English. Jim now wondered what role he would take in the surgical procedures. "It was already very hot and humid, and my uniform was soaked," Jim recalled.

Jim asked the trainer to trot the horses on a lead back and forth. "I immediately picked up on the classic breathing sounds," Jim said. He announced to the trainer "This horse has roars, also known as laryngeal hemiplegia."

The trainer replied excitedly, "You are so right!" Next, he had the trainer trot three other horses in question and decided that all three were suffering from chronic laminitis. He explained to the trainer that he was not qualified to do any corrective procedures.

As it turned out, all the Spanish veterinarian was willing to do was to restrain the horse with a twitch while Jim did the surgery. *We've got a twitch, so now all we need is some confidence!* Jim then began digging deep into memories of his equine surgery classes. And so the magic show began. "Somehow, I located the landmarks, blocked the nerves and performed neurectomies on the three lame horses. I was thinking, *This is too easy! Maybe I should have become a surgeon!*"

The sweat rolled down his face and dripped from his nose. "I knew that the procedure wouldn't cure the laminitis, but it might help the horses to be more active and possibly even sound. Next, I anesthetized the throat of the horse with roars, opening up the larynx, and the respiratory sounds ceased. My luck was really running good that day."

After the procedures, Jim had a brief conversation with the trainer and the Spanish veterinarian. He then went back to the hotel to finish his report for the health department. All night he worried that he would never leave the island. "I stared at the phone for hours in the dark expecting it to ring," Jim recalled. In the morning, he checked out of the hotel and hailed a taxi to take him to the airport. As he was being cleared at the ticket counter a man ran up to him calling, "Dr. Steele, Dr. Steele!"

The police are here to detain me! Jim thought. He stood there in disbelief when the messenger presented him with a fine leather briefcase. Inside was a personal thank-you card from President Trujillo. As he boarded the plane he thought, *Something will still go wrong with those broken-down horses and they'll come get me!* But he never heard another word about the horses or President Trujillo. "I decided to not even mention the episode in my report," he said.

As it turned out, Jim had excellent relations with the Dominican Republic commissioner of health for many years. President Trujillo was assassinated by his own staff seventeen years later, gunned down in cold blood. They had had enough of him. *Maybe he asked one of them to tend to his horses!* Jim thought.

Jim's next stop was Port-au-Prince, Haiti, childhood home of the Nazi, Hermann Goering who would become a defendant in the Nuremberg War Crimes Trials. Malaria was endemic there, and Jim was taking prophylactic chloroquine. Blurred vision and eye pain are side effects of this medication, but Jim can't remember ever having any problems. Upon arrival, he was taken to the Hotel Belvedere, near the edge of the city. They had a curious tradition of serving chocolate cakes and sweets before dinner. "Everyone wanted to know if I spoke French, but I knew only a few words and phrases," Jim stated. There were no practicing veterinarians in the country at the time as far as Jim knew. The few who had studied at a school in Montreal or at Cornell became businessmen importing veterinary supplies and medications they sold to the dairies and ranchers. For some reason, they didn't want to go into practice, probably because there was little income potential.

As he traveled around the country he couldn't remember a filthier place. "It literally reeked of human and animal waste," Jim recalled. Anthrax was common in both animals and people in Haiti. Jim had heard that they were still using the anthrax vaccine developed by Louis Pasteur in the late 1800s. He wondered about the vaccine's efficacy and the possibility that they weren't even using one. Jim examined animals that had died in the northern regions of the country. In some instances, the animals were field slaughtered and consumed by villagers. "I saw the black eschar lesion characteristic of cutaneous anthrax in several people. Many simply died of the intestinal form after ingesting the meat," Jim said.

Agricultural officials took Jim to a dairy built on the outskirts of Port-au-Prince. They also visited some abattoirs. "One had a great pavilion that appeared like a replica of the Eiffel Tower with beautiful iron grillwork. It was probably designed by French architects. It must have been four stories tall and looked as if it had been in a world's fair somewhere. The animals were killed by pithing, a skillful severing of the spinal cord at the occipito-atlantal joint with a sharp knife. The slaughterers never seemed to miss their mark, and it appeared to be a very humane means of killing the animals," Jim stated. These activities occurred in the early morning hours, often without sufficient light. The hygiene in the facilities was terrible, and Jim decided that his report to the government was going to be straight to the point. Every day by mid-morning, all the animals had been slaughtered and processed. The market quickly sold all the fresh meat. "The only reason they probably didn't have more food-borne illness was because, like the Chinese, the time from slaughter to consumption was so brief," Jim deduced.

Next he visited an area near Port-au-Prince, where a human anthrax outbreak occurred in 1943 involving at least forty people. The Haitian sanitarians who were traveling with him stated that the mortality rates in the rural areas were higher. The gastroin-testinal anthrax cases came as no surprise to Jim, as meat was rare during the war. "To be sure, animal protein was considered a lux-ury. The animals that died during an anthrax outbreak were often cold slaughtered and processed. This resulted in both cutaneous and intestinal anthrax cases in people. None of these cases were ever confirmed on autopsy or in the lab," Jim said. Physicians in Haiti attributed the outbreaks to unknown factors. "I heard stories from the villagers of people dying with severe abdominal pain, but I never saw a case firsthand. It can't be a nice way to go," declared Jim.

"One day I was in a small rural community market area where I saw two large local women wrestling over a big cracker can about 16" across and 24" tall. It was filled with something very hot and steamy, a stew possibly, and the contents were being slung all around. I guessed that they must be burning their hands as they tried to wrest the can from each other. Food was scarce and peo-ple were fighting for it," he said. Glass bottles were also a valuable commodity and were sold in the markets. "The most wholesome food available was probably the indigenous fruits and vegetables, but understandably, the people were craving animal protein," Jim stated.

To this day, Jim believes that Haiti was the most poverty-stricken country he has ever visited. He recalled seeing a boy in a village with saber shins. "Saber shins is a thinning of the tibia due to a disease called Yaws, also known as *Frambesia tropica,* thymosis or *Polypapilloma tropicum.* Yaws is caused by the spirochete *Treponema pertenue,* and is transmitted by direct contact with infected pa-tients through poor hygiene or gnat infestation. Sometimes the nose is affected, which resulted in horrifying deformities," Jim ex-plained. Later, back in the states, a colleague mentioned to Jim he was lucky not to have become infected himself. "Most of the diseases I was encountering I had only read about in textbooks. But now I was beginning to see many of them in real life."

Dr. John Mason was a former USPHS field veterinarian and a friend of Jim's. USAID assigned Dr. Mason to monitor malaria in Haiti. He described how hurricanes disrupted the ecological balance and established widespread breeding places for mosquitoes. They used DDT as the only effective way to control the mosquitoes and malaria. Dr. Mason confirmed many of Jim's observations. "Eastern encephalitis was another disease known to be in Haiti, but no one knew the incidence," Jim stated.

Many years later, in the eighties, Dr. Frank Mulhern, who became the director of APHIS, led the eradication of African swine fever on Haiti through identification and depopulation of herds. Today, Haiti is suspected of being a site of the introduction of AIDS into the Americas. Another friend of Jim's, Boris Velimirovic MD, made a good case for this theory. He described how Haitians were recruited by the United Nations to teach in French-speaking African countries. After about ten years, he theorized, they came home to Haiti and introduced AIDS, ultimately transmitting to visitors through male prostitution.

Over the years, Jim was concerned about people coming in to the US from Haiti and other countries. "I tried to balance my empathy for people fleeing totalitarianism and abuse with risks of the introduction of diseases they may be carrying," Jim said. President John Adams created the USPHS in 1798 for the express purpose of prohibiting the entry of people with obvious diseases into the US. There were and still are no clear answers to these questions in Jim's mind. "I believe public health programs should be in place to identify and treat these people as they enter the US. Once they are proven non-contagious, that is the time for integrating these folks into society," Jim stated.

Jim was invited by the Haitian president Élie Lescot to a party that was held at his palace. Lescot would later be overthrown in 1946. To begin the festivities, rum drinks were served along with French pastries and hors d'oeuvres. Then it was announced that the guests must move into the next room for a multi-course sit-down dinner. *I am already full! How can all these skinny people eat so much?* Jim wondered.

After dinner, Jim went back to the Belvedere Hotel and listened to FDR on the radio. "He was addressing a joint session of Congress and I didn't want to miss it," Jim said. He recalls FDR saying something like, "Peace is now on the horizon. Our biggest struggle now will be to put the world back together again. Tonight, I will sit down—I've been wearing these braces too long." FDR died about a month later, on April 12, 1945. After his death, all military and USPHS personnel wore black armbands out of respect for the president. Jim said that at the time there was a shortage of black material to make the armbands. Jim returned to Puerto Rico and filed reports of his observations on the Dominican Republic and Haiti.

Back in Puerto Rico, Dr. John Porterfield replaced Dr. Haldeman as chief of the sexually transmitted disease program. Jim and John roomed together until John brought his wife down to the island. Jim then traveled to Washington, DC to take care of some business. At a meeting with Joe Dean, they talked about all the new medical programs being launched. Public health nursing and dental public health programs were just being created. Jim suggested that a new program be established within the USPHS entitled veterinary public health. "Joe Dean liked the idea and said he would support me on the concept," Jim said.

Jim drove to the PAHO office on Seventeenth and Constitution in Washington, DC to deliver his report on the Dominican Republic and Haiti. The surgeon general of PAHO (the title was later changed to director, PAHO) was Dr. Hugh Cumming. To Jim's delight, Dr. Cumming received him personally and was very interested in his report. The meeting was special, as it was the first time that Jim had recommended that an international organization build a program in veterinary public health. "It was also the first time I used this phrase publicly!" Jim said.

After Jim's PAHO briefing, Dr. Cumming wrote a letter to Surgeon General Parran thanking Jim for his services in DR and Haiti. Jim's only regret about his service in this part of the world was he did not have time to tour Cuba. That would have to wait.

Aina's health had taken a bad turn about the time Jim returned stateside in August 1945. "I decided to spend a month with Aina in Michigan to assess her situation and to see what I could do to improve her care and well-being," said Jim. During his stay, he attended a DDT demonstration on MacInaw Island. First used in 1939 for controlling mosquitoes and malaria, DDT was also effective for controlling flies. "There were many horse-drawn vehicles present at the demonstration to ensure that there were plenty of flies around," Jim said. Jim also took this opportunity to visit Dr. Stafseth at Michigan State College.

"I didn't want to make a decision regarding my next assignment until I knew what was going to happen in Japan. Of course, in August, Nagasaki and Hiroshima went up in flames after the US dropped atomic bombs. Surrender was imminent."

With the end of the war nearing, important new challenges awaited Jim.

CHAPTER 11:
ENCEPHALITIS AND POLIO IN PANAMA

The War to End All Wars was all but finished. Emergency contingency plans, painstakingly written to protect public health and to take care of potential mass casualties in the United States were being filed in the historical archives. Jim had visited Haiti and the Dominican Republic as the war wound down to determine what kinds of public health problems would be found in isolated countries in the postwar era.

In November 1946, Dr. Bustamante of the Pan-American Sanitary Bureau (PSB) called Jim to discuss a disease outbreak and to ask for his assistance. He wanted Jim to investigate an outbreak of Eastern equine encephalomyelitis (EEE) in the Panamanian horse populations. At the same time, some hospitals were seeing a neurological syndrome in children. "Dr. Bustamante suspected that the outbreak might be spilling over from the horses to the kids," said Jim. The PSB staff knew about Jim's work in the Dominican Republic and Haiti and decided that he was the man for the job. Dr. Mountin followed up on the request. He said, "Jim, this sounds like a real challenge. You know what to do." Once again, Jim was surprised that an international public health agency would ask for his services. *People are already seeing the value of veterinary public health!* Jim thought.

Jim had been interested in EEE since his visit to the Mayo Clinic in 1941 to learn more about the epidemiology of the disease as it related to outbreaks in western Minnesota, Nebraska and the Dakotas. He knew that it was a mosquito-borne disease, and he also knew that horses were sentinel animals. Veterinarians were diagnosing the disease routinely in clinical practice. "Typically, people became infected two to three weeks after the horse outbreaks," Jim recalled. Horses were thought to be reservoirs of infection, but the epidemiology was still poorly understood. Later, it was determined that people and horses were both infected by mosquitoes from a common source, songbirds.

It was known that EEE had been diagnosed earlier in Panama by a US Army medical researcher, Dr. B. G. Kelser. Jim didn't feel he knew enough about the disease in humans, so he consulted with Dr. Karl Habel, a researcher with the National Institutes of Health. Dr. Habel had developed excellent tests for evaluating rabies vaccine and had become one of Jim's trusted consultants on viral diseases. Based on the confidence Jim had in Karl, Jim invited him to travel to Panama to assist with the investigation. Dr. Habel's superior, Dr. Charlie Armstrong, was quite interested in the investigation as was Dr. Joe Mountin. "Dr. Armstrong was concerned that we would contract EEE while in the field. He pre-pared a crude vaccine by growing the virus in embryonated eggs and then modified the virus chemically. About a week before we left for Panama, the material was injected intradermally in our forearms. We both developed small, noticeable vesicles in the skin but experienced no other side effects," Jim said.

The impending trip to Panama was very exciting for Jim. He was still a relatively new USPHS officer and, of course, a veterinari-an. This was a totally new concept for the USPHS. "Dr. Bustamante apparently had a high level of confidence to ask me to conduct this investigation. I just didn't want to let anyone down!" Jim said.

Jim arranged for air travel early on a Sunday morning. Both Karl and Jim were somewhat hung over from a National Institutes of Health (NIH) party on Saturday night. "The parties were fun and were great networking opportunities, but they sometimes took their toll," Jim stated. Jim and Karl made it to the airport late, and their military DC-3 flight had already lifted off. Jim always took these kinds of situations on as a personal challenge. In this in-stance, he arranged for them to board another plane at Patuxent River Naval Base and flew directly to Jacksonville Naval Air Station. In spite of this maneuvering, their arrival in Panama was still de-layed a full day.

The Panamanians had arranged for a large delegation to meet them at the airport, including the ministers of health and some high-ranking military officials. But Jim and Karl didn't reach their destination on schedule, and the crowd finally broke up and went home. When they finally arrived the next day, there was no one to meet them. So they continued on to the town of David near the Costa Rican border. Jim made a flurry of telephone calls and a Panamanian public health officer came to meet them. "He took us to a local hotel and we checked in," Jim said.

"The next day we drove north to begin our investigation. We set up our headquarters in a bungalow with a bedroom and a kitchen in a small village. During our briefings, we were warned to not drink the water, so they provided us with the unique combination of Scotch whisky and coconut milk. I had friends who drank scotch with ginger; that was bad enough! But warm coconut milk and scotch—not my favorite!" said Jim. Regardless, they knew that they couldn't touch the water or the ice. The scotch and coconut milk became their evening drink for cocktail hour. In the mornings, they boiled water for coffee and tea.

"It didn't take long before we confirmed a diagnosis of EEE in the sick horses. This was the first time I had actually seen clinical cases of EEE. It was hard to watch the horses on the ground struggling, almost totally paralyzed in lateral recumbency. Once they reached this stage of the disease, there was simply no treatment. I humanely euthanized the sick horses I examined with Nembutal. Karl harvested brain tissue for mouse inoculation. The season was wet and bugs were everywhere. We asked the Panamanian health workers to collect plenty of mosquitoes for us. The insects were ground up and injected into mice. Dr. Habel later easily isolated the EEE virus upon return to NIH," said Jim.

But the question remained regarding the illness in the children. Jim wondered, *Is there epidemiological support for EEE virus as a cause of disease in these children? It doesn't quite add up for me.* But from Jim's visit to Mayo Clinic, he knew there had been a human outbreak of EEE in Minnesota in the 1930s.

Dr. Habel asked, "Where are the human patients?"

The locals responded, "They are all in the hospital!" Jim had great confidence in Karl. He was not only a viral expert; he was a clinician as well.

Dr. Habel walked a little ahead of Jim through the wards. The hospital was crowded. There were patients on mattresses on the floor between the regular beds. Dr. Habel picked up the arms of several children. When he let go, their arms quickly dropped back to the bed, flaccid. There was no muscular resistance. Dr. Habel announced with some reserved excitement in his voice, "This is not encephalitis Jim; this is polio!" The realization that there were two independent, non-related outbreaks occurring in Panama at the time, one in horses and one in people, was quite a discovery. Dr. Habel began consulting with the local doctors and helped in managing the patients in the hospital.

Jim wired their findings to Washington. Everyone was impressed, but the job was not done. It fell on Jim to do more necropsies on the horses and to collect additional brain specimens to bring back for testing. "I had performed lots of necropsies on chickens, calves and pigs, but horses were quite a different animal indeed!" Jim reported. A local veterinarian volunteered to help Jim do the necropsies and collect the samples. "It would be my pleasure if I could do this for you!" he said with a smile. Jim appreciated the offer of help. Once all the specimens were collected, the mice were inoculated and prepared for the trip back to the US

The local officials were jubilant. It was Thanksgiving back in the US, and the Panamanians wanted to have a fiesta for their American heroes in the town of David. It was to be a true *Día de Gracias de norte americanos.* First, they had a Panamanian wild turkey dinner. "It was tough as shoe leather! They served us vegetables and rum pudding as side dishes. I saw them chasing the turkeys for miles before catching them. That's probably why they were so tough. The Panamanians were obviously very proud that they were able to serve a native turkey to us," said Jim. After the meal, they decided to host a Latin dance . Of course, all the señoritas wanted to dance with Jim. "Most of the girls were barely five feet tall and had to stare squarely into my full belly. I know these ladies never could see where they were going, dancing with me. But we had a great evening. I hope they had as much fun as we did."

Jim then began planning their trip back home to Washington, DC. The Panamanian minister of health and the US Army provided excellent support, to include the use of facilities, jeeps, trucks and even airplanes. Jim recalled the audacity of the clout he had in Panama considering he was still at the rank of O-3. "I made several calls emphasizing that we had been investigating outbreaks of both human and animal disease and that we had an urgent need to transport critical specimens back to a diagnostic laboratory in the US. We finally boarded a plane that departed from David. But the aircraft stopped at every garrison along the way," Jim said.

To make things worse, Jim was experiencing a bad case of di-arrhea, the "tropical trots." The airfields had some nice conces-sion facilities, and he saw a dairy counter. "Give me one of those milkshakes" he said, thinking that would straighten out his gut. The first one was so good he ordered another. "The next airfield also had a nice dairy counter; so I ordered a third shake!" Jim ad-mitted. While they waited, he listened to the Army-Navy football game on the radio. The Army was having a great year with run-ning back Glenn Davis and fullback "Doc" Blanchard.

They finally set down in Balboa, southwest of Panama City. The capitol was located in central Panama, near the big canal the Unit-ed States built from 1904 to 1914. Panama City has been called "the moveable city," since it has been relocated a few times throughout history. Because of its proximity to the great canal, it has also been named "crossroads of the world." The word "Panama" literally means an abundance of fish. It was Saturday night and their hosts wanted to take them out and show them the town.

"My gut was still wrecked. I spent most of my time being sure I was close to latrine facilities," he said. The next day, they were taken out to see the sights of Panama City and the Canal. "I really enjoyed watching the boats pass through. The Canal Zone is truly a unique place."

By Monday morning, Jim was confident that their travel was all set for their trip back to the States. But upon arrival at the Panama City airport, there was no plane awaiting them. Jim talked with the airport clerks and called the tower but still no plane. Jim asked one of the airmen, "Who is in charge here?" He didn't know it at the time, but the airman gave him the name of the commanding gener-al of the US Army based in Panama. Jim called the general's office, but they quickly referred him to the office of the senior surgeon.

He asked Jim, "Can't you just buy a ticket like everyone else?" Jim replied point-blank, "We are here on military orders. We have laboratory specimens that require special handling. Sir, we need a military plane to fly us back to the US!" He then asked Jim in a very serious tone, "Is this important to the Canal Zone defenses?" Jim replied, "Good Lord, man, we've got encephalitis and polio; this is important to the defense of the western hemisphere!" These were the magic words. Things started to happen.

When Jim and Karl arrived back at the airport from the Army base, a US Public Health Officer was waiting for them. A telephone call came to the dispatch officer. He looked at Jim and said, "Sir, we now have a plane for you!" Jim breathed a sigh of relief. The officer then asked, "Is there anything else I can do for you?" Jim replied, "Yes, you can notify our offices in Washington we will be coming in with sick mice." The officer asked Jim to write out the message: Drs. *Jim Steele and Karl Habel are arriving with two hundred infected, sick mice and one man with severe diarrhea.* Only Jim and Karl knew the identity of the diarrhea patient. Jim addressed the message to Dr. Dunnahoo, the chief quarantine officer of the USPHS; the military commander; Dr. Joe Dean; and Dr. Dyer of the NIH. "I wanted to be sure we would get adequate clearance into Washington," Jim stated. Jim knew from past experience that it is best to keep all concerned parties informed, especially with something as important as this.

As they were collecting their luggage, Jim learned that a special aircraft had been diverted to assure the quickest and safest trip back to the US. A few of the mice were already dying. To preserve the tissues, Jim and Karl placed them in thermos bottles with ice. After boarding the plane with all specimens and animals loaded, Jim said to Karl, "Well, it looks like we are going to get out of here after all!" Suddenly, the dispatch officer came bounding onto the plane and announced that there were several American soldiers trying to get back to the US on leave. "Can the soldiers hitch a ride with you Dr. Steele?" the dispatcher asked. "I don't want anyone fooling around with these mice, do you understand? Tell these soldiers that the mice are dangerous!" Jim had the cages labeled *Dangerous Material* just to be sure. Jim then personally invited the soldiers to board the plane and briefed them on the important nature of the cargo.

After takeoff, Karl checked on the mice at the back of the plane. Several more had died. He quickly transferred them to a thermos filled with ice. "The soldiers on the plane were probably wondering what mysterious cargo we had on board!" said Jim.

Their portal of entry into the United States was West Palm Beach, Florida. With their stated mission of *defending the entire western hemisphere,* their next plane was patiently waiting to fly them direct into Washington, DC. "We felt as if we were returning from the moon with specimens that needed to be handled with great care!" Jim reflected. In Florida they were met by an impressive USPHS delegation. One officer bounded up to the plane and said, "We are so glad you had a successful mission! Please tell us, does this disease truly pose a danger to the United States?" As they transferred the *dangerous materials* from one plane to the next, onlookers were probably thinking that they were carrying the deadliest germs on the planet.

The next thing they knew, Jim and Karl were delivered to a grand reception. "Everyone was asking us for our autographs and offering drinks. I told them that we were sorry we couldn't join the party but our mission wasn't complete. We were really worried about our mice," Jim said.

The captain of the plane that was to fly them to Washington, DC walked up to Jim and solemnly announced, "You are in command of this aircraft. I will follow all of your orders with the exception of ditching the plane." After takeoff from Palm Beach, they learned that the temperature in Washington was twenty-one degrees Fahrenheit with snow flurries. Fortunately, they had their winter uniforms in their bags. They changed from their tropical uniforms into the warmer gear en route.

Unfortunately, Jim had no antacids or Kaopectate in his possession. "I was very nauseated, I needed some relief," Jim stated. The first officer came back to the cabin and asked, "Do you have any instructions for me to radio to Washington, sir?" Jim replied, "Yes, please get a message back to Dr. Joe Dean that Steele and

Habel are coming in with 200 sick mice and a sick man, meaning me!" Jim was thinking that if his gut continued to go downhill, he might need more than antacids. The flight in the DC-3 traveling at about 170 knots per hour from Palm Beach to Washington, DC was about five hours. "The flight seemed like forever, and it was so damn cold!" Jim said.

At last, they landed at Andrews Field with blowing snow on the tarmac. There was electricity in the air. "This is really something, Karl: We left Panama at noon, Florida at sunset, and we reach Washington in the dark of night. Gosh, we really pulled this one off, not a thing gone wrong!"

Suddenly, Joe Dean bounded up the aircraft steps to greet him and Karl in the cabin. "Jim, what exactly happened down there?" Dr. Dean asked impatiently.

"Everything went well; no real problems to report!" Jim replied.

"What do you mean, everything went well? Where are all the sick men?" asked Joe.

"What sick men? Me, I'm the sick man!"

Joe responded, "I got a message you were flying in with dozens of sick men and mice!"

Jim was flabbergasted. He stepped out the door of the plane and his jaw dropped. There were ambulances as far as the eye could see—one for each mouse. The press was there in full force. Jim and Karl were both interviewed at length. The story made the rounds in Washington, DC for weeks and even made national radio news programs.

PUBLIC HEALTH SCIENTISTS BRING BACK STRANGE
NEW DISEASES FROM PANAMA!

Somehow, their message was scrambled in transmission. As it turned out, the message as it was received in Washington stated:

JIM STEELE AND KARL HABEL ARE BRINGING BACK 46
SICK MEN AND SOME SICK MICE....

At first, the incident created panic, but it was followed quickly by amusement. Fortunately, Jim had held on to his original written message. "I figured that someone might have gotten in real trouble over the event, but no one ever even asked me about it!" Jim said.

A quarantine officer cleared the entry of the mice and the other diagnostic specimens. Karl went to work immediately. Within a few days, he isolated and identified the virus as Eastern equine encephalitis. The mosquitoes they collected turned out to be a new species whose larvae could acquire oxygen underwater by attaching to the stems of reeds, genus Mansonia. Later, Jim submitted his report to the journal *Veterinary Medicine*. "This article was my first scientific contribution as a public health officer," said Jim.

Jim was invited to discuss veterinary public health at the state health officers' meeting in December 1946. The surgeon general was present. This was the first time a USPHS veterinary officer had ever addressed the group. Dr. Halveron, the public health officer from California, instructed all the speakers to keep their remarks as brief as possible, but when he introduced Jim, he stated, "Jim, please take *all the time you want* to present your important data!"

After Jim's presentation someone asked, "Aren't you the one we heard just came back from Panama with a new disease?"

Jim said, "No, I did not come back with a new disease."

"But didn't you come back with a lot of sick men?"

Jim replied, "No, we came back with sick mice!" In spite of all the confusion, it was a great opportunity for Jim as a USPHS veterinary officer to inform the public health community about the contributions he was making with his special medical training and background. "I then spent the next twenty-five minutes answering questions and talking about how veterinarians can have an impact on public health," recalled Jim.

Shortly thereafter, Dr. Bustamante asked Jim to participate in a postwar meeting of public health officers that was to take place in Caracas, Venezuela. "Our four-engine DC-8 caught fire en route, and we were forced to turn around and land back in Miami. I vividly recall the silence of the passengers in the cabin. One engine caught fire and had to be shut down by the pilots. I remember watching the flames licking at the engine, a very scary site indeed!" he said. Jim was disappointed that he could not present at the international meeting but was ecstatic to touch down safely in Miami. The fact that he had been invited to speak at the meeting gave Jim the self-assurance that he was beginning to be respected in the public health community.

"The trip to Panama was an outstanding learning experience and earned me a lot of brownie points!" Only a year earlier, Jim had prepared a report on zoonotic diseases for Dr. Mountin at his request. Now, Jim felt confident that the stage was set to launch a revolutionary new program.

CHAPTER 12:
THE GENESIS OF VETERINARY PUBLIC HEALTH

With the Puerto Rico assignment behind him along with exceptional field experiece in Haiti, Dominican Republic and Panama, Jim was ready to move onward with his plans for the future of veterinary public health. He was a bit distracted by some interesting peace-building opportunities that he could explore in Europe at the time. But first and foremost, he wanted to implement his ideas in the United States.

Jim is the quintessential history buff. In his younger days, he especially enjoyed reading the chronicles of public health and veterinary medicine leading up to his own career. "In the late nineteenth century, British veterinarians had measured success in dealing with foot and mouth disease and rinderpest. American veterinarians were duly impressed with how the British packaged and delivered veterinary services to protect cattle and other food animal species from disease," Jim stated. This set the groundwork for veterinary medicine as a public health science. "The Scottish veterinarian James Law was the first professor of veterinary medicine of the Cornell College of Veterinary Medicine. He later served as the college's first dean from 1891 to 1916. In one of his famous reports, James Law pointed out the value of veterinary services in protecting the public health. There was similar work going on in France and Germany. Dr. Law had the distinction of awarding the first doctor of veterinary medicine degree in the US to Daniel E. Salmon. He went on to found the US Bureau of Animal Industry in 1884. Dr. Salmon fully understood the public health responsibilities of veterinary medicine. At the time, there was a strong debate on whether veterinary services should fall under agriculture or health. Politically, the 'ags' won. The BAI was created to serve the meat industry and to promote health and trade. The US Public Health Service (USPHS) incorporated its commissioned corps in 1889. This enhanced quarantine programs, which aided in keeping certain diseases out of the US," Jim explained.

Until about 1900, the USPHS was heavily engaged with diseases such as typhoid, Vitamin B deficiency (beriberi) and malaria. "President Theodore Roosevelt became concerned about milk-borne disease during a large typhoid outbreak in DC in 1905. He turned to the USPHS because they demonstrated that typhoid was a waterborne disease. Dr. Milton J. Rosenau of the USPHS came up with a milk protection program. This was the first attempt at dealing with an animal-borne disease. The USPHS then turned to the BAI of the US Department of Agriculture to help build a program for bovine tuberculosis control," said Jim. Dr. John R. Mohler and Dr. Daniel Salmon were two of the first scientists to recognize the need for this kind of agency cooperation.

"The first institution to offer training in public health in the US was the Army Medical School established by Surgeon General George M. Sternberg in Washington, DC in 1893," Jim stated. At about the same time, a school of sanitary hygiene was created at the Massachusetts Institute of Technology. Eventually, the Army Medical School joined with Harvard and MIT in 1913, forming the Harvard-MIT School of Public Health. This was the first civilian school of public health in the US. Johns Hopkins University School of Hygiene and Public Health began its operation in 1918. This helped to provide the impetus for other schools of public health in US universities. These new schools trained most of the specialists that were needed in the US at the time.

"During the Spanish-American War of 1898, US soldiers were fed what they thought was 'embalmed beef' during military operations in Cuba. They also believed that the meat was making them ill," Jim said. This elicited the sympathy of the American public and suspicion by U. S. Army General Nelson A. Miles. President McKinley appointed the Dodge Commission, headed by General Grenville M. Dodge, a well-known veteran of the Civil War, to investigate. Most of the meat in question was ostensibly produced and canned by Chicago packing plants. Although the investigation did not prove that the meat was embalmed, it was found to be of very poor quality and nearly inedible. Upton Sinclair later referenced the scandal in his book *The Jungle,* which led Congress to pass the Pure Food and Drug Act of 1906.

Initially, meatpackers were not receptive to the idea that all meatpacking operations and products would be inspected. "Dr. Salmon used this resistance to push for the Food and Drug Act of 1906. Fortunately, President Teddy Roosevelt and the US Congress supported the idea and it passed. Milton J. Rosenau, MD, of the USPHS proposed that milk be harvested only from disease-free animals. This was the first time that the USPHS was complementing programs in the BAI," Jim said. Dr. John R. Mohler, chief of the US Bureau of Animal Industry, led the bovine TB control program, carrying Dr. Daniel Salmon's leadership forward.

"Interestingly, the USPHS milk pasteurization program moved quite slowly after its beginnings in 1910. Many communities did not buy into the concept of pasteurization," Jim said. The perceived virtues of raw milk continued until the 1920s. The USPHS reorganized their milk pasteurization program and began firmly advising against raw milk consumption. The veterinary profession took the leadership in certifying herds free from bovine tuberculosis. Once the Sanitary Code was implemented in 1907, states were soon allowed to move their programs along independently. "The southern states were very slow to adopt Dr. Mohler's programs. Many large cities were reluctant to relinquish their control over milk," said Jim.

"After several delays related to World War I and the 1918 influenza pandemic, the FDA established a small veterinary office in 1920 to liaise with agriculture. At the same time, the dairy industry decided not to support the program for the eradication of bovine tuberculosis. As a result, the USPHS hired four veterinarians between 1924 and 1929. They were Drs. Clarence E. Smith, William H. Haskell, Rex D. Bushong, and Franklin Clark. They all became milk specialists. This was the first time that the USPHS recognized the need for veterinary services. Prior to that, the USPHS had had only sanitary engineers, entomologists and nutritionists to augment the expertise of the medical officers. These four veterinarians formed a small corps, working closely with the sanitary engineers within USPHS, and cooperated with the BAI on bovine TB control. I had some interaction with these four veterinarians through the years, but I didn't know all of them personally," Jim said. When Jim was in Ohio with the USPHS as a sanitarian in 1942-43, he was assigned to an engineer who signed off on all of his inspections. The role of veterinarians in the public health arena was slow to evolve, but Jim Steele vowed to change that.

Jim's efficiency report for his time in Puerto Rico finally arrived in Washington, DC. "I could hardly believe my eyes. The report was average in all respects despite my positive accomplishments. It also mentioned a mishap with one of my superiors that questioned my loyalty." Jim said. The report was written and signed by Elmer Herringer, Sanitary Engineer, his boss and rater. It turned out that Mr. Herringer believed that Jim had abused his position by supporting a local Puerto Rican businessman who marketed milk pasteurization equipment on the island. Jim provided a positive recommendation for this company to Dominican Republic officials. "I did this only because believed the company offered the best solution to the pasteurization problems in the country." Jim said.

Jim reported his dilemma to several colleagues, including Joe Dean who exclaimed, "I can't believe it. Jim, talk to your friends in Puerto Rico!" Jim knew in his heart that he had done an outstanding job in Puerto Rico. "I heard that Surgeon General Thomas Parran received a call from the White House to look into the issue of my report. Governor Tugwell of Puerto Rico, and his chief of staff, Mason Barr were visiting the Truman White House that very week. I have no doubt that the governor initiated the inquiry," said Jim.

The assistant surgeon general, Charlie Williams, Sr., invited Jim over to his office and asked him to tell the story. Dr. Williams told Jim that it was disturbing for Dr. Parran to receive a call from the White House about the problem. "This is my career hanging in the balance, will I survive?" Jim asked.

Dr. Williams replied, "What is happening to you happened to me forty years ago. While a sanitation officer in New Orleans, I did a favor for someone and received a bottle of whiskey. As a result, I was accused of all kinds of unscrupulous deeds!"

Dr. Williams recommended that Jim go back to Puerto Rico to see Mr. Herringer face to face. "Well I can tell you I'm plenty mad about this. I want it off my record one way or the other," Jim said. So Jim did travel back to Puerto Rico to meet with Mr. Herringer. Soon, the report disappeared from Jim's files permanently. The only remnant of the event was a note stating, "Certain documents in this file have been destroyed."

Joe Mountin told Jim with a grin, "Jim, I guess you know how to take care of yourself!" Jim mused, *Did a dog in Puerto Rico with bladder stones make the difference? I don't suppose I will ever know for sure!*

Jim would often stay at Joe Dean's home when he was in Washington, DC. During one of these visits he announced, "I am thinking about leaving the USPHS to seek an academic position—possibly teach public health and epidemiology."

Joe Dean replied, "Let's talk to Joe Mountin about this. He is seeking out fresh, new ideas for the future of public health. He has created many new programs such as tuberculosis control, nursing and dental services. It makes sense for you to tell him your ideas, Jim."

On September second, 1945, Japan surrendered. Dr. Joe Mountin invited Jim to meet for what he called "an important discussion."

"What would you like to talk about, sir?" Jim asked with interest.

"I'd like to hear your thoughts about farm life, the importance of animals, veterinary medicine and how this all ties in with public health. What will you vets do now that the war is over?" he asked. Such an open-ended question might have posed a difficult challenge for some, but Jim had been thinking these things through for a long time. He responded by reciting some of the diseases transmissible from animals to man that he believed to be of real importance. Jim went on to explain how little was known about the epidemiology of some of the zoonotic diseases and how few physicians received any training or had clinical experience with them.

"Toward the end of this meeting, Dr. Mountin asked me to prepare a comprehensive list of zoonotic diseases that he could take to Congress. He felt strongly that this would generate ideas and momentum for future directions," Jim said.

Dr. Mountin suggested that Jim visit the National Institutes of Health (NIH) to meet Dr. Charlie Armstrong. He was a well regarded scientist who had worked extensively on psittacosis and other bacterial diseases in people. He received Jim warmly. "During our meeting, he told me about a perplexing disease problem that had just emerged in Cincinnati, Ohio. This was one of the first recognized cases of cat scratch disease," Jim recalled. Soon Jim met with Dr. Carl Larson, a *Brucella* researcher for the NIH, who helped Jim gather data on brucellosis. "I made a lot of valuable contacts in the NIH that helped me to build my extensive table of zoonotic diseases.

Jim worked on his special assignment for roughly a month. The final product was a thirty-eight-page report that he forwarded immediately to Drs. Mountin and Williams. Dr. Williams then posed another question. "The Army says that about twelve million soldiers will be returning from overseas, many with pets. What should our guidelines be?" Jim responded that as far as he knew there were no such guidelines. "My job security was piling up!" Jim said with a grin.

Dr. Williams called a meeting with key representatives of the Army to discuss the issue. At the gathering, Jim was introduced as the head veterinarian from the Public Health Service. "I'm sure this was the first time I was introduced in this way. It took me a little off-guard, but I really liked the sound of it!" Jim said.

In 1947, Jim recommended to Dr. Mountin that a veterinary public health program be established within the USPHS that would focus on zoonotic diseases. "The precedent was already set with programs in public health nursing and dental public health. Veterinary public health would effectively round out the existing programs. I further proposed that we establish a corps of veterinary officers in the Public Health Service. Many titles for the new corps officers were tossed around, such as "veterinary public health officer," "veterinary surgeon," "veterinarian," and "veterinary science officer." "'Veterinary medical officer' was the title that finally stuck," Jim said.

Joe Mountin replied, "Sounds interesting, Jim; see if you can sell it. If you get in trouble, don't call me!" This was still over a year before CDC was created.

Jim was assigned an office next to the dental public health group in the T-6 temporary building at the NIH. "The first thing I did was order a sign for the office that read 'Veterinary Public Health,'" Jim said. He then wrote to the *Journal of the American Veterinary Medical Association* (JAVMA) and the American Public Health Association (APHA) to announce that he would be leading a new program in veterinary public health for the US Public Health Service. His announcement was very well received by the veterinary medical profession. "This was a key milestone that helped to launch my career," Jim remembered.

After considering many names for the new health agency, the Communicable Disease Center (CDC) was born in January of 1946 with Dr. Joe Mountin as its founder. The new agency inherited the mission of the wartime agency known as Malaria Control in War Areas (MCWA), which worked to control malaria through the use of DDT to eliminate mosquitoes. But Dr. Mountin had a much grander vision for the future of his new agency. "I actually participated in the discussion to name the new agency along with Mark Hollis, the director for the MCWA, and several others. This was a very exciting time in my career!" Jim stated. The CDC start-up was composed of about 400 employees who occupied one floor of an old building on Luckie Street in Atlanta and some other buildings on Peachtree road.

In 1947, representatives of the CDC, the USDA, the Departments of Commerce and the Interior, the military and other agencies with animal health missions met to help consolidate support for the new program in veterinary public health. Dr. Mountin ordered Jim to move to Atlanta, which he did in September 1947. "My new title was to be Chief, Veterinary Public Health Division, Communicable Disease Center, U. S. Public Health Service," Jim said. Dr. Mountin promoted Jim to the rank of O-4, equivalent to a US Army Major, just before he was relocated to CDC in Atlanta.

The new Veterinary Public Health Division was initially located on the seventh floor of the Luckie Building, across the hall from the Epidemiology Division. "My first secretary was a Ms. Pearl. She was an elegant, buxom southern lady," Jim reminisced. "I lacked experience in dictating letters, so my solution was to write things out in longhand." Both divisions began as one-person operations. "I can remember discussions on diphtheria as a possible zoonosis, questions about pellagra in dogs, and parasites shared by animals and people. The list of veterinary public health problems to research was seemingly endless." Jim was asked to look into radiation as a possible preventive for trichinosis in meat. Jim recalled that the sanitary engineers weren't quite sure what he was up to. "The sanitary engineers were protective about diseases like typhus, dengue, and malaria that they had been working around for many years. It was not surprising," he said.

"Everyone seemed to be interested in my ideas and expertise, including Dr. Justin Andrews, the deputy director of CDC. He was a very well known parasitologist at the time. We became great friends," Jim said. In March 1947, Jim and Dr. Andrews made a road trip through the Midwest together to learn about zoonotic diseases and public health problems in rural communities. Jim brought along one of his papers on schistosomiasis he had written at Harvard for Dr. Andrews to read. "We naturally hit it off," Jim recalled. Along the way, Jim experienced a public health problem firsthand. "I had this habit of hanging my arm out of the car window. The next thing you know, a bee flew up the sleeve of my shirt and started stinging me!" he said, laughing. "We stopped somewhere in the Kentucky horse country that evening. A fellow at the hotel said that horse manure was a great treatment for beestings, but I decided I'd just suffer with it!"

Jim established the new office in Atlanta as the solo employee. "I was actually becoming somewhat lonely intellectually. There was no one I could talk veterinary issues with," Jim said. That all ended with the arrival of Jim's first hire, Dr. Ernest Tierkel, who was recruited in mid-1946. Jim dispatched Dr. Tierkel to Montgomery, Alabama to establish a rabies program at the old Rockefeller Laboratory. In the late 1940s and early 1950s, some of the other the early USPHS veterinarian recruits were assigned to Florida, New York, Texas, Ohio, New Jersey, Oregon, Washington, California and West Virginia to develop rabies control programs. These veterinary officers were attached to state health departments and assigned to laboratories or to sanitation programs. In some states, the state veterinarian was assigned the additional duty of oversee-ing veterinary public health. "The New England states were slow to become involved, but eventually developed their own programs and did quite well. Eventually, nearly all of the USPHS veterinary public health positions in the states were converted to state health department positions," said Jim.

Dr. Raymond Vonderlehr, under whom Jim had served in Puerto Rico, became the first medical director of CDC in 1947. Mr. Mark Hollis was the founding director until that time. "Dr. Vonderlehr was a mild-mannered person and wasn't one to discipline or dress folks down when problems occurred," Jim said. In 1949, Dr. Vonderlehr, with the help of Dr. Justin Andrews, dep-uty director of CDC, recruited Dr. Alexander A. Langmuir from Johns Hopkins University to lead the epidemiology division. Dur-ing World War II, Dr. Langmuir had researched respiratory diseas-es in military personnel, particularly influenza, pneumonia and, later, Q fever.

"Dr. Langmuir knew little about veterinary medicine but was truly interested in my ideas and activities," Jim said. In 1951, the Veterinary Public Health and Epidemiology divisions were consoli-dated into the Division of Epidemiology in 1951. This effectively downgraded Jim from a division head to a section chief. "I wasn't totally in favor of this change, but Dr. Langmuir assured me that he saw the importance of the new veterinary public health pro-grams and would support them implicitly. He also let me know that I could operate independently of the epidemiology division as needed," Jim stated.

Later, people would ask Dr. Langmuir, "Was Jim Steele a part of this program?"

Langmuir would reply, "Yes, but I could never tell him what to do!" Jim took this as a compliment.

Ultimately, Dr. Langmuir became a devotee of the power-ful links between veterinary and human medicine. "In 1953, Dr. Langmuir began including veterinarians in the Epidemic Intel-ligence Service (EIS)," Jim said proudly. "Now that I was no longer under Joe Mountin, Dr. Langmuir became my greatest ally. He promoted my ideas and activities every chance he got. It had the effect of legitimizing the importance of veterinary public health."

In late 1953, Dr. Langmuir invited Jim to attend a review of the new *American Public Health Association Handbook* at the an-nual meeting in New York. The meeting was led by Dr. Haven Emmerson, former New York City Commissioner of Health and was a professor of public health at Columbia University. "Dr. Langmuir introduced me and lavished praise on all the con-tributions that I could make to the book. This began more than a forty-year stint on the editorial board for the book. Thanks to him, a veterinarian will always be a part of the editorial board. This was just another example of how much Dr. Langmuir believed in the skills of veterinarians," Jim said.

The first state crisis that Jim became involved in at CDC was an outbreak of Q fever in Los Angeles, California that was recog-nized in 1946. "The disease was named thus because the etiology was not known. The name 'query fever' was used following the first outbreak in Queensland, Australia in 1935. Its victims, usually stockyard or dairy workers, suffered with severe flu-like symptoms. The Los Angeles outbreak began in 1946 and was continuous, kill-ing a number of people, even infecting undertakers handling the bodies," Jim said. Jim ultimately assigned a veterinarian to inves-tigate. "I recruited Dr. John Wynn as a USPHS veterinary officer. He was working in California at the time. Dr. Wynn later rose to become the head of the laboratory division of CDC."

Dr. Ben Dean, the California State public health veterinar-ian was upset when he found out that Jim had assigned Dr. Wynn to investigate the outbreak without clearing it with him first. "Dr. Langmuir told me he didn't want that to happen again. I was learning the new ropes in Atlanta, sometimes the hard way!" Jim said. Later, Dr. Francis Abianti, a veterinarian, joined the Q fever project led by Dr. Robert Huebner, a physician from the NIH.

In 1951, Dr. Langmuir and Jim took a long train ride together to visit the Rocky Mountain Laboratory in Hamilton, Montana. "We wanted to learn more about the Q fever research that was in progress there. In addition, Fort Detrick was funding a vaccine project for me at the lab. The extended time we spent together on this trip really helped to cement our relationship," Jim recalled. When they boarded the train, Dr. Langmuir told Jim, "You are going to teach me about veterinary medicine on this trip. I especially want to know how you feel veterinary medicine can make contributions to public health."

"Dr. Langmuir sometimes questioned my ideas, especially at WHO and PAHO meetings. But overall, it was a positive relationship. He supported me immensely in my work. Dr. Langmuir connected me to all the right physicians and other scientists at the CDC, NIH and the medical community. Many of the physicians told me I was their only exposure to veterinary medicine and zoonotic diseases. Countless physicians stated that they learned a lot from me during consults and seminars. Dr. Langmuir became one of my greatest champions for veterinary public health. He provided me with the crucial support and credibility I needed to launch the new discipline," Jim reported.

Jim believed that a successful program in veterinary public health needed to be implemented at the state level whenever possible. "This became my primary strategy. I learned so much from successful state programs for things like tuberculosis control, sanitation engineering, water and air standards, non-zoonotic disease vaccination strategies, public health methods, and sexually transmitted disease programs. This helped me to construct a plan for a comprehensive program in veterinary public health," he said.

In 1942, Aina entered the Ingham County Sanitarium in Lansing, Michigan. No matter how busy Jim was, he visited Aina at least six times per year. "Aina was the eternal optimist, an avid reader and a strong Christian. Whenever I arrived at the sanitarium, she always put on a grand reception for me with her hair perfectly done. She was always genuinely happy to see me," Jim recalled. He would usually stay for two or three days on each trip. "During the visits, we would mostly sit and talk. I shared all the exciting stories about my work and colleagues. Aina would talk about the books she was reading and would introduce me to the friends she had made. These visits were very nice," Jim said. Unfortunately, Aina shared a room with one or two other patients, so there wasn't a great deal of privacy.

In 1945, Aina was moved to the first floor of the sanitarium with the terminal cases. Streptomycin soon became available after World War II; she was placed on the drug in 1946. "A USPHS colleague, Dr. Herman Hilleboe, chief of the tuberculosis control unit, arranged for the drug for Aina. It was like a miracle; the streptomycin stopped the progression of her disease. Soon she was feeling so good she registered for a correspondence course in literature at the University of Michigan," said Jim. Her prognosis improved considerably after they injected her sputum into guinea pigs. The lack of growth of the tuberculous bacillus in the animals meant that she was no longer releasing the live organism into the environment. "I suddenly regained hope that Aina could be cured," Jim said. She was released to go home in March 1949. She spent her first month with aunt Gommy Palm in Chicago. In April, Jim picked Aina up to go home to Atlanta with him.

At the time, Jim was living in the bachelor officers' quarters at the Chamblee Naval Air Station. It was time to find a home that he and Aina could call their own. "I was making about $12,000 per year and was confident we would be able to find something nice," Jim said. Dr. Tom Sellers, the state health officer, told Jim there were some nice homes for sale in the Buckhead area just north of town. "I finally found a nice white clapboard house with green shutters and gas heat. It had three bedrooms, a living room, a kitchen, dining room and a full basement, all for $11,000. I took some photos of the house and went back to Chicago to show Aina. She was very pleased!" Jim recollected.

Jim drove to Chicago to pick up Aina in a 1948 Oldsmobile. Upon his arrival, Aina told him that she decided against the long car trip back to Atlanta, so Jim booked their travel by air. "The house wasn't ready to be occupied on arrival, so we stayed at the Biltmore hotel, a beautiful facility with a friendly staff. Aina was really enjoying herself in Atlanta," Jim remembered. Later, Aina's cousin Elsie and a friend drove the Steele's Oldsmobile back to Atlanta from Chicago. "Next, we bought new furniture for the house. I still have most of it in my home in Houston today," Jim said. After cousin Elsie went back to Chicago, Aina's Aunt Gommy Palm came down in May and spent about four months. She helped with the cooking and setting up the house.

Jim traveled alone to attend the World Veterinary Congress in London in August 1949. Afterwards, he went on to Stockholm, Sweden for some meetings. About a week after his arrival, Swedish doctors diagnosed him with chronic appendicitis. Jim remembered having recurrent lower right quadrant abdominal pain for a long time. "When I heard that the hospital was still using chloroform for anesthesia, I quickly arranged for a flight back to New York. I scheduled the surgery at the Stanton Island Public Health Service Hospital," Jim said. Aina was in Atlanta and wanted to come to be with him, but he asked her to stay at home. Aunt Palm was still with her, so Aina was in good hands. The surgery was uneventful. Jim was discharged in a few days and flew back to Atlanta.

Jim and Aina traveled to Cuba in December of 1949 to enjoy their first holiday together. It was a time of relative order and political freedom during the presidency of Carlos Prio Socarras. They stayed with Bessie and Bill Schaum, whom Jim had met while in Washington, DC. Bill was an engineer from Ohio and was managing a sugar plantation in Mayaguez where they processed their own cane and even raised cattle. Bill's wife, Bessie, was the sister of Dr. Joe Dean's wife, thus the connection. "I had a marvelous time fishing and learning to golf. Aina had just been released from the sanitarium and was feeling better than ever. She didn't know it yet, but she was already pregnant with Jay at the time," Jim said.

Investors on the eastern seaboard of the US owned many of the plantations in Cuba after the Spanish-American War of 1898. Bill encouraged Jim to buy about 100 acres of land in Cuba, which he did. "I signed a promissory note with a $500 down payment and made payments on the property until 1956. That's when the Cuban revolution led by Fidel Castro to overthrow the Batista regime got into full swing. The revolution was supposed to end with democracy for the island, but Fidel had some other ideas. The investment became a total loss when the parcel was nationalized by Castro," Jim said. He had to leave in late February but Aina stayed in Cuba to avoid the winter weather in Atlanta.

After Aina was discharged from the sanitarium in 1949, Dr. Springer advised Jim to be sure she did not become pregnant. Dr. Springer was concerned that the hormonal influences during pregnancy might cause her tuberculosis to recrudesce. Regardless, she began missing her period in January and February of 1950. "Aina was insistent about having a child. We both decided to let Mother Nature take its course and, of course, we were glad we did!" said Jim. Aina flew back from Cuba to Miami at the end of February. "I drove down from Atlanta to pick her up. When I saw her, she was feverish, nauseated and, in general, not feeling very well," Jim recalled. Aina underwent the "rabbit test" and they learned she was pregnant. Back in Atlanta, Jim consulted with a Dr. Wolf. He thought Aina could do well through the pregnancy with proper medical management. "We both wanted the baby very much," Jim stated. Jay Steele, a healthy boy, was brought into the world on October 10, 1950. Jim later employed a nurse by the name of Anne who had also recovered from tuberculosis. "She stayed with us for about for about two years and ran the household like a drill sergeant. Everything seemed to be finally coming together. Aina's health was much improved and we were now able to live under the same roof. And, of course, I had my dream job with CDC!" he said.

By 1954, requests for veterinary public health assistance by the various states were coming in regularly. Jim found himself lacking sufficient resources to respond. Brucellosis, rabies, tuberculosis, and psittacosis were among the many diseases that states were concerned about. Dr. Langmuir asked Jim to explore the possibility of bringing on more veterinary medical officers. "I got on the phone and began calling veterinary schools and other animal health institutions to see if any veterinarians would be interested in a career in veterinary public health," Jim said. Jim was able to recruit two promising new veterinary graduates. "I was so fortunate to get

Dr. George Beran from Iowa State and Dr. Dan Cohen from Illinois on this round," Jim stated.

In 1949, Dr. Fred Soper, head of the Pan American Sanitary Bureau, established his own program in veterinary public health. Jim recruited his friend and colleague Dr. Benjamin D. Blood, to lead the new program. At the time, Dr. Blood was just finishing his MPH at Harvard, something that Jim had strongly encouraged him to do. These early interactions with the PASB led to a lifelong relationship with the organization for Jim. In 1958 the name was changed to the Pan American Health Organization, with the PASB continuing on as the executive arm of the organization. "Ben visited me once in Atlanta. He had just returned from Korea. After he saw my nice office he told me he wanted my job! I thought, gosh, this guy really lays it on the line. I think he really meant it!" Jim said with a smile.

Within just a few short years, Jim had overseen the birth of veterinary public health and the birth of his own first son. Jim commented, "Life was good!"

CHAPTER 13:
INVESTIGATING BRUCELLOSIS, THE CHRISTMAS DISEASE

"Sir David Bruce, a Scottish pathologist and microbiologist, first isolated and identified the bacterium *Brucella melitensis* in 1887. A Maltese doctor and archaeologist, Sir Temmi Zammit, subsequently associated the organism from unpasteurized milk and a human with the disease in 1915, thus the name Malta fever. The disease would eventually assume over seventeen names, including geographically-linked titles such as Mediterranean fever, Cyprus fever and Gibraltar fever," said Jim. He worked making *Brucella abortus* antigen for diagnostic testing in the attic of the anatomy building as a student. He also experienced firsthand the dangers of *Brucella melitensis* after the accident that occurred in Dr. I. F. Huddleston's laboratory at Michigan State College, infecting almost an entire class of veterinary medical students resulting in one fatality (see chapter 4). This incident made Jim wonder if other *Brucella* organisms could be transmitted by aerosol.

In January 1946, Jim was working as a scientist at the NIH. "I was sent to Salisbury, Maryland to investigate an outbreak of human brucellosis that had occurred one month earlier," he recalled. Another cluster of human cases was identified shortly after the New Year holiday. The outbreak was blamed on pastries infected with *Brucella abortus*. However, the exact source of the infected pastries was still not known.

"Pastry makers know that unpasteurized cream whips up firmer than its processed counterpart and results in a more desirable and marketable product. It was guessed that some dairies were selling raw cream to local bakeries, but we didn't know which ones," Jim said. Jim interviewed all of the affected patients to try to verify a common source of exposure. "I quickly figured out that almost every patient had purchased products from one bakery. I remember some colorful discussions with the management. The owner said that he had been using unpasteurized cream for many years without any problems. I also learned that state law did not prohibit selling raw milk products. The cream only had to be from an accepted, accredited farm," Jim reported. Somewhat later, Jim used the results of this investigation to work for a stricter interpretation of the milk ordinance to ensure that dairy herds are disease free. Jim wrote an article about the investigation and published it in *Public Health Reports.* "This was my first scientific paper," Jim said.

As has already been described, Jim moved to Atlanta, Georgia in September 1947 to establish the veterinary public health division of CDC. CDC headquarters was in the Luckie Building, with Jim's office on the seventh floor. He would stay there for several years before moving to a federal office complex in a new building nearby. Dr. Mountin visited Atlanta in March of 1948 to evaluate what Jim and others were doing with their new health programs. Jim discussed his concern regarding the public health risks of brucellosis in the Midwestern states. Dr. Mountin suggested that they take a field trip to Indiana and Michigan to learn more about the problem.

Their first stop was Michigan. They met with the state health officer and Dr. Art Wolff, who was a USPHS Veterinary Officer in Michigan at the time. He later became the deputy chief for the Environmental Protection Association (EPA). Dr. Wolff explained the history of problems with *Salmonella* in several Michigan hospitals during the war. "Many of the nursing assistants were carriers and easily infected infants. Michigan was also struggling with brucellosis at the time. Dr. Wolff wanted to learn more about the brucellosis program that I started in Indiana.

From there, Jim took Dr. Mountin to meet Dr. Huddleston and Dean Giltner at Michigan State College. Dr. Huddleston voiced his concern regarding *Brucella abortus* in Michigan dairies. "He told the story of Edsel Ford, president of Ford Motor Company, and how he died at age forty-nine from complications of brucellosis. "Henry, Edsel's father, did not test their dairy herd for the disease. They also didn't believe in pasteurization. His thinking was that since none of his animals were aborting, how could his herd have brucellosis? Mr. Ford frequently invited his top executives to the farm for parties. Many of his guests came down with clinical brucellosis. A few died of the disease. As a result, brucellosis became a societal disease as well as an occupational disease of the time. People were talking about it, especially in Michigan," said Jim.

Their next stop was Indiana. First they attended a roundtable discussion on *Brucella suis* at Purdue University in Lafayette. Dr. Fred Blankenship, the regional USPHS officer, joined the meeting. Also present was Dr. Pat Hutchings, a classmate of Jim's whom he had worked with in the *Brucella* laboratory. He was now head of brucellosis investigations in Indiana. Many representatives of the Purdue Veterinary Medicine Division were also present.

The Indiana state health officer informed Dr. Mountin that brucellosis was endemic in the Indiana pork industry. At the time, farmers were striving to improve the genetics of their stock. Therefore, they were using the best boars without testing for brucellosis. "This lack of testing essentially created a manmade epidemic. *Brucella suis* cases were common in packing house workers," Jim learned. Farmers were also being exposed to *Brucella suis* in their farrowing operations. Interestingly, there was a state law on the books that offered occupational compensation for infected workers.

Jim assigned Dr. Ray Fagan, a USPHS veterinary officer, to work under Dr. Lee Burney, the Indiana state health officer, to study the epidemiology of brucellosis in Indiana. "Dr. Fagan was the first USPHS veterinary officer to be appointed to a state position. The initial version of the Uniform Methods and Rules (UMR) for brucellosis was not released by APHIS until 1947. "The successes in Indiana became the model for other states. Human cases of brucellosis declined drastically. Brucellosis in the swine industry also declined with the increased testing of swine. I wasn't aware of any cases of *Brucella melitensis* in the Midwest with the exception of the laboratory accident outbreak at Michigan State College," said Jim.

Jim attended the first Inter-American Conference on Brucellosis in Buenos Aires in 1948. Dr. Louis William, head of foreign quarantine for the US Public Health Service, personally invited Jim to attend the meeting. Dr. Carol Mingle, also attended the meeting. He was in charge of the brucellosis program within the BAI. Jim arranged for a meeting with the American ambassador in Buenos Aires. "I made it a point to tell him about the brucellosis meeting.

I was amazed when I realized that the embassy was totally unaware of the animal health problems in the country," Jim said. Argentine physicians and scientists told Jim that brucellosis in people was common in rural areas, mostly from occupational and farm exposure.

"The surgeon general of Argentina was very cordial to all of the American guests. This surprised me a bit, as relations between the United States and Argentina were fragile at the time. I was assigned a translator. She took Dr. Mingle and me on a tour of Buenos Aires. Somewhere in the middle of the city, a soldier approached us with his gun drawn. He said that we were under arrest and escorted us directly to a guardhouse. Our translator tried to explain our situation, but the soldier paid no attention to her. I could tell that Dr. Mingle was quite concerned. I asked our translator to call the surgeon general's office and let them know about our predicament. Fortunately, he was able to arrange for our immediate release. He apologized profusely and invited us to be his guests. Apparently, the soldiers patrolling the streets were somewhat out of control in those days," Jim said. "Why not let us show you our beautiful countryside!" said the Surgeon General. After the unexpected arrest and jail time, Dr. Mingle decided it was best to return to Washington, DC as soon as possible. "I stayed on to take the surgeon general up on his generous offer.

We traveled to Bariloche in the southern Andes Mountains and then returned to the seashore. It was a very beautiful and memorable trip," Jim recalled. The surgeon general asked Jim what the American embassy said about the arrest. "I told him that I wouldn't bother the American embassy with such a small incident. The surgeon general's face lit up with relief. We remained great friends for many years," Jim said.

Jim attended the World Health Organization (WHO) meeting on brucellosis in Washington, DC in 1951. "It was an extraordinary opportunity to hear discussions on the prevalence of human brucellosis around the world," Jim said. In his presentation, Dr. I. Forest Huddleston estimated that there were about 25,000 cases of human brucellosis in the US from 1945 through 1946. "I was skeptical about his data, but everywhere I traveled people were talking about human brucellosis. I was trying to figure out how to verify Huddleston's numbers. There were reports of up to 2,000 cases in Iowa and maybe 500 cases in Indiana at the time. Dr. Ray Fagan was conducting field studies to confirm the cases in Indiana. The state health department was performing serological testing, but the problem was how to interpret the titers. Many rural people in Indiana had low titers. We didn't want to make the error of diagnosing brucellosis on a simple titer and no clinical history. I wanted the diagnosis to be consistent with a person's occupational and/or environmental exposures. It was very frustrating that we couldn't adequately collect and sort out the data," Jim concluded.

Dr. Pat Hutchings, Purdue scientists, the Indiana State Laboratory, the University of Minnesota, and the Iowa Health Department collectively agreed that a titer of 1:320 or greater could be considered a suspect case assuming the appropriate clinical signs and exposure potential were also present. With this concept in place, case numbers declined significantly. "Unfortunately, arriving at a sound case definition that would be consistently utilized in the field wasn't resolved for a long time," Jim said.

During the roundtable discussion, the topic of *Brucella orchitis* in boars was discussed. "In particular, we talked about venereal transmission of brucellosis by boars. This topic really piqued the interest of Dr. Joe Mountin," Jim said. Dr. Mountin asked, "How did you say this is spread?"

The Purdue University staff members then started talking about the copious ejaculatory discharge of the boars, up to several ounces. Dr. Mountin asked, "What do they mean, ounces?"

Someone responded, "The boar ejaculate can be up to 300 milliliters!"

Dr. Mountin looked at everyone with amazement. He then said, "Good God, that's ten ounces, enough for a lifetime!" At this point, Dr. Blankenship looked at Jim as if to say, "Did you set this up?"

As they walked out of the meeting Dr. Mountin commented to Jim, "There sure is a lot to learn about these critters!"

Next they traveled to Indianapolis to meet with Dr. Lee Burney at the state health office. "He became the surgeon general ten years later. Dr. Burney felt strongly that since streptomycin and PABA were now available to treat tuberculosis, brucellosis control should become a higher public health priority. He predicted that sanitariums for tuberculosis victims would eventually be filled with brucellosis patients," Jim said. Earlier, Dr. Burney had traveled to Washington, DC to speak with Dr. Mountin about brucellosis. "Dr. Mountin asked me what my thoughts were. I never really subscribed to Dr. Burney's predictions on brucellosis. There was no question brucellosis was a serious problem in the US but I never thought it would have the same impact as tuberculosis," Jim said. At the end of the meeting, Dr. Mountin reiterated his stories about boar semen. "Dr. Burney looked at me for an endorsement. I simply smiled and nodded to the affirmative," Jim said.

Jim then returned to Atlanta. Dr. Blankenship and Dr. Mountin drove to Cincinnati to tour an engineering research center that later evolved into the Environmental Protection Agency. Jim learned much later that after Dr. Mountin returned to Washington, DC, he recited the boar semen story at numerous social gatherings. "Imagine that, 300 cc's, enough for a lifetime!"

Dr. Blankenship later told Jim, "My God Jim, while we were on the road he doffed his hat every time we passed a pig farm. I was expecting him to salute next!"

"This is one of my favorite humorous animal stories," Jim said with a smile.

Jim later traveled to Iowa to report on the success stories in Indiana. The public health veterinarian in Iowa at the time was Dr. Stanley Hendricks. The commissioner of health for Iowa, Dr. Hendricks's boss, had worked in Pasteur's lab. "Iowa seemed worse than what I saw in Indiana," Jim said. However, implementation of the same swine test-and-slaughter program in Iowa caused human cases to decline quickly. With each victory, Jim became more confident in his evolving veterinary public health program.

In 1952, Jim was called to Chicago during a rabies outbreak. Upon arrival, he met Dr. Herman Bundeson, commissioner of the Chicago Department of Health. Dr. "Bundeson knew how to get things done politically," Jim said. Dr. Roy Davenport was the state public health veterinarian at the time. Dr. Davenport had been quite active in brucellosis control in the Midwest, so he and Jim stayed in close touch. In 1924, the USPHS developed the Standard Milk Ordinance, which later evolved into the Pasteurized Milk Ordinance (PMO). The intent of the Pasteurized Milk Ordinance was to prevent milk-borne disease in people. The ordinance stated that all Grade A milk would come from disease-free cows. "Of course, the early emphasis was on tuberculosis in cows," Jim said. The USDA began a national campaign to rid the US of bovine tuberculosis after World War I. At that time, Dr. Bundeson was a young health officer in Chicago, and he was totally in support of the program. "If it is doable, let's do it!" he said.

"Dr. Bundeson had plans to run for governor of Illinois. He explained to me that he lost the election because of his support for the bovine tuberculosis eradication campaign. I thought that was quite a tale!" Jim said. Dr. Bundeson made a bet with Colonel Robert McCormick, owner of the Chicago Tribune. "He told Colonel McCormick that he was going to rid the Chicago milk shed of tuberculosis," Jim said. In 1923, Dr. Bundeson had put forth a ruling that all milk coming into Chicago would be free from tuberculosis within four years. "Wisconsin was cooperative, as it was a progressive dairy state. Minnesota and Iowa followed suit to a somewhat lesser extent. With only one year remaining, Bundeson turned up the heat on Illinois. The farmers were telling him that he was ruining their dairy herds. At the same time, we learned that the other states around Illinois, Wisconsin especially, were selling their tuberculosis reactor cows into Illinois at less than market value. Illinois was inundated with infected dairy cows!" Jim explained. In 1930, when Dr. Bundeson ran for governor, the farmers campaigned against him, stating, "Bundeson killed our cows!" Dr. Bundeson told Jim, tongue-in-cheek, "That's why I never became governor. Does this mean that I can't be elected president of the United States if I support your new brucellosis eradication program?"

Jim explained the importance of enforcing the milk code. Dr. Bundeson asked, "What is the actual situation here in Chicago?"

Jim replied, "I don't know, but there are several surrounding states with a serious brucellosis problem, such as Wisconsin, Illinois, Minnesota, Indiana, Ohio, Michigan and Iowa. All of these states send milk to Chicago."

Dr. Bundeson asked, "What should we do about it, Jim?"

Jim replied matter-of-factly, "Well, you simply must insist all milk has to come from states that are *Brucella*-free!" Jim used the term "free." The phrase "accredited free" was not yet in use. "Dr. Bundeson put out the word that Chicago was not going to purchase any milk from a state unless it could demonstrate the milk was from *Brucella*-free herds. He gave the states four years to meet the requirements," Jim said. Dr. Roy Davenport, the Public Health Veterinarian for Illinois later told Jim how delighted he was with Dr. Bundeson's ruling, as he was in total agreement with the recommendation.

"Everyone in Washington thought I was trying to take over all the milk hygiene programs. Nothing could be further from the truth!" Jim said. When the Chicago and Illinois programs began moving forward, people began to believe his strategy was sound. At about the same time, Jim began receiving letters from health officers in other states asking why pasteurization wasn't sufficient. In his work with Dr. Huddleston, Jim learned that laboratory workers could have severe allergic reactions even when they came in contact with dead *Brucella* organisms. "Practicing veterinarians backed me up with letters stating that because they were sensitized to *Brucella*, they had to avoid drinking market milk," Jim said. Jim had dinner with a dairy veterinarian from Providence, Rhode Island, who told him the story of having to give up his practice because he had severe allergic reactions when he was exposed to *Brucella* organisms, live or dead.

"I also understood that pasteurization was not a perfect process. It could never solve the human brucellosis problem alone. So I presented the idea of disease-free status in animals much like a public health insurance policy," Jim said. Chicago turned out to be the first major city to enforce brucellosis control. Jim was later able to promote the same program in other major cities, and it was finally adopted throughout the country. "I worked with Dr. Henry Holle to help clean up the dairy herds in Texas. Tuberculosis and brucellosis eradication came slow in Texas until the interstate shipment of milk was involved, and other states required Texas to comply. Beef herds were the last to comply," Jim said. Jim's leadership and in-depth knowledge of brucellosis enabled him to have a huge influence on reducing public health risks from the disease. As the states implemented the disease-free-herds model, human cases of brucellosis continued to decline.

President Truman initiated the Federal Civil Defense Act of 1950. The act was signed into law in January 1951. "Interestingly, the US Public Health Service was to have a large role," Jim said. At the AVMA meeting in Milwaukee, Wisconsin in 1951, it was announced that the USPHS was moving forward to help establish the Civilian Defense Administration in Washington. "The focus on civil defense emerged during the McCarthy era when there was a burgeoning anti-Communist movement in the US Russia detonated its first atomic bomb in 1949. The Communist nuclear threat now existed, and the civil defense program was to be the protector of the American public," Jim explained.

"Interestingly, I was accused of having contacts with Communists during this period. In 1952, I had a lot of correspondence with people behind the Iron Curtain, mainly from Yugoslavia. The State Department invited several veterinary scientists from Yugoslavia to the US and the NIH and they were assigned to me. I showed them around Washington and introduced them to many people. Without my knowledge, my personal secretary reported to my superiors her suspicion that I was a Communist sympathizer because of my correspondence with the Yugoslavians. She was an old Southern lady who believed any Yankee was bad. I was called to the office of the CDC director, Dr. Ted Bauer. He explained everything to me. A politically appointed lawyer from Washington was demanding that I account for all the time I was spending with the people in question. I was ordered to make copies of my files and all my correspondence with the Eastern Bloc scientists and submit them to the attorney, which I did. Apparently this cleared me of ay suspicion as nothing ever came of the charges. After that incident, my reputation around Washington was stronger than ever. Folks knew not to mess with me as I will respond strongly. My secretary was reassigned to a minor job and retired soon," Jim said.

"I didn't buy in to the civil defense program totally. But I had to play the game. I oversaw many staff involved in the program around the US," Jim said. He remembered a unit in Georgia that was responsible for setting up medical facilities to be utilized if a major city was evacuated. "Many of these plans involved evacuation to farms. I envisioned hundreds of thousands of people sleeping in barns around animals where they would be exposed to Q fever and brucellosis and God knows what else. I cited the story of the US Army moving through Italy in 1945, succumbing to the so-called Balkan grippe or Q fever. The soldiers were incapacitated with severe flu-like symptoms and pneumonia. The German army experienced similar problems as they moved into Greece. I made these risks clear to the civil defense authorities in Washington," Jim said.

A world conference on brucellosis was held in Washington, DC in 1952. Sir Weldon Champney, the deputy administrator of health for Great Britain, was elected the chairman of the meeting. "At the time, I was working fiercely to try to accurately characterize the human brucellosis problem in the US by collecting and analyzing serological data from state health departments," Jim said. This meeting served to bring together scientists from all over the globe with an interest in human brucellosis. "I compared the data I was collecting to the data from other countries. In the fifties, we were definitely making progress on brucellosis control in cattle in the US. Of course, I continued to work closely with Dr. Mingle in the USDA. He understood the epidemiology of brucellosis and was an excellent consultant as we moved the USPHS programs forward," Jim said.

In 1953, Jim pushed for an even stricter interpretation of the Public Health Service Milk Ordinance. He argued that Grade A milk should come only from cows that were free from brucellosis, mastitis, tuberculosis and other identifiable infectious diseases. "This was not a new concept. But I didn't see that the job was getting done. The sanitary engineers thought I was elbowing my way into their lane, and feared that veterinary public health wanted to take over the milk program. This was not my intent. I only wanted to communicate that the Public Health Service was totally in favor of stricter animal disease control programs because the end result would be improved public health. This strategy got me in a little hot water from time to time, but everything eventually worked out well," Jim said.

Dr. Charlie Williams, assistant surgeon general, called Jim one day and asked, "Look here, Jim, aren't you being a little too aggressive about saying you don't want *any* diseases in the cows? Do you want a veterinarian on every farm?"

Jim responded, "Sir, it is not a matter of a veterinarian on every farm, but I want every herd under veterinary supervision."

Jim invited Dr. Lee Burney to speak at the AVMA meeting in Cleveland, Ohio in 1957. Dr. Burney spoke highly of the efforts of veterinarians in public health roles. After his speech, Jim was approached by Dr. Sam Scheidy, the chairman of the AVMA executive board and later president of the AVMA. Dr. Scheidy told Jim, "Jim, thanks to you, no one can ever say again that veterinarians do not have a role in public health!" Jim later devoted four chapters to brucellosis in his *CRC Handbook Series for Zoonoses.*

Jim attended another international brucellosis meeting sponsored by WHO in Poland in 1957. "I learned about a Russian program for vaccinating humans against the disease. This gave me caution as I knew from Huddleston's work that this could not be done effectively or safely," Jim said. Dr. Wesley Spink, a physician at the University of Minnesota, worked out a plan for testing the Russian vaccine on federal prisoners at the Minnesota State Penitentiary just outside Minneapolis. "The test was a total disaster. The vaccine itself caused clinical brucellosis. Then they challenged the inmates with the live organism. It was unbelievable." Jim said. Dr. Spink later served as the director of the Brucellosis Research Center for the WHO Coordinating Laboratory. "The

Russians claimed that the trial of their *Brucella* vaccine was done to discredit their research. Another trial was organized to be conducted in Iran under Dr. Spink's direction. This trial also failed," Jim said.

Jim traveled to Russia in 1963 and saw just how widespread and devastating human brucellosis could be. He also witnessed just how misdirected the Russian public health policy was. In 1966 he went to Peru and observed an outbreak of over 5,000 human cases of *Brucella melitensis* infection. "These were all related to goat cheese made from unpasteurized milk," Jim said.

"I am pleased that human brucellosis is relatively rare in the US today. But I am discouraged that it is still a significant public health problem in so many developing countries of the world. It is amazing how war and politics can stand in the way of achieving a good level of health for the people of the world. If politicians only understood the simple fact that as you improve people's health and animal health, you virtually eliminate poverty at the same time."

CHAPTER 14:
OLD YELLER REVISITED

Set in Texas in 1869, the 1957 hit Disney movie *Old Yeller* is about fifteen-year-old Travis Coates, who has to run the family farm while his father is on a cattle drive. His younger brother, Arliss, has adopted a stray dog, Old Yeller, who got into a fight with a mad wolf. Unfortunately, Old Yeller contracted rabies, forcing Travis to kill him with a rifle. "Unfortunately, rabies is still a significant problem in the world. The following 19th Century poem by English poet William Sommerville, is apropos. The first verse calls for vigilance against rabies, while the others speak of the dumb and furious forms of the disease," Jim explained.

The Chase
…. Visit thou
Each ev'n and morn with quick observant eye
Thy panting pack. If, in dark sullen mood,
The gloating hound refuse his wanted meal,
Retiring to some close, obscure retreat,
Gloomy, disconsolate; with speed remove
The poor infectious wretch, and in strong chains
Bind him suspected. Thus that dire disease
Which art can't cure, wise caution may prevent.

…. Or in some dark recess the senseless brute
Sits sadly pining; deep melancholy,
And black despair, upon his clouded brow
Hang lowering; from his half-opening jaws
The clammy venom, and infectious froth,
Distilling fall; and from his lungs inflamed
Malignant vapors taint the ambient air,
Breathing perdition; his dim eyes are glaz'd.
He droops his pensive head, his trembling limbs
No more support his weight; abject he lies,
Dumb, spiritless, benumbed; till Death at last
Gracious attends, and kindly brings relief.

> …. His glaring eyes
> Redden with fury, like, like some angry boar
> Churning he foams; and on his tail incurved
> He drops, and with harsh broken howlings rends
> The poison-tainted air; with rough hoarse voice
> Incessant bays and snuffs the infectious breeze;
> This way and that he stares aghast, and starts
> At his own shade….
> …. Whate'er he meets
>
> Vengeful he bites; and every bite is death.

In the early 1880s, Pasteur performed several experiments demonstrating that a virus that replicates readily in central nervous system tissues causes rabies. This work led to the development of the first rabies vaccine. In 1903, the Negri body was characterized as a distinct pathological lesion seen in the brain cells of most people and animals that succumbed to the dreaded disease. In the 1920s, the Semple vaccine was adapted for dogs in Japan in hopes of controlling canine rabies. "This helped set the stage for the establishment of a veterinary public health program to combat rabies in the 1940s and after the war," Jim said.

"During my small animal clinical rotation in veterinary school, I did a thorough physical examination on a sick puppy. The next day it died and was confirmed rabid. I wasn't vaccinated at the time, so I had to take the complete series of injections at the Michigan Health Department. Later, I received the chick embryo vaccine. To this day I empathize with anyone who has to go through this. Getting stuck with needles is no fun nor is it entertaining to lie in bed at night wondering if you are infected!" Jim stated.

Jim had been concerned at first about leaving the Washington, DC area for Atlanta. He was convinced that Washington was where he could develop the most support for his new program in veterinary public health. "But as it turned out, I still spent as much time in Washington as I did in Atlanta. I was fortunate to have a generous travel budget. This allowed me to promote my programs and to build a valuable network of colleagues and collaborators.

OLD YELLER REVISITED | 135

This became very important as I worked to help establish state programs to control rabies," Jim said.

"At the end of the war, stray dog and cat populations in the US posed a colossal public health problem," Jim related. The situation was aggravated by military calls to duty and repeated assignments from one base to another. Pets were popular, but too often they were left behind. "The city streets and the countryside were full of unvaccinated animals. Animal control services were almost nonexistent at the time," Jim pointed out. Rabies was endemic in all states, and Georgia was no exception. Jim understood the challenge, and he quickly convinced his superiors, including Joe Mountin, that important work had to be done to evaluate new vaccines that would become the underpinning of a nationwide rabies control program.

Dr. Mountin asked Jim to scout out vacant US government and other properties that might be suitable for conversion into a rabies research laboratory. "I looked at hunting lodges, resort homes, vacant government buildings—anything that might be suitable," Jim said. In 1946, Dr. Harold Johnson from the Rockefeller Foundation told Jim about their lab that was going to be closed that might be suitable.

The CDC Rabies Investigation Laboratory was ultimately established in the old Rockefeller laboratory in Montgomery, Alabama. "This was selected as the site where the rabies vaccine studies on animals would be accomplished. The facility was donated by the Rockefeller Foundation for one dollar," Jim recalled. Dr. Harold Johnson and others adapted the rabies virus to embryonated chicken eggs at the Rockefeller rabies laboratory in the late thirties. "It was decided that these legacy laboratories should be shut down and all rabies projects transferred to the CDC," Jim stated. Jim recruited Dr. Ernest Tierkel to head the new veterinary rabies laboratory operations in Montgomery with Ms. Martha Edson as his lead technician. "I was astonished to be given such a nice facility. We couldn't possibly utilize all the space," Jim said.

The first task was to evaluate the work that Dr. Johnson and his colleagues had done. Next, they created a prototype vaccine that they would use for challenge studies. "The rabies control consultants were Drs. Tom Sellers, Charlie Leach, Karl Habel and myself," Jim explained. Jim knew Dr. Sellers as head of the Georgia State Health Laboratory. He developed the famous Sellers stain that enabled the visualization of Negri bodies in tissue sections. Dr. Leach had been a virologist at the Rockefeller lab. Dr. Habel was a physician at NIH who developed a test to evaluate the effectiveness of a killed rabies vaccine in mice. "I did some work with Dr. Habel at NIH. He went to Panama with me in 1946. Tragically, in the 1980s Dr. Habel became infected with Monkey B virus and died," Jim reported. In the late 1970s, Dr. Robrt E. Kissling did the work in applying the fluorescent antibody (FA) technique for rabies diagnosis at CDC in Atlanta. "This really excited me. The FA test eventually became the most valuable diagnostic test ever for confirming rabies cases," Jim said. Later Dr. Maurice Schaeffer, a physician, was recruited to be the director of the Montgomery lab with the mission of making it an all-virus research facility. "The laboratory was in very good hands. CDC carried on rabies studies for more than fifty years, evaluating vaccines and improving diagnostic methods," said Jim.

The second challenge was to learn how to improve on the existing rabies vaccines. Sir David Semple founded the Pasteur Institute in Kasauli, India, and developed a killed vaccine utilizing sheep brains in 1911. A modified Semple phenol killed vaccine was still being used for vaccinating dogs in the US and around the world in the 1940s. "The US Army recommended a semiannual vaccination protocol with the Semple product that seemed to provide adequate immunity. But was it practical to believe that people would vaccinate their animals twice a year?" Jim said. Practicing veterinarians in the US adopted the same practice, more than happy to bring their clients back in the clinic twice every year.

Dr. Harold Johnson's adaptation of the rabies virus to embryonated eggs was a huge leap forward for vaccine technology. "This was based on work done at Vanderbilt University, where they had successfully adapted the vaccinia virus. Unfortunately, Dr. Johnson was a perfectionist and a procrastinator and never published his work," Jim said. Dr. Sellers did the first work with the Flury strain. This strain was isolated from the vulva of a young girl who was about twelve years old by the name of Flury. She acknowledged having allowed a dog to lick her genitals. Unfortunately, the dog was rabid and she developed clinical rabies and died. The story was verified by Dr. Sellers, who investigated the case. It is a bizarre and sad story, but it verifies that mucous membranes are a suitable portal of entry for the rabies virus. The virus isolated from Ms. Flury is the one that Dr. Sellers adapted to embryonated eggs. This strain was later used to challenge dogs vaccinated with the chick embryo product in the CDC trials.

A young Polish researcher, Dr. Hillary Koprowski, heard about Dr. Johnson's work from friends at the Rockefeller Foundation. He had fled Poland to Brazil. Dr. Koprowski took the Flury virus to Lederle Laboratory, a division of American Cyanamid, to conduct further studies. Dr. Harold Cox, a former USPHS officer, was recruited to be the director of the laboratory to help produce Rocky Mountain spotted fever vaccine. Lederle Laboratories was located in upstate New York on the Pearl River across from New Jersey. Dr. Lederle was chief of the public health laboratories for New York City in the early 1900s.

Apparently Dr. Harold Cox knew who Jim Steele was. "I knew him by reputation only," Jim said. Dr. Cox cornered Jim at an American Public Health Association meeting at a hotel room get-together and stated matter-of-factly, "I've got the answer to your national rabies vaccination program, Jim. We have developed an efficacious live virus rabies vaccine!"

Jim pulled him over into the bathroom and asked, "A live virus vaccine, you say? You would have to demonstrate it is not only efficacious but safe!" Jim added, "Don't forget about all the deaths related to the German louse-borne typhus live vaccine."

"I was dumfounded!" Jim said. He knew that Dr. Johnson was working with rabies virus, but he had had no idea that anyone was thinking along the lines of a live rabies vaccine. From the winter of 1947 into the spring of 1948, Jim was getting lots of questions. "Many of my colleagues were really skeptical about a live product. But all I could think of was the potential of inducing a long duration of immunity. I wanted to be open-minded, but I kept returning to my cautious side," Jim said. Finally, outside pressures reached a point where Jim had to make a move.

In the spring of 1948, Drs. Sellers, Leach, Johnson, Tierkel and Steele met to discuss new directions for their rabies research. "My objective was to evaluate the new Flury strain vaccine. There was no other way to learn if the product could be protective and safe. And I was anxious to see what the duration of immunity would actually be—six months or maybe even six years! I was actually hoping for lifetime immunity at the time," Jim said.

He heard that the trials of the Flury product at Pearl River had gone well—no vaccine-induced rabies. "Inducing rabies through vaccination was my worst nightmare," Jim said. Jim's group finally designed a trial that spring to focus primarily on duration of immunity. Dr. Tierkel was the principal investigator. "I asked him to conduct the rabies vaccine trials, comparing the Lederle product against other available vaccines. Dr. Karl Habel joined the advisory committee and we met regularly to monitor progress," Jim said.

"By 1951, the data on the Lederle vaccine was looking very promising, and most of the committee members were voting to discontinue the study. I was uncomfortable with this, as we had agreed to continue the trials for a minimum of five years," Jim said. He reminded the committee about what they had originally agreed to but was overruled. Dr. Schaeffer encouraged them to end the experiment. "I was concerned that it would be difficult, if not impossible, to ever conduct another trial like this one. Why not take it as far as possible?" Jim said. But the decision was final. The study would be terminated within six months in the spring of 1952, a year early.

Jim gave the nod for Dr. Tierkel to continue his work until the bitter end. He acquired sixty dogs for the last trial–thirty for vaccination and thirty controls. He challenged the control group with a live virus street strain, and all of the dogs subsequently died of clinical rabies. When he challenged the vaccinated group, 80 percent of the dogs survived. "The vaccine certainly wasn't perfect, but it had to be the best available at the time. We learned later that we were able to achieve thirty-nine months' duration of immunity in the dogs. I was very pleased," Jim said. They published the study in the proceedings of the AVMA meeting in July 1952. Jim continued using the Flury strain live virus chick embryo vaccine for his canine rabies control programs for the next twenty years and is still being used in Asia and Africa.

Jim oversaw CDC's first major field test of the Flury vaccine in Memphis, Tennessee in 1950. Even though trials were still in progress to ascertain the duration of immunity, the product was approved by the USDA for use in the field. "Memphis had been experiencing periodic rabies outbreaks in dogs for decades. The Tennessee Department of Health finally asked for USPHS assistance. I dispatched the charming and very competent Dr. Tierkel to their rescue," Jim said with a smile. He convinced city officials and the media to conduct a rabies awareness campaign, emphasizing the importance of vaccination and stray dog control. "Veterinarians conducted vaccination clinics at fire stations, schoolyards, and parking lots for little or no charge. Stray dogs were captured and euthanized if their owners could not be quickly identified. The goal was to vaccinate at least 75 percent of the dogs in the city. At the time, we made the assumption that there was approximately one dog per ten residents," Jim said.

The control program was a huge success. An article summarizing the program was written by a Memphis health officer and was published in the *Journal of the American Public Health Association* in 1952. "The number of dogs with confirmed rabies decreased precipitously and cases in people were nonexistent. To say we were pleased is a major understatement!" said Jim.

With his growing reputation, Jim was increasingly in demand to speak on rabies prevention and control. For example, he was asked to be a keynote speaker at the Inter-American Public Health Association Convention held in Havana, Cuba in October 1951. "The meeting was a big affair with about three thousand attendees. It turned out to be the first international public health forum where veterinarians were asked to host their own scientific program," said Jim. Justin Andrews, PhD, a well-known parasitologist and a colleague of Jim's at CDC, had been quite involved in program planning for the meeting. Dr. Andrews was the Director of CDC. Jim presented an overview of rabies in domestic animals and discussed how urban expansion into rural areas was resulting in more human exposure to animals. "I referred to this phenomenon as the 'edge,'" Jim said. Jim also presented on the success of his rabies programs around the US and described how his team had achieved up to thirty-nine months of protective immunity in dogs with the Flury strain vaccine. "Mongoose rabies was a real problem in Cuba at the time and still is in most of the Caribbean Basin. I met many Cuban veterinary scientists while at the meeting. Most of them were quite impressive," Jim reported.

Jim visited the University of Havana School of Veterinary Medicine. "It was the only veterinary school in Cuba at the time. We had a meeting with the faculty to discuss collaborative projects with CDC. I felt that the Cubans could be a timely source of alerts regarding outbreaks of diseases in animals or people which might spread to the US from the south," Jim said. Jim also visited several dairies while in Cuba. "They were employing high-quality pasteurization methods. But I was primarily interested in learning about mongoose and bat rabies, which was prevalent in western Cuba. Cuba became my first true CDC outpost," Jim said.

In 1952, Jim was presented the Carlos Finlay Prize for his work in veterinary public health at the Pan American Health Congress in Havana. Carlos Finlay was of Scottish descent. He attended Jefferson Medical College in Philadelphia, Pennsylvania and became the chief health officer for Cuba from 1902 to 1909. He discovered the link between the mosquito and yellow fever and pushed for insect control to help eliminate the disease. "I found it interesting that the Latin American countries grasped the importance of the zoonotic diseases well before the concept was embraced by English speaking countries," Jim said.

The WHO established a committee to review Dr. Tierkel's work after his success with rabies control in Memphis. In 1953, he was invited to Geneva along with Dr. Karl Habel to help WHO promote the Flury strain chick embryo rabies vaccine worldwide. Dr. Tierkel ultimately traveled throughout Europe, Asia, the Caribbean and South America on this mission. Along the way, he learned that many countries had decided to develop their own vaccines. "Dr. Tierkel looked at other vaccines developed utilizing embryonated eggs. He also studied the Fuenzalida suckling mouse brain vaccine, a killed project developed by a veterinarian by the same name in Chile. But for that period in time, no vaccine was as safe and effective as the Flury vaccine evaluated by Dr. Tierkel and Martha Edson." Jim stated.

The next significant outbreak of canine rabies was in Denver, Colorado in 1954. Dr. Robert Anderson was the public health veterinarian in Denver at the time. With Jim's guidance, he implemented the same program that had been so successful in Memphis. "He had the same level of success in Denver as we did in Memphis," said Jim. Dr. Anderson later became a professor at the University of Minnesota College of Veterinary Medicine and taught public Health. Dr. Anderson, along with veterinarians Dr. Leo Bustad and Dr. William McCulloch and physician Dr. Michael McCulloch (William McCulloch's brother) became founders of the Delta Society, an organization that first studied the importance of the human-animal bond and the public health value of animals as companions. Jim was inspired by his colleagues' careers and how they evolved creatively from one facet of veterinary public health to another.

Subsequently, a rabies outbreak erupted in St. Louis. Jim dispatched Dr. Tierkel immediately to plan and execute a control program. "The outcome was once again extremely successful. One or two dollars was charged for the rabies vaccination to help cover the cost. Hundreds of thousands of dogs were vaccinated. This generated a lot of cash that the city didn't know exactly what to do with. The community was quite upset. I suggested that we move on to the next epidemic. We didn't need to get in the middle of a political firestorm. Our jobs were done!" The *St. Louis Post Dispatch* newspaper ran an editorial condemning the veterinary profession for saying the funds should be paid to them for helping the city to augment dog control. Jim thought his colleagues were unwise. "There are times when our profession should do things for the community, give something back."

The El Paso, Texas outbreak hit next. The Colorado State veterinarian, Dr. Martin Baum, was dispatched from Denver to help out. "He had worked with Dr. Anderson on previous outbreaks and had gained some good experience," Jim said. However, a local El Paso veterinarian, Dr. Duane Cady, who represented his local veterinary medical association, had other ideas, "This is a local, private issue and we will run this program. We don't need any state, federal or military assistance!" Dr. Cady said.

"Dr. Cady and his team initiated a citywide program, but soon became overwhelmed and requested help from the Fort Bliss Army post. Fort Bliss first decided to restrict their vaccination program to the post, but later did pitch in and assist with the city program," Jim said.

This turned out to be one of the worst rabies outbreaks in US history. "There were pockets of problems all around the city. To complicate things, there was the Mexican border with plenty of free-roaming, rabid dogs spilling over into Texas. The local veterinarians vaccinated many dogs, but not enough," Jim said. The epidemic stretched on for months until finally the local veterinarians began working with government officials. "This is a classic, excellent example of how things can go wrong if there is an anti-governmental attitude or poor cooperation and coordination in response to an outbreak," Jim said.

"The big Chicago rabies outbreak occurred in 1953. A man had died of rabies near the Indiana state line. An investigation revealed that the dog probably originated in Indiana," Jim said. Herman Bundeson, MD, was the city health officer at the time. He phoned CDC and requested assistance. Ernie and I went to Chicago to help with the delicate situation which was evolving. I assured Mayor Martin Kenneley we would bring the rabies epidemic under control. We were very confident in our control strategy by this time." Jim said.

The *Chicago Tribune* and the *Daily News* gave their support with special articles covering the outbreak and the planned control strategy. "The chick embryo vaccine was successful in Memphis, Denver, St. Louis and even in El Paso. We knew we wouldn't let my hometown down!" Jim said. By now, the entire US public health community held a growing interest in the new vaccine.

"I believed in the vaccine so much that I was accused of being a promoter for Lederle Laboratories. In addition, the veterinary profession was speaking out against the chick embryo vaccine because it was made available to lay groups like breeders and kennels. It was all a little hard to juggle. But I fell back on the excellent success record of the product every time," Jim said.

One morning a prominent veterinarian called Jim at home in Atlanta and asked, "Why are you supporting only the Lederle vaccine?"

Jim replied, "It is the best vaccine available!"

The veterinarian then asked, "How much are you getting paid for your support of this product?"

Of course, Jim didn't receive a dime from any company. But these accusations were a source of irritation and frustration for him. "In reality, numerous vaccine types were used during these outbreaks. The veterinarians that participated in the rabies control programs were free to choose the vaccine they wanted to use. There was no way we could control this. There was a new ultraviolet attenuated vaccine from Pittman Moore of Indianapolis. The vaccine was not properly attenuated and may have resulted in vaccination-induced rabies. The vaccine caused a dumb form of the disease, which was not well recognized at the time. There were rumors of the furious form of rabies induced by vaccination, but this was never confirmed," Jim said. The ultraviolet attenuated vaccine was finally removed from the market. Jim remembered thinking how lucky he was to have distanced himself from the ultraviolet vaccine. "The gods were looking after me again!" Jim said.

Several special vaccination clinics were established around Chicago in the spring of 1953. The city offered free vaccinations while private veterinarians charged a small fee. "The city clinics were held mostly in fire stations. Hundreds of thousands of dogs were vaccinated, and the outbreak stopped. I remember that my name appeared in newspaper stories almost daily," Jim said. One headline he recalled stated:

PUBLIC HEALTH VETERINARIAN COMES HOME
TO SAVE CHICAGO FROM RABIES!

"There were several human deaths associated with this outbreak. But there have been no other major outbreaks in Chicago
since. It was a real honor to be able to come back to my hometown and make this kind of contribution. Dr. Bundeson was very
pleased with the outcome. He took our entire team to his favorite
Italian restaurant one night and told us stories of his adventures as
a public health officer in Chicago," Jim said.

"Unfortunately, the humane societies and another group led
by Irene Dunne, the famous retired actress, singer and dancer,
claimed that veterinarians were promoting the rabies control program only to increase their profits. She was essentially saying that
the rabies vaccination program was equivalent to animal abuse,"
Jim said. A citywide meeting open to the public was scheduled to
discuss the rabies vaccination program. The meeting was held in
the city health department offices. Ms. Dunne arrived with her
well-dressed entourage. She made some opening remarks: "This
rabies program amounts to nothing but a means to promote the
business of veterinarians. There's no telling how many animals
have suffered in the development of this vaccine. The British
don't vaccinate their dogs; why should we?"

"Technically she was correct, but the British didn't have rabies
in their country, either. What happened next, I would never forget," said Jim.

Dr. Tierkel quietly moved to the podium and began to speak.
"I am a special advisor to the queen of England on rabies control. I have advised the queen to vaccinate any and all animals
coming to them from overseas in order to keep rabies out of the
United Kingdom. She is implementing my recommendation as we
speak." This statement drastically weakened Ms. Dunne's defense
and served to defuse the whole situation. "Dr. Bundeson and I
got along famously from then on. Later we worked together to
ensure that Chicago utilized milk from brucellosis-free animals,"
said Jim.

Colonel Robert Rutherford McCormick, the owner of the Chicago Tribune and the WGN radio and television networks, im-
plored a Congressional delegation to introduce a bill that would
lead to the eradication of rabies in the US. The bill mentioned

Jim's rabies control program specifically. States were to receive funds based on a well thought out formula. The whole program would be administered by CDC. "If the Truman administration had been reelected, the bill would have passed. Eisenhower refused to sign the bill, and no rabies control bill was ever passed," Jim said. However, funds were eventually found to fund the state programs. Jim worked primarily with state public health officers and local and regional veterinary associations to implement their programs. "At one point, the USDA wanted to oversee rabies control and to approve the vaccines that would be utilized. But this was a stretch of their mission, as the principal goal of rabies control was to protect public health, not animal health," Jim said.

"In 1952, rabies began to rear its ugly head in Houston, Texas. For reasons unknown to me, our control program wasn't put into place immediately and things were getting out of hand," Jim said. President Eisenhower took office in January of 1953 and appointed Oveta Culp Hobby as the first secretary of the newly formed Department of Health, Education and Welfare (HEW) in April. "Prior to accepting the position, she had served as president and editor of the *Houston Post.* One of her most notable contributions to public health was her decision to legalize the use of the Salk polio vaccine in the US," Jim said.

Soon she recognized that rabies was becoming a real problem in Houston. Jim thought to himself, *Gosh, this is Secretary Hobby's city! We can't mess this one up!* "I did the necessary coordination and dispatched Dr. Tierkel to Houston to get things moving. Dr. Tierkel hooked up with Dr. Burke, the Houston city veterinarian. There was excellent cooperation with the Houston veterinary profession. Using our standard one dog per ten citizens ratio, we estimated that there were roughly 100,000 dogs in Houston based on a human population of about one million at the time. By the time we had vaccinated 80,000 dogs I felt the outbreak would be over soon," Jim said. But something was terribly wrong this time; cases continued to emerge. "There we were in the hometown of the new HEW secretary and things were not going right. Rabies cases continued through the summer and into the fall. I was truly baffled," Jim said.

Jim recommended that they reexamine the dog population data. "We decided to take another look at the dog license data and also did an informal block-to-block census of animals and people. This exercise revealed Houston had twice the number of dogs than what they had estimated in the northern cities. Instead of a 1:10 ratio of dogs to humans, the correct ratio was closer to 1:5!" Jim said. So the 80,000 dogs we had vaccinated represented only 40 percent of the population. "The vaccination program had to be vastly expanded," Jim concluded.

Eventually, the City of Houston, Harris County, the Texas public health veterinarians and the private practitioners brought the situation under control with an aggressive vaccination campaign. "Never take the denominator lightly! Decisions like this must be based on accurate epidemiological data!" Jim admonished. When Jim began consulting outside the US on rabies control, he found that a ratio of 1:10 was usually a good rule of thumb. But he would never forget his experience in Houston, Texas. "The life expectancy of dogs in developing countries was very short, and rabies control programs based on our original ratio were always successful. But we always conducted an informal census just to be sure," Jim said.

The last major rabies epidemic that Jim had direct involvement occurred in 1954 in Los Angeles County, California. "Q fever was also a problem in the area at the time. In those days, most small towns in southern California had their own small public health offices. This resulted in poor coordination of services. The Q fever outbreak caused the small towns to relinquish their authority to the county health department. Ultimately, the small health departments were consolidated into a county health department," Jim said. He learned that most counties had a veterinarian on staff along with animal control units. "With all these resources available, I thought this outbreak would be an easy chore, but it was not to be," Jim said.

"There was strong opposition to the vaccination of dogs in the region. I tried my best to resolve the situation from Atlanta. I spent countless hours on the phone with California staffers. Finally, they asked me to fly to California to meet with the county commissioners face-to-face," said Jim. The night before the meeting, Jim met with the Los Angeles County Veterinary Medical Association. "They just wished me a lot of luck! The press had somehow convinced the local community that the rabies vaccine was not safe for their animals," Jim explained.

A retired Hollywood starlet by the name of Marion Davies was intimately involved in the emerging humane movement in California at the time. She had starred in popular movies in the thirties, such as *Ever Since Eve* and *Hearts Divided*. Ms. Davies and Estelle Taylor, the ex-wife of boxer Jack Dempsey, organized a campaign to oppose the vaccination program. "They were a force to be reckoned with," Jim recalled. Ms. Davies attacked Jim viciously in the *Los Angeles Examiner,* one of William Randolph Hearst's early successful operations. She was rumored to be Mr. Hearst's mistress at the time. "They were presenting me as a mad scientist who conducted cruel experiments on dogs. I was being tarred and feathered by Mr. Hearst. In one of Hearst's editorials I remembered something to the effect that I had no sympathy or compassion for animals—I only wanted to glamorize myself. Who was going to listen to me?" said Jim.

Fortunately, Jim was able to establish contact with Dr. Phillip Olson, a prominent Hollywood veterinarian, whom he had met as a senior in veterinary school. Dr. Olson helped Jim to organize local veterinarians who pledged to support the rabies control program. The next day Jim met with the county commissioners. "They were probably the most politically powerful group in Los Angeles at the time," Jim said. Present at the meeting was the wife of another popular movie star. Jim never did learn her name, but she obviously had the ear of the movie industry. "She was clearly good friends with Ms. Davies and Ms. Taylor," Jim recalled.

Jim spoke with great confidence as he addressed the commissioners. "I laid out exactly what the rabies vaccination program was and how it worked in concert with animal control efforts. I also explained how the same program had been successful in major cities like Memphis, Denver, St. Louis, El Paso, Chicago and Houston," Jim said. The program was endorsed by the AMA, the AVMA, and the APHA. He told the commissioners, "It is a good vaccine. It is a safe vaccine. We can eliminate rabies in the greater Los Angeles area if we can mount a sound, government-supported program. I don't mean the federal government; I mean the Los Angeles local government. This vaccine will protect human life from dog-borne rabies, including helpless children on the streets who can be easily attacked and bitten. It will also save the lives of thousands of helpless dogs!"

The discussion continued until about 3:00 p.m., when the meeting broke with no conclusion. "I was frustrated and concerned," Jim said. However, he was encouraged that they were willing to meet with him again the next day. The next morning, they met for about an hour and still couldn't come to a decision. Jim learned later that this was a simple stall tactic designed to give the commissioners time to evaluate him. They were making inquiries to public relations and other agencies on the eastern seaboard to better understand what the CDC was, who was Dr. James Steele, and what was his role? Jim was relieved when the commissioners agreed to meet with him once more the following day.

"The next morning, I felt that the commissioners and their public relations people were beginning to understand and trust me. We had a positive discussion on the importance of an awareness campaign to help the public learn what the vaccine could do for the community," Jim said. At the end of this short session, it was announced that the next meeting would be held in Palm Springs the following day, about 100 miles east of Los Angeles. "Phil and I were really confused by this move. Why would they want to sequester us away from the city?" said Jim.

The next day, Jim and Dr. Olson drove over to Palm Springs together. "Phil and I got along quite well. He was invaluable in garnering support for the vaccination program. When we arrived in Palm Springs, there was a luncheon in progress. Guests were engaged in small talk and gossip but there was no substantive conversation," said Jim. Many of the commissioners didn't make it to the meeting, but Jim noticed that the wife of the movie star was at the table. "I still hadn't learned her name and never did," Jim said. After lunch, they moved to some tables in a reserved area of the club and she stood to speak.

"Our veterinarian from the CDC has explained to us how we have been brainwashed by the animal welfare people," she stated, displaying almost no emotion. Jim was apprehensive. He was thinking, *Did they really understand me?* She continued, "They are the people that want to make issues with the animal control department. We have checked Dr. Steele's credentials with the Public Health Service and believe that his proposed strategy is sound. We are recommending to the county commissioners that they support the proposed rabies control program to be overseen by the Los Angeles County government."

"To say the least, I was elated. This earmarked the beginning of one of the largest rabies control programs ever conducted in the United States. With over two million people and nearly one-half million dogs, this city was the biggest challenge yet," Jim said. There was some skunk rabies at the time near the ocean, but the vaccination program was so successful, skunk rabies never became a major issue. Occasionally a cat would be found to be rabid, but cats were not a part of the control program at the time. From Los Angeles, the program continued south to Orange County and on to San Diego County. "This program lasted for almost four years," Jim said.

Much later, Jim spoke to a San Diego County health officer who was complaining about dog rabies coming in from Mexico. "He wanted to build a fence across the US and Mexico border at the lower end of California to keep the dogs out," Jim stated. The health officer and his colleagues worked with a US congressman from southern California to introduce a bill to build the fence.

Acting Surgeon General Paul Peterson asked Jim, "What are we going to do about this?"

Jim replied, "It is an insane idea. I do not concur with the bill." The surgeon general replied, "Well, you had better do something about this now. We don't want to have the issue come up before naïve congressional committees that will end up voting to build this ugly, expensive and useless fence!"

Jim returned to California and met with a group of health officers in San Diego. Jim explained that a border fence was not going to be the solution to rabies in Southern California. He reasoned, "US immigration tried to build a fence, and it was torn down as fast as it went up. The materials were sold on the black market in Mexico. Earlier when food and mouth disease appeared in Veracruz, Mexico, there was also talk of a fence, but nothing ever came of it." But Jim had another plan, and the health officers listened.

Jim proposed to assign a USPHS veterinarian to every area along the border of southern California, Arizona, and New Mexico, and to also place two veterinarians on the Texas border. "I told them I didn't have all the funding and resources to do everything I wanted to do. But I recommended that we move forward with a program," Jim said. In the meantime, a bill was introduced to the U. S. Congress to provide one million dollars to build a fence between southern California and northern Mexico. "I approached the congressional staffers who introduced the bill and explained to them that this was not the right approach. I suggested that they delete language about the fence and strengthen the wording about how a rabies prevention and control program would operate and be funded. Funding was then made available by a special congressional appropriation for California, Arizona, New Mexico and Texas. PAHO committed to assist the Mexican states. All the vaccine and supplies were purchased with local money. I assembled a team of competent veterinarians, including Drs. Ted Baker, Dick Parker, James Glosser, Robert Huffaker, and others to help administer the program," Jim said.

Soon, Jim and his colleagues battled for and received a $1 million federal appropriation to assist Dr. Pedro Acha of the Pan American Health Organization to build a joint US-Mexico rabies control program. The bill that originally included provisions for building a fence across the Mexican border with the US was rewritten to contract with PAHO for hiring veterinarians and animal control personnel; to purchase vehicles, vaccine and supplies; and to construct impounding facilities on the Mexican border. "The program continued successfully until 1977 when CDC was satisfied that rabies had been adequately controlled on the border states," Jim said.

The first bat rabies case that Jim became involved with occurred in Florida in 1953. "The case was confirmed by Dr. Bob Kissling at CDC. Bat rabies was also reported in Pennsylvania and Texas during the same year. Bat rabies was recognized in South America in the early 1900s and the spread of the disease across rivers suggested that there was a flying reservoir. Vampire bats were causing rabies in cattle there and still are to this day," Jim said.

Jim heard an interesting story about a rancher outside of Tampa, Florida. "This fellow read a story about bat rabies in Mexico in *Life* magazine. At the same time, he had observed some local bats acting erratically on his ranch. He called the regional health office, and they investigated. Dr. Arthur Lewis, a public health veterinarian in Florida knew how to conduct a proper investigation and confirmed rabies in the bats. Both the Jacksonville and the CDC labs were involved in the testing," Jim said. This case was the first confirmation of bat rabies in the US and North America. Subsequently, rabies was found in more bats that had died on the ranch. Rabid bats were later found in Pennsylvania, Texas and in New Mexico near Carlsbad Caverns. "Of course, the national parks were concerned that bat rabies would have a negative impact on tourism. Eventually, bat rabies was confirmed in the forty-eight contiguous states," Jim reported.

"I was a co-investigator on a Texas study which demonstrated that bats were becoming infected shortly after birth by aerosols in caves. We then learned that aerosols from bat urine and saliva could transmit rabies to humans as well," Jim said. One of the earliest known human cases was a spelunker in Frio Cave in Texas in 1956, apparently infected by aerosolized bat urine while exploring caves. "Further bat studies were conducted by Dr. Denny Constantine and Dr. George Baer, both public health veterinarians at CDC. It was almost comical that they had to conduct the bat studies in their homes because there was no suitable laboratory space at CDC. Imagine something like that happening today," Jim said. The veterinarians built their own cages for the bats and kept them in vacant closets. These studies lasted until 1967.

"Later, a bat research laboratory was established in New Mexico. I remember receiving a call from Commissioner of Health Peavy in West Texas in 1968. A Boy Scout troop had broken into the Frio Cave, where there were signs posted: DANGER—RABIES. The scoutmaster had used the cave as an initiation for Eagle Scouts. The scouts were required to stay in the cave overnight. Commissioner Peavy asked me how to handle the situation. I recommended prophylaxis for the boys as a part of the routine for anyone entering the caves. However, the scouts did not receive the vaccines. Fortunately, no rabies cases occurred," said Jim.

Jim was involved in another unusual rabies outbreak near Christmastime in the late 1950s in Idaho. A pet shop raccoon dam died of rabies after the kits had been sold to families. "The Idaho department of health called me and asked for advice on how to handle the situation. I was concerned and alerted the CDC public relations team to be ready to travel. Fortunately, we were able to trace all of the animals to the homes where they had been sold. We were very firm with the families. All of those exposed had to undergo the prophylactic vaccination program. At the time the treatment consisted of twenty-one intradermal injections in the abdomen," Jim said. Fortunately, the incident did not result in any human rabies.

In 1971, Jim was appointed to the faculty at the University of Texas, School of Public Health (UTSPH) by Dr. Reuel Stallones, the school's first dean. In 1978, a biologist and consultant by the name of Alan Beck advised Dr. Stallones, "We don't need to be spending all this money down on the border for rabies control. Just let the dogs die out naturally, the disease will be self-limiting!" Dean Stallones endorsed his suggestion and made a recommendation to CDC to shut the program down, which they did. "He had a lot of clout at CDC. I couldn't believe it. The Texas Department of Health was bewildered by the loss of the program. Dean Stallones and I didn't have much to say to each other in those days, nor in the days afterward," Jim said. In the early eighties, a severe coyote and fox rabies problem emerged in Texas from El Paso to Brownsville. Jim still believes that if the cooperative program in Texas had continued, rabies would not have reestablished itself in Texas.

"Of course, Dean Stallones didn't put me in for professor emeritus status when I retired. In 1983, Dr. Roger Bulger, president of the University of Texas Health Science Center graciously got the job done. I subsequently heard that Dr. Stallones was not pleased with this. In 1984, the faculty recognized me with a University of Texas inscribed chair. Everything turned out well!" said Jim.

Eventually, all major cities and hundreds of smaller cities adopted the US Public Health Service rabies control program that Jim developed with the help of his USPHS veterinary officers. Ironically, Atlanta was one of the last major cities to implement a program. Jim was asked repeatedly, "Why don't you do something about the Atlanta situation?"

Jim explained, "There was a strange dynamic going on in Atlanta at the time. The City of Atlanta did not have good relations with CDC in the early days." CDC statisticians did a study on dog population estimates for Atlanta so they would be well prepared to implement a sound program when the time came. The ratio of dogs to people in Atlanta turned out to be 1:6. With that knowledge, a vaccination program commenced in 1960. "Some of the local practicing veterinarians in Atlanta were upset, as many of the vaccination clinics were conducted on federal property on weekends. In addition, CDC veterinarians were vaccinating dogs owned by federal employees at no charge. The local veterinarians didn't like this. Some were threatening lawsuits. Fortunately, it all worked out and no one was ever charged that I am aware of," Jim said.

As early as 1949, Jim received a telephone call from a veterinarian in west Texas. He was concerned about the risk of rabies exposure for practitioners and wondered whether prophylactic vaccination should become a routine preventive measure for the profession. "I started thinking that something needed to be done about developing a better human vaccine. I brought this idea to the attention of the physicians at CDC," Jim said. His inquiry raised many questions. How safe would prophylactic vaccination be in people? Would it be worth the risks? What is the duration of immunity in people? "It was known that some individuals who had been vaccinated thirty years earlier still had strong titers and that one booster would usually increase titers significantly," Jim recalled.

Jim asked Dr. Tierkel to investigate the idea of vaccinating veterinary students with the duck embryo vaccine prior to entering the clinical phase of their education. This practice was adopted in 1953 and continued for more than twenty years. In the late 1970s, the duck embryo product was replaced with the monkey and human diploid cell vaccines. "The duck embryo vaccine didn't always produce a good titer. Many booster shots were often needed and titers had to be monitored closely. The diploid cell products produced excellent titers and produced few allergic reactions. I believe the last practicing veterinarian to die of rabies through occupational exposure was in New Jersey in the 1950s. He was bitten while examining a dog. Rabies prophylaxis for our profession has undoubtedly saved many lives," Jim stated.

"I look back on my adventures with rabies, and I am thankful that I was able to make good decisions that led to mostly positive outcomes. Rabies control programs were ultimately transferred to the states with USPHS in the background in a support role," Jim said.

Dr. Tierkel was ready for new challenges, so Jim brought him to Atlanta to be his deputy. "There was no other work on dog rabies vaccines in the world at that time," Jim said. The USPHS rabies control projects that Jim masterminded became a model for the world. "Dr. Tierkel traveled the globe lecturing on rabies control programs and helped many countries implement their own. He also wrote special rabies reports for the World Health Organization. He did a superb job!" Jim said.

"Tierkel's work was comparable to Pasteur's, but was a switch from treatment to prevention of rabies. Drs. George Baer, Bob Kissling, and others succeeded Dr. Tierkel at CDC. Dr. George Baer argued for the development of an oral bait rabies vaccine to be used in wildlife as far back as 1961. I also laud the outstanding work of Dr. Robert Crandell, who helped to characterize Arctic strains of the rabies virus in his work with the USAF Epidemiology Laboratory in the early sixties. The Montgomery Rabies Laboratory was moved to East Atlanta in 1964 and is conducting rabies studies to this day under world renown Dr. Charles Rupprecht, a Public Health Service veterinarian," Jim observed.

In 1963, veterinarian Dr. Shananwat Devakula cabled Jim from Thailand. "He asked me to secretly send him some rabies serum. He further requested that we not notify the press. Dr. Devakula had studied me at CDC with Jim in 1951. A Thai prince in Bangkok had been exposed to rabies. I sent the serum in a package marked "royal shipment" and did not notify the press, as requested. I never really knew if he was exposed or not, but he did not develop rabies," Jim said. Word finally leaked out in government circles about the incident. The assistant secretary of health, Dr. Phillip Lee, admired Jim's decision. In 1967, it was Dr. Lee who appointed Jim as the deputy assistant secretary of health for veterinary affairs and assistant surgeon general, the first veterinarian ever to hold this position in the US.

On the plane to Paris for the World Veterinary Congress in 1967, Jim reminisced about the trials, tribulations, and successes associated with the rabies control programs. "All I could do was smile. There were so many examples of things that went right!" said Jim.

On November 30, 1946, President Manuel Avila Camacho of Mexico stepped down. Soon thereafter, Jim received an urgent call from Dr. Maurice Shahan, a Bureau of Animal Industries (BAI) virologist. He was working with Dr. Lee Giltner, a brother of the dean of the Michigan State Veterinary College, Dr. Ward Giltner. Dr. Shahan said, "Jim, keep this to yourself for now. We have an outbreak of foot and mouth disease in Mexico, and we need assistance in setting up a program down there. Do you have a Spanish-speaking veterinarian trained in public health?" A new president was to be inaugurated soon, but President Camacho didn't want to make the outbreak public. Dr. Shahan explained to Jim there was a tripartite pact among Canada, the US and Mexico to report immediately any occurrence of foot and mouth disease (FMD) in one of the countries. Dr. Shahan went on, "We are expecting an official report from Mexico shortly, but we would like to promptly organize an official team to travel to Mexico to measure up the situation."

"I knew a Peruvian veterinarian by the name of Dr. Aurelio Malaga Alba who was a visiting scientist at NIH. He was fluent in Spanish and well-versed in public health. Dr. Alba was educated in Edinburgh, Scotland and had been an officer in the Peruvian military. He had a really unique Spanish-Scottish accent!" Jim said. Jim asked Dr. Alba to meet with Dr. Shahan. Dr. Alba subsequently joined the team to visit Mexico with Dr. Shahan as the team leader.

"My curiosity was piqued," said Jim. He asked Dr. Shahan, "How big is the outbreak, and where and how did it start?"

Dr. Shahan responded, "There are reports the disease has appeared in the harbor area of Vera Cruz. The Mexican veterinarians feel that they have confirmed it as FMD. It was probably introduced by a gift animal from the Brazilian president to the outgoing president of Mexico. The animals were clearly not routed through the usual quarantine process. We don't know the scope of the outbreak at this time." Jim was totally immersed in his rabies and brucellosis programs at the time and didn't have the time to take any action on the report immediately. "But this event marked the beginning of a campaign that would cost the US at least four hundred million dollars over an eight-year period," Jim stated. By the spring of 1947, the BAI had a team in Mexico. "A year later, in the spring of 1948, health officers on the Mexican border reported FMD was now spreading to people in the area and was causing male impotence and loss of libido." Jim said.

Then Assistant Surgeon General Charles Williams informed Dr. Joe Mountin of a request for a government investigation. Dr. Mountin responded, "Tell Jim Steele to go down to Mexico and investigate. He's the man for the job!" Dr. Williams called Jim right away. "Jim, Humble Oil Company has some operations near Mexico where the foot and mouth outbreak is. Their doctors have requested a government investigation to confirm if the disease is spreading to people. They are concerned about their employees. What do you know about this?"

"I traveled to Mexico City immediately. This was June 1947. The scientific information I had at the time was that FMD was a disease that rarely affected people," said Jim. He recalled Dr. John Mohler's BAI investigation of the FMD outbreak in 1914 near South Bend, Indiana. As part of his investigation, Dr. Shoening had screened people for the disease, as it was still unknown if it was an occupational hazard. Veterinarians and field staff who worked with the infected animals during the 1914-1915 outbreak sometimes complained of acquiring a vesicular disease. These cases were supposedly verified as clinical FMD by dermatologists at Johns Hopkins Medical School. The few reported cases presented with mild fever and vesicles on the hands or occasionally on the legs. The outbreak was finally traced to packing material from Argentina.

Jim went to see Dr. B.T. Simms, a veterinarian and chief of the BAI at the time. Jim asked, "Can man be infected with FMD virus?" Dr. Sims was aware of a few cases involving laboratories and laboratory accidents, but no natural infections. He also related to Jim a story about German veterinarians in the 1830s who reportedly acquired blisters around the mouth from working with FMD in animals and drinking raw milk. Jim contacted Dr. Chester Manthei, a veterinarian who had graduated from Michigan State Veterinary College five years before Jim. He was now the BAI laboratory director in Mexico and was a good friend of Dr. William Thorpe, Jim's cousin. He believed the Mexicans were experiencing vesicular stomatitis, not FMD. He later confirmed that vesicular stomatitis can be an occupationally acquired disease.

Jim's singular mission in Mexico was to learn more about the reported human cases. Ms. Florence Ullman, a registered public health nurse from the USPHS, was working along the Mexican border. "She told me that she had not heard of any human cases of vesicular disease. After a week of trying to find clues leading to clinical cases, I had come up with nothing except rumors," said Jim.

Jim spoke once again with Dr. Manthei from BAI. He reiterated, "Jim, I'm telling you, this is all rumor. There is no human FMD problem in Mexico!" Jim was becoming convinced that FMD was not an occupational disease and was certainly not anything for the oil companies to worry about.

Jim made a report to Drs. Mountin and Williams regarding his investigation in Mexico. "Both were happy and complimentary," Jim said. About two years later, Dr. Manthei published a report on vesicular stomatitis in man. Later Jim asked Ms. Ullman about the vesicular disease in the patients she had seen. "She told me she had seen some vesicular disease in people in rural Mexico, but it was never linked to FMD. I still wondered if Mexico was experiencing an FMD outbreak and a VS outbreak at the same time in 1953," Jim said. Later, Dr. John Mason confirmed that vesicular stomatitis was present in Mexico during this timeframe.

Surgeon General Thomas Parran asked for a report from Jim on his FMD investigation in Mexico. "I was happy that Dr. Williams accompanied me to the meeting that day. I was told Dr. Parran never greeted anyone with a smile, only a handshake and a nod.

That is precisely how he greeted us that day!" said Jim. Dr. Parran came from a well known family with roots in the Chesapeake Bay area. They spent the next thirty minutes chatting about the FMD situation in Mexico. "Dr. Parran seemed very curious about me. He listened closely to my report. I told him that there is no human disease to speak of related to FMD. I explained to him about how severe economic losses occur when the animals have vesicular lesions in the mouth, on the tongue and the hooves, causing sloughing. They stop eating, have difficulty walking, lose weight and often die," Jim said. He cited the veterinarians he had interviewed and discussed Nurse Ullman's observations. "I also told him that the Mexican veterinarians were saying there were human cases. But I told Dr. Parran that I passed that off as an attempt to collect indemnities from the government," Jim reported.

Dr. Parran chimed in, "I have heard they are replacing oxen with mules as beasts of burden. They don't have any experience with mules, do they? Will this cause management problems?"

Jim agreed it could be a somewhat difficult transition. "FMD is an agricultural problem, sir, one that interferes with raising and marketing animals. Even if an occasional FMD infection does occur in people, it is not anything to be concerned about."

Dr. Parran responded, "I understand this is a serious animal health problem, but I am glad to hear it is not a public health problem." During their meeting, all Jim could think thinking about was the astonishing fact that at the rank of O-3, and as a veterinarian, he was directly advising the surgeon general of the United States.

There was a veterinarian congressman from Fort Wayne, Indiana, by the name of Dr. George Gillie, whom Jim had met in Washington. "He told me about his days in practice testing cattle for tuberculosis," said Jim. Dr. Gillie was appointed chairman of a subcommittee for the congressional investigation of foot and mouth disease. He called Jim and asked him to come over to testify to the committee. Jim first cleared the request with his superiors and then asked, "What am I supposed to do?"

Dr. Williams pointed at Jim and said frankly, "Just tell your story honestly and try not to get the Public Health Service in trouble!"

"I arrived at one of the administrative buildings at the Capitol around mid-day for the meeting. There were about seven members present," Jim said. Congressman Gillie seemed very proud to introduce Jim to the subcommittee members. "Congressmen, this is Dr. Jim Steele. He is the chief public health veterinarian of the United States Public Health Service, a distinguished expert who has just returned from investigating foot and mouth disease in Mexico. Jim, please report your findings to the subcommittee." Jim thought to himself, *Holy cow, imagine a congressman saying all that about me!* Jim had to struggle to keep his feet on the ground.

One of the committee members asked, "Is foot and mouth disease an occupational problem?"

Jim responded firmly, "There is no evidence for that."

The committee member then asked, "Then what is the disease in animal handlers that is occurring in people in Mexico?"

Jim responded, "This is a vesicular disease but it is not FMD." In less than an hour, Jim put the entire subcommittee's fears to rest. FMD would was not a direct threat to human health in the US or anywhere else in the world.

In the early fifties, Dr. John Mason, a former USPHS officer, went to Mexico and confirmed that there was endemic vesicular stomatitis in animals that sometimes spilled over into the human population. "Vesicular stomatitis in people could be a debilitating disease lasting several days," Jim said. Drs. George Beran and T.M. Yuill would report this finding in their chapter on vesicular stomatitis in the *CRC Handbook Series in Zoonoses* in the seventies.

A few days later, Congressman Gillie invited Surgeon General Parran to be the speaker at a Republican congressional dinner. Twenty high-level agricultural industry representatives were in attendance to hear Surgeon General Parran. Dr. Parran made a small statement about FMD and then introduced Jim. "I stood right up and told the group about my conclusion that FMD was not a public health hazard. I detected instant relief on their faces. This was followed by some other really good questions. This was just another one of those situations where the moon and the stars were all lining up. I was really disappointed when Congressman

Gillie was defeated in the next election, as we had also gotten along famously," Jim recalled fondly.

Jim and Dr. Parran enjoyed a professional relationship and friendship until Dr. Parran died in the early seventies. About ten years after the congressional dinner, Jim and Dr. Parran had a chance meeting at the Drake Hotel in Chicago at a brucellosis meeting. Many years later, at a CDC meeting, Jim invited Dr. Parran to his home for lunch. During the meal, Jim told him about his impending lecture tour of Europe, and that he would take his son, Jay, along with him. "This was in 1960. That was the last time I saw Dr. Parran," Jim said.

Sometime around 1949, Jim was invited to be a member of an advisory team sponsored by the American Public Health Association (APHA) to visit the western states. The team went to Colorado, then to Arizona and finished up in San Francisco. There, Dr. K. F. Meyer hosted a luncheon that included then retired Surgeon General Parran. During the luncheon, Dr. Meyer stood up and spoke about FMD and what a serious problem it was. He stated that the USDA wasn't sufficiently concerned about border inspection. "Their idea of border control is sodium hydroxide foot baths for people coming into the US from Mexico!" he said angrily.

"K. F. was quite scornful of the work being done by the USDA in Mexico, and I thought he was going a bit overboard," Jim said.

Almost automatically, Jim stood up and disagreed with Dr. Meyer, and voiced his support of the USDA's efforts. Jim remembered Dr. Parran looking at him with amazement that he would correct his distinguished host. What was even more amazing was after Jim sat down, Dr. Meyer got up and said, "Jim, thanks for setting me straight on that!" Jim thought, *Gosh, instead of getting shot down I am getting a little praise!*

Later one of the guests said to him, "You sure know your stuff!"

Jim replied with the usual warm smile, "He was one of my visiting professors at Harvard; we are good friends."

Jim and K. F. did have a good relationship, although they would sometimes go to battle. Dr. Meyer criticized Jim on his rabies vaccine experiments when he learned that CDC was satisfied with 80 percent protection. Jim said, "K. F. thought we should go for 100 percent. I told him that he should recall one of his own lectures, where he said to never make your experiments artificial by striving for a 100 percent success rate. That's why diseases survive in nature! K. F. graciously accepted my remarks once again."

At about the same time, Jim was promoting the importance of having a veterinary public health presence within the Pan American Health Organization (PAHO). Dr. Fred Soper was the new director of the Pan American Sanitary Bureau (PASB), the oldest international health agency in the world. The PASB later effectively became PAHO. Dr. Soper believed strongly that veterinary medicine would have an important role in public health in the Americas. Dr. Soper had a great reputation as a leader in the quest to eliminate yellow fever in the Americas through mosquito control in urban areas. Unfortunately, the disease persisted in the forest and rural areas. He later demonstrated the zoonotic potential of the virus in his work with primates as the reservoir. "Reservoirs are necessary to perpetuate many diseases in nature. Dr. Soper felt strongly that if you fully understand the epidemiology of a disease, your goal should be eradication," said Jim.

Dr. Soper once asked Jim, "Why don't you suggest to the BAI that PAHO has much experience with infectious diseases in this part of the world and let us take care of the FMD problem?" The question worried Jim somewhat, as he didn't want to undercut the BAI team already in place in Mexico. At the same time, Jim knew the team was having its own set of problems.

"The Mexican officials were talking behind Dr. Shahan's back. They were saying that his team wasn't doing an effective job, and that it was difficult to deal with him. In reality, he was just being an honest scientist, but they were essentially degrading his reputation," said Jim. Dr. Shahan was soon sent back to Washington only to be replaced by a retired Army National Guard general from Texas. About two years later, Drs. Frank Mulhern and Robert Anderson, both from the BAI of the USDA, took over the FMD program. Later they would file a confidential report on the FMD situation in Mexico that highlighted the corruption in the Mexican government. Dr. Anderson became director of APHIS, followed by Dr. Mulhern. In 1953, the Department of Agriculture and the BAI reorganized and some programs were transferred into the Agricultural Research Service (ARS). The remainder of the BAI fell under the Animal Plant Health Inspection Service (APHIS).

In 1952, Dr. Soper submitted a PAHO budget item for a program to investigate FMD. Veterinarian Dr. Ben Blood then established a PAHO center for FMD investigations and surveillance in Rio de Janeiro with Dr. Ervin Eichhorn, who was then the chief veterinarian at the FAO division in Rome. They asked Jim if he would defend their premise of FMD as a public health problem. "My thoughts evolved on this disease over the years. FMD denies people access to high-quality protein, limits the availability of beasts of burden and can be devastating economically. Economic health is tied to public health. I told them you cannot have good human health without good animal health. Inversely, you cannot have good animal health without good human health," Jim said.

Dr. Blood had also been directed to establish a zoonoses center in Azul, Argentina, about one hundred miles south of Buenos Aires. "On my first visit to Azul, I learned that some of the vaccines tested by the FMD center in Brazil were based on viruses isolated in the 1920s. In addition, there had been no evaluation of the viruses used in the vaccine," Jim said. The PAHO lab in Rio de Janeiro was responsible for evaluating the vaccines. In 1958, Dr. Soper established a technical committee to evaluate progress on FMD control in the Americas. Dr. K. F. Meyer was appointed chair of the committee. "My responsibility was to determine the best strategy for disease control in Central America," Jim said. This committee was Jim's first exposure to Dr. Pedro Acha, who had just graduated from the University of California, School of Public Health. "I later recommended Dr. Acha for the position of director of the veterinary public health program for PAHO," said Jim.

Jim's FMD public health program was successful. He became an expert at explaining to public health officials around the US and beyond that FMD was not a human health problem. "I remember addressing a US and Mexico border health meeting in

Laredo, Texas with Assistant Surgeon General Williams in attendance," Jim said.

After Jim's presentation, Dr. Williams said, "Jim, that was excellent!" He broadcasted his approval and admiration of Jim's work all the way back in Washington, DC.

In 1958, Jim traveled to Peru, Argentina and Brazil. "I was surprised to learn they weren't really concerned about FMD but were devoting hefty resources to the control of bat rabies," Jim said. In Argentina, he learned for the first time how the FMD virus could survive for several days in lymphatic tissues. Many years later, the Plum Island Foreign Animal Disease Laboratory would ask students and visiting scientists working with FMD in the lab to avoid contact with agricultural animals for a week after their last exposure. "The virus could be harbored in tonsilar tissue and possibly be a source of infection to animals," Jim said. He also learned there was much indifference to FMD in South America at the time. After outbreaks on the farms, the animals would recover and would still be allowed to move to slaughter. "This was of concern as South American countries wanted to market cured meats to the US. These countries had so much land and wealth, but they just didn't seem to get concerned about animal diseases" Jim said.

"Argentinean veterinarians and scientists asked me if irradiation might be used to pasteurize meat for export," Jim said. He had attended a conference in 1951 in Chicago that focused on the possible use of radiation to clear meat of trichinosis. "That was the extent of my knowledge and I let the Argentine veterinarians know this. Later, I learned that an unacceptably high dose of radiation was necessary to kill the FMD virus in meat. Dr. John Rust, a colonel in the US Army Veterinary Corps, later became the military authority on the value of irradiation of food meant for consumption by US troops," said Jim. In the eighties, the USPHS and the Food and Drug Administration conducted their own food irradiation studies. In 1984, Dr. Margaret Heckler, secretary of health services, spoke at the American Grocers Convention. She stated that irradiation of food was a practical means of protecting the public health and should be used.

Dr. Franklin Todd, a USPHS veterinarian, traveled with Jim on a trip to South America. He was the CDC liaison with APHIS. They left Argentina and traveled to Brazil to meet with Drs. K. F. Meyer and Fred Soper in Rio de Janeiro, where they presented their findings. Jim felt there were many challenges in South America that needed attention, including FMD, brucellosis, tuberculosis and various parasitic diseases. "I felt strongly that a program to bring FMD under control with a goal of eradication should be established," Jim said. Dr. Soper agreed with Jim wholeheartedly. Jim returned to Washington and was very vocal about the many challenges that FMD posed in South America. "I also spread the word on the inferior vaccines being prepared by foreign and domestic companies," Jim said.

Dr. Earl Chamberlain, a Public Health Veterinarian at PAHO, rejected Jim's philosophy, saying, "What are you going to do, slaughter a million animals a year?"

Jim responded firmly, "No, we are going to do good epidemiology and implement good control programs."

"I truly believed that quality vaccines could eventually control the disease. There was definitely a place for them. I also believed that control programs should be based on the physical removal of diseased animals and a vaccination ring of healthy animals around the infected farms. This design was not much different from our rabies control programs. Exports would have to be shut down until the country could demonstrate it was free of the disease for a year or more. This fact would be verified by animal health officials on the sending and receiving ends," Jim said.

Some twenty years later, Chile was the first South American country declared free of FMD, with Uruguay following soon after. Other countries have had short periods of months or years when FMD has not been present. "Much later, in 2007, Dr. Albino Balotto, chief veterinary officer of PAHO, assured me that most of South America would one day be free of clinical FMD," Jim stated.

Drs. Joe Held, Pedro Acha, and Primo Arambulo became strong advocates of FMD eradication under Jim's guidance. "I give

Dr. Soper much credit for his leadership and work in this area," Jim said. At one point, PAHO set the goal of eradicating FMD in the Americas by 2000. Jim encouraged the leadership to set these goals. Although many of the goals weren't met, much progress has been made. "As of 2009, most of South America is FMD free except for Venezuela and Ecuador," said Jim.

In 1999, Jim attended a meeting in Rio de Janeiro at PANAFTOSA, the PAHO FMD headquarters, on the invitation of Dr. Primo Arambulo. The congress at the meeting declared Southern Brazil free of FMD. "Unfortunately, FMD reappeared later and was blamed on Bolivia. Some researchers contend that Bolivia remains infected and FMD is not under control. Dr. David Ashford, on loan from USPHS to APHIS, reported outbreaks as late as 2006 in the area," said Jim. Dr. Ashford continued to keep Jim informed on the status of FMD in South America until he left that assignment in 2008.

I invited Martha Roses, MD, the Director of PAHO, to speak at the FMD meeting in Houston in March 2005. At the meeting, I provided a historical perspective on my role as spokesman for Dr. Soper and how I encouraged him to stand fast on the goal of FMD eradication," Jim said. Dr. Roses gave an update on FMD in South America. "She did an impressive job!" said Jim. He told her, "If we hadn't had good leadership from PAHO, we would never have made this progress."

Dr. Roses told Jim, "Dr. Steele, I think you know now that the FMD program would not have survived if the physicians weren't supporting it!"

Jim felt she was implying that veterinarians in South America were not influential enough or appointed to high enough positions to have authority to make the big decisions. "She was correct. A veterinarian has never sat on the PAHO medical board. I bragged on the veterinary involvement in the FMD program in South America. This statement from her was an indication she wanted to be sure I knew the medical doctors had a strong role as well. Her pride in being involved with the FMD program and making a difference was evidence that my legacy has carried through to the present day," Jim said. In July 2007, at the AVMA meeting in Washington, DC, there was a joint session to report the global FMD situation. "There were many excellent papers presented with lots of progress.

"In the early sixties, President Kennedy worked to improve relations with South America," Jim said. Jim remembered being called to Washington one day to meet with a White House counselor. "He asked me to explain my philosophy on helping countries to eradicate FMD and its importance to public health," Jim said. Within a few months, a delegation of six South American veterinarians arrived at CDC and stayed for an entire month. "The program was part of a public health exchange that President Kennedy had established with several South American countries. The president was literally using FMD as an example of an animal disease that affected public health. Obviously, I loved his approach!" Jim said.

Jim is very proud of his interaction with PAHO and with the legacy he has left behind. He is also proud of the more recent outstanding leadership of Dr. Primo Arambulo, past PAHO director of veterinary public health, and Dr. Albino Bellotto, a Brazilian veterinarian and director of veterinary public health at the time of the writing of this book.

"I think that sometimes people see me as Don Quixote tilting at windmills. Yes, I am idealistic, but I have always felt, for the most part, I was standing on firm ground with sound epidemiology. Yes, FMD is a public health problem. You can't have good human health without good animal health!"

CHAPTER 16:
SALMONELLA WARS

"In 1885, Daniel Elmer Salmon, an American veterinary pathologist, along with Theobald Smith, a physician, discovered a bacterium in pigs that was later named *Salmonella* in honor of this distinguished scientist," Jim said. Dr. Salmon helped to organize the Bureau of Animal Industry and served as its chief officer from 1884 to1906. He went on to head the veterinary department at the University of Montevideo, Uruguay, and held that position from 1907 to 1912.

"I enlisted Dr. Leslie P. Williams to write the chapter on salmonellosis for the *CRC Handbook Series in Zoonoses*," Jim said. His opening statement reads, "The most important zoonosis in developed countries is salmonellosis." Over 40,000 cases are still reported in the US each year, costing an estimated $3 billion and untold human suffering. Worldwide, millions of cases are reported annually, resulting in thousands of deaths. At the time of this printing, over 2,500 serotypes of *Salmonella* bacterium have been identified, 1,200 more than Dr. Williams reported in his revised CRC chapter published in 1990. "Our knowledge of this organism continues to grow, but our ability to deal with it in the public health arena remains a difficult challenge. I did my best to fight some of the battles against this disease in the twentieth century," Jim said.

Dr. Henrik J. Stafseth, Jim's microbiology professor in veterinary school, worked with *Salmonella* extensively at Michigan State College. "He wanted to resolve the *Salmonella pullorum* problem in poultry. I feel very fortunate to this day to have been a student of this outstanding scientist. Because of Dr. Stafseth, I acquired a strong foundation in microbiology that served me well throughout my career," said Jim.

Jim's earliest professional involvements with *Salmonella* as a public health problem occurred in Michigan while he was still a veterinary student. "Several salmonellosis outbreaks were diagnosed in 1941 by the Michigan State Health Department while

I was on the laboratory staff. I gained an early respect for the bacterium," Jim stated.

In 1944, multiple outbreaks of meningitis in infants, with three fatalities, occurred in hospital nurseries in Battle Creek, Michigan. *Salmonella panama* was isolated from the patients. "*Salmonella panama* was first isolated from soldiers stationed in Panama in 1934. At first it was thought that the Battle Creek nursery infections were due to back-siphonage of waste material from a bedpan-washing system into the fresh water sources. Further investigation revealed that there had been four previous infant deaths in the same hospital from July 1943 to March 1944," Jim said. "I met with Michigan public health officials frequently to discuss this outbreak and other *Salmonella* issues when I came home to visit Aina. But I wasn't serving in an official capacity. One explanation was the infection was spilling over from the hospital patients, especially the children, where they had been experiencing some fatal infections. I suspected possible carriers among the hospital staff."

The Michigan state epidemiologist ultimately found a *Salmonella* carrier in a nursery staff member. "Once the carrier was removed, the outbreak ceased. Later, *Salmonella panama* was isolated from a total of 138 people, 57 of whom were infants. The adults were hospital employees and family members. The full investigation uncovered eighteen tragic deaths by the bacteria from 1943 to 1944," Jim said. This outbreak is documented in the *Seventy-second Annual Report of the Commissioner of the Michigan Department of Health (June, 1944)*, and in the *Annals of the New York Academy of Sciences* (1956).

"Sporadic hospital-borne *Salmonella* cases continued to occur in Michigan. But there were no sound epidemiological explanations," Jim said. The Michigan State Health Department asked Jim to get involved in an outbreak in 1948. As mentioned in the chapter on brucellosis, Dr. Joe Mountin traveled to Michigan with Jim in the spring of 1948 to meet with health department officials. After their meetings, Jim assigned Dr. Art Wolff, a new Public Health Service veterinary officer, to study the *Salmonella* issue in Michigan. "Art graduated in the veterinary class in 1942, one year after me. He served as a US Navy officer until 1946. Michigan was his first assignment in the Public Health Service. This led him to an outstanding career," said Jim.

During his investigations, Dr. Wolff found *S. panama* in suburban and rural water wells. He was curious to understand how the bacteria could have spilled over into the community hospital in Battle Creek, Michigan. Mildred Galton, a microbiologist who was then working with the Florida State Health Department in their microbiology laboratory and who would later join CDC, found *Salmonella*-contaminated rural water supplies in Florida. "Dr. Wolff's findings were not unprecedented. These incidents caused me to order further CDC studies on rural water supplies around the country. These studies went on for many years," Jim stated. Recycled animal waste and contaminated feed were incriminated as helping to perpetuate carrier states in animal populations which were the source of the water contamination. "I believe that the carrier state in animals will be a major challenge in the future as the world's populations grow," Jim said.

At about the same time, *S. panama* was also found in turkeys in Ohio. "The US was exporting turkeys to Poland. When an outbreak of turkey salmonellosis occurred in Poland, we suspected the exportation of the bug. Most pig herds were infected with *Salmonella* at the time. Outbreaks often occurred in conjunction with hog cholera. Mildred Galton had a theory about swine slaughterhouses. If *Salmonella* carriers entered the processing line early in the day, everything processed after the infected pig would be contaminated. This, of course, was later proven to be true," Jim said.

Salmonella pullorum was a major focus of early veterinary research in the 1920s. "We were taught that it wasn't possible to have a profitable poultry industry until the disease in chicks could be controlled," Jim said. *S. pullorum* disease in poultry was also known as bacillary white diarrhea, or BWD. BWD caused up to 80 percent mortality in young chicks. The etiological agent was first identified in poultry by bacteriologist Dr. Leo Rettger in 1899. "A serological test which could detect carriers was developed by veterinarian F. S. Jones in 1913, the year of my birth. These major breakthroughs marked the beginning of the control of *S. pullorum* in chicks and gave hope to the scientific community about the disease in other species, including people," said Jim.

Statewide pullorum testing programs were initiated in the early 1920s. Testing programs revealed that hatcheries and vehicles were contaminated and carried the bacteria between farms. In 1935, industry, along with state and federal governmental agencies, initiated the National Poultry Improvement Plan (NPIP). "The primary mission of this group was the eradication of *S. pullorum* in poultry, and is still in operation," Jim said. An interesting microbiological side note is that *S. pullorum* is species specific and is only an incidental problem in people.

"When I came to CDC, I was interested in the challenges that *Salmonella* brought to the public health arena. There I met physician Dr. James Watt of the NIH shortly after arriving in Atlanta. Dr. Watt did some of the early investigations of *Salmonella* during World War II, studying the disease on Army posts and troop ships. He also investigated *Salmonella* outbreaks involving eggs in New Orleans," Jim said. Dr. Watt was impressed with Jim and wanted to work with him on a collaborative *Salmonella* research project. Jim told Dr. Watt, "One prerequisite: I need a lab!"

Jim and Aina traveled to Cuba in 1949 over the Christmas holidays. Jim left her behind with friends soon after New Year's Day to meet with the Florida State Health Department to discuss *Salmonella* issues. Dr. Watt told Jim about an excellent microbiologist in Florida. He met Mildred Galton on this trip. "She held a Master of Science in microbiology and was a first-class bench scientist. I recruited her to CDC to head the new veterinary public health laboratory. For fifteen years she reported to me almost daily on her laboratory activities," Jim said.

In the 1950s, Jim helped recruit Dr. Phil Edwards, who headed a well known *Salmonella* laboratory at the University of Kentucky. "Dr. Edwards was known for his work on animal *Salmonella* in horses and cattle. I wanted to build a body of scientific evidence about the public health risks of *Salmonella,* so we needed to recruit the best microbiologists." Jim recalled.

And so the work began. "One of the first things I asked Mildred Galton to do was to help out the baking industry. She surveyed powdered eggs for bacterial contamination and found a high incidence of *Salmonella*. Powdered eggs are basically air-dried whole eggs. If the drying temperature was not high enough, Salmonella would survive the process. Mildred Galton's recommendation to the powdered milk industry was to reduce the moisture in the powder. This greatly decreased the problem of *Salmonella* growth in powdered eggs," Jim said. Next, CDC began investigating the baking industry. Raw egg yolks used in baked products were found to have *Salmonella*. Ms. Galton recommended that all egg "meats" to be used in baking products be pasteurized. "This greatly decreased public health risks from bakery products," Jim said.

"Mildred Galton was a heavy smoker and, unfortunately, died of lung cancer in 1968. I am so pleased that prior to her death, she received the K. F. Meyer Gold-Headed Cane Award for her outstanding work as a veterinary public health scientist and investigator. She was one of our very best public health team members. She helped to promote the improvement of hygiene all the way down to the farm level. She applied the concepts of hospital hygiene to the farm. She was an astute, innovative scientist who made many significant contributions to public health," Jim said.

Jim remembered receiving a telephone call from Dr. Cliff Carpenter, president of one of the national poultry associations. "Do you *really* think *Salmonella* is a problem in poultry?" he barked.

Jim responded firmly, "Yes, I think it is a huge problem!"

"Who is your boss?" Carpenter asked.

Jim replied, "The surgeon general!" Dr. Carpenter backed off quickly.

Jim received irate phone calls frequently in the days when he was studying public health problems that were tied to the food industries. "It wasn't my favorite part of the job, but I was always up to the task!" Jim said.

In the mid-sixties, there was an outbreak of salmonellosis in patients at the Philadelphia General Hospital. After CDC isolated the bacteria, she typed it as *Salmonella derby.* "It was suspected to have come from shell eggs supplied by local contractors. We got an investigation going quickly," Jim recalled. He knew *S. derby* had been isolated from poultry. CDC and USDA sampled farms in southeastern Pennsylvania and found *S. derby* in laying hens. "We discovered that fecal waste was being fed back to the chickens on these farms, creating the perfect environment to produce a carrier state in a high percentage of the birds. Eggs from some of these farms were found to have supplied Philadelphia General Hospital, resulting in sickness and some deaths," Jim reported.

EIS medical officer Phil Brockman was sent by CDC to lead the investigation of environmental contamination in the hospital. "It appeared that much of the facility had become contaminated with *Salmonella. Salmonella* was even discovered in rooms that had undergone a rigorous cleaning,"Jim said. Field investigators later found *S. derby* on pig farms in eastern Pennsylvania. "The lawsuits started flowing in from patients and their families. Many of the suits were directed against the City of Philadelphia and eventually cost the city over $200 million," Jim recalled. These events led to new USDA inspection programs in the 1960s designed to eliminate *Salmonella* in all broiler and egg products. Jim watched as old-fashioned practices disappeared, such as the New York dressed chicken. This involved leaving the intestines in the body cavity to keep the carcass "fresh."

Following World War II, there was enormous growth in the poultry industry. The elimination of pullorum disease helped to fuel this growth. The market for ready-to-cook poultry products expanded fast. "I lobbied the USDA to establish a national poultry inspection service. I attended many meetings in Chicago and several conventions with the poultry industry to discuss the issue," Jim remembered. Initially, the USPHS was the agency being considered to establish a poultry inspection system. "I was against this idea. This belonged under the USDA," Jim said. Administrators in the surgeon general's office told Jim he was turning down 5,000 jobs and a $50 million budget. "While that sounded attractive, it just was not the right fit. I held my ground that poultry inspection should not be a CDC or USPHS function," said Jim. Congress finally passed the Poultry Products Inspection Act (PPIA) in 1957. Thanks to Jim's efforts, poultry inspection became the rightful responsibility of the USDA.

After World War II, the pet industries burgeoned and the pet turtle trade was born in Louisiana. "Entrepreneurs gathered eggs from the wild and placed them in sandboxes covered with burlap sacks. In about sixty days, the eggs hatched, and the baby turtles were shipped throughout the United States to be marketed in pet stores," Jim reported. In the late sixties, it was recognized that children handling the turtles were contracting *Salmonella* infections. "I became concerned and got involved. I quickly learned that the dealers were feeding the turtles cattle offal from packing houses in Louisiana and elsewhere. *Salmonella* contamination in these byproducts was widespread. I recommended that the feed be cooked. But the proprietors of the pet industries responded that this practice would put them out of business," Jim said.

It was not until Dr. Steve Lamm, an EIS officer from CDC, investigated an outbreak of turtle salmonellosis in 1971 in Connecticut that the pet industry finally admitted it was a problem. Enforcement of the turtle trade was then turned over to the FDA. "Unfortunately, *Salmonella* infection in pet turtles remains a problem today," Jim lamented.

On a visit to the University of Kentucky, Jim learned of the danger of human carriers of *Salmonella* on farms. An outbreak of *Salmonella* occurred in Lexington in 1969 through 1970 in newborn foals. "I always wondered if this could be caused by man-to-horse transmission. The horse industry kept everything quiet due to the fact that most of the animals were insured. Today, horse nurseries utilize strict biosafety and hygiene practices to protect both animals and attendants. Even with this, *Salmonella* is difficult to control.

This turned out to be my last formal field investigation with CDC!" Jim recalled.

Stahl/Steele Selected Family Tree

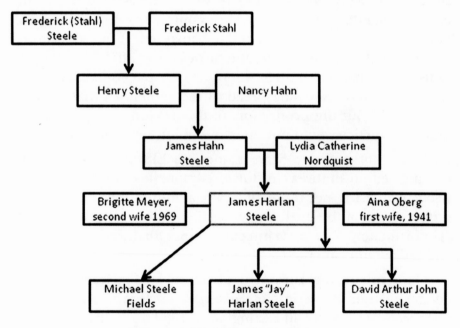

Abbreviated Stahl-Steele family tree.

April 3, 1913, James Harlan Steele's birth certificate and
first certificate of vaccination.

Circa 1898, left to right, back row: Uncle Ira Steele, dentist; Aunt Luella
Steele, schoolteacher; James Hahn Steele, father and dentist; Aunt Sara
Steele, dentist; Uncle Frank Nelson Steele, veterinarian. Front row: Aunt
Alice Steele Snider, dentist; Grandmother Nancy Hahn Steele, homemaker;
Aunt Mary Letha Steele Thorp, schoolteacher.

Circa 1900, Dr. James Law, 1838-1921, a pioneer veterinarian and leader whom Jim considers to be the first spokesperson for veterinary public health. He was memorialized by Jim Steele in a James Law Centennial Lecture at Cornell in 1983.

Circa 1910, Lydia Nordquist, Jim Steele's mother. For his graduation from
elementary school she wrote, "There is a dawn that wakes you to truth. It is
conscience, the dawn of the soul." She taught Jim to read at an early age,
which led to his love of books, the arts and history.

Circa 1917, James Harlan Steele, Chicago.

Circa 1920, Dr. Cecil Drinker, professor of physiology and dean, School of Public Health, Harvard University. "He advised me to literally fly under one flag. In other words, to keep veterinary medicine as my focus as I moved forward in my career in public health," Jim said.

Circa 1925, James and brother John Steele in the backyard on Berenice St, Chicago.

Circa 1927, James Harlan Steele, Chicago.

Circa 1938, Dean Ward Giltner, professor of bacteriology and dean, School of Veterinary Medicine, Michigan State College. "A man of vision and depth of thought, he was my mentor who encouraged me to pursue a career in public health and helped to make it possible," stated Jim.

Circa 1941, James H. Steele, veterinary student working in the Michigan State *Brucella* laboratory on campus. "This experience stimulated a lifelong interest in the epidemiology of brucellosis in man and animals," said Jim.

Circa 1947, Dr. Jim Steele as a National Institutes of Health intern.

Circa 1948, Dr. Joe Mountin, physician and Assistant Surgeon General for
States Relations, US Public Health Service, Washington, DC. He challenged
Jim with the question, "What are you veterinarians going to do for public
health now that the war is over?" He dispatched Jim Steele to Atlanta to be a
part of the newly formed CDC.

Circa 1950, Dr. Martin Kaplan, veterinarian and first Director of Veterinary Public Health at the World Health Organization. "He was a valued colleague who helped promote veterinary public health worldwide," Jim said.

December 1950, left to right: Professor J. Verge; Dr. Martin Kaplan; the WHO representative, unknown name; Sir Daniel Cabot; Dr. Jim Steele; Dr. K. V. L. Kesteven at the first meeting of the WHO Expert Committee on Zoonoses in Geneva, Switzerland. The meeting was chaired by Sir Daniel Cabot, who was the CVO of the United Kingdom during World War II.

Circa 1954, Dr. K. F. Meyer, Professor of Bacteriology, University of California, San Francisco Medical School and Director, Zoonoses Center. "He was a valued pioneer in the study of zoonotic diseases and my close colleague," Jim said. In 1964, Jim presented Dr. Meyer with the Gold-Headed Cane Award of the American Veterinary Epidemiology Society.

Circa 1955, Dr. H. J. Stafseth, Professor of Bacteriology, Michigan State College. "He helped me to pursue my graduate study in public health at Harvard," Jim said.

Circa 1956, Dr. Jim Steele is being interviewed for a training film on leptospirosis at CDC in Atlanta.

Circa 1958, Dr. Alexander Langmuir, physician, founder and chief of the Epidemic Intelligence Service (EIS) of CDC. "He was a great supporter of veterinarians in the EIS," Jim said.

Dr. Robert J. Anderson

Circa 1958, Dr. Robert J. Anderson, veterinarian, became director of
USDA-APHIS. He nurtured good relations between the USDA and the CDC.

Circa 1959, left to right: Myrna and Myrle Steele, Jim Steele's twin cousins, at the World Veterinary Congress, Madrid, Spain.

Dr. Francis J. Mulhern

Circa 1960, Dr. Francis Mulhern, veterinarian, became director of
USDA-APHIS. He established excellent relations with USDA and CDC and was
the first to send a USDA veterinarian to train in the EIS program of CDC.

Circa 1963, left to right: Dr. Robert Courter; Dr. Ernie Tierkel; Dr. Jim Steele.
Drs. Courter and Tierkel were Jim's deputies. Taken at the CDC building,
Atlanta, Georgia.

May 1964, Dr. Jim Steele and Dr. K. F. Meyer. Dr. Meyer received the
Gold-Headed Cane Award on his eightieth birthday.

May 1964, Aina, Jim's first wife, receiving flowers from Dr. Malaga Alba, former
Chief Veterinary Officer of Peru. This was taken in Atlanta on the same day
that Dr. K. F. Meyer received the Gold-Headed Cane Award.

October 1964, left to right: Dr. Jim Steele; son Jay; wife, Aina; and son David. Picture taken in the garden of the Steeles' home on Old Ivy Lane, Atlanta, Georgia.

November 1967, left to right; Dr. Jim Steele and Dr. Aurelio Malaga Alba. Jim is addressing a group of microbiologists and parasitologists at a congress in Lima, Peru.

Circa 1967, left to right, front row: Dr. K. F. Meyer; Dr. Jim Steele; Dr. Louis Jacks; Dr. Paul Arnstein. A meeting in Washington, DC, where the strategy for controlling psittacosis in pet birds was decided.

June 27, 1969, Jim and Brigitte's wedding day, taken in George Baer's home in Mexico City, Mexico. "We were veterans of two worlds coming together, the holocaust and the free world," Jim stated.

Circa 1970, Jim's cousin Dr. William Taylor Steele Thorp, 1914–1984, Dean,
College of Veterinary Medicine, University of Minnesota. Dr. Thorp
persuaded Jim to transfer his studies from forestry to veterinary medicine.

Circa 1970, Dr. Joe Dean, 1899-1974, Assistant Surgeon General for States Relations, US Public Health Service, Washington, DC. "He was initially skeptical of the concept of veterinary public health but later became my strongest supporter," Jim said.

Circa 1970, left to right: Ms. Virginia Knauer; Dr. Jim Steele. Ms. Knauer was the consumer consultant to President Richard Nixon. Jim advised her and the White House staff on veterinary public health issues. This relationship afforded Jim and Brigitte the opportunity to dine at the White House.

Circa 1968, Dr. James H. Steele, assistant surgeon general of the United States for veterinary medicine and deputy assistant secretary for veterinary affairs.

Circa 1974, left to right: Dr. Jim Steele and son Dr. Mike Fields sharing time together in Atlanta, Georgia. Mike is a professor of animal science at the University of Florida.

Circa 1975, Dr. Ernie Tierkel. Dr. Tierkel succeeded Dr. Jim Steele to become the second assistant surgeon for veterinary affairs at CDC.

Circa 1975, Jim Steele and Max Stern, founder and CEO of Hartz Mountain.
"He was a strong supporter of veterinary research at Rutgers University and in
supporting Dr. K. F. Meyer in his research to control psittacosis in pet birds,"
Jim said.

1983, Jim and Brigitte Steele at the University of Texas, where a Norwegian maple was planted to honor Jim's seventieth birthday. The event was planned by Dr. Charles Oke, a former student of Jim's.

April 1989, Dr. Jim Steele and Dr. Max Sterne, developer of the Sterne anthrax vaccine, together in Southampton, England.

July, 1991, Dr. Jim Steele and BG (Ret.) Tom Murnane at the American
Veterinary Medical Association Meeting.

Circa 1993, Dr. Jim Steele in his office at the University of Texas School of
Public Health on his eightieth birthday.

Circa 2001, left to right: Dr. Craig Carter, biographer, and Dr. Jim Steele, both in military dress, Hilton Hotel, College Station, Texas.

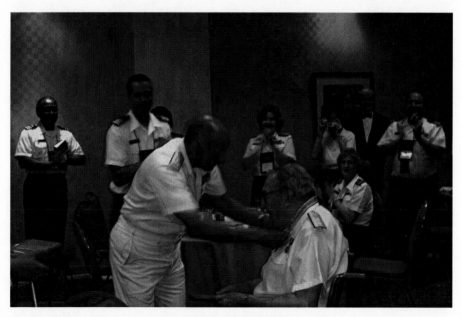

June 2005, Dr. Jim Steele receives the Surgeon General's Medallion from then Surgeon General Richard Carmona, Commissioned Officers Association meeting, Philadelphia, Pennsylvania.

June 2005, left to right: Dr. Dan O'Leary; Dr. Jim Steele; Dr. Doug Ashford;
Surgeon General Richard Carmona. Jim is presenting the fiftieth anniversary
edition of the Merck Veterinary Manual to Surgeon General Carmona,
Commissioned Officers Association meeting, Philadelphia, Pennsylvania.
Dr. Steele edited the zoonoses section in the manual for fifty years.

June 2005, left to right: Brigitte Steele; unknown; Dr. Julius Richmond, twelfth surgeon general of the United States; Dr. Richard Carmona, seventeenth surgeon general of the United States; Dr. Jim Steele; Dr. Herry Farrel, executive director, USPHS Commissioned Officers Association; Dr. Everett Koop, thirteenth surgeon general of the United States; Dr. Antonia Novello, fourteenth surgeon general of the United States, Dr. Kenny Moritsugu, acting surgeon general, 2006–2007, at the Commissioned Officers Association meeting, Philadelphia, Pennsylvania.

June 2005, Dr. Jim Steele and wife, Brigitte, just after receiving the Surgeon General's Medallion, Commissioned Officers Association meeting, Philadelphia, Pennsylvania.

June 2005, Dr Jim Steele and Brigitte on the roof of the Metropolitan Museum of Art on holiday in New York City. Central Park is in the background.

Circa 2006, Dr. Jim Steele on holiday with Brigitte in northern France at the Matisse Art Gallery, where they purchased a copy of this painting by Henri Matisse. "This painting by Matisse signifies the relationship of man and animals," Jim explained.

July 2007. Drs. Jim Steele and Craig Carter at the annual meeting of the American Veterinary Medical Association in Washington, DC. "For years, Craig and many other friends help me to get around at meetings in a wheelchair when I could no longer do it on foot," Jim said.

CHAPTER 17:
MYCOBACTERIOSES—TOO CLOSE TO HOME

In the *CRC Handbook Series in Zoonoses*, for which Jim served as editor in chief, he wrote about how long *Mycobacterium tuberculosis* has cursed the world. Vertebral fragments from mummies in Egypt dating back to 2400 B.C. display the classic lesions of bone decay seen in cases of tuberculosis. In about 460 B.C., Hippocrates described *phthisis*, Greek for consumption, as one of the most prevalent diseases of the era. "Hippocrates even warned other physicians not to visit patients in the late stages of the disease as it would damage their professional reputations. Almost all patients died of the disease in the early days," Jim explained.

Other phrases have been used through the centuries to characterize the disease, such as "captain of the men of death" and "the great white plague. "I believe tuberculosis was one of the most important diseases of the nineteenth and twentieth centuries and it has endured into the twenty-first century worldwide. Most adults living today can recall a family member who was affected by this disease," said Jim.

The epidemiology of tuberculosis was advanced in the eighteenth century. In 1720, an English physician, Benjamin Martin, wrote in his book *A New Theory of Consumption* that the disease might be caused by "wonderfully minute living creatures."

"As part of his research, he worked out the epidemiological principle of person-to-person transmission," Jim said. The term "tuberculosis" was not used until the nineteenth century. It is derived from the word "tubercle" which is a nodule full of lymphocytes and epithelioid cells that is characteristic of the lesions seen with the disease. In 1850, Herman Brehmer, a Silesian botany student, suffered with tuberculosis. "He decided to move to the Himalayas to further his studies. Fortunately, his new, clean-air environment nursed him to a cure," said Jim. He returned home and attended medical school. In 1854 he wrote a paper entitled *Tuberculosis is a Curable Disease*. In 1859, he established what is considered the first sanitarium, in Gobersdorf, Germany. Patients there received a highly nutritional diet. In addition, the facilities had spacious balconies where residents could breathe in clean air. "Soon, sanitariums were established throughout Europe and North America to treat consumptive tuberculosis patients in the early stages of the disease," Jim reported.

Jim's grandfather Henry Steele, born in 1832, died in 1888 of what was called "galloping consumption," a form of tuberculosis that runs its course rapidly. Jim suspects that his grandfather had subclinical tuberculosis for years and later developed fatal pneumonia. Jim's Aunt Mary Letha Steele, born in 1862, developed tuberculosis forty years later and had to retire early as a teacher in the Chicago school system. She relocated to western Michigan and recovered, living into her late nineties. Apparently the disease was arrested, but there was some concern that she could be a source of the disease for her adopted son, William Taylor Steele Thorp, and her nephews, Jim and John Steele. Her distress about the possibility escalated when she learned there was tuberculosis in the Thorp dairy herd. The family drank raw milk from the farm for many years, but fortunately, none of the boys ever developed any signs and remained tuberculosis negative.

Jim grew up in Chicago in a middle-class neighborhood. "A few of my boyhood friends with whom I played football and baseball developed tuberculosis," Jim said. Aina came with Jim to visit one of his friends who was suffering with tuberculosis. "This was Bob Hedrich. He was living in one of the Chicago tuberculosis sanitariums. I never dreamed Aina would come down with tuberculosis. To this day, I wonder about the source of her infection. Interestingly, with all my career exposure, I didn't become skin-test positive until late in life," he said.

"After Brehmer's work, the next major milestone in the understanding of tuberculosis came in 1865 when a French military physician, Jean-Antoine Villemin, thought tuberculosis could be transmitted from people to cattle and from cattle to rabbits. He hypothesized that a microorganism was involved in the disease," Jim said. In 1882, Robert Koch developed a bacterial stain that allowed visualization of the organism *Mycobacterium tuberculosis*, marking the beginning of scientific diagnosis. Dr. Koch also discovered tuberculin which he created through a glycerin extract of the tubercle bacilli. He had hoped tuberculin could be used as a treatment for tuberculosis, but it turned out to be ineffective.

"In 1895, Dr. Wilhelm Konrad von Roentgen discovered the x-ray, launching the field of radiology and providing a tool that could be used to evaluate the progress and status of tuberculosis patients," Jim said. In 1906, Dr. Clemens von Pirquet, an Austrian physician, noticed that patients who received a second dose of smallpox vaccine had a quicker and more severe reaction. He soon learned that the same reaction occurred with tuberculin injections. In 1907, Charles Mantoux, a French physician, then expanded on Dr. Pirquet's work by recognizing that tuberculin injected into the skin could be used as a diagnostic test for tuberculosis.

"In 1908, the French physician and bacteriologist Albert Calmette and veterinarian Camille Guerin at the Pasteur Institute learned how to attenuate the tuberculin bacterium so it could be used in a vaccine," said Jim. The vaccine was ultimately named the BCG vaccine (Bacille Calmette Guerin) and was first used in people in 1921. It was used sporadically in some European countries until after World War II. The vaccine was never tried in the US, but was used extensively around the world with variable results. The tuberculosis bacterium was resistant to sulfa drugs and penicillin, which were available at the time. Actinomycin was found to be effective against tuberculosis but was too toxic for use in humans at the time. However, in 1943, streptomycin was developed and used in the first tuberculosis patient in November 1944. This patient made a miraculous recovery. "Physicians finally had a drug to treat this dreaded disease," Jim recalled. But there was still much work to do regarding mycobacteria and their risks to public health and Jim Steele would have his own important role.

Drs. J. Arthur Myers and Al Karlson at the University of Minnesota and Mayo Clinic, helped Jim to grasp the pathophysiology of *Mycobacterium bovis,* an organism that causes disease in most warm-blooded vertebrates, including people. "This species causes lung lesions morphologically indistinguishable from those caused by

Mycobacterium tuberculosis. However, extrapulmonary lesions can occur in the meninges; bone, especially of the spine;, and lymph nodes," Jim recited. The bony and arthritic form of the disease is also known as Pott's disease, named after an eighteenth-century British physician, Percivall Pott, who was one of the first to describe the lesions. *Mycobacterium bovis* is recorded in medical history during the Grecian and Roman empires and throughout Europe into the twentieth century.

The US program to control and eradicate bovine tuberculosis was led by Dr. John R. Mohler, a famous veterinary pathologist who served as the BAI chief from 1917 to 1943. He understood very well the risk of milk-borne tuberculosis, especially in young people. "In his mind, there was no option but to stamp out the disease in cattle," Jim said. Dr. Mohler worked closely with city health officers such as Dr. Herman Bundeson of Chicago. As has been described, Dr. Bundeson decided that he wouldn't allow milk to enter Chicago that was not from accredited tuberculosis-free herds. The announcement had a major impact on Dr. Mohler's program, including delays induced by belligerent farmers in Iowa and California. The National Guard was called up to protect the federal veterinarians in Iowa who were being greeted by farmers with firearms when they tried to enter their properties for inspection.

In spite of the resistance, the BAI control measures were put into place and were very successful. In 1941, the US was declared free of bovine tuberculosis. "This, in my opinion, is one of the greatest veterinary public health achievements in history." said Jim. He had the honor of inviting Dr. Mohler to speak at a Junior AVMA meeting (now the Student Chapter of the AVMA) at Michigan State College in 1941, when he was a veterinary student and president of the organization. "The eradication of bovine tuberculosis is one of my fondest memories of contributions to public health by veterinarians," Jim said.

At the World Veterinary Congress (WVC) in August 1949 in London, Jim heard reports of overwhelming *Mycobacterium bovis* problems in Western Europe. "I spoke with a veterinarian from Holland who said he was routinely diagnosing the disease by finding acid-fast organisms on microscopic milk smears. It was quickly becoming clear to me that this disease was still a huge problem for the whole world," Jim said. He listened to presentations by the French on the use of BCG in the control of bovine tuberculosis. "British and American army veterinarians serving in Europe had to turn to Denmark in 1947 to acquire a safe milk supply for the troops," Jim said. There were papers describing the practice of extending the milk with water with much concern about how clean the water was. "The sessions at this meeting were truly dramatic," Jim claimed.

Jim met Dr. Martin Kaplan at the London congress. He was a graduate of the University of Pennsylvania. After a brief teaching stint at Brandeis University, Dr. Kaplan joined the United Nations Relief and Rehabilitation Administration (UNRRA). "Following Victory in Europe (VE) Day, he was sent by boat to Greece with six genetically superior bulls donated by the Brethren Society of Pennsylvania to help restock cattle populations around Europe. Most breeding animals were killed during the war. He also traveled to the eastern Mediterranean and Lebanon to buy stallions and mules," Jim recalled. Dr. Kaplan also helped to establish laboratories to produce animal vaccines and to train the local veterinarians. Jim and Martin became great friends and colleagues. Dr. Kaplan was awarded the Nobel Prize for Peace in 1995 and shared the prize with Joseph Rotblat.

While at UNRRA, Dr. Kaplan learned about a job opportunity for a veterinarian in the newly established WHO office in Geneva. He inquired, was hired and established a veterinary section at WHO in 1949. Dr. Kaplan organized the WHO Expert Committee on Zoonoses with the support of the members residing on the WHO Expert Committee on Tuberculosis. A meeting was held in Geneva in 1950 to provide guidance on zoonotic diseases for WHO and FAO. This committee was created at the request of the WHO Committee on Human Tuberculosis by Dr. Herman Hilleboe of the US Public Health Service. He was the physician who helped Jim acquire streptomycin to treat Aina's tuberculosis. Dr. Hilleboe came from Minnesota, a state that was home to one of the first tuberculosis eradication programs. "He brought the important message about bovine tuberculosis to the new WHO committee," Jim said. It was then decided to form a committee to ascertain how extensive bovine tuberculosis was in Europe and around the world.

"I was invited to be on the newly organized Expert Committee on Zoonoses and served as a consultant. One of my jobs was to write the reports of the committee. This job turned out to be a real learning experience." Jim said. Dr. B. Plum, the Danish chief veterinary officer, described how Denmark kept their country free of bovine tuberculosis. "When the Germans occupied Denmark, they required a certain number of animals be turned over to the Germans daily to feed the occupational forces. The Danes gave them all their tuberculosis-infected animals," Jim said with a grin.

Physician Franklin Top, professor of infectious diseases at the University of Iowa medical school and a US Army military consultant, told Jim that one-third of all human tuberculosis in Germany after World War II was due to *Mycobacterium bovis*. "This firmed up my resolve to forever speak out for tuberculosis control based on solid science. The French recommended vaccinating cattle in the dewlap with BCG. But I knew that vaccination would not protect all animals. It certainly did not constitute an effective eradication program. They were saying that a golf ball-sized mass in the dewlap would identify all positive animals. But I knew there were lots of false negatives," he said.

There was some discussion about other zoonotic diseases such as Q fever, salmonellosis, and leptospirosis at these meetings. But when they were through, Jim held his ground, "I won't sign this report if we say that BCG is a recommended preventive measure for bovine tuberculosis!" Most of the committee members were Europeans. The French, Italians, Poles, and some Asians and Africans all supported the BCG solution. Dr. Kaplan had done some excellent work in Greece with UNRRA and in Poland with FAO. He believed that the test-and-slaughter method for tuberculosis control and eradication was the only successful strategy. Dr. Ben Blood wanted Jim to withdraw his objections. "I lost a little respect for Ben on this one. I wondered why Ben would ask me to go against my best judgment. Maybe he had different experiences with the disease than I," Jim said.

"I stood fast till the bitter end," Jim reported. At the age of thirty-seven, he was the youngest member of the committee. He was opposed by everyone except Dr. Kaplan and Dr. Plum, the Danish veterinarian. Dr. Plum brought Jim aside during a tea break and said, "Europeans don't want to offend each other, Jim. You are the only one who can solve this. I will support you!"

This gave Jim the confidence he needed. "I will not sign an endorsement of BCG, and that's the end of it!" he resolved. But he ultimately made a minor compromise with the group. The report was revised to say that BCG could be used as a "last resort" control strategy.

A Danish veterinarian asked Jim why he was so against the BCG option. "The epidemiological evidence speaks for itself. We've got to stick with good science on these issues," Jim responded. In Mexico, children were being given BCG at birth, but they were still come down with bovine tuberculosis. Elsewhere he read similar reports.

By 1957, Dr. Top had brought the Germans around to Jim's point of view. This change occurred at the first WHO Expert Committee on Zoonoses meeting behind the Iron Curtain in Warsaw, Poland. "Dr. Ervin Eichhorn, the FAO chief veterinary officer, agreed with my evaluation of BCG. I was beginning to feel like I would receive more support on the topic. There was a report to the committee that a South African had completed a study in Malawi. The conclusion was that BCG sensitized the animals making them *more* susceptible to the bovine tuberculosis organism. The body was apparently walling off the bacteria," Jim stated.

The issue was never brought up again. Most of the administrative work for the committee was done by Jim and Dr. Kaplan. "I was appointed as the reporter. I often had to tone the verbiage down in some of the reports. I told Ben Blood that infected animals should be removed from the herds. The British were removing infected animals because some of the rural children were becoming infected with tuberculosis," Jim noted. The committee asked the WHO for reports on the status of bovine tuberculosis from many countries of the world. "I knew that some of the countries were fabricating their statistics regarding the incidence of the disease. Unfortunately, we really couldn't do anything about that," Jim said.

When Jim visited India in 1970, the cattle population was nearing 300 million. Government veterinarians were reporting a tuberculosis reactor rate as high as 20 percent. At a meeting in Delhi, in 1972, Muslim veterinary scientists were found to be receptive to the idea of culling TB reactors from the herds. "This brought cattle populations down to about 200 million and resulted in a healthier food source. India was at war with Pakistan at the time. Indian Muslims would eat beef but not pork. Cattle were being sold primarily at large markets in Calcutta and Lahore," Jim said.

At the same time, Indian veterinarians were allowing tuberculosis-positive carcasses with no lesions to be sold to Iraq. However, these sales were soon blocked by the Indian secretary of agriculture. "The small state of Karala in the southwest corner of India was planning to cull all their reactors and had worked out an arrangement to sell them to Iraq. Dr. Calvin Schwabe was in India at the time and was helping the government to devise a plan to deal with bovine tuberculosis. A meeting was arranged with the Indian minister of agriculture. I congratulated him on his plans to begin identifying infected animals," Jim said.

But the minister later decided against the plan. He told Jim, "Remember, I am a politician and I have to support my religion."

Jim replied solemnly, "You are missing a great opportunity to improve animal agriculture and to save human lives. In 1980 I heard that they were identifying the TB reactors but were still selling the carcasses illegally to Muslim populations. I simply couldn't believe it," Jim said.

Jim traveled to South America and Mexico in 1981 as a governmental consultant. On this trip, Jim had yet another encounter with BCG. "The Mexicans were still using BCG to vaccinate people, but had stopped using it in cattle. I figured that the Mexican veterinarians had never been trained on how to read the skin test properly," Jim stated. The USDA sent veterinarians to Mexico to provide training. "I knew that tuberculosis-positive cattle would always leak into Texas from Mexico, so I wanted to do everything possible to help the Mexicans eradicate bovine tuberculosis," Jim said.

"The Argentineans told me that their tuberculosis infection rate was low in beef cattle, but for some reason they hadn't been testing their dairy animals. As it turned out, almost 7 percent of the Argentinean dairy herds were infected in spite of vaccination with BCG. This was just more evidence that BCG could not control bovine tuberculosis. I told them that there is a lot of research going on to develop an effective BCG vaccine that will protect people. If this ever works out, the veterinary profession should be quite interested!"

Dr. William H. Stewart, a USPHS officer who was to become surgeon general in 1965 asked Jim, "How did you get away with condemning BCG?"

Jim replied matter-of-factly, "There is no scientific basis for it!" Dr. Stewart had a brother who was a veterinarian in Minnesota who was involved in control programs for animal diseases.

In 1959, Jim recommended to the Japanese and Taiwanese that they test and eliminate their TB reactors. He supported the US Army veterinarians who were in these countries trying to make some progress on bovine TB control. At a WHO meeting in Tokyo the same year, Jim did not endorse BCG for the Asian nations, including Korea, Thailand, Hong Kong, and the Philippines. Jim met Dr. John Francis, a British veterinarian and professor of infectious diseases at the University of Brisbane, Australia, who was working on bovine tuberculosis control and eradication in Australia. He endorsed the test-and-cull method. "Dr. Francis was the first to suspect that tree-climbing marsupials might be a reservoir of tuberculosis, and it turned out that he was right," Jim said.

Jim co-authored a book published in 1969, *Bovine Tuberculosis in Man and Animals* with Dr. J. Arthur Myers, a physician and professor of internal medicine and public health at the University of Minnesota. The book is a comprehensive review of bovine tuberculosis, outlining the disease in man and animals, control programs, economic factors and worldwide prevalence. It also covers the importance of physicians and veterinarians working together to attempt to eradicate the disease.

To this day, Jim is still fascinated with the disease and the many species that are affected. "In 1998, multi-drug-resistant TB strains appeared in South Africa, with some infecting the wild herbivorous animals such as the Cape buffalo. The buffalo were apparently infected by commingling with cattle herds starting in the 1950s. When animals become weak, lions hunt them down and eat them. The lions then become infected with the intestinal form of tuberculosis. In some areas, especially Kruger National Park, South Africa, lion populations have fallen significantly. Elephants can also succumb to the human form of tuberculosis. Between 1994 and 1996, three elephants on an exotic farm in Illinois died of the disease," Jim reported.

"World Tuberculosis Day is held on March 24 of each year and is designed to raise awareness about the disease. Tuberculosis is endemic around the globe and still causes the deaths of millions of people and animals each year. March 24 is the day that Robert Koch announced in Berlin his discovery of the *Mycobacterium* bacillus. Many groups, including the World Health Organization, have adopted the goal of eradicating the disease worldwide. I sincerely hope that eradication of tuberculosis will be possible. It will be up to you bright young veterinary scientists out there!" he urged.

"Dr. Charlie Thoen has been my expert bovine tuberculosis consultant for some forty years, since I left CDC. He has helped me gain a much better understanding of this complex disease. He co-authored the update of J. Arthur Meyes's *Man's Greatest Victory over Tuberculosis* in 1994 and has contributed so many other significant articles and books on tuberculosis. I considered it a great honor when he asked me to co-author his book, *Mycobacterium bovis Infection in Animals and Humans*. The second edition of this excellent work was published in 2006. I recently reviewed his excellent tuberculosis update for *Veterinary Italiana* that came out in 2009. I will always have a very healthy respect for these unique, acid-fast organisms that have learned to adapt and survive so well in nature," Jim said.

And he will never forget what they did to his first love, Aina.

CHAPTER 18:
SETTING THE STAGE FOR THE FUTURE OF
VETERINARY PUBLIC HEALTH

As Jim's new veterinary public health (VPH) program was being launched at CDC after World War II, he learned about various specialty groups that were being organized in such fields as preventive medicine. "I had a close relationship with the Army preventive medicine officers and was intrigued with the direction they were taking to improve the image and value of their group of professionals. As these officers retired and went back into civilian life, many continued to work in the growing field of preventive medicine. They were of the opinion that they should be given respect and pay comparable to physicians," Jim said.

Jim met an MD at the University of Louisville who was working to form a specialty board of preventive medicine physicians. The board grew out of a joint committee composed of representatives from preventive medicine, industrial medicine and public health within the American Medical Association. It was incorporated under the laws of the State of Delaware on June 29, 1948 as The American Board of Preventive Medicine and Public Health, Inc. (ABPMPH). In 1949, the board was recognized by the Council on Medical Education and the Hospitals of the American Medical Association as a medical specialty board that would certify specialists in public health. In 1952 the name was changed to The American Board of Preventive Medicine.

Jim stayed in touch with members of this group and monitored the progress of the organization. "I noticed that these groups were very well organized and seemed to help their members get recognition for their special set of medical skills. In addition, the ABPMPH enabled better pay for their physician members," Jim observed. Jim also believed that veterinarians working in VPH should also be paid on a scale with clinicians, not as sanitarians. "My exposure to the ABPMPH planted the seed in my mind that a similar organization might be appropriate to nurture the field of veterinary public health," Jim said.

Jim discussed his ideas with veterinary colleagues in health agencies around the country. The consensus was that a specialty organization was needed for VPH to attract young veterinary scientists to the specialty and to advance the scientific knowledge base in the new discipline. "I was receiving lots of encouragement from my colleagues at the time. They wanted me to be their spokesperson," Jim said. The whole process came to a head at the American Veterinary Medical Association (AVMA) meeting in Detroit in July of 1949. At this meeting, twelve veterinarians convened with the express purpose of organizing the American Academy of Veterinary Public Health (AAVPH), which was modeled after the ABPMPH.

The twelve organizing council members were a distinguished mix of US Army Veterinary Corps (VC) officers, public health veterinarians, and academicians, including Jim as the US Public Health Service representative. Representing the Army were Lieutenant Colonels Frank A. Todd, Phillip R. Carter, and Mervyn B. Starnes. From city and state public health offices came Dr. L. W. Rowles from Kansas; Dr. Martin D. Baum from Denver, Colorado; and Dr. Alexander Zeissig from Albany, New York. Dr. Zeissig was the public health veterinarian from New York. Three academic institutions were represented, by Dr. Ival A. Merchant of Iowa State College, Dr. Franklin A. Clark of Alabama Polytechnic Institute and Dr. Henrik J. Stafseth of Michigan State College, Jim's former professor of microbiology. Also in the organizing group was Dr. Benjamin D. Blood from the Pan American Health Organization, whom Jim had met shortly after opening his office at CDC in Atlanta. Rounding out the team was Dr. John G. Hardenbergh, who was then serving as executive director of the AVMA. "Dr. Hardenbergh had an illustrious career in the military and academia. I was so pleased that he participated with the group," Jim said. Colonel Carter died in 2006, making Jim the last remaining member of the organizing council. He preceded Jim in receiving an MPH at Harvard, the first veterinarian to do so. Jim was the second to earn this academic credential from Harvard.

"I was asked to serve as the first secretary to the AAVPH organizing council. At the first meeting, Dr. Todd was elected the temporary chairman of the council. Dr. Todd immediately appointed two working committees. The charge of the first committee was to write a definition of veterinary public health. The other committee was charged to write the by-laws of the organization and to decide upon credentials for eligibility as a member of the specialty," Jim recalled. The council met next on Sunday, October 23, 1949 in Jim's room at the Statler Hotel in New York City. They were all there for the annual meeting of the American Public Health Association (APHA). "I was careful to point out to those present that attendance at the organizational meetings did not automatically confer founding member status in the AAVPH," Jim said.

Shortly after the New York meeting, the council voted to change the name to the American Board of Veterinary Public Health (ABVPH). "As I recall, this went back to our physician counterparts, who used the term 'Board' in naming their organization. It seemed a better fit at the time for an organization that would be certifying specialists by examination," Jim stated. The first constitution and by-laws were published and were dated November 30, 1949. The organization was incorporated in the District of Columbia on February 3, 1950. "During the official organizational meeting, Colonel Todd was elected the first president," Jim said.

An examination committee was then established to be chaired by Dr. Zeissig. His committee worked closely with the APHA to help establish the prerequisites for examination eligibility. In addition, all members of the examination committee contributed questions for the exam which were reviewed by the APHA. It was decided that to be eligible to sit for the ABVPH exam, an individual had to be a licensed graduate of a veterinary school recognized by AVMA, have completed an APHA-recognized master's of public health degree program, possess a license to practice veterinary medicine issued by a recognized national or state licensing agency, and have six years of relevant experience in the field. "I believe that four years of additional experience could substitute for the graduate degree requirement initially," Jim said.

The first official meeting of the ABVPH was held in Miami Beach, Florida, in August 1950. At this meeting, thirty-three applicants were approved as charter fellows. Their next meeting was held in Milwaukee, Wisconsin, in August 1951. At this assembly, the AVMA formally recognized the ABVPH and the American College of Veterinary Pathologists (ACVP) as the first two veterinary specialties in the US "The other very significant event at this meeting was President Todd's announcement of our definition of veterinary public health, which was approved by the board of the ABVPH," Jim said. It read as follows:

> Veterinary Public Health is all community efforts influenced by the veterinary medical arts and sciences applied to the prevention of disease, protection of life, and promotion of the well-being and efficiency of man.

Dr. Todd also announced that the definition had been adopted by the World Health Organization and the Food and Agricultural Organization of the United Nations during the meeting of the FAO/WHO Expert Committee on Zoonoses held in December 1950. "I couldn't have been more pleased!" Jim said. The first examination of candidates was conducted at the APHA meeting in Cleveland, Ohio in October 1952. Seven military veterinarians were eligible to take the exam. All of the applicants passed and were then certified as ABVPH specialists.

"I continued to be active in the ABVPH on into the sixties. However, by that time, I was becoming so busy at CDC that I decided to step down and let the next generation nurture and grow the organization. Everything was running smoothly, so I didn't feel bad about taking a more passive role," Jim said. In the early days, the Army veterinarians led the charge toward ABVPH board certification.

In 1959, the AVMA Council on Education recommended that an advisory board on veterinary specialties (ABVS) be formed. This came into being in 1961. Beginning in the 1970s, the AVMA began to see a lot of interest in forming additional veterinary medical specialties. At about the same time, many agricultural and regulatory-oriented veterinarians were of the opinion that the ABVPH was narrowly focused and should be broadened to include other disciplines besides epidemiology, food hygiene, statistics, and zoonotic diseases. "The debate between those in veterinary public health and regulatory veterinary medicine was often lively," Jim reported. The regulatory veterinarians later approached the AVMA about establishing a new board of veterinary preventive medicine to reach their goals of building a broader specialty.

The AVMA was quick to point out that the ABVPH already embraced many of the concepts that the preventive medicine group envisioned and asked that the two groups work together to see if the existing board could be expanded to fulfill everyone's goals and objectives. Dr. John Helwig of Ohio State University and Colonel William E. Jennings of the US Army Veterinary Corps led the initial effort. "With my prominent role in veterinary public health, I decided to stay on the sidelines. Dr. Helwig was concerned that I would be upset over the change in scope and name of the organization. On the contrary, I believed in what John, Bill and the others were trying to do. They only wanted to expand the scope of the organization and make it stronger. Retrospectively, it was certainly the right thing to do. The new certifying group can easily embrace relatively new and important fields like molecular genetics and bioinformatics as they apply to epidemiology, preventive medicine and veterinary public health," Jim said.

The debate and evolution of the organization, which has been so very well documented by BG (Ret.) Tom Murnane in his paper entitled *Historical and Future Perspectives of the American College of Veterinary Preventive Medicine (2000)*, continued from 1966 to 1978. Several specialty groups were proposed during this timeframe. These included the American College of Veterinary Public Service Practitioners (1966), the American College of Regulatory Veterinary Medicine (1971), and the American College of Veterinary Preventive Medicine (1973). The latter specialty was only given probationary status by the AVMA ABVS in 1973. Between 1971 and 1978 there was much discussion amongst the groups. Graciously, the ABVPH board ultimately agreed to revise its constitution to satisfy the goals and objectives of the other proposed specialty groups so that they could all operate within one organization.

For historical clarity, it must be stated that the outcome of these transactions was not a simple merger of the ABVPH and the

ACVPM group that was provisionally recognized in 1973. In actuality, the members of the probationary ACVPM group were inducted into the fully recognized ABVPH. At the same time, the ABVPH constitution was revised along with a unanimous vote to rename the American Board of Veterinary Public Health (ABVPH) the American College of Veterinary Preventive Medicine (ACVPM). As part of this process, twenty-six veterinarians of the provisional college were invited to become charter diplomates of the new ACVPM. Twenty-three of these accepted the offer. Interestingly, although an amendment was passed to recognize subspecialties in public health, public administration, and regulatory medicine, this clause was never exercised. The ACVPM was formally recognized by the AVMA ABVS on July 16, 1978 and was incorporated in the District of Columbia.

The first meeting of the fully approved college was held on July 17, 1978 and was presided over by Dr. John H. Helwig, who was the president at the time. He was succeeded by Dr. William E. Jennings, who served his term from 1979 to 1982. The ACVPM obtained approval for the subspecialty of epidemiology in 1984. The college continues to grow and has about 700 certified diplomates at the time of the printing of this biography. The epidemiology subspecialty also continues to grow.

"I have so much pride in the board and, subsequently, the college through the years. I very much appreciate the hard work of the executive directors and the outstanding officers and committee members. I am delighted with so many of the diplomates that have had and are having such productive careers in veterinary public health, epidemiology and other fields. I congratulate and thank Dr. Tom Murnane for acting as the official ACVPM historian. I am very humbled to have had a role in getting it all get started. When the ABVPH evolved into the ACVPM, it was definitely tough to see the phrase "veterinary public health" be eliminated from the organization's name. But I knew that this was just necessary progress and that the expanded role of the college would pay huge dividends for veterinary medicine in the future," Jim stated. True to form, Jim Steele simply did what was right for the future of veterinary public health and veterinary preventive medicine.

Jim has made many contributions toward bringing together veterinarians with an interest in public health. In 1950, he became concerned that university veterinarians involved in public health didn't have an adequate forum for intellectual exchange. To help correct this, he organized the first CDC Conference for Public Health Veterinarians in Atlanta, which was held in April 1950. Dr. Justin M. Andrews, CDC director from 1947 to 1951, complimented Jim on being proactive in organizing the meeting. "He really liked the idea and thought it was the right thing to do," Jim said. This was the first time that the CDC had hosted a conference designed with university professors and veterinary scientists in mind.

At the first meeting, veterinarians came from the National Institutes of Health (NIH) and delivered lectures on brucellosis. Drs. James Watt and Luther Terry, both physicians lectured on atherosclerotic plaques in pigs, and Dr. Ernest Tierkel spoke on rabies. Dr. Terry went on to serve as Surgeon General from 1961 to 1965. "Representatives from roughly thirty universities and state public health veterinarians were in attendance. At later meetings, Canadian scientists attended from the University of Guelph and elsewhere," said Jim. Jim reached out to veterinarians at Tuskegee and encouraged them to attend the meetings. Tuskegee veterinarians were well represented at the first and subsequent meetings. This started a rich relationship between CDC and the Tuskegee College of Veterinary Medicine. This also led to Jim's recruitment of Dr. Norman Hayes, a Tuskegee graduate, in 1962. He became the first African-American veterinarian employed by CDC.

"I also invited in representatives of the Pan American Health Organization (PAHO) like Drs. Pedro Acha and Ben Blood and later, Peter Schantz, who was working in Argentina at the time. These productive conferences continued for more than twenty years. The meetings eventually led to the formation of the National Association of Public Health Veterinarians (NAPHV) and the National Association of State Public Health Veterinarians (NASPHV), two associations in which I have continued involvement," Jim reported.

Jim has also given freely of his time, leadership, and energy to recognize those individuals who have made outstanding contributions in the fields of veterinary public health and epidemiology. His drive to create the American Veterinary Epidemiology Society (AVES) stemmed primarily from his desire to recognize Dr. K. F. Meyer, an outstanding scientist, mentor, colleague and friend. "I patterned the AVES after the American Epidemiology Society (AES), an old-line, honorary epidemiological society that dates back to its origin in 1927," Jim said.

"The AES was composed of epidemiologists in human medicine that did so much of the early, significant work in the field. The AES also became an advisory group to the Armed Forces Epidemiology Board (AFEB), which was formed in 1940 during World War II," Jim stated. The board members were primarily civilian and academic medical scientists who advised the Army regarding the epidemiology of infectious diseases that were threatening deployed military personnel. "Dr. John Herbold, a leading veterinarian and professor at the University of Texas School of Pubic Health, San Antonio, Texas, and a very close friend of mine, is currently an advisory member of the AFEB," Jim said. The establishment of the Armed Forces Epidemiological Board was a milestone in the history of epidemiology in the US. "I wanted to create a similar forum to recognize leaders in veterinary epidemiology and public health." Jim stated.

"The school of medicine at the University of California, San Francisco initiated a Gold-Headed Cane Award in 1939. The award has its beginnings in the seventeenth century and was awarded by the king of England to his personal physician," Jim explained. The cane was passed on from doctor to doctor for honorable service and eventually became a symbol of the highest learning and medical excellence. The head of the cane has a special significance as outlined in the following passage:

> The head of the cane had a hollow compartment into which herbs and potions could be placed which would repel contagion. The physician could place the head of the cane beside his nose to breathe the potent smell

instead of the terrible necrotic smell of his patients. The canes awarded by the California School of Medicine contained an illuminated scroll in the compartment. On it was an inscription symbolizing the ideals of the true physician.

–From *The Gold-Headed Cane* by William Macmichael, 1953

The Gold-Headed Cane Award is presented to the graduating medical student who, according to the faculty and his/her class, is judged as displaying the qualities of a "true physician." As outlined in the chapter on Hartz Mountain, "I established the American Veterinary Epidemiology Society (AVES) in 1964. Based on my knowledge of the history of the award created at the University of California for physicians, I initiated the K. F. Meyer Gold-Headed Cane Award in Dr. Meyer's name on his eightieth birthday. I believed strongly that this was a fitting way to honor K. F.'s work and contributions in veterinary public health. The Hartz Mountain Company provided full sponsorship of the AVES from the beginning until the present," Jim stated. He will always treasure Hartz's outstanding support of the AVES and veterinary public health.

"I learned about all of this through K. F. Meyer, who was working in the University of California system. He planted the seed for me to recommend a similar award to be given by the AVES. The K. F. Meyer Gold-Headed Cane Award is the highest honor given to a veterinarian by the AVES," Jim said. K. F. Meyer, of course, was the first recipient in 1964 on his eightieth birthday. Dr. Donald Dean of the New York State Health Department also received a cane in 1964. Dr. Raymond Randall was awarded the cane in 1965 for his long and successful career at Walter Reed Medical Research Center. Dr. Jim Steele received the Gold-Headed Cane Award in 1966, followed by his friend and colleague Dr. Martin Kaplan in 1967. The Gold-Headed Cane Award recipients are a veritable *Who's Who* of veterinary public health throughout the years.

In 1967, the AVES began awarding one honorary diploma each year to a distinguished veterinary scientist. The first went to

Dr. George Beran in 1967, followed by Dr. Henrik J. Stafseth in 1968. After that year, one or more diplomas were awarded each year until the 1990s, when five became the standard number to be given out in any one year. "I stayed on as president until 1989, when I suffered a minor heart attack. I felt that it was time to get someone new onto the podium!" Jim said. Subsequently, Drs. Joe Held, Robert Jorgensen, Harry Mussman, Lonnie King and George Beran have served as AVES presidents. Dr. Beran has been presiding since 2008.

"In 1995, the AVMA included the awarding of the AVES Gold-Headed Cane in the opening ceremony of the meeting each year. However, the private AVES award luncheons and breakfasts have carried on until the present time and are still sponsored by the Hartz Mountain Company. A special dinner for the awardees is held the night before the awards are presented," Jim said. In 2006 at the meeting in Honolulu, the AVES award luncheon was combined with the AVMA president's luncheon. Jim and Brigitte, his second wife whom he married after Aina's death in 1969, could not attend the meeting this year. "The only other time we missed was Baltimore in 1998," recalled Jim. There were two vacant chairs placed at the table in their honor. Surgeon General David Satcher (1998-2002) lavished praised on Jim as he spoke at the meeting. "Somehow, an AVES event isn't the same without Jim and Brigitte!" he lamented.

CHAPTER 19:
JIM STEELE, ALEXANDER LANGMUIR AND THE EPIDEMIC INTELLIGENCE SERVICE

"Dr. Alexander Duncan Langmuir was recruited by the late Joseph Mountin, as I was, after World War II, with the challenge to explore new areas that related to public health. Mountin was a leader who gained fame by challenging the old order and anticipating future needs. He foresaw the need for an agency such as the Communicable Disease Center, now the Centers for Disease Control and Prevention or CDC, to service the states," Jim wrote in the *American Journal of Epidemiology* (1996). Dr. Justin Andrews, deputy director of CDC, helped Dr. Mountin identify Dr. Langmuir, who was an assistant professor at Johns Hopkins University at the time. Their strategy was to identify a leader who could build a strong body of well trained epidemiologists for CDC in the early Cold War years. Dr. Langmuir came to CDC in the spring of 1949.

"Dr. Langmuir was a medical consultant to the Department of Defense during the war. He couldn't get a commission in the military, as he had a chronic middle ear infection. After the war, Dr. Langmuir accepted a position at Johns Hopkins University. But he told me later that academic life wasn't providing the opportunities he had hoped for. He was brought to CDC in 1949 as the head of the epidemiology branch. Dr. Langmuir was very interested in what I was doing, especially with rabies. We later made our memorable trip by train to the Rocky Mountain Laboratory to learn more about the Q Fever research being conducted by Dr. Herb Stoner and others in relation to the outbreaks in California. We had long discussions about many zoonotic diseases on the trip. Back at CDC, Dr. Langmuir continually queried me about my program in Veterinary Public Health," Jim recalled.

"He told me that his only exposure to veterinarians had been in New York State, where they were running the milk program. I gave him a copy of my compendium of zoonotic diseases. He was always asking me questions about specific diseases," Jim stated.

Dr. Langmuir once visited the CDC Rabies Investigation Laboratory in Montgomery, Alabama. As has already been described, it was established in the 1930s to study rabies in people and dogs by scientists of the Rockefeller Foundation. "Dr. Langmuir liked my epidemiological approach to rabies control, which utilized population estimates, mapping, the calculation of incidence and vaccination rates, and other epidemiological methods. He encouraged me to continue to spotlight diseases like brucellosis, leptospirosis and salmonellosis, and Q fever," Jim recalled.

"In 1951, my program in veterinary public health was moved under the epidemiology branch. Some were concerned that this would eclipse my work. But that view was totally unfounded. In my discussions with Dr. Langmuir, he assured me that it was his intent to fully integrate veterinary public health into the epidemiology program at the right time," Jim explained.

The Epidemic Intelligence Service (EIS) was also established in 1951, as a joint training and service program. It was designed to be focused on the use of epidemiological principles and methodology in the furtherance of public health. The idea for the EIS was initiated by Dr. Joseph Mountin, the assistant surgeon general and founder of the CDC. "It is my understanding that Dr. Mountin coined the phrase 'Epidemic Intelligence Service,'" Jim said. Dr. Alexander Langmuir was selected to launch the new program. Twenty-two physicians and one sanitary engineer reported to Atlanta in July 1951 to begin their training.

"Dr. Langmuir asked me to lecture to the first EIS students on animal and zoonotic diseases. He was intrigued with many of the case studies that came out of the veterinary public health program. At this time, I began to suggest to Dr. Langmuir that veterinarians should become a part of the EIS program. When it was announced that the nursing program was to be included, my argument got even stronger." Jim said.

With Dr. Langmuir's support, Jim started a seminar series in veterinary public health that was held at CDC in 1951. "The audience consisted of state public health veterinarians, industry veterinarians, university professors and practitioners. Initially, the seminars focused on emerging zoonoses. Rabies got a lot of attention in the early seminars. Dr. Langmuir would sometimes participate to emphasize the importance of sound epidemiology," Jim recalled. The outbreak of Western equine encephalomyelitis in southern California in 1953 all but canceled the conference that year. Dr. Langmuir dispatched all available veterinary officers to the scene along with medical and entomology officers. This was the first major operation that involved many medical and veterinary officers.

Jim and Dr. Langmuir got along very well for the most part. "We agreed most of the time. The only time I recall that we had a total falling out was at a biological warfare conference at Fort Detrick, Maryland. At the meeting, reports were presented on disease outbreaks that were investigated jointly by agencies in the US and Canada from 1942 to 1950 that were suspected to have possibly been biowarfare attacks. The veterinary delegations that presented were all in support of the traditional control approach of test-and-slaughter. Dr. Langmuir challenged this view based on the work of the nineteenth-century English statistician Dr. William Farr, who described an outbreak of rinderpest that moved through Europe in the late 1850s. Dr. Farr didn't believe a carrier state could be established in survivors of the disease. Dr. Langmuir was in agreement with his findings. The idea of a carrier state for rinderpest was not known at the time but was later proven to be true. We had a nice time debating this one!" Jim said grinning.

In the spring of 1953, Dr. Langmuir asked Jim to identify some outstanding veterinarians who would be screened for matriculation into the EIS training program in July. "He kind of put me on the spot, but, of course, I was all for it. Most new graduates had already accepted positions. Regardless, we pulled together an outstanding list of candidates. I called the deans of the veterinary schools and asked for nominations. The nominees were then interviewed. They were going to train side by side with physicians. This was a very exciting time. It added a whole new dimension of opportunities available to veterinarians," Jim recalled. The veterinarians in the first three EIS classes are as follows:

Dr. Robert Courter, 1953
Dr. Paul Arnstein, 1954
Dr. George Beran, 1954
Dr. George Fischer, 1954
Dr. Harvey Hearn, 1954
Dr. Charles Hilbers, 1954
Dr. Keith Maddy, 1954
Dr. John Richardson, 1954
Dr. Richard Tjalma, 1954
Dr. Gordon Wallace, 1954
Dr. John Clayton, 1955
Dr. Daniel Cohen, 1955
Dr. Denny Constantine, 1955
Dr. Douglas Hawkins, 1955
Dr. Joseph Held, 1955
Dr. Merlin Kaeberle, 1955
Dr. Richard Parker, 1955
Dr. Kenneth Quist, 1955
Dr. Gordon Solomon, 1955
Dr. Robert Watson, 1955
Dr. Daniel Weiner, 1955

"After Dr. Robert Courter graduated as an EIS officer, I assigned him to Greece to support the Truman policy of maintaining an American presence in the country. He was assigned to the veterinary school at the Aristotle University of Thessaloniki, Greece, where he taught veterinary public health and preventive medicine. He did an admirable job for us." Jim reported. When Dr. Courter returned from his assignment in Greece, he became Jim's deputy for several years.

"Dr. George Beran was headed for the Army Veterinary Corps. But when he heard about the EIS program, he became very interested. George Beran was a member of the second EIS class that began in 1954. He served as an EIS officer until 1956. At that time, he went on to complete a PhD in microbiology at the University of Kansas Medical School," Jim said with pride. Dr. Beran and Jim continue to share a strong friendship and have collaborated a great deal along the way.

In the early 1950s, there was an outbreak of cholera in India. "Dr. Langmuir asked me if there could be an animal reservoir. I told him that a British study in the early twentieth century demonstrated none. I didn't believe there was one myself. Dr. Langmuir and I dispatched Dr. Kenneth Quist, a veterinary EIS officer, to look into the epidemic. It was centered mostly in the cities. He helped to link the outbreak to potable water tanks. Dr. Langmuir began including veterinarians in the investigation of all emerging diseases. Dr. Frank Mulhern from the BAI sent Dr. Saul Wilson down to observe the EIS program and to learn about how epidemiology was being used in disease investigations. It was all coming together so nicely!" Jim said. Because veterinarians were included in the EIS program, many veterinary schools began to offer courses and degrees in epidemiology.

Salmonellosis was a big problem in pigs and poultry in the 1950s. Dr. Langmuir decided to establish a national surveillance program. Earlier, Ms. Mildred Galton joined the CDC and worked in Jim's veterinary public health laboratory as a bacteriologist. "She had done some outstanding work on salmonellosis in Florida. She trained many EIS officers in laboratory methods to culture and identify *Salmonella*," Jim said.

According to a paper in the *Journal of Veterinary Medical Education* (2003) by Dr. Marguerite Pappaioanou et al, from 1951 until 2002, 195 veterinarians completed the EIS program. This comprises 7 percent of all EIS officers in that timeframe. The first female veterinarian EIS officer, Dr. Grace Clark, was admitted to the program in 1971. By the 1990s, over half of the veterinarians in the EIS program were women. The first minority veterinarian EIS officer was Dr. Roscoe Moore, an African-American, who also entered the program in 1971.

"In the early decades of the EIS program, veterinary officers were mostly assigned to state health departments with a few to rabies or other field stations. Later on, many veterinary EIS officers were assigned to headquarters positions. In the beginning, most were involved in infectious disease problems. But eventually there were officers assigned to study occupational and environmental health issues," Jim said. An article by Dr. Stephen B.

Thacker et al in the *American Journal of Epidemiology* (2001) states that EIS officers started out almost strictly as white, male physicians. Today the EIS is composed not only of physicians and veterinarians, but also includes nurses, epidemiologists, public health specialists, statisticians, biologists, microbiologists, anthropologists, industrial hygienists, dentists, chemists, biochemists, toxicologists, pharmacists and more. This includes a mix of men and women, minorities, and non-US citizens. The core activities for learning (CAL) in the EIS Program as outlined in Dr. Thacker's paper are:

> The Epidemic Intelligence Service (EIS) Officer will perform the following activities:
>
> CAL 1. Conduct or participate substantively in a field investigation of a potentially serious public health problem that requires a rapid public health response.
>
> CAL 2. Design, conduct, and interpret an epidemiologic analysis on a new or preexisting database that has a sample size that permits assessment of confounding and effect modification. As a result of the analysis, appropriate public health recommendations should be made.
>
> CAL 3. Design, implement, or evaluate a public health surveillance system and deliver a written and/or verbal report on this system as required during the fall EIS course.
>
> CAL 4. Write (as first author) a scientific manuscript for submission to a peer-reviewed journal.
>
> CAL 5. Write and submit a report to the *Morbidity and Mortality Weekly Report* (MMWR).
>
> CAL 6. Participate in the EIS Conference by giving an oral presentation or a poster presentation.
>
> CAL 7. Give an oral presentation at the Tuesday Morning Epidemiology Seminar at the Centers for Disease Control and Prevention or at a national scientific meeting with a substantial epidemiologic constituency (such as the Society for Epidemiologic Research or the American Public Health Association).

CAL 8. Respond appropriately to written or oral public health inquiries from the public, the media, government officials, or other health professionals.

Dr. Thacker's article also states that the EIS program has had an enormous impact on public health practice. In the early years, only 35 percent of graduates stayed in public health careers. Today, nearly 90 percent of EIS graduates stay in public health at the local, state, university, national or international level. Further, in 2000, 43 percent of state epidemiologists were graduates of the EIS program. As of 2001, at least three CDC directors had graduated from the EIS program, as had nine of eleven directors of CDC units. In addition, former EIS officers are deans of ten schools of public health. Two EIS officers have served as surgeon generals of the US. Finally, in 2001, 160 EIS graduates were working in fifty-four countries on six continents. "Many of the veterinary EIS officers went on to excel. Dr. Joseph Held established a laboratory animal medicine program that is the envy of the world. EIS officers like George Beran and so many others wen on to be recognized at the state, national and international levels for their outstanding contributions," Jim said. The following tribute to Dr. Langmuir is excerpted from Dr. Thacker's paper:

The impact of Alexander D. Langmuir on CDC and global public health was extraordinary, but his greatest legacy was undoubtedly the EIS program. It continues to evolve as we grapple with new health problems such as interpersonal violence and chronic disease. A large, closely knit group of alumni often work together to address new public health problems, including the emergence of new pathogens and infectious diseases as well as the practice of new areas of applied epidemiology. The EIS officer is an applied epidemiologist who uses epidemiologic practice and research to improve public health. Because the EIS Program is rooted in public health practice and is based on a philosophy of "learning while doing," it maintains a spontaneity and relevance that are essential to addressing the public health challenges of the 21st century.

Jim concluded, "I was named an honorary member of EIS in 1975 by Dr. David Senser, the director of CDC, and Dr. Phil Brockman, the CDC director of epidemiology. This was a very special honor to me. Dr. Langmuir and I worked very closely to carefully integrate veterinarians into the EIS program. Retrospectively, I don't see how it could have turned out any better. Wherever you are, Alex, I am sure that you are very pleased. Thanks for your many contributions. Special thanks to you for your support of veterinary public health!"

CHAPTER 20:
THE CIA, THE IRON CURTAIN
AND BIOWARFARE

Jim's earliest direct experience with a potential biowarfare agent occurred when he was in veterinary school at Michigan State College. The accidental infection of students in the bacteriology building with *Brucella melitensis* in 1938 (see chapter 4) helped to crystallize his thoughts about the importance of zoonotic diseases and public health. Initially, the consensus was that students became infected via contaminated drinking water. However, Professor Maxcy of Johns Hopkins School of Public Health found overwhelming evidence that the infections were caused by an aerosol created by broken test tubes in a centrifuge. He presented his data at the US Army Surgeon General's Epidemiology Conference on Biowarfare in early 1942. The event fueled the concept that the *Brucella* organism might be suitable as a bioweapon. "After World War II, I attended several biowarfare seminars at Fort Detrick and participated in research plans on biowarfare," Jim recalled.

Later Jim realized the potential for aerosol rabies transmission when he learned about human cases associated with spelunkers in bat caves in Texas and with various laboratory accidents. "Glanders is another disease I struggled with through the years as a possible biowarfare agent. In many wars, glanders decimated military horse populations and there were also human cases. But overall, the idea of biowarfare was questionable to me at the time," Jim said. But he could certainly see how foot and mouth disease would affect human health through the loss of the food supply. "I also believed animal agents might be used to wage psychological warfare. The deaths of large numbers of animals can be very distressing to people. But as I thought it through, I came to the conclusion that it is as difficult to start an epidemic as it is to stop one. Biowarfare wasn't as feasible as many were thinking in my opinion," Jim stated.

The Central Intelligence Agency (CIA) was established in September 1947 to evaluate and coordinate the intelligence activities of governmental departments in the interest of national security. As soon as the CIA was operational, Jim was approached by medical officers who were recruiting for the agency. "I found this kind of comical. I always thought of the CIA as a bunch of tough guys packing pistols. I learned later that many veterinarians have done work for the CIA over the years. I rarely had firsthand knowledge of their activities. I assumed that most of them were keeping track of animal pathogens that might be used in a biological attack," Jim said.

It was the beginning of many experiences Jim would have with the CIA, mostly related to his travels behind the Iron Curtain. This phrase marked the start of the Cold War and was introduced by Winston Churchill in his historic "Iron Curtain speech," delivered at Westminster College in Fulton, Missouri on March 5, 1946. "He was referencing an imaginary boundary separating Europe ideologically into two regions after World War II. This lasted until the end of the Cold War in 1989 with the fall of the Berlin Wall," Jim said. Most of the countries west of the Iron Curtain were aligned with the United States, while those to the east were under the influence of the Soviet Union.

Jim attended World Health Organization (WHO) meetings in Geneva in the 1950s. During these meetings, he learned that Dr. Martin Kaplan, the first director of veterinary public health for WHO, was a champion for human rights and public health. "He was working to building bridges into the Eastern Bloc countries," Jim said. One of the positive outcomes of his efforts was the WHO European Symposium on Veterinary Public Health held in Warsaw in 1957. This was the first WHO meeting behind the Iron Curtain that focused on veterinary public health.

"The CIA handed me a list of questions concerning new developments in biological research before I left for Poland in November 1957. I was one of the keynote speakers for the meeting. The Poles had constructed a number of new laboratories. The CIA wanted to gather intelligence regarding what sort of research was being conducted in them. The Communists had taken over some of the large estates of the Polish aristocracy and converted them into laboratories. I could only conclude that the CIA's concern was that they were working on biological weapons. There was research being conducted in the US toward developing a strain of anthrax resistant to antibiotics. The Japanese were also working toward this goal, and one could only assume the Soviets were, too," Jim said. This was Jim's first excursion behind the Iron Curtain.

"When I arrived in Poland, they seemed delighted to see me. They thought I was toting big bags of money to fund research under the Public Law 480, also known as PL 480. This program was created in 1954 during the Eisenhower presidency," Jim said. Title I of this law provided US funding for the sale of US agricultural products to developing countries under special credit terms with low interest rates. "A developing country was eligible if it could not meet all of its food needs through normal commerce," Jim recalled. At the time, Stalin forbade any collaboration with the US, which included financial assistance programs.

"So I had to break the news that I was not there to distribute any agricultural funding. During my tours, I was appalled at how woefully inadequate the laboratory facilities were. Most were fortunate to have a few Bunsen burners and Petri dishes. Their scientists didn't even have journals to read," he said. Jim reported back to the CIA that it was highly unlikely the Polish scientists would be developing any viable biological weapons.

Dr. Kaplan led the Warsaw meeting. "It was attended by many western medical and veterinary scientists along with hundreds from the USSR and Eastern Bloc countries, including Poland. We all stayed in a hotel that formerly was the Prudential Insurance building. We all lost weight on the trip as food was very limited. But there was plenty of vodka throughout the day served in little chilled glasses!" Jim said with a grin.

Dr. Joseph Parness, a Polish veterinarian, was head of the Lublin Institute. The institute was established to provide veterinary public health services in Poland, including supporting rural public health, improving the water supply, and tuberculosis and brucellosis control. "I inquired about the incidence of salmonellosis in Poland. Dr. Parness replied that there was a *Salmonella* laboratory up north in Danzig. I knew that tuberculosis was a colossal problem in Poland, but I didn't learn the extent of the disease until about 1960," Jim said.

During the time of this meeting, Jim was selling his house on Ivy Road in Atlanta and was expecting some closing paperwork in the mail. Dr. Parness delivered some mail to Jim which had obviously been opened. Jim inquired, "Why has my mail been opened?" and Dr. Parness replied, "We are protecting you from being discredited, Dr. Steele!"

Jim walked into the conference center in Warsaw on the day he was to present a paper on the international implications of veterinary public health. "After I was introduced, I walked to the podium and looked out at the crowd. It was then that I noticed that all the attendees were sitting on their hands. I thought this was a bit peculiar, but I proceeded to deliver my talk," Jim said. Two hours later he finished his lecture, thanked the delegation and the attendees and sat down. "There was no applause, not a sound. You could hear a pin drop!" Jim said. Later that afternoon, the Soviet speakers delivered a treatise on Leninism and extolled the great scientific achievements that had been accomplished through the years. After the Soviet speakers were done, the moderator asked Jim if he would like to make any additional remarks. As Jim recalled it, he simply stood up and began to talk. "This is all illusory. Let's get down to reality. If we are to have solid veterinary science and epidemiology, we have to know history. Epidemiology has made its contributions through good data collection and sound mathematical analysis, from John Snow in England to Pasteur and Smith and through the great scientists leading up to the present time. The most important concept in public health is that we must remain truthful to ourselves!" Jim concluded and sat down. Instantly, everyone in the room rose and gave Jim a standing ovation. "I knew I had won the audience, and the Soviet official sitting next to me couldn't do a thing about it. It was one of my greatest moments! It was one of those times where the timing was just right. Every time I turned around, people in the crowd were toasting me and encouraging better relations among all countries. I still wonder what ended up in my KGB file that day," Jim said with a smile.

After the meeting, Dr. Parness asked Jim to sponsor him to become a WHO officer in Geneva. Dr. Parness fell out of favor with the Communist Party, probably because of his close association with Jim and Dr. Kaplan. "Dr. Parness wanted to leave the country with his laboratory technician, a lady named Crystal. Dr. Stableforth, a British WHO veterinary representative, asked me if I would recommend Dr. Parness to be appointed to a position with the veterinary laboratories in Weybridge. At the time, I just didn't feel comfortable with the idea. There was something about him that didn't set well with me," Jim said.

Dr. Parness ultimately found refuge in Denmark and continued his work on serologic diagnostic methods for detecting the *Brucella* organism. He tried to persuade WHO to use his methods even though the Danes already had their own testing techniques. "The more I examined his work, I found that I couldn't endorse his science or his laboratory methods," Jim said. But Dr. Parness continued to write to Jim frequently. "Later I was also approached by a veterinarian in Czechoslovakia who wanted me to sponsor him to come to the United States. I was very cautious. Some of these guys may have been secret agents. But my main concern was that most of these individuals weren't well trained scientists," Jim said.

In 1958, Jim was invited back to Poland as part of a five-man team for the purpose of trying to establish some PL 480 contracts. "The Centers for Disease Control and the National Institutes of Health were both reaching out to many parts of the world at the time. On this trip, I met some good scientists in the laboratories, but none of them were veterinarians," Jim said. Several had visited CDC earlier for training, and subsequently served as liaisons on enteric diseases.

"In 1960 I was invited to conduct a lecture tour through Yugoslavia and throughout the Eastern Bloc. I came up with the idea to bring my son Jay along for the ride. He was ten years old at the time and had a good level of maturity. I was still recovering from my bout with fowl plague that I had likely picked up during a visit to Cairo in 1959. I was feeling better but was definitely still not back to my old self," Jim said.

Jim's director at the time, Dr. Larry Smith, asked him, "Aren't you stretching your health a bit?"

"I tended to agree with Larry, but I saw this trip as an incredible window of opportunity to advance veterinary public health in Eastern Europe. The veterinary public health meeting in Poland in 1957 really stimulated my interest in the Eastern Bloc," Jim said.

Jim crafted an ingenious plan to acquire some time for recuperation during the trip and to spend some quality time with Jay. "I traveled so much in those days and I felt like I was missing out on precious family time. It was great to have Jay with me!" Jim said. He decided they would travel to Europe by ship and booked tickets on the S. S. Independence. "Construction began on this grand vessel in Massachusetts in 1949. It took its maiden voyage in 1951, was almost 700 feet in length and could carry over 1,000 passengers. The berths were comfortable, the food was good and there were many activities on board. President and Mrs. Truman had traveled on the ship in the summer of 1958. Iwas looking forward to the slow paced cruise and the time with my son," Jim said.

Beyond the much needed father-son time, Jim thought having Jay with him would help to prevent any misreading of Jim's intentions in the Eastern Bloc countries. "Aina reluctantly agreed to let Jay travel with me. I also had to clear it with WHO and the foreign health division of the US Public Health Service. But this didn't turn out to be a big problem. I also had to get Jay excused from elementary school," Jim said. Most of the teachers were enthused about the trip as an educational opportunity. "We departed from New York City bound for Naples. There were many friends present to see us off. One of the bon voyagers was the chief of USPHS quarantine at Ellis Island for New York City. The trip across the Atlantic was delightful and healthful. I exercised a lot, read and played bridge along the way. The attendants on the ship repeatedly said that Jay was the most well behaved child they had ever seen, calling him a model child!" Jim said.

"By the time we entered the Strait of Gibraltar, where the Atlantic Ocean meets the Mediterranean Sea, Jay knew every crew member on the ship. The captain even allowed him to steer the ship through the strait. I can still see the beautiful, classic rock formations in the distance," he said. Jim and Jay placed a message in a bottle stating their route and explaining their veterinary public health mission. "We tossed it into the ocean. Our note asked any person finding the bottle to contact us back in the US. No one ever did, but it is a fond memory. We stopped in Gibraltar for a few hours but didn't have time to go ashore," Jim recalled.

"After a brief stop at Nice, France, we went on to Genoa, Italy where we went ashore and took an enjoyable tour of the city. We met an Italian couple who helped guide us. We were having such a good time we almost didn't hear the whistle of the boat. We ran back to the ship and nearly didn't make it aboard. We were the last passengers to get back on the ship. If we hadn't made it aboard, we likely would have had to travel by train to Naples," said Jim.

"I remember the trip down the Italian coast like it was yesterday. There were endless coves and bays lined with pine and oak trees. There were lavender orchids and lots of rugged rocks and cliffs," Jim reminisced. They enjoyed the exquisite scenery all the way into Naples, their destination. There, Jim and Jay were met by U. S. Public Health Service (USPHS) quarantine officers. "They entertained us and showed us around Naples, including a trip to Pompeii," Jim said. Jim was fascinated with the history of the area. Naples was the first city where the USPHS had established a quarantine section to clear Italian immigrants for travel to the US. From Naples, Jim and Jay traveled to Rome to meet with the US embassy staff. "Upon arrival in Rome, we checked in at the Grand Hotel," Jim recalled.

"One day when Jay was drinking some milk at the hotel, he found some broken glass in his cup. The hotel management was appalled and provided us with free tickets to the opera that night," Jim said. That evening at the opera, featuring *Girl of the Golden West* by Puccini, turned out to be "grandfathers' night." The idea was that attendees were supposed to bring their grandchildren with them. Of course, Jay's blond hair stood out. "Many of the young girls his age were flirting with him," Jim said.

Jay asked his dad with a puzzled look, "What would a girl want with me?"

The hotel staff took Jay to the zoo one day while Jim was working. Jim still has a picture of him with a lion at the Rome Zoo. "Jay enjoyed the zoo more than he did the opera. He was having a grand time!" Jim said with a smile.

After Jim finished his business in Rome, he and Jay flew to Belgrade, Yugoslavia. They were received warmly by local veterinary officials. Jim spent a few days visiting and meeting with Yugoslavian veterinarians, primarily on the topic of hydatid disease. Dr. Martin Kaplan had tried to institute a program there to eliminate the parasite in dogs. "He was also working to implement a rabies control program. Martin asked me to conduct an assessment of how the Yugoslavians were doing in managing these two diseases. I was also interested in learning about the incidence of brucellosis in Yugoslavia," Jim said.

"I also wanted to investigate a mysterious renal disease that was being reported south of Belgrade. I was told that people were succumbing to an acute nephritis that reduced the kidneys to walnut size. This led to renal failure and death in most of these patients. I couldn't think of anything infectious. I surmised it must be some kind of toxicity," Jim said. He asked the veterinarians in the area if they had seen anything similar in animals but was not able to obtain any positive reports. Yugoslavia had a system of rural medical clinics where people could come for diagnosis and treatment. "I visited a few of these clinics and learned that there truly was a high incidence of patients in renal failure." Later Jim would read about a similar problem that occurred among Confederate soldiers during the Civil War in the US "I never did find out what was causing the problem. Every now and again I think about this and wonder what could have been going on there!" Jim exclaimed.

Jim and Jay then traveled to Zagreb, Yugoslavia, now the capital of Croatia. Jim was scheduled to teach a course in veterinary public health at the University of Zagreb for two weeks. "Veterinarians, physicians and microbiologists from all over the country had enrolled. I lectured for about two hours each day with one hour for questions and discussion. I turned Jay over to caretakers who kept him entertained while I was working. I made several excursions to Novi Sad, north of Belgrade, to visit laboratories where they were producing a rabies vaccine.

The minister of health arranged for a luncheon one day in Ljubljana, the capital of Slovenia. Jim was lecturing to a group of government veterinarians and ran over, showing up about an hour late for the luncheon. Jay explained to the U. S. State Department representative, "Dad is always a little late!" During the meal, Jim learned from a local veterinarian that an outbreak of tick-borne encephalitis occurred every spring at nearby Lake Bled. "I remember wishing I had the time to follow-up on these reports." said Jim.

After Yugoslavia, Jim and Jay went on to Vienna for a short stop before completing the next leg of their trip to Prague, Czechoslovakia. "We needed clearance from Moscow to travel into Czechoslovakia, but this was not coming through. I called Geneva to see if they could resolve the problem. Two days later we still did not have clearance for Prague. The WHO advised me to abort the mission to Prague and return to Geneva," Jim explained.

Before leaving Vienna, Jim and Jay visited St. Stephen's Cathedral to see an artifact alleged to be the tablecloth from the Last Supper. From there they flew to Milan, Italy, en route to Geneva. There, on the Fourth of July, Jim gave an extensive report of his findings to Mohammed Abdusallam, Dr. Martin Kaplan's WHO deputy at the time. This officially completed Jim's charge. Jim and Jay joined the American staffers at WHO for a celebration of the American holiday.

With the WHO mission completed, Jim and Jay traveled to Copenhagen, Denmark, where they visited Ms. Annie Anderson and her family. She was a translator at the WHO Copenhagen office. "She was enormously helpful to me through the years. Annie spent six months with us in our household in Atlanta in 1958," Jim said. Jim also visited the WHO regional office for Europe in Copenhagen, the University Veterinary Research Center, Tivoli and the famous *Little Mermaid* statue. This statue was commissioned in 1909 by the founder of Carlsberg Breweries to commemorate the fairy tale written by Hans Christian Andersen.

From there they traveled to Stockholm, Sweden, where Jim made contact with Dr. Kjell Tullberg, a Swedish veterinarian. "Dr. Tullberg was my first postwar contact in Sweden. This established a working relationship between the Swedes and the CDC and beyond. He visited me at NIH in 1948 and CDC in 1957," Jim said. They also visited Jim's cousin, Mr. Olaf Forsberg, who was a school principal in the Stockholm suburbs. Mr. Forsberg had traced his family back to the eighteenth century by researching church records. "I was hoping to trace the Nordquist family, my mother's lineage, but unfortunately these efforts were in vain," Jim said.

The Swedish veterinarians held a nice reception for Jim and Jay. Jay was asked to play chess with Jim's cousin Olaf. Jay had learned chess in Yugoslavia, and he demonstrated his newfound skills by beating his cousin. "We had no idea Americans played chess so well!" his cousin said.

"Jay went on to play chess in high school and became a class champion. I guess the Yugoslavians can take the credit for getting him off to a great start!" Jim said.

From Stockholm they traveled to Paris to visit with Dr. Ray Ravenholt, who was an EIS officer in Europe. "Ray briefed me about Europeans returning from Africa with salmonellosis and other enteric infections. I asked him questions about the nephritis syndrome that was reported in Yugoslavia, but he didn't have an answer," Jim said.

"The USPHS quarantine officer arranged for us to attend a Bastille Day ceremony. We watched an impressive parade with French cavalry from Africa on Arabian horses followed by tanks, trucks, flags and a display of their nuclear capability," Jim said.

"From Paris we went to London to visit Dr. Ian Beveridge and his wife, Patricia, at Cambridge. He was a brilliant Australian veterinary pathologist who wrote *The Art of Scientific Investigation,* a book widely read by epidemiologists. He also wrote *Influenza: The Last Great Plague,*" which told the story of the 1918-1920 influenza pandemic," Jim said. Later, Dr. Beveridge worked with Jim and Dr. Kaplan to gather data on influenza and potential animal reservoirs. Jim and Jay had a nice time in Cambridge, and flew home from London in late July. The trip lasted over two months.

"This tour was very satisfying for me, as it provided an opportunity to spread the concepts of veterinary public health throughout Europe and even behind the Iron Curtain. However, I was disappointed not to make the trip to Czechoslovakia. I guess Moscow didn't want the Czechs to collaborate with the West," Jim said. Apparently, the Soviets somehow feared Jim's scientific leadership in veterinary public health. "I felt strongly then as I do now that freedom of science is an extremely important facet of our personal freedoms. Veterinary public health was feared by the Communist states because it represented volition, independent thought and curiosity. Furthermore, my philosophy was to raise the veterinarian's role to the level of the physician in line with the 'one medicine' concept. This notion was not embraced by the Soviets," Jim explained.

Jim made several trips to Poland over the years, primarily to assist with bovine tuberculosis and with trichinosis control and eradication. "Every time I made a trip to Poland, the CIA liaison officer knocked on my door for a report. I told them repeatedly that there was no evidence of biological weapons development that I could discern. My trichinosis studies in Poland continued for about twenty years," Jim said. He also studied beef and pork tapeworm problems, which were a major concern in Poland at the time. "The slaughterhouses either did not care or did not know how to screen for parasitic diseases. I arranged for PL 480 funds to help them solve some of these problems," Jim stated.

In 1958, the USPHS liaison to the WHO executive board asked Jim to write a review of the status of brucellosis in the Soviet Union. "The Soviets reported an incidence of the disease in people and animals that didn't make sense to me. They were reporting fairly high levels of animal brucellosis yet very little in people. I thought they were covering it up. I also wondered if they had a covert scientific research program on the *Brucella* organism," Jim said. He organized the data he had collected in the USSR in the fifties and wrote a paper for the Journal of the AVMA that was published in 1959.

Four years later Jim visited Moscow. He ran into a Soviet medical director at the Ivanoski Institute in Moscow who had read Jim's AVMA article. She growled through her translator, "How could you write such nonsense?"

"The whole time she was beating a magazine on the table. It reminded me of Nikita Khrushchev!" Jim said.

She continued, "This is not true; we do not have a brucellosis problem in the Soviet Union–it has been resolved! Where did you get this data?"

"I just used your data," Jim responded. "Needless to say, we didn't part friends," Jim said.

With Jim's assistance, the CIA had conducted a sophisticated analysis of Soviet epidemiological data from the thirties forward which demonstrated that there had been at least 100,000 human cases of brucellosis by 1958. "The data was out there but the Soviets didn't want to make it public. I simply used their data in my paper, we just put it all together," Jim said.

From June 19 through July 31, 1963, Jim traveled in the USSR as chief of a scientific exchange program arranged by the US State Department. Representatives of the United States Department of Agriculture (USDA) and the U. S. Public Health Service (USPHS) were invited to participate. "Premier Nikita Khrushchev, who was in power from 1958 to 1964, admired American agriculture and wanted to model some of his own programs after ours. Because of his intense interest in US agriculture, all expenses for the delegation while traveling in Russia were covered. I was chosen to head the USPHS mission and hand-picked my delegation," Jim said.

Among Jim's selectees were Dr. Carl Brandley, the dean of the College of Veterinary Medicine (CVM) at Illinois; Dr. Bill Thorp, Jim's cousin and dean of the CVM at Minnesota; Dr. Howard Dunn, a swine disease expert from Pennsylvania State; and Dr. Eugene Papp, a veterinary pathologist from the University of Georgia who would serve not only as a subject matter expert but also as their interpreter. "Unfortunately, Bill Thorp had to drop off the team. His wife, who held a PhD degree in bacteriology, insisted that she wanted to accompany her husband, but the Soviet government would not approve her travel. Bill understood and bowed out gracefully," Jim reported. Jim then selected Dr. Herb Stoenner to replace Dr. Thorp. At the time, Dr. Stoenner was the director of the Rocky Mountain National Laboratory in Hamilton, Montana. The purpose of this trip was to study the progress of research and teaching on zoonotic diseases in the Soviet Union.

After stops in Vienna, Austria; Budapest, Hungary; and Warsaw, Poland, the delegation boarded an Ilyushin 114 turbojet bound from Warsaw to Moscow. "We arrived at Sheremetyevo International Airport on June 19 on a mild, cloudy afternoon. A welcoming committee consisting of Soviet veterinarians from the Ministry of Agriculture greeted us upon our arrival. Professor M. M. Ivanoff and Dr. Victor Nazarenko, a translator, were with the group. Both had visited the CDC and the University of Georgia School of Veterinary Medicine previously. Two veterinarians were assigned to accompany our group wherever we traveled. One was Dr. V. V. Pavlovsky, and the other, Dr. Neal Shilikov," Jim said. The balance of the US delegation arrived from Amsterdam an hour later. They were taken to the Hotel Leningradskaya, a magnificent, ornate hotel. "My translator stated that the furnishings reminded him of his grandmother's parlor. The first thing our hosts did was collect all of our passports. This made everyone uncomfortable, to say the least," Jim said.

"The beds in the hotel were Stalin-style, designed for someone about five feet, six inches. I asked the translator if the hotel staff could provide an extension to the bed. My legs hung at least a foot over the end of the bed. The hotel staff in Moscow and every other hotel I stayed at for the next six weeks accommodated me by extending the bed with footboards or some other fix without any prodding from me. Communication around the country was obviously efficient!" Jim said.

At the end of every day of the tour, the team congregated in Jim's room and toasted the light fixture above, "Sorry our comrades couldn't be here to share a drink with us!" In good spirits, the team members all assumed and accepted the fact that every room was bugged. "One evening, the floor maid came to my room with a bottle of brandy and just laid it on my bed. I was a little perplexed and called my translator and asked him what to do. He asked me if I was afraid of a maid. He also told me that it should be pretty obvious what to do with the brandy," said Jim.

At the time, it was estimated that there were thirty-three schools of veterinary medicine and approximately 40,000 veterinarians in the USSR. "We learned of the class of health professionals called *feldsher*, which was derived from the German word *Feld* which means 'field' and *Scher* meaning 'doctor.' The literal translation is 'field doctor.' These professionals did primary care and preventive medicine work in rural areas. They referred the more serious cases to higher-level institutions. Feldshers were present for both human and veterinary medical care. The training for this field was not as rigorous as for the medical degrees. In 1963, there were an estimated 70,000 feldshers operating in the Soviet Union," Jim recalled.

"And so began a once-in-a-lifetime opportunity for all of us to see veterinary medicine and research in the Soviet Union first-hand. The day after our arrival, we met with the chief veterinarian of the Soviet Ministry of Agriculture, Dr. A. A. Boyko. He was a well dressed man with cufflinks and fine Italian shoes. He spoke excellent English. He told us that their anthrax animal vaccination program was working well. They were apparently using a modified Sterne vaccine. He also told us that they had built several scientific institutes dedicated to anthrax control since the turn of the twentieth century. I asked him where the vaccine production center was and he responded that it was in Tbilisi, Georgia," Jim said. Later, in Tbilisi, Jim learned they had adapted the Sterne vaccine for use in people and published this information in their main journal of infectious diseases. "By all indications, they had tested the vaccine on human volunteers. I was really curious why they were making a vaccine to protect people. When I asked them how much human anthrax vaccine they were making, their scientists replied that they made as much as the minister asked for. I didn't feel that the Soviets were being forthright with us. At one point, I just asked them to simply tell me what the heck was going on! I think that most of them were all happy when I left, quite relieved!" Jim said. He also asked to visit the laboratory where they were working on glanders. "I never saw that lab, either. I knew that the CIA would be really disappointed when I came home," Jim reflected.

"I learned from a colleague that Dr. Boyko had received the Stalin Award for his work on foot and mouth disease. I quizzed him about his research. Dr. Boyko replied that he had made his vaccine from the whole blood of infected animals. I knew that the Germans had gone down this same path in the early 1900s, attenuating the virus with arsenicals. Dr. Boyko had likely plagiarized this work to gain recognition in his own country," Jim said. He soon realized that wherever he turned, there were dishonest scientists trying to make names for themselves through any possible means.

"Next, we visited the Moscow Institute for Experimental Veterinary Medicine. We also got a brief tour of the Kremlin and, on Sunday, attended the Bolshoi Theater. This was a special treat, as everyone knows what a fan I am of the theater, ballet and the opera. One of the pieces we enjoyed was the opera 'Boris Godunov' by Modest Mussorgsky," Jim said.

For the next six weeks, they toured distant provinces, visiting a seemingly endless number of veterinary institutes, laboratories, and farms, and meeting with dozens of prominent Soviet veterinary scientists and researchers. What follows is a sampling of some of the stops on their itinerary:

Moscow Veterinary Academy

Moscow Institute of Helminthology

Milk plant, Ostankino

Institute of Epidemiology & Microbiology, Galalaya

Ivanovsky Institute of Virology

Institute of Poliomyelitis

Kazakh Research Institute of Veterinary Medicine and Animal Husbandry

Uzbek Research Institute of Veterinary Medicine, Tashkent

Armenia Veterinary Institute

Georgian Zootechnic Veterinary Institute, Tbilisi

Leningrad Research Institute of Veterinary Science and Zoology

"Throughout our travels, the meals were generally good. However, vodka was served and consumed all day, including at lunch. Everyone was inebriated by 1:00 p.m. After about the third day of this, I imposed my own set of rules for the day with each new group. Alcohol was to be prohibited until scientific discussions were completed for the day. I don't think the locals appreciated this very much," Jim said. This rule backfired somewhat when one of the scientists accompanied Jim up to his room that evening. When he saw all the liquor that had been provided by the US embassy, he said, "Sir, how can you complain about our habits; you have enough alcohol here for an army!"

Jim replied quickly, "This is only for guests after hours!" Of course, Jim knew that the fellow didn't believe a word he said.

Jim was aware that all research in the Soviet Union at the time was centrally planned and directed from Moscow, with the exception of Armenia. During a news conference with the Soviet press in Yerevan, the capital of Armenia, reporters asked Jim, "Do you have anything to recommend regarding the Soviet veterinary scientific program?"

Jim replied, "I am very impressed with the Armenian veterinary scientists in that they have shown more independence and are pursuing their own scientific curiosity. Maybe if they were left alone, they could accomplish much more." The reporter was not happy with this statement and immediately packed up his camera and left. Jim was wondering how much trouble this would cause, as it had been a live broadcast. "I just couldn't resist sending a strong message to Moscow!" Jim said. While in Armenia, Jim suffered from heat exhaustion. "I was treated with wet towels and sent on my way," Jim said.

"During my visits with the Soviet veterinary scientists, I did my best to gather information regarding the incidence of infectious diseases in animals, what their prevention and control programs were, and what was the extent of spillover of zoonotic diseases into the human population. It was amusing to see that many of the scientists had old copies of American journals like the *Journal of the American Medical Association* or the *Journal of the American Veterinary Medical Association* lying around. It was obvious that they prepared their lectures and reports from these journals," Jim said.

Brucellosis was reportedly widespread in cattle and sheep, especially in the southern regions. It was even being blamed for killing wild rabbit populations. The Soviet veterinary laboratories were trying to identify all reactors before inoculation with the Strain 19 vaccine. "I tried to explain that the vaccine would not prevent brucellosis in animals or people. Everywhere we went, we heard reports about how widespread human brucellosis was. But when we questioned the high-level authorities about it, they only replied that over four million people were vaccinated for brucellosis in 1961. They also reported a very low number of 33,000 human cases in 1962, with decreasing incidence. I didn't buy it. The Soviets called their vaccine the 'Moscow attenuated human strain.' What they also did not report was the high incidence of gangrenous cold ulcers at the site of the vaccination," Jim said. The ulcers were large, sloughing, painful lesions. Jim suspected the cause was either a vaccine contaminant or a variant of the *Brucella* Strain 19 organism, especially among those with a history of brucellosis.

"I also learned that leptospirosis was a problem in people on farms in the southern areas. There were over 5,000 human cases reported in 1962. No telling what the actual total was. Serovars Pomona and Tarsowi were considered to be the most predominant in the region. The Soviets developed a polyvalent vaccine for animals that they touted as effective. The animal vaccine was not of any value for people," Jim said.

"I also tried to learn about the extent of bovine tuberculosis. The Soviet government told me that attempts to eradicate the disease had begun in 1928 on state farms. They claimed the incidence in 1963 was no more than 0.57 percent and attributed this progress to their animal health programs. They also reported a low incidence of tuberculosis in packing house workers. All children in the Soviet Union were supposedly being vaccinated for tuberculosis with BCG at the time. I was also aware that the Soviet medical community had numerous sanatoriums in operation," Jim said.

The CIA was really interested in what Jim could learn about anthrax on this trip. The Soviets had been conducting anthrax research since the turn of the twentieth century, and the CIA was concerned that they were building bioweapons. "When I questioned scientists at the various institutes that I visited, they told me that anthrax was a sporadic disease. In areas where animal anthrax was found, they were vaccinating animals with the STI (Ginsberg) and Sinkovsky vaccines, non-encapsulated and non-virulent. When I inquired about human vaccines, they replied that there were two products available to physicians that were administered by skin scarification. The scientists that I spoke with claimed that most of the anthrax cases in people was the skin form resulting from environmental contamination, including working with animal products," Jim said. He learned about a professor of microbiology in Moscow who believed that people could become chronic carriers of anthrax, and the disease could recrudesce when the person was stressed, causing neurological symptoms and sometimes death.

"For rabies control, I was told that the Biological Control Institute had developed a formalin inactivated vaccine made from spleen, lung, and lymph nodes of sheep and rabbits. The Soviet scientists claimed that human cases of rabies were rare since the 1930s. If rabies was detected, they vaccinated all dogs in the affected area. They quizzed me about the safety of the Flury vaccine that we were using in the United States," Jim said.

"We also visited the Institute of Poliomyelitis and Virus Encephalitides in Moscow. They professed that polio was sporadic but that there was some increased incidence after World War II. The Soviets studied the Salk and Sabin vaccines produced in the US and selected the Salk in 1957 for their use," Jim said. Fifty regional polio laboratories were established across the USSR. In 1960, over seventy million children were vaccinated. "Tick-borne encephalitis, also known as Soviet spring and summer encephalitis, was also studied at the institute. Six hundred thousand people were supposedly being vaccinated annually for this disease. The incidence apparently was much higher in the eastern regions," Jim reported.

While in Kazakhstan, Jim asked their scientists about echinococcosis. "There were about 30 million sheep in the state at the time with populations expected to rise significantly. The Soviets were working on immunological tests to detect the disease in humans. Arecoline was the drug of choice to eliminate the tapeworm from dogs. Feces from infected dogs were, by all accounts, collected and buried," Jim said.

"I also inquired heavily about toxoplasmosis. Dr. Leveet from the Institute of Zoology in Kazakhstan told me toxoplasmosis was widespread but little work had been done to characterize the disease in people. They said they had identified over fifty wild animals that were carriers of the protozoan. An interesting report was that porcupines were believed to be a carrier," Jim said.

"I was very curious about the meat and dairy processing plants and their markets in the Soviet Union," Jim said. He and his team visited the main Moscow slaughterhouses. "At the time, one facility we visited was killing 3,500 cattle, 8,000 swine, and 3,500 sheep per day. The plant employed 8,000 people. The animals were killed in groups by electrocution, and I was concerned that the animals weren't being bled out adequately," Jim said. The team also visited one of forty-one meat markets in Moscow. "I recall that the market was well lit, and the facilities seemed to be clean. I asked about trichinosis in the slaughtered pigs, and they assured me that the pigs were all tested for the parasite with few positives. Milk was available for sale in shops by street vendors and in produce markets. We visited an experimental milk bottling plant that was not in active production. I noticed that milk taken directly from the cows was being placed in a large bulk tank that was not chilled. They told me that within an hour and a half, the milk would be in town at the plant for processing. I was somewhat skeptical about that claim as you might imagine," Jim said. The team visited many milk processing plants in several towns. Only a few of the plants were equipped to do pasteurization. In southern Russia they were amazed to find a pasteurization plant that had been a part of the 1939-1940 World's Fair exhibit in New York City. "How they got a hold of this equipment I don't know. It was amazing to see that the Soviets were still using this technology, which was over twenty-five years old at the time," said Jim.

In mid-July, Jim and the team made a long journey to the far-away city of Alma Ata, now known as Almaty, in Kazakhstan, over 2,500 miles from Moscow. "While en route by airplane, my feet just about froze. I don't think there was any heat on the aircraft. Somehow I think this may have spurred some of the neurological problems in my lower extremities," Jim said. The name "Alma Ata" refers to apples, one of the big crops in the area.

"The scientists were very proud of their zoonotic disease research program on wild animals. They made reference to water pollution, deforestation and other environmental concerns. We took several all-day field trips, beginning at 7:00 a.m. and sometimes lasting to 11:00 p.m. near the frontiers of southeast China in northern Kazakhstan. The area reminded me of Pennsylvania with large green hills, pine trees and deciduous trees," Jim stated. Plague and tick-borne Soviet spring and summer encephalitis were endemic in the area. "Many scientists there spoke of how they admired the work of K. F. Meyer. That was really nice to hear. They also told stories of Korean hemorrhagic fever in the region. They were speculating that it might be a viral or fungal disease. The disease wasn't fully characterized until about 1970 and, of course, is now recognized as one of the diseases caused by a hantavirus," Jim said.

"We then took a brief trip into Siberia. It reminded me of the northwest US. With all the stories you heard growing up about Siberia; I couldn't believe I was actually there. Our primary reason for going there was to inquire about diseases in wildlife. I recalled my history lessons on how Stalin transferred Estonians to Siberia as a penalty for surviving the war and cooperating with the Germans. So-called "banning" to Siberia actually began in Czarist times of the 1700s. The great explorer Vitus Jonassen Bering almost died as he traveled through Siberia, later exploring Alaska," explained Jim.

Finally reaching the end of six busy weeks of tours, Jim's team summarized their findings. "One thing that really stood out was that there seemed to be almost no collaboration or communication between veterinary and human medicine. The Soviet medical profession viewed veterinarians more as technicians than medical professionals. Overall, their veterinary research programs appeared to be lagging significantly behind those in the US regarding scientific methods and quality of facilities and equipment. One of our conclusions was that Soviet authorities were understating their statistics regarding disease incidence and overstating the effectiveness of their vaccination programs. Finally, we believed they were definitely downplaying the public health importance of zoonotic diseases," Jim said.

Quite unexpectedly, Jim got to meet Premier Nikita Khrushchev on the Fourth of July, 1963 at the US embassy. This day was a holiday for the team. The premier commented to Jim, "You are one of those big Americans they grow."

"I am a blend of the best European stock," Jim replied grinning.

The embassy hosted a Fourth of July reception for hundreds of scientists, distinguished visitors, and Soviet officials. "Somehow, I attracted a lot of attention in and around the embassy. One day I pulled up in a car and got out and was surrounded by Soviet police, not in a threatening way but as if to protect me. I suppose they thought I was a local dignitary. In broken Russian I would ask them, 'Hey, what do you guys want?'" Jim recalled.

The team then traveled to a resort city, Sochi, on the Black Sea, where the Soviet nobility took their holidays. "We stayed there for three days of rest and relaxation. On the second day we were walking on a rocky beach and saw a young girl. We all voiced our greetings to her and she responded in good English asking who we were. I thought she might be on staff with one of the foreign embassies. But she turned out to be a well known Soviet radio singer who had been provided a vacation to the resort as a reward for a job well done. I asked her if she knew any American songs," said Jim. She responded to the group that she knew "Chattanooga

Choo Choo," made popular by the famous Glenn Miller Orchestra. "This was difficult for us to believe, so we asked her to sing it. She did and did it quite well. We were amazed! All the while we were all standing knee deep in the Black Sea. It made for a very interesting memory," he said. From there, they moved on to Leningrad, passing areas where some of the World War II tank wars had occurred.

"A banquet had been planned for us the day before we were to depart the USSR for Finland. But out of nowhere, a Soviet officer announced the event was canceled due to my bad behavior. Apparently, our hosts didn't appreciate my criticism of the antiquated scientific methods being employed at the Soviet institutes that we visited. I just shrugged and suggested to the team that we eat a nice dinner at the hotel restaurant. Many years later, in 2001, at the dedication of the Veterinary Public Health Institute in Berlin, a former Soviet scientist approached me in a restaurant. I did not recognize him," Jim said.

The man looked Jim right in the eyes and said, "We have been on two different sides for a long time, Dr. Steele. Let me salute you as a great opponent!" Then he raised his glass as a salute.

"Then I realized that it was Dr. A. Koulikovskii of the Ivanovsky Institute of Virology in Moscow, whom I had met in 1963. I guess I made an impression on somebody while I was there. I saw him again at a WHO meeting in Geneva and at the WHO Salmonellosis conference in the Netherlands in 1981," Jim said.

"I was beginning to wonder if were going to be allowed to leave the Soviet Union. On August 1 we queued up at the Sheremetyevo Airport. A cadre of military clerks asked us for every kind of document imaginable. As we walked to the plane, I saw an armed soldier at the bottom of the steps and another at the top. I was thinking to myself, *They are going to get me yet!*" But at last, the team was airborne headed for Helsinki, Finland. "On the ground in Helsinki, we all breathed a big sigh of relief. We were greeted by a delegation of Finnish veterinarians who offered us drinks," Jim said.

One of the Finnish vets said with a big smile, "You are free once again and can say whatever you want!"

"That proclamation was the start of a party that lasted for three days. One of the Finnish veterinarians had studied at Kansas State University and had developed a taste for American-style drinks. One night, he entertained the team with a sauna and a swim at a lake along. The staff kept bringing us what seemed like an endless string of martinis. Then they served us frozen vodka with dinner." Jim said. After dinner, Jim was standing up making a toast to his host and the next thing he knew, he was on his back. "The floor just came up and hit me! I think we were all enjoying a little too much of our newfound freedom!"

CHAPTER 21:
ZOONOSES ON THE WORLD STAGE:
THE HISTORIC JOINT WHO/FAO EXPERT
COMMITTEE MEETINGS

The first joint meeting of the WHO/FAO Expert Committee on Zoonoses in December 1950 resulted from numerous requests to the World Health Organization (WHO) and the Food and Agricultural Organization (FAO) for assistance in the understanding of zoonotic diseases by member countries. "I was aggressively recruited to participate by Dr. Martin Kaplan," Jim said. Dr. Kaplan was hired by the WHO in 1947 to establish a section on veterinary public health. Jim and Dr. Kaplan had met for the first time in London at the World Veterinary Association Congress in London, in August 1949.

Dr. Kaplan told Jim, "Whenever I hear about your progress in veterinary public health in the US, I make sure that everyone in WHO is aware of it!" He went on to say, "I am putting together a working committee next year on veterinary public health in Geneva, and I hope you will join us!"

Of course, Jim had recently established the new section of veterinary public health at CDC. "It was so heartwarming to see how veterinary public health was being embraced at WHO and around the world," Jim said proudly.

"I was very excited about the invitation, as I was the youngest member of the committee," Jim said. The group of seventeen veterinarians that Dr. Kaplan assembled was an international *Who's Who* of public veterinary medicine representing Italy, Sweden, France, Brazil, England, Israel, Argentina, Denmark, Indonesia, Switzerland, and the USA.

"Embarking on the trip to Geneva, I arrived in New York only to be greeted by a wintery snowstorm that shut the airport down for a day," Jim recalled. The next day, a special plane was arranged for the president of Trans World Airlines (TWA) bound for Europe. "Somehow, I talked my way onto this flight. I even got to meet the

TWA president. We had a nice chat," Jim said. The plane made a refueling stop in Gander, Newfoundland as was customary in the days of propeller transports. They then headed for Ireland. "I needed to make a courtesy visit with some colleagues there. The TWA president's car drove me to Dublin the day after we arrived. The chief veterinary officer of Ireland was waiting there for me," Jim said. He provided Jim with a tour of the city and the countryside. "Every couple of hours we stopped for a hot toddy. The weather would chill you to the bone!" Jim said.

Jim then traveled to London to visit with a Dr. Ian Beveridge, professor of veterinary pathology at Cambridge University. "Dr. Beveridge wrote some excellent books on disease investigation methods. I met him at the World Veterinary Congress in London in 1949. During my visit, we had some great discussions on the future of WHO and veterinary public health. Ian was a very sharp scientist," Jim said. He later recommended to Dr. Kaplan that WHO consider hiring Dr. Beveridge as a consultant on influenza.

"I then moved on to Holland to investigate the status of foot and mouth disease (FMD). All of Europe was struggling with the disease at the time," Jim said. While in Holland, Jim met Dr. Jerry Callis, a Bureau of Animal Industry virologist on loan to Europe. There was a lot of concern about how to eradicate the disease from Europe and to manage the movement of animals around the continent.

"The next stop was Paris, France," Jim said. The Marshall Plan was being established in Europe, headquartered in Paris. Jim met with a veterinarian from California who was part of a working group there. "This is where I learned what was being done to control bovine tuberculosis and brucellosis in Europe. This knowledge helped me to gain a perspective on the problems on the European continent before joining the WHO meeting in Geneva. It was perfect timing," Jim said.

Jim arrived in Geneva, Switzerland on December 10, a day before the meetings were to commence. "The weather in Geneva was breezy, with the temperatures in the thirties, as I recall. I marveled at the beautiful architecture of the city's buildings and streets. Geneva is situated where the Rhone River flows into Lake Geneva. It is considered to be one of the most global of cities, with many international organizations headquartered there. The International Red Cross was founded in Geneva in 1863," Jim explained.

Dr. Kaplan met Jim at the airport and exclaimed, "Jim, can you believe that this meeting was organized to explore our interests and goals in veterinary public health! Isn't it great?"

Jim was elated to see veterinary public health growing in the international arena. "Our meeting had its seeds from another WHO assembly on tuberculosis that was held in Geneva a few months prior. Dr. Herman Hillable was the chief of tuberculosis for the US Public Health Service at the time and chaired the meeting," Jim said.

The meeting was kicked-off on December 11 by Dr. Andre Cavaillon, one of France's foremost public health officials, who helped to prepare the drafts of the constitution for WHO in 1946. At this time, Dr. Cavaillon assumed the role of secretary general of the ministers of public health for WHO. "You have a very important mission, to identify and study diseases of animals that are a problem in public health. Bovine tuberculosis should be a high priority!" he said. The distinguished members of this first WHO Expert Committee on Zoonoses were as follows:

> Professor Iginio Altara, director general, veterinary services, Rome, Italy
>
> Professor A. Ascoli, director, Institute of Pathology, University of Milan, Milan, Italy
>
> Dr. Hans Bengtsson, medical officer, Royal Medical Council, Stockholm, Sweden
>
> Dr. Ben Blood, chief, veterinary public health, Pan American Sanitary Bureau (PASB), Washington, DC.
>
> Sir Daniel Cabot, president, OIE, Paris, France (chairman)
>
> Dr. Victor Carneiro, Institute of Biology, Sao Paulo, Brazil
>
> Professor T. Dailing, chief veterinary officer, MOA, London, England

Dr. J. Francis, Imperial Pharmaceutical Laboratories, Cheshire, England

Dr. J. van der Hoeden, director, State Veterinary Institute, Tel-Aviv, Israel

Dr. R. M. Mendy, director of zoonoses, MOA, Buenos Aires, Argentina

Dr. N. Plum, State Veterinary Serum Laboratory, Copenhagen, Denmark

Dr. James H. Steele, chief, veterinary public health, CDC, Atlanta, Georgia, USA

Professor J. Verge, National Veterinary Ecology Institute, Seine, France (vice chairman)

Dr. F. K. Waworoentoe, chief veterinary officer, MOA, Jakarta, Indonesia

Dr. M. M. Kaplan, veterinary officer, WHO, Geneva, Switzerland (joint secretariat)

Dr. K. V. L. Kesteven, chief, animal industry branch, Division of Agriculture, FAO, Washington, DC, USA (Joint Secretariat)

Dr. H. T. B. Hall, veterinary consultant, animal industry branch, Division of Agriculture, FAO, Washington, DC, USA

"I was staying in a nice hotel next to a railroad station in Geneva. It wasn't luxurious, but it was quite comfortable. The hotel was far enough from the site of the meetings that cars were needed to shuttle the participants back and forth," Jim recalled. Early in the trip, Jim was invited to Dr. Kaplan's home, where he met his wife, Lenna. "She was a strong supporter of Martin in everything he was trying to accomplish. They both had sympathy and support for the social movement in Europe and the postwar reconstruction. Dr. Kaplan was particularly interested in fostering communication and cooperation with the Eastern Bloc countries," Jim said. Jim's son Jay had been born October 10, 1950. Jim remembered showing off pictures of his son to the Kaplans and others in Geneva.

The meetings were held in the League of Nations building, which had been built in the 1920s. "The conference room was nicely paneled, with green table covers and lots of refreshments. This was my first introduction to hot goat cheese fondue. It was delicious. Our committee members had the support of a full secretarial staff to keep the proceedings of the meetings recorded and transcribed. Everything was well organized," Jim said.

The committee members were equally impressive. Professor A. Ascoli from Milan, Italy was famous for his thermo precipitation anthrax test, which he developed for the detection of anthrax in hides and meat. "He was direct and outspoken in defending the Italian contributions to the advancement of veterinary medicine and public health," Jim said. Dr. Hans Bengtsson from Stockholm was a strong supporter of controlling and eradicating zoonotic diseases for the betterment of public health. Dr. Ben Blood created the first zoonosis center for the Americas in Argentina with the Pan American Sanitary Bureau. Sir Daniel Cabot was the chair of the committee and was a former chief veterinary officer for the United Kingdom. "Sir Daniel Cabot provided me with valuable guidance on the importance of bovine tuberculosis in the world. During the World War II years, many children contracted the disease as they moved to rural areas from the cities to avoid the bombings," Jim said.

Dr. Dailing became chief veterinary officer of the United Kingdom after World War II. "He fully supported Sir Daniel Cabot on the importance of bovine tuberculosis as a public health problem and carried on his work," Jim said. Dr. J. van der Hoeden from Israel was very enthused about the future of veterinary public health. Dr. R. Mendy of Buenos Aires was the first veterinarian from South America to bring veterinary medicine and human medicine together in the struggle to control hydatid disease. "He worked diligently to educate farmers and physicians on the epidemiology of the disease. He also helped Ben Blood establish the Pan American Zoonoses Center in Azul," Jim said. Dr. N. Plum of Denmark would later support Jim in his opposition to vaccination with BCG for the eradication of bovine tuberculosis. "He helped to design a test-and-slaughter program that led to successfully eradicating the disease. Drs. K. Kesteven and H. Hall of FAO were both outspoken scholars and supportive of veterinary public health. At the time of the writing the first draft of this chapter, Jim is the only surviving participant of this first historic meeting.

"After Dr. Cavaillon's opening remarks, the working sessions continued for the next six days. The sessions lasted two hours on average, followed by a break. The day's sessions were followed by the transcription of notes, writing of reports, and seemingly endless proofreading. The output of this historic meeting was profound. It helped to define the zoonoses, veterinary public health and its contributions to human health and the 'one medicine, one health' concepts," Jim said.

The following is excerpted from the report of the 1950 meeting written by Dr. Martin Kaplan:

1.1 Zoonoses are those diseases which are naturally transmitted between vertebrate animals and man. A list of the zoonoses, comprising more than eighty diseases, is contained in the Appendix.

1.2 The field of zoonoses is the major responsibility of veterinary public health and includes the etiology, pathogenesis, diagnosis, transmission and control of these diseases.

1.3 Veterinary public health is all community efforts influencing and influenced by the veterinary medical arts and sciences applied to the prevention of disease, protection of life, and promotion of the well being and efficiency of man.

1.4 Traditionally, veterinary medicine is responsible for the protection of human life against these hazards which result from contact with diseased animals, and animal products contaminated during the processing and delivery of such foods to the consumer. These functions are of basic importance in the public health program. The practice of veterinary public health forms an important consideration in the attainment of health as defined by the WHO: "Health is a state of complete physical, mental and social well being and not merely the absence of disease or infirmity."

1.5 The term veterinary public health is relatively new in the English language, but it has already gained wide acceptance. The group feels that the term describes well the modern concepts of the responsibility of veterinary medicine to the health of the public.

1.6 The public health veterinarian is responsible for a variety of duties which include the following:

(a) Promotion of activities to eradicate animal diseases transmissible to man.

(b) Supervision of inspection and hygiene of all foods of animal origin.

(c) Consultation and liaison with voluntary or official agencies, such as farm organizations, professional groups, and health and agriculture departments.

(d) Development of special statistical services with reference to zoonoses.

(e) Research activities in public health science.

1.7 The above activities are veterinary public health functions regardless of the institution or agency which assumes or is charged with the responsibility for their performance. It is not necessary that they invariably be performed under the direction of a public health agency. The group feels, however, that these functions can be most effectively pursued by specific administrative units within governmental public health organizations, whether in economically advanced or lesser developed countries.

1.8 Effective performance of veterinary public health services depends upon the employment of properly qualified personnel trained to work as an integral part of a public health organization. For this reason advanced public health training is a highly desirable part of the educational background for veterinarians engaged in these activities. Suggested educational qualifications for public health veterinarians will be found in Appendix 1.7.

"Many significant zoonotic diseases were discussed at length during the six days of meetings. This information is well documented in the committee's report which included recommendations on methods for prevention, control and eradication in some instances. The control of tuberculosis in cattle was the first and most important topic on the group's agenda. Bovine tuberculosis was already recognized as one of the most important zoonoses in the world at the time," Jim stated. The WHO Expert Committee on Tuberculosis, which had its fifth session in Geneva from 11-16 September, 1950, made the following statements in their report:

> The Committee recognizes the seriousness of human infection with bovine tuberculosis in countries where the disease of cattle is prevalent. There is danger of transmission of infection by direct contact between diseased cattle and farm workers and their families, as well as from infected food products.

> Reduction in bovine tuberculosis helps to improve the economic and nutritional standards of a country by improving the quality of the milk and the productivity of the cattle.

"I fully agreed with these statements and supported efforts to eradicate bovine tuberculosis worldwide. Recent Scandinavian studies had demonstrated the risk of tuberculosis by droplet infection in cowsheds, especially in children," Jim said. The committee calculated that the bovine population of most countries turned over about every six years, and that the prevention of the disease in young animals could result in significant reductions in human disease in about the same timeframe.

"The recognized method for eradication at the time involved tuberculin testing of all cattle and the slaughter of infected animals," Jim said. Furthermore, the committee concluded in their report that vaccination with BCG or the vole bacillus vaccine should only be considered a "temporary expedient." Jim did not agree and wanted the vaccine to be for research purposes only. "I was adamant about the misuse of the vaccine. This was a heavily debated issue within the group and was a very strong point of contention for me," Jim said. The development and use of tuberculin testing was also discussed. The advantages of the purified protein derivative (PPD), described in the literature as the "purest and most uniform product" used in tuberculin testing was analyzed. "It was also recognized that infection with other mycobacterial organisms such as *M. johnei* and *M. tuberculosis avium* could cause non-specific reactions in animals being tested," Jim said.

The group ended their report on bovine tuberculosis with an 1892 quote by Bernhard Bang, a Danish veterinarian and microbiologist, regarding the use of tuberculin:

> It is found that the tuberculin test is no more perfect than are other things in this world. Sometimes it fails. Animals with a very real degree of tuberculosis will sometimes fail to react, and the same applies to animals with a very slight degree of the disease. Further, a positive reaction has been observed several times in animals in which no tuberculous changes were found on examination of the organs when the animals were slaughtered...but it would be the greatest folly to reject this method because it is not able to give everything we desire.

Much discussion and deliberation were also dedicated to Q fever during this first meeting. The committee concluded the disease had been identified in many countries and could possibly have worldwide distribution. "We also stated that it is an insidious disease that does not usually cause clinical signs in infected animals," Jim said. In addition, *Coxiella burnetti* often survived pasteurization methods in use at the time (142-145° F for ½ hour or 160° F for 15 seconds). "I was pleased that the Third World Health Assembly asked the WHO director-general to conduct a study of the prevalence of Q fever in the world and to better characterize the epidemiology of the disease. It was agreed that research was needed regarding diagnostic tests, assessing the effectiveness of available vaccines and in therapeutics for animals," Jim said.

Anthrax was the next worldwide disease covered by the expert committee. "There was considerable evidence to show that anthrax can be transferred into some countries by feed and fertilizers contaminated in ships which have recently conveyed infected bones and hides," Jim said.

On the topic of anthrax, the committee concluded, "Despite familiarity on the part of farmers with anthrax in livestock where this disease recurs periodically, the onset of an epizootic is frequently difficult to recognize because of the lack of diagnostic signs in the peracute or apoplectic form of the disease found at the beginning of an outbreak. For economic reasons, agricultural workers are loath to lose the value of hides which are salvaged from dead animals, even where anthrax is recognized as the cause of death. Animals are often slaughtered at the first sign of illness for meat salvage as well as for their byproducts. These practices are highly dangerous and must be condemned."

The expert committee also reported that the lack of diagnostic laboratory support for anthrax was the most significant shortfall in obtaining a rapid diagnosis of the disease. "I recommended that countries consider providing low-cost or free vaccination programs to aid in prevention of outbreaks," Jim said. By 1938, the avirulent vaccine developed by Max Sterne, a veterinary scientist and bacteriologist trained at the Onderstepoort Veterinary Institute, South Africa, was in widespread use. Sterne had successfully recognized that the so-called "rough" strain of the organism was not pathogenic when injected in animals. The group also recommended public education programs for agricultural workers on the "dangers of contaminated wounds, scratches and abrasions, the eating of meat from infected animals and the necessity for proper handling and disposal of carcasses." Much detail was provided by the committee in their report on prevention and biosafety in the industrial environment and on the importation of animal byproducts. "I took a listen-and-learn approach during much of this discussion, as I really hadn't had much training or field experience with anthrax. This discussion was quite an education for me!" Jim said.

Psittacosis was thrashed out extensively by the group. It was then described as "a disease of birds and man caused by a virus of the psittacosis-lymphogranuloma group...the disease is world-wide in distribution, with the highest reported prevalence in North America." The complement fixation test was recognized as a valuable diagnostic tool, but the difficulties and labor-intensiveness of the test were also pointed out. One statement in the report described Java Rice Birds as sentinels for detecting psittacosis in aviaries as they are very susceptible to the disease. "I brought up the fact that psittacosis in household birds is recognized as a human health risk," Jim said.

Hydatid disease was the next disease to be addressed. "First, we talked about the global distribution of the disease. At the time it was thought that the highest incidence was in southern South America and the South Pacific regions," Jim said. Based on reports Jim had been hearing, he was concerned that the disease was more widespread and moving into areas that were considered hydatid-free. "I pointed out that wherever domestic ruminants, swine and domestic or wild canids existed, epidemiologically, it is possible to perpetuate the disease in nature," Jim said.

The committee's recommendations focused on eliminating the infection in the reservoir, i.e. wild or domestic dogs. "Iceland once had the world's highest incidence of hydatid disease, but it was just about eliminated through public education campaigns, veterinarian inspection of all slaughtered meat, and treatment of all dogs at least once a year with an approved anthelmintic. At the time the drug of choice was arecoline hydrobromide. Elimination of the stray dog population also was a priority, along with improved practices to prevent the availability of slaughterhouse offal to canidae. Dr. Mendy was invaluable during this discussion, as he had a lot of experience educating farmers and slaughterhouse staff in the handling of offal in Argentina to prevent exposure to domestic and wild canids," Jim said. The committee also proposed a public awareness campaign to be primarily focused on children of school age.

Many other diseases were discussed by the committee during the six-day meeting. "We recommended surveillance studies be undertaken to determine the prevalence of the viral encephaliti-des to include eastern, western, Venezuelan, Japanese B and other dangerous pathogens in this class. The group also recommended that surveys be conducted in all countries to determine the inci-dence of human leptospirosis and to develop better procedures for typing the various strains of the Leptospira organism," Jim re-called. Other questions addressed were:

> What is the role of animals as reservoirs of schistosomiasis?
> What is the best method for the control of trichinosis?
> Can glanders be eradicated in countries where it exists?
>
> How much human salmonellosis is being transmitted from animals to people via food products?
>
> What is the role of animals in the transmission of diseases to man such as influenza, histoplasmosis, toxoplasmosis and various parasitic and fungal diseases?
>
> How significant is the transmission of disease to humans by food of animal origin?

The committee also discussed the importance of veterinary bi-ologic products in the successful prevention of disease in animals. "We recommended the development of internationally recognized standards to assure products are efficacious and safe," Jim said.

Various appendices were developed and attached to the report of this first meeting. "I provided an abbreviated copy of our zoo-notic disease table which identified the etiology, animal reservoirs and more, to be included in the report," Jim said. Another appen-dix described what the group believed was the "basic educational background" for a public health veterinarian. Other appendices covered topics such as the appropriate use of tuberculin in differ-ent species; the Ascoli anthrax test; the Sterne anthrax vaccine; a procedure for ridding wool, hides and hair of the anthrax spore; and treatment of dogs for hydatidosis.

All in all, Jim felt this first meeting of the WHO Expert Com-mittee on Zoonoses had done an excellent job considering that there were only six days of working sessions. "Overall, I was quite pleased with the way things went down. However, I was somewhat disappointed that the committee paid so little attention to brucellosis. The Scandinavian representatives were the only ones that seemed to have any concern about the disease," Jim stated. It was common knowledge that the French were consuming raw dairy products and had a high incidence of Malta fever. Jim knew that Latin America and many other parts of the world also had significant brucellosis problems. This knowledge, along with Jim's experiences at Michigan State, caused him to press for more emphasis on the disease. Interestingly, brucellosis would not be a major topic in either of the later meetings of the committee, in 1959 or 1967. "However, a special committee formed that was devoted totally to brucellosis in Washington, DC, in 1952," Jim said.

"Dr. Kaplan and I worked into the wee hours writing the final reports summarizing the meetings. Dr. Ben Blood provided excellent oversight in this task," Jim said. Toward the end of meeting, it became apparent that the committee lacked in-depth of knowledge of some diseases, such as leptospirosis.

The closing session was somewhat tumultuous. Dr. Kaplan re-emphasized his desire to put a sentence in the report supporting vaccination for bovine tuberculosis. "I was opposed and did not endorse this idea at all. But the committee ultimately compromised and agreed to language stating that vaccination for bovine tuberculosis was to be used for research only," Jim said.

"After the meetings and the reports were completed, I did a little shopping. I bought a crèche for Jay along with some other trinkets. As a favor, I also picked up some gifts from a veterinarian, Dr. Julius Fishbine, at the Paris airport that he wanted delivered to friends and family in the US. I ended up with so many bags I needed assistance at the airports," said Jim.

"I remember being amazed when I learned how many American scientists were studying at schools around Europe on this trip. I wanted to learn all about where they were and what kind of projects they were working on," Jim said. He boarded a Douglas DC-6 in Geneva for the trip home. He traveled back via Ireland,

Newfoundland, and New York, and then on to Atlanta for the Christmas holidays. "I was really looking forward to spending some quality time with my new son, Jay!" said Jim.

The second meeting of the Expert WHO/FAO Committee on Zoonoses was held in Stockholm, Sweden, 11-16 August, 1958. "I asked Aina to travel with me this time, and she happily agreed. We were both hoping to learn more about our family histories during the trip. We were very excited to be traveling together on this adventure. We booked our trip to Stockholm on the Norwegian Steamship Line," Jim recalled.

While in New York before embarking on the steamship, Jim visited the Staten Island quarantine station to try to learn about which diseases were a problem for the immigrants. The United States had to be vigilant for diseases such as typhus, cholera and smallpox that could be imported into the country. As early as the mid-1800s, physicians inspected passengers on ships arriving at New York Harbor. "Up to one in six immigrants were held in quarantine. Interestingly, the quarantine service was slowly phasing out and many federal employees were being transferred," Jim stated.

"We had a nice stateroom on the ship. We spent a lot of time on the deck enjoying the sun. I recall that Aina didn't have a lot of energy and took frequent naps during the six-day trip. All in all, the voyage was nice, with near perfect weather. The service on the ship was excellent. It was almost like a vacation, as part of my expenses were being covered by the WHO and the Public Health Service," Jim said. They met a number of Americans on the ship, including some viral experts from the University of Michigan and the New York Health Department who were traveling to attend a WHO meeting on viral diseases.

On one of the last nights of the trip, Jim hosted a cocktail party for some of the Americans aboard ship. "I asked the chef to prepare and serve steak tartare, which is basically ground meat topped with a raw egg. This delicacy has always been one of my favorite foods. Many people are surprised that I would eat such risky food as a public health man!" Jim said. The captain joined them for the party, and a great time was had by all. Of course, there was a lively discussion about veterinary public health. The boat docked at Bergen and later in Copenhagen, to discharge passengers. "I met with friends at the WHO office in Copenhagen, but there wasn't enough time to visit the central office. I remember wearing a new blue flannel suit that brought quite a few compliments," Jim recalled. The next stop was Oslo, Norway, which was the home port for the ship.

"Aina and I spent two nights in Oslo in a fine old hotel. On one of the evenings, the chief veterinary officer of Norway and his wife entertained us. We had a marvelous time. We then boarded a train that took us from Oslo to Stockholm. It was a six-hour journey in a parlor car. Aina loved the train ride. We were both enthralled by the magnificent scenery," said Jim. Along the way, Jim pondered the history of how a Swedish king had ruled Norway until the country achieved independence in 1905. Sweden remained neutral during World Wars I and II, but provided high quality iron ore to Germany from 1940 to 1945.

Upon arrival at Stockholm, they checked into the hotel. "Aina didn't waste any time calling her cousins. I was going to be very busy with the World Veterinary Congress, and she was looking forward to visiting with relatives. It was a perfect opportunity for her." Jim stated.

Aina's cousins lived in a Stockholm suburb. She had to take a commuter train to get close to their neighborhood. The cousin she met told her, "My home is just a few steps down the road." A "few steps" turned into a very long walk. Aina explained her medical condition, and they took a taxi the rest of the way. "During the ensuing week, Aina spent practically every day with a different cousin. She could speak Swedish, so there were no language problems. They treated her like royalty," Jim said. Since Aina was not staying in the hotel room during the meeting, Jim invited John Miles, a physician and virologist on the committee from New Zealand, to stay with him.

"I was so happy to be able to attend most of the meetings of the WHO Expert Committee on Viral Diseases. This was held just before the meeting of our WHO/FAO Expert Committee on Zoonoses," Jim recalled. He remembers sitting with a Russian military scientist who supposedly had developed an intranasal modified live virus vaccine for avian influenza. "This intrigued me. This was the first time I had ever heard of an intranasal vaccine," said Jim. Most of the participants were leading physicians from around the world with special knowledge in virology. Dr. K. F. Meyer was probably the most distinguished veterinarian attending.

"Only four of the original members of the committee from the 1950 meeting attended the second session in 1958, including Drs. Mendy, Blood, Dalling, and, of course, me," Jim said. Dr. Martin Kaplan was with the WHO as the chief veterinary officer and served as the joint secretary for the meeting. Several new distinguished members joined the group. Professor M. Abdussalam represented the College of Animal Husbandry from Lahore, Pakistan. He had an excellent reputation as a veterinary parasitologist and later became Dr. Kaplan's deputy. Dr. Abdussalam later replaced Dr. Kaplan when he stepped down to become the chief science officer and deputy director for the WHO. Dr. W. Charles Cockburn was director of the Epidemiological Research Laboratory in London, England and was a *Salmonella* and enteric disease expert. He was intimately involved in the laboratory outbreak of Marburg disease in Germany in 1967. Dr. K. F. Meyer was one of the most noted veterinarians and scientists alive at the time. He had retired from the University of California, San Francisco in 1954 but was still very active. Jim was responsible for inviting Dr. Meyer and recommended that he chair the committee, which he did.

Dr. J. A. R. Miles was a professor of microbiology from the University of Otago, New Zealand, and served as the vice chairman of the committee. He had published extensively on psittacosis. This disease was to be a major topic at this meeting. Jim and Dr. Miles became longtime friends and colleagues. Dr. Jorgen Muller was head of the *Salmonella* department of the State Veterinary Serum Laboratory in Copenhagen, Denmark and was considered a world-renowned *Salmonella* expert. He was also researching the use of irradiation for pasteurization. Thirty-five years later, Jim talked to him again about the use of radiation in food. Dr. Jorgen commented, "Jim, you can't get people to think about irradiating food when they won't even accept electricity that comes from nuclear power!"

Dr. A. W. Stableforth was director of the UK Veterinary Laboratory and Investigation Service in Weybridge, Surrey, England. He and Jim had many in-depth discussions about leptospirosis. "Jim, do you think this could become a significant worldwide problem?" he asked. At the time, Jim thought the disease was definitely worldwide but more of a sporadic problem. Professor K. Wagener was dean of the College of Veterinary Science at Hanover, Germany. He had done his PhD under K. F. Meyer and was a botulism expert.

Dr. Earl Chamberlayne was a public health veterinarian with the Pan American Sanitary Bureau in Washington, DC. Jim thought he was a good administrator, but he didn't seem to contribute much to the meetings. Sir Thomas Dalling had retired from his position as the chief veterinary officer for the UK and was now a consultant to the Food and Agriculture Organization in Rome, Italy. He told Jim, "Well, you somehow got me invited to this meeting, but you and Kaplan are the only ones that know what you are talking about!" Dr. Ervin Eichhorn was the head of the Animal Production Branch of the FAO in Rome and a noted foot and mouth disease specialist.

"I was very pleased with the members of this second committee. I knew in my bones that we would make lots of progress!" Jim said. Of course, the first meeting in 1950 had been a great success. Since that historic event, the Pan American Health Organization had started its veterinary public health division; Jim's rabies vaccination programs were up and running in the Americas with much success; and veterinary public health programs were emerging in many American universities. "But I was concerned that little had been done in Asia and Africa," Jim lamented. Jim felt he was widely accepted in the scientific community, and he believed veterinary public health was becoming well established in the world. He wanted to continue to branch out across the globe. "At that year's American Veterinary Medical Association meeting, Surgeon General Leroy Burney strongly endorsed the concept of veterinary public health to a large general audience. I was so proud. Things were really beginning to work," Jim said.

"Our first order of business at this second meeting of the Joint WHO/FAO Expert Committee on Zoonoses was to reevaluate the definition of a zoonosis," Jim said. The definition from the 1950 meeting stated that zoonoses were defined as "those diseases which are naturally transmitted between vertebrate animals and man." The following is an excerpt from the 1959 report on this discussion:

> Views have been expressed in the literature proposing such terms as antropozoonoses (diseases transmitted from animals to man) and zooanthroponoses (diseases transmitted from man to animals). The Committee considers that the introduction of such terms into general use would have many drawbacks, including the fact that the definition as given above is now widely recognized and accepted as delineating a very important group of diseases common to man and animals. Recent findings, however, have shown that, apart from microorganisms and parasites causing latent infection, there are other isolates, as yet not clearly defined in nature and of which many cannot so far be incriminated as producers of disease, which can be recovered from both man and animals. Some of these isolates have common characteristics, and there is good reason to suspect that they can be transmitted between man and animals. The Committee, therefore, has slightly modified the definition of zoonoses given above, namely, "Those diseases and infections which are naturally transmitted between vertebrate animals and man."

"At this time, more than one hundred diseases were being recognized as zoonotic. I had put a lot of effort into compiling this list," Jim said. The committee stated in its report that the prevention, control and eradication of these diseases "are responsibilities of considerable magnitude in every country" and went on to state that "attention to zoonoses must be given at all levels of government—local, municipal, provincial, and national." The report reflected on successes with bovine tuberculosis, brucellosis, and rabies and stated that the committee now wished to focus on programs that could be useful in the battle against zoonoses throughout the world. The committee also recommended routine reporting of zoonotic disease outbreaks by physicians and veterinarians on the global level so to assess the severity of the diseases and to develop appropriate disease control programs.

In their report of the second meeting, the committee noted the Pan American Zoonoses Center that was established in 1956 in Azul, Argentina. The committee lauded the work of the new center and recommended that it "be supported to the fullest possible extent."

Unlike the 1950 meeting, where it was barely mentioned, salmonellosis became a major topic of discussion at the second meeting. More than 500 different serotypes of *Salmonella* were known at the time, with most of them found in both people and animals. The committee reported that the true incidence of salmonellosis in humans and animals was increasing. The report went on to state:

> The close co-operation of the medical and veterinary professions is required before the problem of salmonellosis on both the national and international scale can be solved.

> Human salmonellosis, therefore, is common in many countries, and in countries where observations have been made over a period of time it appears to be increasing. It causes preventable deaths in the very young and very old, and is responsible for much minor disability and discomfort in persons of all ages. Furthermore, it is an example of the distasteful transfer of bowel pathogens from a man to man and from animals to man.

"Our discussion of salmonellosis was extensive. It included an overview of the disease in poultry, cattle, pigs, sheep, horses, and pet species. An extensive look was taken at food-borne *Salmonella* transmission by poultry, beef, veal, pork, milk, fish, and vegetables. *Salmonella* in animal food and fertilizers was also examined," Jim recalled. Jim's firsthand experience investigating *Salmonella* outbreaks as a Public Health Service officer made him an invaluable contributor to this discussion. The committee's final recommendations for control measures against salmonellosis included reporting of cases, food-handler education, proper refrigeration of foods, effective pasteurization of milk, hygienic production and storage of eggs and egg products, sterilization of animal food that was at high risk for contamination, and high standards of cleanliness for slaughterhouses.

Broadening the list of recognized reservoir hosts for leptospirosis became a major focus of the second meeting. Although rodent species and dogs were traditionally considered the "primary animal carriers" as noted in their report, the committee also underscored the roles of pigs, cattle, sheep, goats and horses in the epidemiology of the disease. In addition, a wide range of wildlife species was listed, including bats, mongooses, bandicoots, shrews, hedgehogs, jackals, foxes, opossums, raccoons, skunks, wildcats and others. Persistent shedding of the organism was highlighted as making this disease especially insidious in nature. The committee also pointed out that some leptospires have a single host while others, such as *L. canicola*, have multiple hosts. *L. canicola* can be found primarily in the dog, but also in cattle and swine. At the time, laboratory diagnosis was achieved primarily by animal inoculation and serial serological tests. Serotyping and serogrouping of leptospires was being done at six WHO/FAO reference laboratories around the world.

For prevention, the committee emphasized disinfecting contaminated environments and preventing exposure of people to infected animals by various hygienic means. "Vaccines were still in their infancy, and we strongly recommended more work in this area. Penicillin was considered the de facto antibiotic of choice in humans at the time. But we agreed as a committee that there was no solid scientific evidence to support this claim," Jim recalled.

Bovine tuberculosis was revisited at the second meeting to document progress with respect to control of the disease and to clarify some of the points from the first report. The committee recognized the considerable progress that had been made since the first meeting in utilizing their recommendations to test and slaughter reactors. "Many countries had achieved near-free or free status, including Norway, Finland, Denmark, USA, Canada, the Netherlands, Switzerland, Great Britain, and Germany. Although there were several known types of tuberculin in use around the world, we still recommended the purified protein derivative (PPD) to be the best option available," Jim stated. The problem of non-specific reactors, or false positives, to the tuberculin test was still a problem in some countries. "We reiterated our opinion that vaccination was still not considered a viable option in cattle tuberculosis eradication programs. We also advised against chemotherapy for the disease," Jim said. The committee also made mention of the bovine form of tuberculosis in animals other than cattle, including monkeys, dogs, cats, parrots, goats, sheep, pigs and horses.

Anthrax had been covered extensively in the first meeting's report and was once again given a lot of attention at the 1959 meeting. The committee noted that this disease was likely being highly underreported in the world; there were possibly ten times as many cases as were being reported. "We approached the disease from the agricultural and industrial standpoints. In agriculture, the main source of infection was by contact with contaminated carcasses, wool, hair and hides. So we recommended that services be made available for rapid diagnoses based on blood smears or the Ascoli precipitation test. We further recommended that carcasses be destroyed by incineration if possible or burial in a pit two meters deep covered with lime. Vaccination of animals at risk in endemic areas was recommended every six months. Anthrax education programs should be instituted to inform those in agricultural enterprises how to deal with the disease. Finally, we made many special recommendations when anthrax was suspected in the abattoir," said Jim.

In industry, cutaneous infection by animal byproducts, hides and skins, was the major risk for workers. Although disinfection appeared to be a practical means of control, the committee knew of no effective means that was backed by good science. A comprehensive annex was included in the report that provided guidelines for industrial operations dealing with the hides and hair of animals. "Vaccines for humans working in this business were showing some promise at the time, but the committee made no specific recommendations," Jim recalled.

Once again, psittacosis was given much attention at this meeting. In its report, the committee provided an overview of the disease, including the species affected, microbiological and serological diagnostic tests and treatment regimens. Free-flying pigeons were noted as a possible, yet rare, source of human infection. The committee recommended a thirty-day isolation practice for birds being moved internationally. Suspicious birds should be tested. "Bird food impregnated with tetracycline was offered as an option to control the disease, but we noted that this option was still being researched. We wanted the industry to wait until this methodology was proven. Dr. Meyer and I would be spending a lot of time on that one." Jim said.

Q fever was once again discussed. "The committee regretted to report that despite research advances on the disease since 1950, recommendations could still not be made for an effective control program. Pasteurization of milk would require increasing routine temperatures by several degrees. In addition, vaccination of workers at risk was recommended, but there were reports of undesirable reactions. Vaccination of cattle was reported to be disappointing as well. Finally, the complement fixation test was not sensitive enough to detect all infected animals," Jim stated. The "good news" reported by the committee was that treatment with broad-spectrum antibiotics seemed to be fairly effective.

Arthropod-borne encephalitides had not been covered extensively at the first meeting but received more attention at this second gathering. With respect to mosquito-borne viral diseases, western equine encephalomyelitis was given the most attention. The committee reported that warm weather and sufficient moisture to nurture mosquito and bird populations aided in increasing the risk for the disease. Tick-borne viral diseases were also covered, including the louping-ill group, Omsk and Kyasanur forest disease, and tick-borne encephalitis. "Mosquito and tick control utilizing airborne DDT dusting was found to be up to 99 percent effective in Russia. The Russian mouse-brain vaccine was being used for timber workers and others that had to work among the tick-infested areas but was causing some severe reactions. Finally, normal pasteurization of milk would not kill the tick-borne viruses," Jim said.

Much attention was given again to hydatidosis. The committee provided extensive recommendations, as in its first report. "The successes in eradicating the disease in Iceland were lauded and considered a model for the world to follow," Jim remembered. Arecoline hydrobromide was still considered to be the drug of choice to eliminate the parasite in dogs. However, the drug caused severe vomiting and did not always clear the infection. Therefore, the committee recommended research to develop a better anthelmintic.

The WHO Expert Committee on Respiratory Diseases asked this committee to conduct a joint session to consider the possible roles of animal influenza in human influenza. "Swine influenza emerged about the same time as the severe human pandemic of influenza in 1918. There was some evidence that the swine infection originated in humans at that time. Recently published sequencing work and phylogenetic analyses now suggests that the genes encoding the 1918 virus were derived from an avian-related influenza agent," Jim stated. In 1957, a human pandemic of type A influenza occurred, which prompted the WHO to conduct a serological survey in animals residing in twenty-five countries. The results of this survey were not compiled at the time of the committee's meeting, but the members were aware of type A influenza in horses, swine, poultry and ducks and recommended that the WHO and FAO continue to conduct such surveys and additional research to try to ascertain the connection.

Several other zoonotic diseases were given attention for the first time at the second meeting. Congenital toxoplasmosis was listed as a tragic cause of human neurological disease. The committee noted that few laboratories in the world were equipped to diagnose toxoplasmosis and recommended that the WHO and FAO work to improve the availability of good diagnostics. Listeriosis was listed as a disease that was being reported with greater frequency, and it was likely being misdiagnosed by physicians. Cutaneous and visceral larva migrans was mentioned as a common source of dermatitis, generalized visceral reactivity and sometimes death in humans around the world. The committee recommended further investigation in countries where the disease was endemic. Dermatomycosis, human and animal ringworm, was discussed; the committee stated that control of the disease would require the "detection and elimination of reservoirs of infection." In addition, it recommended research into better treatment modalities. The committee also discussed liver and blood flukes as problems in humans in some developing countries where food and water contained cercariae. "Cat scratch disease was being reported by several countries at the time. Most infections seemed to be associated with a cat scratch; but, of course, an etiological agent had not yet been isolated. Because cats did not display signs of disease, we surmised that they may be only a mechanical carrier of the agent. There were so many diseases to review and very little time to do it. All we could do was set the stage for further study of many important zoonotic diseases," Jim said.

"We also discussed the importance of wild animal reservoirs of many of the zoonotic diseases. Because wild animals pose a huge challenge for control measures, it was recommended that veterinarians work closely with epidemiologists, ecologists, microbiologists, parasitologists, botanists, geologists and climatologists to better understand their role in zoonotic diseases," Jim observed. The committee recommended further work toward the detection of enzootic foci of zoonotic diseases through studies of topography, soil, vegetation and other environmental factors.

A discussion of what the committee called "emerging zoonoses" was held for the first time at the 1959 meeting. The report included the following passage:

New disease entities or previously unsuspected human-animal disease relationships are being reported with increasing frequency. It is clear that host-parasite-environment interactions are constantly changing, and this, together with the availability of more refined tools for biological study, no doubt partially explains these observations...It is important, therefore, to clarify wherever possible the natural history of specific disease agents and to be alert to the possible emergence of new zoonoses.

The committee was pleased that the WHO/FAO was considering "specific studies in this direction." The report went on to state:

For example, one of the failures in studies on communicable diseases up to now has been our inability to follow the progression of disease in geographical areas at different points of time.

"Based on this strategy, we further recommended that serum banks be created for different species and age groups of animals and humans such that retrospective studies could be conducted in the future to help determine when certain new zoonotic diseases emerged," Jim said. The committee also discussed what it called "animal orphan viruses," such as the entero-cytopathogenic human orphan viruses (ECHO). These agents had been isolated and identified in both humans and animals but were not yet tied to any clinical disease. "So we ended up calling them viruses in search of a disease." Jim recalled. He had heard Dr. Robert Huebner of NIH make that statement sometime earlier.

After the report for the meeting was drafted, Jim was piecing together in his mind the next logical steps for veterinary public health. "I could see the need for a veterinary public health officer in the WHO office in Copenhagen to direct European operations. This appointment would lead naturally to establishing a veterinary public health division in all European and Eastern Bloc countries. Holland had established the first veterinary public health program in Europe, led by Dr. E. H. Kampelmacher. He was doing some excellent work on *Salmonella* contamination of estuaries. But, unfortunately, it would be another twenty years before other European countries would begin establishing programs in veterinary public health," Jim recalled.

"Dr. Kaplan and I had long discussions about the future of veterinary public health. They always centered on the need for more regional offices and more international meetings. We worked closely with Dr. Francisco Dy, a retired Public Health Service medical officer who was the director of the Western Pacific Regional WHO office in Manila, to plan a meeting in Japan in 1959 to focus on the importance of veterinary public health. I also got the US Army Veterinary Corps involved in the planning process. The meeting helped to get things moving in the Far East. My good friend and colleague Dr. Yoshiro Ozawa was working on his PhD at Michigan State University at the time under Dr. Stafseth. Dr. Ozawa became a lifelong friend and a strong champion of veterinary public health throughout his career. He later spent the balance of his career with FAO," said Jim.

Jim and Dr. Kaplan also planned a meeting to discuss veterinary public health in Africa. This event was hosted in October of 1960 in Nairobi, Kenya. Later in 1964, a meeting was held in Lahore, Pakistan to plant the seeds for veterinary public health in the Middle East. "Dr. Kaplan stayed in his position with the WHO for another ten years," Jim stated. At the closing session of the meeting, Dr. K. F. Meyer stood up and announced, "I now turn the leadership over to James Steele."

After the WHO/FAO meeting, Jim and Aina traveled south to Geneva by train. From there they trekked through the south of Sweden by train and on to Denmark, following the Rhine River. "The new chief veterinary officer of Denmark met us in Copenhagen and put on a wonderful reception for us at his home. Next, we rode by train all through Germany. We made a transfer in Cologne and were routed through Frankfort to Geneva. Somehow I lost my ticket and had to buy another one, only to find the original the bottom of our suitcase after we returned home!

"The tour through Europe was marvelous, but Aina was getting really tired. She was delighted to be back in Geneva. Dr. Kaplan arranged a hostel with a big, comfortable room for us. He was such a loyal friend and colleague, always looking after me," Jim recalled.

Jim and Martin met to finish writing the report for the second meeting. "We also worked on a list of priorities for the veterinary public health program. In addition, I wrote some proposals and endorsements for Dr. Kaplan to present to WHO," Jim said. Jim and Aina spent another nine days in Geneva. Aina was spending most of her time enjoying the garden at the hostel, as she couldn't tolerate much walking.

Next, Jim and Aina flew to Madrid, Spain, where Jim visited with Colonel Charlie Munoz. Jim had met Colonel Munoz in Puerto Rico about thirteen years earlier. He had also earned an MPH at Harvard and was now serving in the United States Air Force. "There was considerable interest in veterinary public health in Spain, and with Colonel Munoz's help and the assistance of the WHO, we compiled an excellent framework for their fledgling program," Jim said. Spain was still in the grips of the fascist regime of Francisco Franco, who remained head of state until his death in 1975.

After their stop in Spain, Jim and Aina flew to the Portugal World Tropical Medicine meeting. "It was now the first week of September and Aina was anxious to get home," Jim remembered. After the meeting, they flew out of Lisbon and made the grueling propeller plane ride back to Atlanta.

"I was thrilled with the outcome of this second historic meeting of the Joint FAO/WHO Expert Committee on Zoonoses and believed veterinary public health was now on very solid ground," Jim said. In addition to the international meetings and visits he was making, Jim, Mildred Galton and other collaborators were publishing many scientific papers together at the time. "Things were really going our way. And it was so nice to have Aina along to share in the experience and to keep me company. I think she really enjoyed this trip," said Jim.

The third session of the Joint FAO/WHO Expert Committee on Zoonoses was held in Geneva, Switzerland on December 6-12,

1966. "I traveled alone to this meeting. On the way in, I traveled to Langenegg, Austria to meet with Dr. Konrad Eugster and his family. Konrad is an Austrian veterinarian who wanted to immigrate to the US to complete his graduate studies. I later sponsored him to become a US citizen. He went on to have a very successful career in diagnostic veterinary medicine at Texas A&M University as a virologist and later as an administrator," Jim said. The Eugster family members were farmers, but were avid skiers. "Somehow they found some large ski shoes for me and we headed for the slopes! Forty years later, a picture of me skiing was presented to me as a remembrance by Kathe Eugster, Konrad's wife." Jim said smiling. The picture is still hanging on the wall of Jim's home at the time of this writing.

Only six of the committee members in attendance at the second meeting attended this session, including Dr. Raul Mendy, Dr. K. F. Meyer, Dr. John Miles, Dr. Ervin Eichhorn, Dr. Martin Kaplan and Jim. Just before the meeting, Dr. Kaplan discussed the appointments for key positions for the session. In no time, the committee had appointed Jim as committee chairman. Drs. Kaplan and Eichhorn served as joint secretaries. The new additions to the committee were as follows:

> Professor B. Babudieri, Instituto Superiore di Sanita, Rome, Italy (vice chairman)
> Dr. M. R. Dhanda, Director, Indian Veterinary Research Institute, Izatnagar, U. P., India
> Dr. E. H. Kampelmacher, head of the Laboratory for Zoonoses, National Institute of Public Health, Utrecht, Netherlands
> Professor G. S. Nelson, Department of Parasitology, London School of Hygiene and Tropical Medicine, London, England
> Professor A. Rafyi, dean, Faculty of Veterinary Medicine, University of Tehran, Tehran, Iran (vice chairman)
> Dr. B. Rosicky, director, Institute of Parasitology, Czechoslovak Academy of Sciences, Prague, Czechoslovakia
> Professor C. W. Schwabe, chairman, Department of Epidemiology and Preventive Medicine, School of Veteri-

nary Medicine, University of California, Davis, CA, USA
Professor E. J. L. Soulsby, chairman, Department of Veterinary Biology, School of Veterinary Medicine, University of Pennsylvania, Philadelphia, PA, USA
Dr. M. Abdussalam, Veterinary Public Health, WHO, Geneva, Switzerland
Dr. P. N. Acha, Communicable Disease Branch, Regional Office for the Americas, Pan American Sanitary Bureau, Washington, DC, USA
Dr. R. F. Fagan, Wyeth Laboratories, Philadelphia, PA, USA
Dr. E. S. Tierkel, National Institute of Communicable Diseases, New Delhi, India

Once again, the committee members were leaders in veterinary medicine from around the globe. Professor Babudieri was known for his fine work to gain a better understanding of Q fever in cattle. The spread of the disease had been blamed on American troops from the North Africa campaign in World War II but was indigenous to the Italian countryside. Dr. Dhanda confirmed that cholera had no animal reservoir. Dr. Kampelmacher did some excellent work with *Salmonella* and was a staunch supporter of food irradiation for years. Dr. Nelson was a parasitologist and an old friend of Jim's from Kenya who was a tapeworm expert.

Dr. Rosicky, a PhD parasitologist, had argued that *Pneumocystis carnii* was zoonotic and had a rodent reservoir. Dr. Schwabe was an internationally known veterinarian and also a parasitologist and epidemiologist. He would later become known as the father of veterinary epidemiology. He and Jim were great friends for years. Dr. Soulsby was an expert in veterinary parasitology and later became dean of the School of Veterinary Medicine at Cambridge University. Dr. Acha, a renowned public health veterinarian, was serving as the chief of the Pan American Sanitary Bureau's (PASB) Veterinary Public Health since 1960. "I considered the PASB's veterinary public health program the best in the world at the time," Jim stated.

On the first day, Dr. P. Dorolle, deputy director-General of WHO, opened the meeting and welcomed the participants. The committee decided to update the topics covered in the second session and to review some new diseases, including parasitic diseases of major public health importance. "I pushed the committee to put special emphasis on characterizing the epidemiology of the zoonotic diseases in the next report. There had been some debate on whether or not ectoparasitic diseases constituted zoonoses. The committee decided to list only those that penetrate into the body of the host. We were getting down to some of the nitty-gritty stuff," Jim said.

Once again, the committee commenced its session by reviewing the definition of a zoonosis. The latest version read, "...those diseases and infections which are naturally transmitted between vertebrate animals and man." Although there was some argument that this definition excluded diseases produced by non-infectious agents (e.g., toxins) and some infections that animals might acquire from humans, the decision was made to leave the current definition alone. "I reported to the committee that the number of recognized zoonoses was now over 150. In our report, the committee once again laid heavy responsibility on the governments of the world to establish prevention, control and eradication programs for this class of diseases. We also cited success stories with bovine tuberculosis, brucellosis and rabies as examples of what can be accomplished with well designed, well funded programs," Jim recalled.

The committee also prepared definitions of other important terms in this report for the first time. These included the following:

> *Prevention* consists of measures to protect man or animals against disease. These may frequently be independent of measures aimed at bringing the disease under control.

> *Control* consists of measures to reduce the prevalence or incidence of disease or infection in animals and man.

> *Eradication* is the total elimination of the etiological agent from a region.

The committee's report also included a section on the role of operations research in developing prevention, control and eradication programs. Operations research is an interdisciplinary branch of mathematics which uses modeling and statistics to maximize economic potential or to minimize risks. The committee encouraged countries to train and recruit personnel in agriculture with these skills so that they could be applied as needed. In addition, the committee highlighted the importance of sound disease reporting programs utilizing standard nomenclature and classification systems as established by the National Institutes of Health and the US Public Health Service. "I emphasized that reports of confirmed animal disease should come from diagnostic laboratories and meat inspection services. We also outlined the concept of surveillance as defined by Dr. Alex Langmuir, who created the Epidemic Intelligence Service (EIS) at CDC in 1951," Jim said. Dr. Langmuir was quoted as follows:

> Organizations with the necessary equipment, personnel, and financial support should consider establishing surveillance programmes that would entail "continued watchfulness over the distribution and trends of incidence [of a disease] through systematic collection, consolidation and evaluation of morbidity and mortality reports and other relevant data. Intrinsic in the concept is the regular dissemination of the basic data and interpretation to all who have contributed and to all others who need to know."

A special section of the committee's report of the third session was directed at emphasizing the importance of zoonoses as occupational hazards and the related economic implications. "We spoke about the changes in agricultural and industrial practices and how these changes shift the patterns of zoonotic diseases. I had a special interest in these topics. For example, brucellosis had shifted from primarily a food-borne illness to a disease transmitted by contact or by inhalation in the meatpacking business, or through the practice of veterinary medicine," Jim said.

A much broader range of infectious agents and diseases was reviewed by the committee at this third meeting. What follows is an interesting sampling of observations and recommendations made at the meeting based on new research data at the time:

Arboviruses –The distribution is still unknown in many countries.

Japanese encephalitis virus – May be brought north by migrating birds and possibly overwinters in birds as a latent infection. There is no evidence that pigs are a reservoir. Bats may have a latent infection.

Western equine encephalitis virus – Birds are amplifier hosts. Small rodents can be infected and be unapparent carriers.

Venezuelan equine encephalitis virus – Mammals, rather than birds, may be the main reservoir.

Tick-borne encephalitis – All strains survive transstadially in vector ticks.

Influenza in animals and its relationship to human influenza –

- Swine influenza strains of type A have not changed significantly in the twenty years preceding the meeting.

- Swine can be infected by human strains.

- Man can be artificially infected with the equine strains.

- Numerous type A strains have been isolated from wild fowl and poultry in North America and Europe.

- Influenza type B can be transmitted from man to laboratory monkeys.

- Dogs and cats don't seem to be important in influenza epidemiology.

- Further investigation of animal influenza is warranted to determine if animals are reservoirs of human infection.

Herpes B infection in monkeys – Rhesus monkeys from Southeast Asia have been shown to be naturally infected. New world monkeys do not appear to be infected. Handlers of monkeys should observe strict hygienic precautions.

Poxvirus infections – Cowpox (vaccinia) infection in man is still frequent where hand milking is practiced. Monkeypox transmission to man has not been observed or attempted.

Q Fever – Recently, the indirect fluorescent antibody (FA) technique has become valuable for diagnosis. The direct FA is used to detect infected ticks in nature.

Bedsonial (psittacosis, ornithosis) infections – Ducks, turkeys, and pigeons are major sources of infection for man. Psittacine birds moving internationally should receive 45 days of prophylactic treatment with tetracycline.

Salmonellosis – Special attention should be given to the resistance of *Salmonella* to antibiotics. Irradiation of food and feed may become an effective means of preventing *Salmonella* infections.

Bovine tuberculosis – Extensive field trials are needed to determine the value of chemoprophylaxis. In the opinion of the Committee, vaccination of cattle still has no place in the control or eradication of this disease.

Anthrax – Further work is needed on the anthrax toxins and on the pathogenesis.

Leptospirosis – Further research is required related to prevention or curing shedder states.

Colibacillosis – A possible hazard to human beings ingesting *E. coli* of animal origin has been revealed by the discovery of the phenomenon of resistance factor transfer from *E. coli* to other intestinal organisms, including pathogens such as *Shigella* and *Salmonella.*

Tularemia – Control is based on avoidance of exposure.

Listeriosis – It is a not uncommon cause of abortion in women and of infections in the newborn.

Plague – The possibility that the human flea, *Pulex irritans,* may be a vector of infection has caused much concern.

Staphylococcosis – There is convincing evidence that some outbreaks traceable to milk and milk products are caused by staphylococci of bovine origin.

Borreliosis – There is still no evidence that every strain of *Borrelia* found in murine animals and some other small rodents is pathogenic in man, and further study of this problem is necessary.

Dermatophytosis – The Committee recommends further surveys and research in human and animal dermatophytoses and systemic mycoses. Epidemiologic studies are also needed, particularly in rural areas. The teaching of these subjects in veterinary or medical schools should not be neglected.

Toxoplasmosis – The Committee recommends that sera of human and animal origin be prepared and made available to diagnostic laboratories as serologic standards. It also recommends that national and other laboratories be encouraged to produce diagnostic antigens.

Leishmaniasis – Further research on the zoonotic aspects of the leishmaniases should include detailed studies of the varying epidemiologic patterns in different geographic areas, with reference to vertebrate susceptibility, host preferences and biting habits of vectors, and possible immunologic and biochemical differences in the parasite strains.

African trypanosomiasis – Methods for clearly distinguishing *T. brucei* from *T. rhodesiense* and *T. gambiense* are urgently needed. Until this has been achieved, there can be little progress in determining the role of lower animals in the epidemiology of this disease.

American trypanosomiasis – Little is known of the vector species involved in the transmission of *T. cruzi* among wild mammals, or of the invasion of human dwellings by sylvatic species of reduviid insects. The zoonotic aspects of Chagas' disease require much further investigation.

Pneumocystis carinii – Further studies are required to clarify intraspecific and interspecific transmission, the influence of nutritional and other stress factors, and pathogenesis in man and animals.

Malaria – It seems that the natural occurrence of simian malaria in man is rare, and therefore the importance of malaria as a zoonosis should not be exaggerated.

Echinococcosis – Since the last meeting, progress has been made in almost all areas of echinococcosis research and there has been demonstrable progress in control, particularly in New Zealand.

Taeniasis and Cysticercosis – Since cattle develop a good level of immunity to re-infection with *C. bovis*, it would appear valuable to investigate the usefulness of artificially-produced immunity as a control measure.

Research is required to determine the importance of cysticerci of taeniids that parasitize carnivores as a cause of human cysticercosis, particularly the cerebral form.

Trematode infections – Unless effective biological control measures are discovered and a major effort directed against the snails, control will probably be impractical.

Nematode infections – There is a need for increased awareness on the part of physicians, veterinarians, and the general public of the danger of infection from dogs.

After the meeting was concluded, Jim, Dr. Kaplan, and Dr. Miles, the appointed *rapporteur*, undertook the enormous task of writing the committee's report. "We also discussed other ideas related to the future of veterinary public health. I was still pushing for having a veterinary public health consultant at the WHO headquarters in Copenhagen. We also debated if such a consultant should be from the Eastern or Western Bloc region. We ultimately became stalemated on this issue. Dr. Kaplan thought he could cover Europe adequately for the time being, and so the topic was tabled. I was also recommending opening an office in Manila to cover the Western Pacific region. I put forward the name of Dr. Ade Ojeniyi, a Nigerian, who had an excellent academic record. He was a DVM, MD, and PhD working at the University of Ibadan, Nigeria, who had researched the effects of the overuse of antibiotics in *Salmonella* infections. Unfortunately, there was prejudice in Asia against Africans at the time, and I couldn't get this candidate appointed. I was truly disappointed about the situation," Jim stated. As it turned out, the Western Pacific office was never created under Jim's watch.

There were other parts of the world where Jim wanted to install effective consultants to build veterinary public health programs. "The medical director for the WHO office in New Delhi was recruiting for a consultant at the time, but it was difficult to recruit a high caliber candidate in Southeast Asia. Dr. Dieter Grossklaus, President of the Federal Health Office for Germany, nominated a German veterinarian. Unfortunately, shortly after his appointment, he contracted an illness that required him to return home to Germany for several years. Later, his assignment was terminated. I then assigned Dr. Ernie Tierkel to India to establish a program in veterinary public health. He did an excellent job." Jim stated. Dr. Tierkel worked out of the US embassy in New Delhi with the India analog of the CDC. In addition, Dr. Oscar Sussman, a retired Public Health Service officer, was recruited to the Calcutta Veterinary College to establish a program in veterinary public health.

"Strategically, Africa sorely needed a veterinary public health consultant. I was doing everything in my power to make this happen," said Jim. Jim could never get the administration to settle on a candidate for the Alexandria office in Egypt. An Egyptian veterinarian worked in the Southern Africa office in the French Congo for a while, but nothing came of the program. "The lack of a consultant for Africa was truly frustrating for me. If it wasn't for the work being done by the Centers for Disease Control, none of the diseases like Ebola in Africa would have been investigated," he said.

One of Jim Steele's main objectives at this third meeting was for the committee to identify and document the critical need for research with respect to a large number of zoonotic diseases. This report served as a historic challenge to the world's leading veterinary and medical scientists to unravel the mysteries surrounding the epidemiology, microbiology and pathology of zoonotic diseases. The committee's work at this meeting undoubtedly set the stage for the next two to three decades of scientific inquiry into the diseases shared by humans and animals. Furthermore, this report served to open the coffers of untold quantities of research dollars to conduct these studies.

The report drafted in 1966 concluded with a brief discussion about emerging zoonoses. It is excerpted here so that it can be contrasted with contemporary thought on this topic:

New diseases or previously unsuspected human-animal disease relationships are being reported with increasing frequency. It is clear that host-parasite-environment interactions are constantly changing, and this, together with the availability of more refined methods of biological study, no doubt partially explains these findings. It can be anticipated that diseases that have been latent or restricted to well-defined areas will become more important with (a) increasing control or eradication of major known diseases, (b) the great changes in human and animal ecologic patterns that are being brought about by development of virgin territories, (c) the increase in human and animal populations, and (d) rapid urbanization. It is important, therefore, to clarify wherever possible the natural history of specific disease agents and to be alert to the possible emergence of new zoonoses.

After retirement from the Public Health Service, Jim didn't have much time to devote to WHO activities. But in 1975, he was invited once again to attend the meeting of the Joint FAO/WHO Expert Committee on Zoonoses chaired by Dr. Calvin Schwabe. In later years, Dr. Richard Parker, one of Jim's successors at CDC, carried on the legacy. "These meetings continued to wave the flag for veterinary public health around the world as a bright new field in veterinary medicine. So many great new programs were beginning toward goals like the worldwide control of rabies, the control of bovine tuberculosis and brucellosis, elimination of many parasitic zoonotic diseases, and the eradication of foot and mouth disease to promote international trade and economic growth. As late as 1969, a WHO group of allied health officers from all the nations of the world met in Boston and passed a resolution stating that veterinary public health should remain a high priority," Jim said with pride.

"My involvement in the WHO was supplanted by my strong support and involvement in the Pan American Health Organization. In my opinion, PAHO's program has become the best veterinary public health program in the world. It has been led by many outstanding veterinary scientists including Drs. Pedro Acha, Manuel Fernandez, Joe Held, Primo Arambulo, and Albino Balotto. To this day, I believe that the world should work to emulate the PAHO program in veterinary public health," Jim pronounced. With PA-HO's leadership, Jim predicts that the eradication of clinical FMD will be possible in the future.

Jim Steele chaired this historic third meeting of the Joint FAO/WHO Expert Committee on Zoonoses with energy, brilliance and pride. At this point in his career, he had over twenty years' experience in developing and promoting veterinary public health. Because of his knowledge and leadership and that of his colleagues on the committee, the course was set toward a better understanding of all zoonotic diseases. This historic achievement has resulted in vast improvements in public health and personal wellness all over the globe. His application of epidemiology to the study of zoonotic diseases has helped veterinary scientists to be cognizant of the dynamics of nature and to be prepared for the changes that are sure to come in the form of emerging zoonotic diseases.

"I'm counting on you bright young kids to carry on from here!" Jim challenged with a smile.

CHAPTER 22:
INTO AFRICA

In 1960, Dr. Van Zellhyde, chief of foreign relations for the U. S. Public Health Service asked Jim to speak at an upcoming WHO/FAO conference in Cairo, Egypt on aid to Africa. At the time, there was U.N. support for programs to assess the economic and social status of Africa. These studies would eventually end up in a comprehensive report in 1962 entitled *FAO African survey: Report on the possibilities of African rural development in relation to economic and social growth.* "I was highly motivated to promote veterinary public health in the region and was delighted to be invited on the program. This meeting was the start of a long and rich relationship with my African colleagues," Jim said.

Upon arrival in Egypt, Jim arranged to visit the Cairo University School of Veterinary Medicine. He wanted to learn as much as he could about endemic zoonotic diseases of Africa prior to the conference. "Hydatid disease was a major problem at the time and had plagued Egyptians throughout history. I was well aware of echinococcosis in sheep and goats but was surprised to learn about the disease in camels," Jim stated. During one of his lectures at the university, he was asked a question about hydatid disease by an Egyptian physician. "Fortunately I had done my homework and was able to respond with the full array of reservoirs, including the camel. This physician was surprised that such a wide range of animals was involved in the life cycle of the disease. This was yet another excellent example of how professionals in veterinary and human medicine were not communicating," Jim reported.

Dr. Van Zellhyde told Jim later, "You really slammed it down his throat!"

While in Cairo, Jim also presented his data on the rabies vaccines that he and Ernie Tierkel had worked on in the fifties. About a dozen people had recently died in Brazil because of a vaccine that was not attenuated properly, so this was a hot topic for discussion. "Egyptian scientists presented papers on the epidemiology of anthrax and the guinea worm," Jim said.

"As I traveled around, I became engaged in debates with my colleagues about the diseases that were taking their toll on animals and people in Africa. At the medical school in Alexandria, Egypt, I lectured on my belief that humans are the only true reservoir for the Guinea worm, *Dracunculus medinensis,* endemic in Africa, the Middle East and India. Many years later, I explained this to Dr. Abram S. Benenson, editor of the APHA *Control of Communicable Diseases Manual.* Some of the scientists there wanted me to endorse their theory that the dog was a reservoir. I was aware that the North American Guinea worm infected raccoons, mink, skunks, dogs and other species. But these animals are not a reservoir for human infection. An abstract of my lecture was published in an Egyptian medical journal. I saw this as an example of how scientists wanted my endorsement to lend credence to their theories on zoonoses," said Jim.

Onchocerciasis, caused by *Onchocerca volvulus,* also known as river blindness, is a filarial disease endemic in western Africa and South America that piqued Jim's curiosity. On the trip, he received many questions regarding the disease, mostly relating to the host range and the vectors. "I knew that the condition had been found in non-human primates, but I really didn't think other species were involved. I also knew several species of the black fly were the main vectors and the L1 larvae ingested by the fly developed in the midgut into the infective L3 larvae. The L3 is deposited on the skin of humans by the fly and burrows into the skin where it molts into an L4 stage and ultimately becomes an adult worm that results in fibrous, subcutaneous nodules. These parasites were fascinating to me and I wanted to learn everything I could about them," Jim said.

"An Egyptian veterinarian who received his MPH in Toronto took me on a tour of the pyramids. This was the first time I witnessed people with the humpback form of tuberculosis," Jim said. Pott's disease is one of the extra-pulmonary forms of tuberculosis characterized by intervertebral arthritis that leads to a hump on the back of the patient. Descriptions of the disease are found in hieroglyphics on the walls around the pyramids testifying to the age-old nature of the disease. This tour was also where Jim first learned about the priest-physician role in early Egyptian society and how some of their clinical techniques were applied to animals. "A papyrus dating back to about 1900 b.c. described cattle, dog, fish and bird diseases. My veterinary colleague told me that royal oxen often lived on the pharaoh's household grounds. The sacred bulls were sacrificed when the pharaoh died. Egyptians believed this practice aided in the bulls' transformation once in heaven," Jim stated. Another story was told about how tetracycline was developed from streptomycetes organisms found in the soil and used for the treatment of animal diseases by tribes in the desert.

From Egypt, Jim traveled on to Khartoum, Sudan. Khartoum became Anglo-Egyptian Sudan after British forces defeated the Mahdists in 1898. Sudan became an independent nation in 1956. "I helped to implement veterinary public health in Sudan with the aid of a new WHO-funded program for human parasite control. The program generated a lot of interest by the local public health scientists. Unfortunately, when an expanded program supported by the US was presented, the tribal leaders demanded a fee of $25,000 US dollars for their participation. This was very disappointing," Jim said. Jim never heard about any successful follow-up. Just before Jim left Sudan, his new acquaintances hosted an evening reception in Khartoum for him.

The next stop for Jim was Entebbe, Uganda. "I met a lawyer on the plane who was a Ugandan politician bound for Kampala. He was telling me about change occurring within the Ugandan government and the potential that he would be elected to a high position. I didn't know whether to believe him. But later I learned that Milton Obote became president of the Uganda National Congress and presided as prime minister during the British withdrawal in 1962. The man sitting next to me must have been a close political aide of Obote," Jim said. Upon arrival in Entebbe, Jim was met by an old British friend, Dr. Patrick Guilbride, who was in charge of the veterinary laboratory in Entebbe.

"I spent the next morning with Dr. Guilbride discussing African trypanosomiasis, also known as sleeping sickness," Jim said. The disease, transmitted by the tsetse fly, claimed 300,000 lives in one of the earliest outbreaks in Uganda in the late nineteenth century. "I had a special respect for the colonial veterinarians of the day. They were particularly competent in developing useful laboratory diagnostic procedures. The problem with the British colonies was there was never enough funding to implement prevention and control programs. Another problem with the colonies as they moved toward independence was that many of the new political leaders were corrupt. I was told that they used the British financial support to line their own pockets rather than investing in the health and welfare of their countrymen. Trypanosomiasis could easily have been under control by the sixties through tsetse control programs, but corruption and political unrest kept it alive," Jim recalled.

Next, Jim flew to Nairobi, Kenya for the meeting of the WHO/ FAO Expert Committee on Zoonoses of Africa. Kenya was a British colony and would not obtain independence until December 1963. Upon arrival, Jim met with Dr. Martin Kaplan, the director of veterinary public health for WHO; Dr. Mohamed Abdusalaam, Dr. Kaplan's deputy; and Dr. Ervin Eichhorn, the first chief veterinary officer of the FAO. Dr. Eichhorn received his veterinary training at the University of Pennsylvania. His father was from the Czechoslovakia/Austro-Hungarian region and came to the U.S after World War I. Dr. Eichhorn was raised as an American. "I really enjoyed his company. We worked together on several WHO conferences and became longtime friends and colleagues," Jim said.

"There were some excellent parasitologists at this meeting. We made several field trips while in Kenya. I especially recall one to a solid waste treatment plant. We saw what looked like scum on the surface of the pit. On closer inspection, the 'scum' turned out to be thousands of scolices of *Taenia saginata*," Jim said, shaking his head. Hydatid disease caused by the *Echninococcus* genus of tapeworms was another sizeable problem in East Africa at the time. The incidence in Southern Africa today can be as high as 220 cases per 100,000 inhabitants. They also visited the Trypanosomiasis Research Centre and the Kenya Agricultural Research Institute in Kikuyu, Kenya. "I remember some strange discussions at the Centre about killing all the wildlife reservoirs of the disease as a control method. I advised that they focus on tsetse fly control utilizing organochlorines," Jim stated.

"Dr. Eichhorn and I visited several meat processing plants and slaughter facilities in Kenya together. These plants were excellent facilities built by the British and operated by the Eastern Africans. Unfortunately, the inspection visits were announced well in advance so the plants were usually cleaned up before our arrival. I wondered how they could compete with the European markets.

"While in the area, we stayed at the legendary Treetops Hotel. Now, that was an experience!" Jim said. The hotel is situated in Aberdare National Park, about 180 kilometers from Nairobi. The hotel began as a two-room tree house. Visitors climbed a fig tree to get into the house for a better view of the area. "Legend has it that a young British princess climbed up into the tree house for an overnight stay in 1952 and woke up as Queen Elizabeth II the next morning. King George VI, her father, had died during the night. We could see Mount Kenya's snow-capped peaks from our rooms. This is Africa's second-highest mountain, at 5199 meters high," said Jim.

One evening, Jim and Dr. Eichhorn went to the Equatorial Club. "You could be north or south of the equator inside the club depending on what side of the room you were on. Just outside the club were all kinds of wild animals. Elephants, cats, bushbuck, and buffalo came up to the waterholes and wandered through the grounds of the Treetops Hotel all night. Eating a meal in Kenya could be interesting. I recall a pitcher of blood on the table that was somehow part of the meal," Jim said.

After the WHO/FAO meeting, Jim traveled by Land Rover with a group of British veterinarians to Tanzania. "I remember passing through the magnificent Nairobi National Park with natives in the field, crossing the border into Tanzania at Moshi and seeing Mount Kilimanjaro come into view. We drove to Arusha in northern Tanzania, an area that is surrounded by beautiful landscapes and national parks. I marveled at the tall, slender Masai tribesmen in their colorful, distinctive dress," said Jim.

"The next morning, we learned that crews were shooting a documentary on location in the Arusha area. We decided to go take a look," Jim said. The movie was about a local British veterinarian who was collecting animals for sale to zoos and wildlife parks. "We were amazed at the variety of animals they had on hand. There were antelope, small cats of all kinds and more. Suddenly, someone sounded an alarm. Apparently, a hyena or an African wild dog had escaped from its cage. One of my colleagues shouted for me to get on top of a cage, which I wasted no time doing! We all watched for the animal, but it never appeared. Everyone was relieved," Jim recalled.

A guard came over and asked Jim and his colleagues if they would mind examining a sick dik-dik, a very small, antelope-like creature. "The animal was in a squeeze cage. One of the British veterinarians examined it and asked me to do the same. I did a pretty thorough physical exam on the creature. The animal had a fever, and the limbs felt cold to the touch. I also detected a distinct crepitus in the muscles. Gas-forming bacteria came to mind. I decided the little guy had blackleg caused by the anaerobic bacteria *Clostridium chauvoei*. I was amazed that my British colleagues had no knowledge of the disease being enzootic in east Africa," Jim said.

The British veterinarians asked Jim if he wanted to confirm his diagnosis in the laboratory. "I saw this as a polite challenge of my clinical skills. We traveled with the animal back to the clinic laboratory in Arusha. The animal died along the way, so when we arrived at the lab I made some muscle and liver smears and examined them under the microscope. What I saw were thousands of straight, round-ended Gram-positive pleomorphic rods characteristic of *Clostridium chauvoei*. The British veterinarians were so impressed they offered the horns of the dik-dik for me to take home!" Jim said.

"Next, we flew to Dar es Salaam, the capital of Tanzania at the time. This city lost its status as the capital in 1996 but is still a center for many governmental offices. There we visited an upscale British laboratory," Jim said. The building consisted of about 3,000 square feet of laboratory and office space for the two resident veterinary scientists and several technicians. There were no necropsy facilities, as these procedures were performed in the field. "With unimproved roads and difficult terrain, it was too time-consuming to transport animals back to the laboratory. I was amazed at the witch doctors that came to the laboratory requesting drugs for sick animals in their villages!" Jim stated. Jim learned that Sweden had provided aid to build veterinary laboratories and schools in Tanzania. "Many years later, in the eighties, I returned for another visit, only to find the laboratory in shambles. However, on that trip I learned about some German animal scientists there that tried to domesticate zebra. Of course, they failed," Jim said.

Jim then made a brief trip to the Isle of Zanzibar, off the coast of Tanzania by light plane. "I traveled with a government veterinarian, a native man, who had graduated from the University of Edinburgh. I spent two days there to assess the dairy industry. While on the island we learned about Space Station Zanzibar, a satellite tracking station built by NASA that was utilized during Project Mercury. The station was closed in 1964 after the government was overthrown in a bloody revolution. You never know what you will stumble on in some of these countries," Jim said. Soon after, Jim returned to Dar es Salaam and flew on to Johannesburg, South Africa.

"WHO asked me to investigate and report on the adequacy of infrastructure for veterinary education and services in South Africa. In 1960, many African countries were transitioning from colonialism to independent nations and cultures. WHO, the United Nations and other international agencies were trying to learn how to position themselves for human and veterinary health programs. At the time, there were only two veterinary schools in Africa, one in Cairo and the other in Pretoria," said Jim. Dr. Martin Kaplan, still the director of veterinary public health for WHO, was also concerned about how Africans would be able to gain access to a quality veterinary education. "This was extremely important to assure a promising future for African animal health and, of course, public health," said Jim.

The French had a small veterinary center in Tunis which Jim didn't know about this at the time. There was also a veterinary laboratory center in Kenya, north of Nairobi, that served Kenya, Tanzania, and Uganda. This was known as British East Africa at the time. "After gaining their independence, and with Rockefeller Foundation support, the Faculty of Veterinary Medicine was established at the University of Nairobi. The Swedes provided aid to Uganda and Tanzania and brought African veterinarians to Sweden for specialized training. Eventually, a Faculty of Veterinary Science was established at Morogoro, Tanzania, about 200 kilometers west of Dar es Salaam," Jim reported.

"Along the way, I saw various human disease problems first-hand. There were many children with mottled teeth in the region due to fluorosis. Apparently, the water there was naturally high in fluorides, and there was no processing in place to correct the problem. I also remember seeing many black children with red hair and pot bellies. These are the classical signs of kwashiorkor or severe protein deficiency," Jim stated. Bovine tuberculosis was also endemic in the populations.

One of the British veterinary pathologists informed Jim that there was a mycobacterial organism resident in some of the African amphibians. They were shedding mycobacteria in the fields during the wet season. When the waters receded, the cattle grazed in these areas and became sensitized to mycobacteria, causing false positives on the intradermal test for bovine tuberculosis. "I always enjoyed my interaction with the British veterinarians. Most of them had a passion for utilizing good science in their projects. They also shared my belief that good animal health was a prerequisite for achieving good human health. The British established an animal research center for East Africa. Rinderpest was a topic of high interest. They eventually tested a vaccine developed in Canada," Jim said.

"I then learned that bovine tuberculosis was endemic in the African buffalo. The disease would slow them down enough to make them good prey for the big cats. In addition, the waterholes were perfect places to spread diseases and parasites," Jim recalled. Jim thought that rinderpest was one of the more epidemiologically interesting diseases. "Rinderpest is caused by a morbillivirus that is closely related to the canine distemper and human measles viruses. If ingested by dogs, the rinderpest virus protected them against canine distemper. This acquired protection had the effect of increasing dog populations during the epidemics. Once rinderpest was controlled, canine distemper resurged," Jim stated. In the mid-nineties, distemper spilled over into lion populations via jackals and hyenas that were exposed to dogs near the villages. Distemper and bovine tuberculosis were responsible for the decrease in lion populations.

Later, Jim traveled to Mozambique in Portuguese East Africa; to Angola, comprising most of Portuguese West Africa; and to Rwanda and the Republic of Congo to continue spreading the word about the importance of veterinary public health. "I evaluated many schools on these trips," Jim recalled. Congo was later renamed Zaire in 1971 but reverted back to the Democratic Republic of the Congo in 1997. Jim also visited the United Nations office in Brazzaville, Congo. "The French had many educational projects in place around Africa. They were proud of their efforts to educate Africans. These were some excellent programs. Unfortunately, in South Africa there was little interest in educating black Africans at the time. Later the South African government established an all-black school for the medical sciences that included human and veterinary medical schools," Jim explained.

"All told I spent about fifty days in Africa on the trip in 1960, arriving back home on Christmas Eve," Jim said. After the holidays, Jim wrote a report for the Secretary-General of the United Nations, Dag Hammerskjöld and forwarded it to his office in New York City. His report outlined the lack of veterinary infrastructure and higher educational opportunities throughout the continent. He also emphasized the tremendous need for more veterinarians and laboratories to help in the battle against animal disease and to develop a program in veterinary public health to address zoonotic diseases in Africa.

During his trip, Jim had been impressed with the Scandinavian veterinarians and scientists he met. "I highly encouraged the introduction of more Scandinavian veterinarians, physicians and other health professionals into the African continent as they were compassionate regarding the natives' well being," he wrote in his report. He also sent a copy of his report to WHO headquarters in Geneva.

"I returned to Africa in November 1978. The University of Ibadan in Ibadan, Nigeria invited me as a visiting professor," said Jim. After his arrival, institutions around the country invited him to visit. Brigitte, Jim's second wife, traveled with Jim on this trip. "Our flight was full of businessmen. We arrived in Lagos from London at about midnight on November 1, but no one met us at the airport. Having no Nigerian currency, I gave a man at the airport a twenty-dollar bill to assist us in getting a flight to Ibadan the next morning. We slept on a bench and woke up the next morning at sunrise to the sound of Muslim chants. It was an impressive scene with hundreds of pilgrims praying. It was a long night," Jim said.

After arriving in Ibadan, they hailed a cab and asked to be driven to the University of Ibadan. "At our destination, the taxi driver said he would not accept American dollars. I went and found a Dr. Esuruoso, dean of the Veterinary College. I have forgotten his first name. He paid the taxi driver what seemed like a reasonable sum. But the taxi driver wanted more money. He explained that it would compensate for him having to deal with demanding Americans!" Jim said with a grin. Dean Esuruoso had received his veterinary medical degree in the United Kingdom. "He said they didn't expect us to arrive until November 4. Dr. Esuruoso arranged for us to be taken to the faculty club quarters. We were both totally exhausted but quite thankful that we made it to our destination safely," Jim said.

Dr. Esuruoso was very pleased to have Jim visit his institution. Jim was to deliver lectures over the next six weeks. In addition, he gave about twenty lectures at several veterinary and public health schools around Nigeria. "I remember being well received by the students. My time there was exhilarating," Jim stated. While at the University of Ibadan, Jim and Brigitte were provided with a car and driver for excursions into Lagos and the surrounding area. Jim visited an animal disease laboratory in the town of Vom in northern Nigeria. "Today, it is the home of the National Veterinary Research Institute for Nigeria. I also visited the National

Trypanosomiasis Research Center and a Veterans Hospital. The hospital was full of crippled and amputee veterans from the many tribal skirmishes over the years," Jim said.

"There is an interesting story of unintentional biological warfare regarding the early Muslim efforts to conquer Africa. As the Moslems rode south from the northern deserts, they arrived at about five degrees north latitude, where the tsetse fly begins to flourish. Many of their horses succumbed to trypanosomiasis. In more recent times, Argentinean horses were shipped to Lagos, Nigeria in the 1970s for a polo match only to suffer heavy mortality from trypanosomiasis," Jim reported.

In his travels around Nigeria, Jim noticed that most of the livestock were thin, with many suffering from skin diseases. "I suspected this was mostly parasitism. Foot and mouth disease was endemic in the swine populations. There was lots of lameness. The SAT, South African, strain caused a mild form of the disease in pigs, and so there was no discussion about eradication. The Nigerian meat was not of good quality at this time, in my opinion," Jim said. Brigitte was having recurring stomach problems during the trip. "I suspected that it was either the water, the food or both. I was lucky this trip as I stayed healthy. I finally found a source of distilled water at one of the Vom laboratories for Brigitte to drink. This seemed to help her stomach to settle down. She also resorted to drinking some of the strong local beer, thinking it would be safer than the water," said Jim.

Next Jim visited with the local emirs. "These were the tribal chiefs of estate in the northern towns, including the desert town of Kano. The desert people are very dark," Jim recalled. They also traveled south to Benin City, where a kingdom flourished from the fourteenth to the seventeenth centuries, and to Makurdi in south central Nigeria. "Makurdi is the current home of the Nigerian Air Force. As we traveled, I was amazed at the number of destroyed tanker trucks on the sides of the roads. Apparently drug abuse was high among the drivers," Jim said. Along the way, Jim met with various government officials. He tried to educate them on the importance of environmental and veterinary public health. "For some reason, although they listened to me cordially, I didn't expect the conversations would lead to action. The Nigerian government was rich in royalties from the oil industry at this time, and there was a lot of corruption. Not everyone in government was concerned about the welfare of the people," Jim said.

"At Ibadan, I met Dr. Ade Ojeniyi from northern Nigeria. He went to veterinary school in Denmark on an FAO scholarship. He returned and completed a PhD. He studied the effects of antibiotics on the control of salmonellosis in chickens at the medical center of the University of Ibadan," Jim stated. Unfortunately, the University of Ibadan wouldn't hire him, so he returned to Denmark and attended medical school. He married a Danish scientist who was a *Listeria* researcher. "Ade has been very compassionate and productive in his career. He has done much work on AIDS and other terminal illnesses. He is a classic example of how education can make the difference in a developing country," Jim said.

Jim and Brigitte were invited to Nairobi, Kenya for the Christmas holidays. They arrived at the airport in Lagos, but the Pan American flight was delayed. Brigitte was wearing classic Nigerian garb that the dean of the veterinary school had given her. "It was complete with a turban!" Jim said. The airport was not modern, and there were only a few chairs. "We found some old tires to sit on. Finally, at about midnight, the mechanics finished replacing the engine on our plane. We both breathed a sigh of relief as the plane took off, headed for Nairobi. We waited ten hours for that plane," Jim recalled.

Dr. Igor Mann met them at the airport. "He was a Polish veterinarian who had worked for the United Nations. Somehow, Dr. Mann managed to have a reception party for us at 4:00 a.m. when we arrived. He was a multitalented consultant to the Kenyan government. Dr. Mann discovered that human cadavers in shallow graves were aiding in the spread of hydatid disease in the country. Wild canids and free-ranging dogs were eating the cadavers, thereby completing the cycle of the tapeworm," Jim said. Dr. Mann was a wonderful host and took much of his personal time to show Jim and Brigitte around Kenya. "He even loaned us a car to drive to the site of some pre-historic primate remains," he recalled.

The time finally arrived to make their way back home to Houston, Texas. "After six weeks of lecturing and traveling, we were definitely ready to get home," Jim said. They returned to Africa in 1983, when Jim lectured at several medical and veterinary schools. On this trip, they spent about thirty days total in South Africa, Zimbabwe, Tanzania, Zanzibar, and Kenya. "We especially enjoyed our visit to Kruger National Park in South Africa. I wanted to revisit Nigeria, but they wouldn't accept my visa.

"During our trips to Africa, I primarily emphasized the importance of veterinary public health, sound epidemiology and good science toward the betterment of both animal and human health. I made many friends and colleagues that I have collaborated and communicated with for decades. Today, there are approximately twenty veterinary schools and programs in veterinary public health in Africa. All of them are working to improve the health of animals and people around the continent. I am proud to have had a small role in it all.

CHAPTER 23:
DR. K. F. MEYER—SCIENTIST, MENTOR, COLLABORATOR, AND FRIEND

Jim's first recollection of Dr. K. F. Meyer was as a visiting lecturer at the Harvard School of Public Health in April of 1942, the year he graduated. "I remember the faculty at Michigan State speaking so highly of him. At Harvard, they talked about him even more," Jim recalled. He was a veterinarian, had earned a PhD and was an honorary MD who became famous worldwide for his contributions to public health. "I was absolutely captivated by this guy. Dr. Meyer spoke so expertly on brucellosis and zoonoses in general. He was, hands down, the best lecturer I had ever heard," Jim said.

Dr. Meyer graduated from the Zurich Veterinary College in 1907. He then accepted an appointment to the University of Pretoria in South Africa. "He suffered a severe malaria attack and returned to Europe to recover," Jim explained. In 1912 he accepted an appointment at the University of Pennsylvania to teach courses on infectious diseases and to serve as director of the veterinary diagnostic laboratory. In 1914 he was recruited by the University of California, San Francisco to the new Institute of Tropical Medicine, where he remained for the rest of his life. "He established the first zoonoses laboratory as part of the Hooper Foundation," Jim said.

The day after the lecture, one of Jim's professors told him Dr. Meyer had an opening for a research associate to work with him on war-related issues. "At this point I was not aware that much of Dr. Meyer's research was linked to biowarfare. I made an appointment to talk with him about the opportunity," Jim stated. At the end of their meeting, Dr. Meyer said with his German accent, "Yes, I think we could set up a program for you with a scholarship and a nice stipend. It will be very interesting!" Jim said, "We got along nicely. I was thrilled by the possibility of working with this great scientist."

Jim and Aina planned to move to California after he completed his studies at Harvard. "I had to figure out what to do next. Should I complete an MD degree, a PhD or possibly both? Regardless, the whole idea of a career in veterinary and medical research was thrilling, to say the least. The chance to work under K. F. Meyer, a veterinarian who had paved the way into the public health arena, was also exciting. The phrase 'veterinary public health' was not being used yet. This would later evolve out of my relations with Dr. Joe Mountin and my work at CDC. But Dr. Meyer was a true pioneer in the application of veterinary medicine to public health, a follow-up to what Pasteur had started," Jim said.

Aina was equally excited. Jim had mentioned her tuberculosis to Dr. Meyer, who responded, "Jim, we will have the best treatment for Aina. You will find yourselves a nice home in the country across the bay, maybe in Marin County. It will be a good life for both of you!" Everything was right with the world. Jim had earned his Harvard degree. Aina's prognosis was getting better all the time. She was gaining weight and feeling good. They made a short visit to his cousin Dr. William Thorp at Pennsylvania State College to tell him of their new, exciting plans. Jim thanked Bill for encouraging him to attend Michigan State College and for helping him to find employment in the Michigan Brucellosis Testing Laboratory. Cousin Bill said, "Jim, you are going to be a pioneer in the public health field. I know you will succeed!"

Jim and Aina traveled to Chicago. Aina moved in with her family and Jim stayed with his brother John. "One night I went out with some friends to a pub. The band was playing "California, Here I Come." I remember the effect this had on me. After all, Aina and I were going to California soon. All I was waiting for was the confirmation from Dr. Meyer and my rail tickets to San Francisco," said Jim. But after about three weeks in Chicago, a telegram came from Dr. Meyer stating that the federal funding had fallen through, and he had to withdraw the offer of the graduate position. "I was crushed. I felt misled, let down. My research stint with Dr. K. F. Meyer was not to be. I wondered what I would do," Jim said.

After Jim joined the Public Health Service, he learned that Dr. Meyer had been under surveillance by US intelligence authorities for years. "He had all the attributes that caused suspicion, a German accent, connections with Germany, and lots of foreign correspondence. Scientists were considered suspicious for much less in the postwar environment," Jim said. Even though he was on an advisory committee for the surgeon general of the US, Dr. Meyer was under regular scrutiny.

Sometime after the war, a naval intelligence officer initiated an investigation into Dr. Meyer's activities which resulted in the loss of his security clearance. "Dr. Meyer had no knowledge of the investigation. He was suddenly and thoroughly cut off from Washington, DC. I learned about all this when I received my top secret security clearance. I asked friends at Fort Detrick, Maryland what Dr. Meyer's status was and why he wasn't doing any research. They informed me about the loss of his clearance," Jim said.

"This atmosphere prevailed during the postwar era near the start of the Cold War. 'Better dead than red' was the catch phrase of the times. The axiom was first coined by Nazi Germany's propaganda minister to motivate the German military to fight the Russians to the bloody end. In 1948, I learned that K. F. Meyer was honored by the surgeon general of the US Army for his service during World War II. I never knew about Dr. Meyer's many military contributions until well after the war. I then realized that if I had gone to work for him, most of my career would have been focused on the war effort. In February of 1950, Senator Joseph McCarthy, a relatively unknown US senator from Wisconsin at the time, announced that he had in his possession a list of over 200 card-carrying Communists employed by the US government. It took me many months and a lot of energy to get Dr. Meyer's clearance restored. We finally had to settle for a lesser clearance with the Public Health Service. Dr. Meyer's access to Fort Detrick was never restored," Jim explained.

Years later, Jim and Dr. Meyer collaborated extensively on psittacosis and ornithosis control in pet birds and turkeys. This work is described in detail in chapter 23. In 1964, Jim organized the American Veterinary Epidemiology Society (AVES). "We established the AVES in Dr. K. F. Meyer's name to honor his work and his many contributions to public health," Jim said. At the same time, Jim created the Gold-Headed Cane Award to be given to one or more scientists each year to recognize outstanding contributions to the fields of veterinary epidemiology and public health. "We held the first AVES award banquet at CDC in Atlanta in 1964. Dr. K. F. Meyer was named as the first recipient of the Gold-Headed Cane Award. Recipients of the award were asked to give a speech. Dr. Meyer spoke that day on the role of public health and veterinary and human medicine in fostering social progress," Jim said.

"After our psittacosis projects, Dr. Meyer and I didn't have much interaction until about 1970, when we began discussing writing a definitive handbook series on zoonotic diseases. He was completely immersed in plague research for the US Army at the time and was trying to get some research data ready for publication. I can remember him trying to persuade me to become more involved in plague research, especially in the area of identifying the reservoirs in nature. At this time, coyotes were being recognized as carriers. Some work in New Mexico identified the dog as a carrier and the cat as a victim of the disease," Jim stated. But Jim had no time to get involved in Dr. Meyer's projects.

Dr. Meyer's plague projects were later transferred to the new CDC Rocky Mountain Laboratory at Fort Collins, Colorado. Dr. Jack Poland, a physician, conducted plague studies in non-rodent species. Squirrels were also found to be a part of the plague cycle as part of this work. "In the 1970s, Dr. Meyer began slowing down. Brigitte and I stopped in San Francisco to visit. We were on our way to Samoa to meet with the WHO Western Pacific Regional Office in 1973. We had dinner with K. F. and Marion, his wife, that evening, but I could tell that he wasn't feeling well," Jim said.

Jim presented an idea to publish Dr. Meyer's plague research manuscripts as a supplemental issue to the *Journal of Infectious Diseases*. Jim and US Army Colonel Daniel Cavanaugh, a veterinarian, were to be the editors. Dr. Meyer retorted, "This is a waste of time and money, Jim!"

In September 1973, Jim returned from his trip to the South Pacific and traveled back through San Francisco to spend some time interviewing Dr. Meyer. In November, Jim finished a draft of a brief biography of Dr. Meyer's life, to be included in the journal along with Dr. Meyer's papers on plague. "I asked him to review the manuscript. I had written how Dr. Meyer left the University of Pennsylvania because of his attack against the Society of Pathologists. The University of California learned that Dr. Meyer was available and offered him a position as a professor at the newly established Tropical Medicine Center. He was furious with me!" Jim recalled.

Dr. Meyer barked, "You don't have to say anything about me looking for a job. I've never had to look for a job in my life. My jobs have always found me!"

Jim also wanted to devote a passage to honoring Dr. Meyer's first wife, but he said, "That will not be necessary. The wives of the scientists will not be at the dinner!"

Jim capitulated and removed the part about what had happened at the University of Pennsylvania. "I also decided to leave out any mention of Dr. Meyer's wife. Later I was criticized by some of the guests for not mentioning Mrs. Meyer. No way to win on this one!" Jim said.

Jim completed the final draft of the paper and sent it back to Dr. Meyer for approval. He wrote back, "I suppose that will do."

"I didn't realize that he was seriously ill at the time," Jim said. Dr. Edward Kass, the editor of the journal, accepted the manuscripts but stated that he needed $12,000 to cover the publication of the supplement. "This was a lot of money. Unfortunately, the Army contracts had been terminated and Walter Reed had no funds. I was running out of options," Jim said..

"I also wanted to have a nice celebration for Dr. Meyer's ninetieth birthday. When Dr. Meyer learned about the plans, he really gave me a hard time," said Jim.

"I don't want all this money spent on me, Jim. It's a waste!" Dr. Meyer would say over and over again. All he wanted was a small get-together at *The Family*, his favorite club in San Francisco.

When Dr. Meyer learned that Jim was having trouble raising funds for the journal supplement, he snapped, "Instead of this extravagant party you have planned for me, let's use the funds to publish the plague reports!"

Jim had raised about one-half of the funds he needed to print the supplement by this time. "I was in the Virgin Islands and was doing all these negotiations by telephone. I called Max Stern and asked if Hartz could cover the balance," Jim said.

Max Stern told Jim straight out, "Don't worry, we've got the journal covered."

"He also committed funds for the celebration as long as I agreed to organize it," Jim said. "Max told me to spare no expense, and I did just that! "It was such a nice gesture. I have so much respect for Max,." Some pharmaceutical firms also offered to help sponsor the party.

After returning from the Virgin Islands, Jim came to San Francisco in February to see Dr. Meyer. "Usually we would go out to his club, have wine with lunch and drink scotch and sodas all afternoon, chatting all the while about science. But it was not to be on this trip. Dr. Meyer was not feeling well. This was the last time I would see him alive," Jim stated.

In March, Dr. Meyer gave a lecture to medical students at the University of California. He spoke on the changing virulence of infections in animals. "This lecture was his last and, unfortunately, it was not recorded," Jim lamented.

A friend of Jim's from Sweden who attended the lecture told him later, "The old boy was ailing, Jim. He was grumpy, not feeling good." About three weeks later, Dr. Meyer checked himself into the university hospital, where surgeons found intestinal bleeding and severe anemia. He was diagnosed with advanced colon cancer. Jim thought, *How stubborn can he be; did he not see that he was passing blood?* Dr. Meyer entered the hospital on a Monday and died on the following Friday. "A legend had passed. He was my idol," Jim said.

Jim received a telegram the evening of April 23 signed by Marion, Dr. Meyer's wife. Dr. Meyer had told her, "There's not much more I can say. Please tell my daughter and Jim of my death."

"So instead of attending a grand birthday celebration on May 24, 1974 for his ninetieth birthday, and to honor his life and career, I was writing his eulogy. I knew that K. F. would have done almost anything to not attend the party. I guess he got his wish!" Jim said.

Jim traveled to a memorial service for Dr. Meyer at the University of California in May. Attending in full US Public Health Service uniform, he spoke about the enormous influence K. F. Meyer had on the development of public health in the US "I read excerpts from the biography I had written about Dr. Meyer's incredible life. He was truly an exemplar in the field of epidemiology. To K. F. Meyer, epidemiology meant going out in the field, getting the facts and sorting them out methodically in your brain. Then you come back into the laboratory to think, to be creative and to come up with solutions. He always taught me to come out with an answer to a question. People want answers, and K. F. Meyer provided them. I learned from him the value of clean, hard data to support a diagnosis. K. F. said time and again, 'There's nothing wrong with statistics, as they can support a hypothesis, but they aren't an end in themselves. Epidemiologists need to work to understand exactly what their findings mean. Will my results help to provide an answer?'" Jim explained.

"The National Library of Medicine and the National Institutes of Health offered grants for someone to write a complete account of K. F. Meyer's life and career. I regret that I was so involved with the *CRC Handbook Series in Zoonoses* and other projects at the University of Texas School of Public Health that I didn't find the time to work on the biography. Of course I knew that if I *had* taken the time, K. F. would probably be cussing me from the afterlife. He would much rather have me work on the handbook series. Of course, everyone missed having the birthday party," Jim said. When the K. F. Meyer supplement to the *Journal of Infectious Diseases*, Volume 129, May 1974, came out, it was well received.

Together, Dr. Meyer and Jim helped save a growing pet bird industry. Dr. Frank Beaudette, the Rutgers University avian veterinarian who worked with them earlier on canarypox, had also died by that time. "I had to finish the *CRC Handbook on Zoonoses* without them. We dedicated the books to Dr. Meyer for his outstanding leadership in the field of public health," said Jim.

CHAPTER 24:
PSITTACOSIS AND HARTZ MOUNTAIN:
JIM STEELE FORMS A UNIQUE PUBLIC HEALTH
PARTNERSHIP

In 1926, Max Stern was twenty-six years old and living in post-World War I Germany near the Harz Mountain range, the highest mountains in the country. The country was experiencing unprecedented inflation and unemployment. He was struggling to get a start in life. Max was from a middle-class family that was in the paint manufacturing business. But with anti-Semitism and post-war inflation, young Max was hoping to find a business opportunity that would allow him to leave Germany. A local pet dealer had borrowed some money from Max and didn't have the cash to pay him back. "The dealer offered to give him about 5,000 canaries instead. He quickly accepted the offer, hoping to start a thriving business. He knew that songbirds were the rage in the US after the war, as they provided a bright spot in the home. He wanted to fill that niche. He decided to try to market his birds in New York City," Jim said.

With very limited English language skills, he traveled with his canaries by steamship to New York. He made his first sale of birds to Wanamaker's Department Store in Manhattan. Later Macy's, Woolworth's, Kresge, and Grant's would follow suit. Hartz Mountain Industries was born. By 1932, Max Stern was the chief importer of birds in the US. Soon he began packaging and selling bird food. The rest is history, and Jim Steele was to have an important role.

"Hartz Mountain experienced sporadic health problems with their birds through the years. The company learned about Dr. Frank Beaudette, a Michigan State College veterinary graduate who specialized in avian diseases. They quickly signed him on as their avian health consultant," Jim explained.

Dr. Beaudette was on the faculty at Rutgers University in New Brunswick, New Jersey at the time. One disease that hit the pet bird industry hard was canarypox. The disease caused such high death losses that Hartz Mountain asked Dr. Beaudette to establish a canarypox research program at the veterinary science department at Rutgers. Dr. Beaudette eventually developed a vaccine to prevent canarypox, publishing his initial work in 1953. His heroic efforts helped to save the commercial canary industry.

As World War II broke out, Dr. Beaudette arranged for canaries to be used at the National Institutes of Health and the US Public Health Service (USPHS) to investigate malaria. "Canaries were an important research tool in studying malaria, as they could be infected with the *Plasmodium* protozoa, albeit not of the same species that infects humans," Jim stated. The USPHS used the birds to test drugs which might be effective in preventing the disease in people, especially soldiers deployed to tropical areas of the world. "Hartz Mountain was always a part of the team, providing canaries for the research and providing matching research funds," said Jim.

After World War II, Max Stern and his brother saw enormous potential for selling pets around the world. Pet birds had become very fashionable in the US. In addition, it was common for soldiers returning from the war to build backyard aviaries to raise canaries and lovebirds.

Through most of the nineteenth century, psittacosis was considered strictly a human disease. Psittacosis in birds, or parrot fever, as it was called then, was discovered in 1892 by Dr. Edmond Isadore Étienne, a French veterinarian who specialized in bacteriology and pathology. Initially, it was thought that parrots were the only carriers, but eventually all psittacine birds and a wide variety of other avian species were found to be infected. "A bird is classified as a psittacine if it belongs to the family *Psittacidae*, which includes parrots, macaws, and parakeets. Canaries are not considered psittacine birds as they belong to the family *Fringillidae*. Pheasants, ducks and geese can be infected, along with seashore birds including gulls, terns and egrets," Jim explained.

"Outbreaks in chickens have been rare. However, turkeys have been a major problem," Jim said. The first case associated with turkeys in the US was recorded in Texas in 1937. Turkey exposure later became a common source for chlamydial infections in humans, especially in turkey processing plant personnel. In 1974, 154 human cases occurred, mostly in packinghouse workers. "Dr. K. F. Meyer described some interesting outbreaks of chlamydial infections in carrier pigeons. Psittacosis, or ornithosis, as it was called in turkeys, needed to be controlled," Jim explained.

"Psittacosis is caused by an infectious agent that is evolutionarily somewhere between a virus and a bacterium. It belongs to the taxonomic family *Chlamydiae*. Dr. Konrad Eugster, an Austrian veterinarian that I sponsored to become an American citizen, did his doctoral dissertation in the seventies on *Chlamydiae* at Colorado State University. He wrote the chapter on chlamydiosis in our *CRC Handbook Series in Zoonoses*," Jim said. "Chlamydia" is a term of Greek origin meaning mantle or cloak and is derived from the word 'chlamydozoa,' originally used in 1912 by a German scientist to describe cellular lesions he saw in trachoma patients. Later, it was recognized that the organisms were not protozoa, so the name was truncated to 'chlamydia.' "*Chlamydia psittaci* has recently been renamed *Chlamydophila psittaci*," Jim explained.

"In 1929, a pandemic of psittacosis occurred. In the U.S., the disease was traced to parrots brought in to sell during the Christmas season. In 1930, stiff restrictions were imposed on the importation of psittacine birds into the U.S. and quarantine stations were established," Jim explained.

"*Time* magazine ran a story on the pandemic of psittacosis in their January 27, 1930 edition. An outbreak of parrot fever occurred in Buenos Aires in which nine members of a theatrical troupe there fell ill. It was learned that their mascot, a parrot, had died of an undiagnosed illness. Cases of psittacosis in people were also diagnosed in Mexico City. The health authorities there ordered a depopulation of all parrots and shut down all parrot imports. In Switzerland, four customers of a hairdresser who kept a parrot in his shop died from psittacosis. Germany immediately halted the importation of parrots. In Balboa, Panama, Rear Admiral Edward Hale Campbell gave orders to his sailors to quarantine all pet parrots. Many of the sailors simply set their birds free.

Psittacosis was quickly recognized as a significant public health problem that needed to be dealt with," Jim said.

Back in Washington, DC, Surgeon General Dr. Hugh S. Cumming ordered the USPHS to conduct a nationwide investigation of psittacosis. The investigation was headed by Dr. Charles Armstrong, a veteran USPHS medical officer. "Dr. Armstrong risked his life investigating diseases such as botulism, influenza, milk-borne epidemics, sleeping sickness, breakbone fever and more. He contracted a case of parrot fever during this investigation and was fortunate to live to tell about it. Interestingly, Charles' case led to saving the life of the wife of Idaho Senator William Edgar Borah, who contracted the disease in 1932. Dr. Armstrong harvested some of his own hyperimmune serum and administered it to her, resulting in a complete cure. This was quite a story," Jim recounted. In Los Angeles, a quarantine was placed on all birds at pet stores. In Manhattan, City Health Commissioner Dr. Shirley W. Wynne halted parrot shipments from South America and developed an awareness campaign that advised parrot owners to thoroughly wash their hands after any contact with their birds.

During Jim's early days at CDC while still working in Washington, D. C., he met Dr. Gilbert L. Dunnahoo, a physician who was the chief quarantine officer for the agency. "I admired his knowledge very much. We got along quite well," said Jim. Dr. Dunnahoo was overseeing quarantined birds being imported into the US. Psittacosis is transmitted from birds to people by the inhalation of infective aerosols. "The disease is insidious because clinically healthy pet birds often shed infective organisms in droppings and other body fluids, thereby exposing their owners and other birds," said Jim.

"Dr. Dunnahoo called a meeting to review the status of psittacosis. He was recommending a reclassification of the disease risk for people," Jim said.

Since Jim had just been named the chief of the new Division of Veterinary Public Health, Dr. Dunnahoo decided to turn the bird quarantine program over to him. He announced, "Steele will take charge of this!"

When the word got out about Jim's new role, Max Stern's brother called and asked if there would be any significant changes to the existing quarantine program. Jim replied, "We need your expert advice on this, Mr. Stern; let's work together!" Psittacosis was the first disease put directly under Jim's new veterinary public health program.

"All I wanted was an effective program to prevent the movement of diseased birds into the United States. The outbreak of 1929-30 in the US resulted in at least 170 human cases with 33 deaths in 16 states," Jim stated. This event led to the signing, on January 24, 1930, of Presidential Executive Order 5264 issued by President Herbert Hoover, which prohibited the importation of parrots into the US. In October 1930, the operational regulations were amended to permit importation of commercial shipments under approved sanitary restrictions. The birds had to arrive with a health certificate signed by a sanitary authority at the place of origin. Jim was surprised to learn years later there was a bird quarantine facility on Ellis Island, New York.

Together, Jim and Dr. Dunnahoo decided that there were not enough resources available to enforce a quarantine of all birds entering the country. At the same time, there was great pressure to prohibit the movement of birds from outside the US and the interstate movement out of states such as California and Texas. "There were large colonies of psittacine birds in these states. In December 1933, additional regulations began restricting the interstate shipment of psittacine birds. Movement of birds was allowed only if shippers complied with a certified inspection and quarantine program. Quarantine officers worked directly with state health authorities in those days. These new regulations created quite an outcry," Jim said.

Jim appointed Dr. John Scruggs, a retired Army veterinarian, to implement his psittacosis control program. "Dr. Raymond Vonderlehr, director of CDC, was concerned about the interstate shipment of birds. We discussed this at great length," Jim said.

Enforcing the interstate movement of pet birds was extremely difficult. California suddenly decided it couldn't afford to certify all the aviaries. K. F. Meyer chimed in, "Too bad; they've got to do it. It's the law!"

"At first, our program just wasn't working. Human psittacosis cases were still on the rise. Pet stores were selling canaries, and taverns were giving them away as prizes," Jim recalled. Next, there was an outbreak in a New Jersey aviary. The New Jersey state veterinarian, Dr. Oscar Sussman, seized a truckload of five hundred birds that were being shipped for sale. "Dr. Sussman wanted the CDC laboratory to test all the birds. I told him that we didn't have the capacity to test that many birds. So he decided that the birds would be killed rather than risk spreading potentially psittacosis infected birds around the country. Later, we developed a random testing program to avert having to test whole flocks," Jim said.

Eventually, Jim and his team implemented a very successful control program with the help of Dr. Robert Kissling and Martha Eidson at the CDC Montgomery Virus Laboratory. "Dr. Vonderlehr was impressed. He complimented us all for our work. I gave a lot of credit to Dr. Beaudette, who provided us with valuable advice along the way," Jim said. Jim's leadership is credited with helping to save the pet bird and research bird industries, and at the same time protecting the public from what was often a fatal disease. Jim utilized Dr. Beaudette as a consultant well into the 1960s.

In 1954, Jim and Dr. Beaudette were instrumental in organizing the first international scientific conference on psittacosis. It was sponsored by the Hartz Mountain Company and held in New York City. "I helped to organize the meeting, but I purposely didn't take the lead role. I co-chaired a dinner session for the delegates with Dr. Richard Shope. He was with the Rockefeller Institute, later renamed the Rockefeller Foundation, at the time. Dr. Shope was a physician and a brilliant virologist. He was well known for his love of animals and interest in veterinary virology. He worked for many years on swine influenza," Jim recalled. The meeting was well attended by state public health, CDC and PAHO veterinarians and scientists.

The proceedings of this historic meeting laid the scientific basis for psittacosis control in the US. "In addition, the primary responsibility for control was placed on industry with the support of the scientific community. I recall the electricity in the air at the time for scientists engaged in the biological sciences. Just a few months earlier, Watson and Crick celebrated in a Cambridge pub that they had found the 'secret of life' through the discovery of DNA," Jim said.

Max Stern was indebted to Jim for his leadership in solving major problems for the bird industries. "I guess I kind of became Mr. Stern's go-to person for all avian issues. At this stage of my career, I was beginning to realize the impact that my work could have, even beyond public health. This realization made me even more vigilant to be sure I was making good decisions that were backed up by sound science!" Jim said.

"Psittacosis vaccine trials utilizing mice were ongoing at Fort Detrick. Chlamydiae were among the agents being considered as potential biowarfare agents. The USDA was also quite interested in the possibility of an ornithosis vaccine for turkeys. Unfortunately, the vaccine that was produced wasn't protective and also induced a perpetual carrier state in the bird. Not the desired outcome!" said Jim. A vaccine developed by K. F. Meyer at the University of California was tried in an ornithosis outbreak that occurred near Gonzales, Texas but was not successful. Most of the support for developing a vaccine waned after these efforts.

In 1952, seven migrant workers died in Houston, Texas from chlamydial pneumonia, even in the face of penicillin therapy. Tetracycline, discovered by Dr. Lloyd Conover of Pfizer, was patented in 1950 and came on the market in 1955. It soon proved to be effective against many pathogenic organisms, including *Chlamydia*. "Within three years, tetracycline became the best selling drug in the world. This set the stage for some of our work on psittacosis prevention," Jim said.

The scientific community and the public would soon learn that ornithosis was the turkey version of psittacosis. The focus for control programs then quickly shifted from pet birds to poultry. "A lot of work was going on. K. F. Meyer was conducting research on ornithosis in turkeys in Oregon. Dr. Jessie Irons, a medical laboratory officer with the Texas Department of Health, believed that ornithosis had been endemic there for possibly ten years. This announcement made national news. Dr. James Grimes, a professor of veterinary microbiology at Texas A&M, was working hard to identify the reservoirs of ornithosis. He had a theory that pigeons might be spreading the disease to turkeys," Jim said. CDC was recommending a positive pressure air-flow system for turkey houses. "I never understood why the disease was being seen in the US but not in South America or Europe," stated Jim.

During the turkey ornithosis outbreaks, Max Stern called Jim frequently to ask, "Will this eventually shut down the pet bird industry?" There was much more work to be done.

Another ornithosis outbreak began in the Midwest in September of 1952 that ranged from Minnesota to Texas. "The USDA implemented a system for quarantining infected flocks. When Thanksgiving arrived that year, consumer confidence in the industry was down and sales of turkey products declined sharply. The US Army Veterinary Corps called me to ask if the turkeys were safe for the soldiers to consume, as they had 10,000 birds on the way to Korea," Jim said.

Jim discussed the problem with his new boss, Dr. Theodore J. Bauer, the new director of CDC. "What the hell are we going to do with all these birds Jim?" Dr. Bauer asked intensely.

"I immediately proposed that we infect some turkeys, cook them and have USPHS volunteers eat the meat. We could always fall back on tetracycline treatment!" Jim said. Dr. Morris Schaeffer, Director of the Virology Laboratory for CDC, quickly approved the trial and Jim moved forward. "I put out a request for volunteers via the grapevine. We didn't want a paper trail for this Thanksgiving party!" Jim said grinning. About a dozen people soon volunteered. "Hey, I felt it was safe to feed the turkey to my own family. Farmers raising ducks on Long Island in New York contracted the disease, but no disease was ever found among consumers of cooked product as far as I knew," Jim said.

Jim brought one of the turkeys home to his family. "We all ate it, even Aina. With her delicate health, I wasn't crazy about her participation, but she insisted. We even fed some to guests, after we told them, of course. We didn't get sick. None of the volunteers did either. I called the Army back and told them to let the shipments go forward. Feed the turkeys to the troops. There was no evidence of risk as long as the birds were adequately cooked. I didn't sleep too well until I got the report that none of the soldiers became ill. Another time when things just went right!" Jim said.

Dr. Bauer wrote in his memoirs, "Could you imagine doing something like that today?"

"I sometimes think, if those soldiers *had* become infected, would veterinary public health have survived?" Jim said.

"K. F. Meyer's laboratory was focused on psittacosis research in those days. I met with him to discuss my idea about psittacosis prevention through feeding birds low levels of tetracycline. I really didn't believe that vaccines held much promise, even though the USDA hadn't given up on producing one. K. F. liked the idea. I assigned Dr. Donald Mason, a USPHS veterinarian, to the Hooper Foundation at the University of California, San Francisco, to work with Dr. Meyer on the project. He followed in the footsteps of Drs. John Richardson and Paul Arnstein," Jim said. Dr. Mason was well versed in the disease and had assisted with the ornithosis outbreak investigations in Texas. "He had taken an experimental vaccine yet came down with psittacosis twice during his time in the laboratory. This further supported my opinion that a vaccine solution was probably not going to emerge," Jim said.

"The psittacosis project marked the beginning of my strong support for Dr. Meyer's laboratory. I had a formal CDC contract drawn up for him to conduct research on methods to control psittacosis in birds. From that point on, I always had a USPHS scientist in his lab. In 1960, Max Stern came to San Francisco to meet Dr. Meyer. They got along famously," Jim recalled. Mr. Stern became very supportive of Dr. Meyer's projects and was generous in helping to fund his research.

"Many techniques were tested for delivering antibiotics to birds. They impregnated muffins, buttermilk, and little bars of seed with the drugs for the birds to peck on," Jim said. Dr. Meyer finally enlisted the help of scientists at the Department of Pharmacy at the University of California, San Francisco to come up with the best method. Several antibiotics were tried, some resulting in embryological defects. "I remember birds with no wings and no feathers. When this happened, the team would shift to a new antibiotic. Finally, hulled millet seed impregnated with chlortetracycline began to look promising," Jim said. A spinoff of this work was that pharmaceutical companies began to see the value of testing antibiotics and other drugs in embryonated eggs.

Within a few years, the University of California pharmacy department, in collaboration with Dr. Meyer's laboratory, successfully developed a millet bird feed which contained a precise amount of chlortetracycline to be used as a preventive measure against psittacosis. The seed was impregnated with five milligrams of chlortetracycline per gram for feeding to parakeets. "Feeding for fourteen days was found to be effective in eliminating the infection in the breeding flocks they tested. The turkey industry finally concluded there was no hope for a vaccine. But it wasn't economical to manufacture chlortetracycline-impregnated turkey feed either. However, feed mills learned to produce a ration mix of 400 grams of chlortetracycline per ton of feed. Early experiments demonstrated that when this mixture was fed for seven to fourteen days, the infection was eliminated in the turkeys," Jim said. Later it was learned that there were some virulent strains that could be resistant to the treatment. "Turkey farmers claimed feeding the mixture was cost-prohibitive to the industry. But the practice was continued by most producers. Curiously, the disease in turkeys seemed to suddenly fall into obscurity. It didn't make any epidemiological sense to me," Jim stated.

By the mid-sixties, Dr. Meyer's research on psittacosis had been validated. "It was time to develop the procedures for controlling psittacosis and ornithosis in the US and to begin implementing control programs. Dr. Meyer graciously shared the technology with industry so companies could begin marketing the medicated feeds. Hartz Mountain became a prime producer and distributor. They sold the seed at cost so as to hasten the eradication of the disease from pet birds," Jim explained.

In 1968, Jim, as chair of the CDC Psittacosis Advisory Committee, proposed a thirty-day quarantine along with medicated feeding as a psittacosis control program. In addition, he stated that blood levels of 0.25 mg/ml of chlortetracycline had to be achieved to clear chlamydial infections in pet birds. "Some of the members believed that the quarantine should be as long as sixty days. But I had huge doubts that such a long period could be enforced. I encouraged the group to keep the program as simple as possible. Otherwise, we would just be overwhelmed with violations. Retrospectively, I am pleased that the approach was sound. After I retired, psittacosis control programs were transferred to the FDA. But the Public Health Service still investigates outbreaks in people," Jim said.

In 1974, Jim attended a meeting in Austin, Texas. Dr. Jeremy Irons delivered a lecture entitled, *What Happened to Turkey Ornithosis?* "We hadn't seen any cases for a decade and were beginning to think it had died out. We spoke too soon. New outbreaks began to occur in about 1975. Mother Nature was effectively saying that she can still throw a stinger at us! The Jeremy Irons Award was initiated in 1974 for his support of veterinary public health," said Jim.

Jim's collaboration with Dr. Meyer helped to generate many business connections that supported veterinary public health, especially Hartz Mountain. In addition, Hartz and other companies were key supporters of the proposal that a veterinarian be recognized at the rank of assistant surgeon general within the USPHS. "Without parity of rank with the other health professions, advancing the cause of veterinary public health would have been very difficult," Jim explained.

Of course, Jim Steele would be the first veterinarian in the USPHS to attain flag rank.

CHAPTER 25:
THE FIRST ASSISTANT SURGEON GENERAL
FOR VETERINARY AFFAIRS

"I remember being invited to attend the surgeon general's staff meetings when I was an O-4 USPHS officer. I was thinking to myself, *Gosh, is this for real?*" Jim said. Dr. Charles Williams, Jr. was the head of personnel for the USPHS in the early years of Jim's career. "For some reason he liked me and the feeling was mutual. To this day, I appreciate the extra attention and guidance that Charlie provided me," Jim said. In 1949, Jim was sent to Atlanta as the veterinary advisor to the surgeon general and was promoted to O-5, equivalent to a US Army Lieutenant Colonel. Two years later, he made O-6, equivalent to a full Colonel.

By 1958, Dr. Alexander Langmuir, the founder and first director of the epidemiology division and creator of the Epidemic Intelligence Service at CDC, was speaking very highly of Jim. Furthermore, he was already recommending that he be considered for a new position as an assistant surgeon general (ASG). They could have promoted Jim into a deputy director position, but this was strictly an administrative job. "I was afraid that I would lose the momentum I had gained in building a program in veterinary public health," explained Jim. Fortunately for Jim and veterinary public health, Dr. Langmuir felt the same way.

When Dr. Langmuir first proposed an ASG position for Jim, Dr. Leonard Scheele was at the helm of CDC. "Unfortunately, he didn't support the proposal. He believed that only medical officers should be considered for ASG positions," Jim said. But Dr. Langmuir didn't give up. Next in line was Dr. Leroy E. Burney, who was appointed surgeon general in 1956. He was an invited speaker on the AVMA program in Cleveland in 1958. "I recall his excellent overview of the mission and recent successes of the USPHS. During his presentation, he personally commended and addressed me directly in the audience. He praised my vision for veterinary public health at the CDC in front of the whole crowd," Jim said.

After the session, the chair of the AVMA executive board approached Jim and congratulated, "There's no question about it, Jim; you are the leading public health veterinarian!"

At about the same time, Paul de Kruif, PhD microbiology, the author of *Microbe Hunters*, which was first published in 1923 and again in 1953, wrote a great tribute to Jim's work in the *Reader's Digest*. *Microbe Hunters* acknowledges many outstanding scientists who have made significant advances in the field of microbiology. "Kruif's review threw me in with the likes of Pasteur, Koch, Ehrlich, and Leeuwenhoek. It was quite humbling," Jim recalled.

Dr. Luther Terry followed Dr. Burney as surgeon general in 1961. Jim arranged for Dr. Terry to be the principal speaker at the AVMA meeting in Chicago in 1963 to help celebrate the hundredth anniversary of the organization. When Jim picked Dr. Terry up at the airport, he arrived at gate K9. He had a great sense of humor and quizzed Jim with a smile, "Wow, you're really something! How did you arrange for me to come in to the doggy gate?"

Jim worked closely with SG Terry to help prepare his talk. They wanted to highlight comparative medical research being done at the National Institutes of Health, Bethesda, Maryland, by physicians and veterinarians on vascular plaques in the hearts of pigs. Dr. Terry also excerpted a medical report in *The Medical Review* from the eighteenth century about animal, human and plant diseases. At the end of the meeting, SG Terry told Jim that he was hearing a lot of great things about his work. He said, "Jim, with twenty-two years of service, aren't you ready to be an ASG?" Jim appreciated the comment very much but still didn't believe it was possible.

Dr. Ray Helwig, USPHS veterinary medical director, chaired the CDC promotion board in 1966. "One of the top agenda items was the creation of an ASG position for me," Jim said. The consensus of the board was that this idea should be presented directly to SG William Stewart, who had become SG in 1965. "A meeting was scheduled for me to meet with Dr. Helwig and SG Stewart. SG Stewart concurred wholeheartedly with the proposal and made a personal commitment to go to the US Congress for an appropriation bill to create an ASG position for me. All this activity was overwhelming to say the least!" Jim stated.

And so the campaign began. Journals such as *Veterinary Medicine* and *Veterinary Economics* ran articles to foster support for the idea and to ask veterinarians to contact their respective senators and members of the house of representatives. Max Stern, CEO of Hartz Mountain, Inc. distributed copies of journal articles and pamphlets to a broad spectrum of influential individuals requesting their support for the new ASG position. "However, the preponderance of encouragement and support was coming directly from CDC, of course," Jim said.

Dr. Phillip Lee, assistant secretary for health and human services (HHS), learned about the proposed veterinary ASG position and voiced his strong support. Dr. Lee was quite impressed with an article that Jim had written on the positive impact that veterinary public health can have on a country's economy. "In 1963 I presented the paper at a meeting in Mexico City for laboratory directors, and the article was later published in *Public Health Reports*. He later wrote to me and asked if I would mind if he sent his article to all the US embassies of the world to help garner support for veterinary public health and the concept one medicine. All the support was really nice," Jim said.

Next, Jim began hearing about Dr. James Lieberman, a veterinarian who was in charge of the audiovisual development unit of CDC. "Dr. Lieberman was also being groomed for a new ASG position. Apparently, he had strong support from a Senator Hill from Alabama. I met Dr. Lieberman when he applied for a position with CDC. I reviewed his credentials and learned that he had graduated from a veterinary school in Massachusetts that was not accredited by the AVMA. Based on this and feedback from some of his references, I decided not to hire Dr. Lieberman," said Jim.

Dr. Lieberman went on to complete an MPH from the University of Minnesota, at which time Jim did hire him for a position at CDC in Atlanta. "I loaned him to the World Health Organization for two years. When it was time to come home, he did everything he could to stay in Europe. I also learned that Dr. Martin Kaplan, director of the WHO veterinary program, was not supportive of Dr. Lieberman's desire to stay. Eventually, he moved his entire audiovisual unit to the National Library of Medicine," Jim said.

Dr. Lee saw this all happening and hastened to secure Jim's promotion. "I finally received my star, giving me the rank of rear admiral, pay grade O-7, in my role as the first assistant surgeon general of the US for veterinary affairs on July 19, 1968. The Public Health Service follows US Navy rank structure. An O-7 or rear admiral lower half wears one star, while an O-8 or rear admiral upper half wears two stars," Jim said. In late 1970, Jim was appointed deputy assistant secretary for health and human services. "This was a two-star billet at the rank of O-8. Unfortunately, I didn't acquire enough time-in-grade to retire at that rank. I retired as an O-7," Jim explained. Jim learned later that Dr. Lieberman had retired and become a public health officer in a small town in Connecticut.

This was during the Johnson presidency. In 1969, shortly after Jim's promotion, Dr. Jessie Steinfeld was brought in from the Mayo Clinic as surgeon general. "We got along famously," Jim said. One day Dr. Steinfeld told Jim matter-of-factly, "The way you handle yourself and with your connections in Washington, you might become the next surgeon general!" Jim thought, *Gosh, I guess I must be doing something right!*

The promotion to ASG launched Jim into a whole new level of eminence, especially around Washington, DC. "Presidential hopeful Hubert Humphrey and I became good friends. It was amusing that he would sometimes get Cousin William Thorp and me mixed up. Senator Humphrey chaired a study on the role of veterinary medicine in public health. He interviewed me extensively. My input became the basis for his study. Senator Humphrey was impressed with the huge impact that veterinary medicine was having on the societies of the world. I often wonder where my career might have gone if he had been elected president. When Richard Nixon was elected to that office, strange things began to happen around DC!" Jim said.

In 1969, Jim was waiting to meet with SG William Stewart to report findings of the recent meeting of the WHO/FAO Expert

Committee on Zoonoses, which Jim had chaired. A call suddenly came in from the Nixon White House. The secretary said, "Dr. Steele, I think you need to take this call."

When Jim picked up the phone, an aide asked, "Would the public health service have any objection to removing the 25 percent limit of fat content in meat products?"

Jim replied, "Why of course we would; $1 billion is being spent to prevent heart disease in this country!"

The aide replied, "Would you be willing to come over and explain the USPHS position on this?"

Jim replied, "Absolutely!" Jim had been working closely with James Watt, MD, director of the NIH Heart Institute, on comparative heart studies on pigs which linked high fat diets to the progression of heart disease in people. Jim and Dr. Watt had worked earlier on a *Salmonella* issue.

The next day, Jim was addressing the PAHO Executive Board when someone tapped him on the shoulder and said, "The White House wants you to come over and meet with the president's staff on consumer affairs tomorrow."

"The next day, I walked from the Army-Navy Club over to the White House for the meeting. Upon arrival, I was greeted by Mrs. Virginia Knauer, who was an assistant to the president for consumer affairs from 1969 to1977. She escorted me in and introduced me to about ten young Nixon staff members. During the meeting, I explained the findings of the NIH pig research and how it serves as a model for heart disease in man. I also made it clear that the regulations addressing fat content in meat were over forty years old and needed to be reviewed before I could make any statements on behalf of the USPHS," Jim recalled. He answered their questions, and the meeting was concluded.

After the meeting, Mrs. Knauer introduced Jim to Ms. Elizabeth Hanford, a new White House intern. "Of course, she later married Senator Robert Dole and became a DC icon." Jim said. Jim was very pleased when he heard that President Nixon had decided not to bow to the meat industry's request to change the old law on fat content in meat. Ms. Knauer asked Jim, "Would you be willing to be a consultant for the president's consumer affairs group?" Jim replied that he'd have to clear it with the surgeon general, which he subsequently did.

Later, Ms. Knauer was invited onto the consumer affairs staff during the Reagan administration and asked Jim back as a consultant to the group. "I often brought the consumer affairs group to the Army-Navy Club. We had some lively meetings. I got to know Elizabeth Hanford quite well during these years, and we became great friends.

In 1970, the question arose whether leukosis, a form of cancer in chickens, was causing leukemia in people. "There were some interesting case reports coming out of Indiana and Ohio. A consumer affairs meeting was quickly convened by Ms. Knauer. I was asked to be an advisor at the meeting in Washington, DC," Jim said. As he looked around the room he saw someone in the audience with a smiling face, waving at him. It was Elizabeth Hanford.

"We listened first to a physician who had no background in poultry diseases propose his theory of a potential link between leukosis in chickens and human leukemia," Jim recalled. Jim then rose and cited a preponderance of epidemiological evidence to the contrary. "How do we explain that the veterinary profession, poultry farmers, and poultry packers have no increased incidence of the disease, despite the intimate contact related to the care and processing of four to five billion chickens a year?" Jim asked. This didn't conclude the international debate, but time proved that he was correct. "Stick with good science and you can't go wrong!" Jim advised.

Through the years, Jim was asked to be an expert consultant on many human health issues and sat on many committees to help protect the public health. One day after retiring from CDC, he and Brigitte were shopping in a Houston store. He looked up to see Mrs. Knauer on television, standing in front of a meat counter saying, "We are protecting you as consumers by not allowing the fat content of meat to be raised to dangerous levels." Jim enjoyed his years consulting with the White House staff.

"The years just seemed to fly by. There were so many projects, studies, committees, trips, meetings, presentations, and publications. Where did the time go? All of a sudden I was facing retirement. It just didn't seem possible," Jim said. Jim was a true-blue, CDC company man and, in some respect, he never wanted the incredible ride to end. In the late sixties, his life seemed to revolve around his job. "I was quite satisfied with what I had accomplished. I had truly achieved all the goals at CDC I had set for myself and beyond. No, I wasn't going to stay on at CDC. I had other aspirations," Jim explained.

In this same time frame, Aina's health was deteriorating quickly and ended up being hospitalized. Her lungs were badly scarred; she had heart problems, and severe allergies; and was also suffering from the effects of long-term steroid therapy. Jim, Dr. William Thorp and his wife were on their way to visit Aina one morning while they were in Atlanta. Jim called to say they were coming, and Aina replied, "Give me an hour; I want to brush my hair." But she died before they arrived at the hospital. The day was March 8, 1969.

"Aina's passing forced me to think hard about my future. I asked myself over and over, what did I really want to do? It was a very difficult time for me," Jim said.

By 1971, the year of his retirement from CDC, Jim's son Jay was twenty, and David was eighteen. Both were attending the Lovett Episcopal High School in Atlanta. Dr. David Senser, Director of CDC at the time, asked Jim to stay on in an administrative role. "The offer was really tempting. It meant staying in Atlanta with little change in my lifestyle. It was the path of least resistance," said Jim. But soon he moved out of his large office on the fifth floor of the CDC building. A colleague of Jim's at the University of Michigan, Dr. Thomas Francis, asked him if he would like to pursue a faculty appointment there. Jim carried on a dialogue with Tulane University for a while as he had collaborated with several of their faculty over the years. "I remember a friend from Tulane warning me that I wouldn't like the New Orleans lifestyle." Jim said. The president of the University of Georgia, Dr. Fredrick Davidson, another good friend and colleague, showed some interest in developing a position, but nothing ever came of this.

"I made some inquiries at Harvard, but I couldn't seem to connect with them either," Jim recalled. The president of Tufts, Dr. Jean Mayer, told Jim, "We are going to establish a veterinary school here in the future; keep us in mind." But once again, nothing became immediately available. "I contacted K. F. Meyer and asked if there was any possibility for me to succeed him at the University of California, San Francisco. Surprisingly, K. F. was negative about the proposal. I think he had experienced a lot of friction with the university trustees over the years and he was possibly trying to protect me from a similar fate," Jim said.

Dr. Paul Peterson called Jim while he was in Washington, DC on business in January 1971. "He was going to be a dean at the University of Illinois Medical Center once he finished his stint as the acting surgeon general. I had worked with him on some projects in Mexico over the years. We arranged for a meeting at the Army-Navy Club in Washington, DC," said Jim..

"Jim, if you are retiring from CDC, why don't you think about joining us at the University of Illinois?" Dr. Peterson inquired. He offered Jim a position as a professor of environmental health in the University of Illinois microbiology department with a starting salary of $25,000.

"When I visited the campus in Chicago, I was definitely impressed. We stopped by Dr. Peterson's apartment on Lake Shore Drive," Jim recalled. We met Dr. Mable Ross, a retired health economist, who was living in the same building. She told him, "You'll be in good company, Jim. You can be close to the university with a beautiful view of Lake Michigan!" At the time, Jim thought that the Illinois position was a perfect fit. "Shortly after my visit to the campus, I left word with Dr. Peterson that I accepted his offer.

Jim was the chair of the American Public Health Association Committee on Standards and Evaluation in 1971. One of the committee members was Dr. Lester Chambers, a distinguished biologist. At a committee meeting he asked, "Jim, we are looking for a professor of environmental health at the University of Texas School of Public Health in Houston. Would you be interested?" Dr. Chambers extended an invitation for Jim to deliver a lecture at the Houston campus and he quickly agreed. The School of Public Health was new, having matriculated its first class in 1969.

Jim traveled by himself to Houston in February to give his lecture. While there, he encountered Dr. Robert Kokernot, an old friend and colleague who was already on the faculty at the UTSPH. "Dr. Kokernot was a very interesting fellow with a rich history behind him. He held both MD and DVM degrees. He was a really bright guy," Jim said.

Jim learned that the research program at UTSPH was in a very early stage of development, and it would take a lot of work to generate funding for research projects. Dr. Kokernot encouraged him, "You would be a part of a fresh, new and growing program, Jim. And you can add your own special touch!"

The following day, Jim gave his lecture. "Dean Rueul Stallones, the first dean of the UTSPH, immediately offered me a position. I had been thinking about the cold Chicago winters and the bad memories of my youth. He was offering me $10,000 above the Illinois offer, and Texas had no state income tax. I told Dean Stallones that I would accept his offer," Jim said.

Jim was shocked to realize that he had now accepted two positions. *How did I get myself into this mess?* he said to himself.

About two weeks later, Jim was at the meeting of the Council of State and Territorial Epidemiologists in Chicago. He was to be made an honorary member of the organization during the event. "At a reception one evening I was having a conversation with the new dean from the University of Illinois when Dean Stallones from the University of Texas walked up and joined us. My stomach was churning. I decided to leave the reception early to avoid a train wreck. It was quite unusual for me to leave a party. Later someone asked why I left so early. I told him I wasn't feeling well. That was the truth." Jim stated.

Brigitte, Jim's new bride, accompanied him to Houston for the second interview in March 1971. "She looked at the community and looked at houses while I was attending to my business on campus. In one meeting, I advised Dr. Martin Cummings, chair of the Health Science Center, and Dr. Stallones that I would need a lot of freedom to travel and consult during the first year. I also told them about the planned zoonosis handbook project, emphasizing that it would represent a high percentage of my effort for a couple years. Soon we reached an agreement on all this," Jim said. After a telephone conversation with Dr. Charles C. Le Maistre, the President of University of Texas at Austin, Jim formally accepted the Texas offer. "I was now a full professor of environmental health with tenure at the University of Texas, School of Public Health. It felt so right. I called Dr. Peterson to tell him that I would not be coming to Illinois. He graciously understood, and we remained good friends and colleagues for many years. Eventually Dr. Arthur Wolff, a veterinarian who had been serving as deputy director of the USPHS Environmental Health Agency, took the Illinois position," Jim said.

Jim notified the Public Health Service that he would retire at the end of August 1971. In April, Jim and Brigitte traveled to Lima, Peru for a PAHO meeting. Jim received a wire from the surgeon general that his application for retirement was approved but they wanted to move the date to June 1. "I thought this was unusual, so I called my secretary. She told me that the promotion board needed my billet to advance someone else. I immediately agreed to this by telegram," Jim said.

Once the meeting in Lima was concluded Jim and Brigitte flew to Iquitos in northeastern Peru for a tour of the Primate Research Center and the Amazon jungle. "It was a one-hour flight from Lima. We landed and booked a nice room at a hotel. After the conferences in Iquitos, we took a boat down the Amazon River. There was lots of wildlife to see, including caimans, which resemble alligators, and piranhas in the waterways. You really weren't free to just jump into a body of water and take a swim! We stayed in a remote camp with native Peruvians, who were very curious about us. The rooms in the huts where we slept were separated only by sheets," Jim recalled. Early in the morning of the next day, Jim went bird watching. "There were beautiful wild parrots, jeweled cardinals, hummingbirds, falcons, hawks and other birds," said Jim. Brigitte and Jim took an evening tour on a small craft with the natives, who pointed out the flora and fauna along the way. "I remember having trouble keeping my balance while walking through a stream. Thinking back, this may have been the first indication of the neurological degeneration in my legs that would continue to worsen through the years," Jim surmised.

After four days in the jungle, it was time to return to Iquitos. Jim and Brigitte boarded one of two boats that were chartered to take them back. About halfway back, one of the boats broke down. "Everyone had to get out and wait on a sandbar. Our predicament was rather interesting, considering all the not-so-friendly creatures in the water. Finally, everyone was loaded on the other boat, but it then got stuck on a sandbar and ran out of gas. The operator of the boat announced the biggest men would have to get out so that they could free the boat. I was in shorts and a shirt. I jumped out and hung on to the side of the boat. Once the boat was loosened from the sandbar, I struggled to chin myself up the side, scraping my stomach pretty bad in the process. But I made it back on the boat.

"It soon turned dark. The natives told us that we could see better in the dark than in the light but somehow this didn't have a calming effect. Finally someone returned with some fuel," Jim stated. When they reached Iquitos five hours late, someone joked, "The barefoot admiral has finally landed!" Jim then realized his size sixteen shoes had been left on the other boat that had broken down. "When we think about the excursion now, we realize just how dangerous it was, especially without life preservers. I did finally get my shoes back. This was a very good thing, considering the improbability of finding size sixteen shoes in Peru!" Jim said.

One day while still in Iquitos, Jim was playing tennis when Brigitte heard a knock at her door. It was a young Peruvian boy who announced that Jim had purchased an Amazon falcon. He was there to deliver it. "I was not going to sleep in a room with a falcon flying around, so I put it in a paper basket with some leaves and covered it up," Brigitte recalled. When Jim returned from the tennis courts Brigitte quizzed him, "Why are you doing this, Jim?"

He replied, "Why, I want to donate it to the United States Air Force Academy!" The falcon was the official mascot of the academy, and they maintained a collection of falcons from all over the world. Jim wanted to add to their collection. "Unfortunately, the bird died in Miami in quarantine," Jim said.

Days later, Brigitte and Jim boarded a DC-4. "We flew at 15,000 feet over the Andes on our way back to Lima. En route, one of the engines caught fire and started smoking profusely. The plane promptly returned to Iquitos. We all kissed the ground! We finally made it to Lima on the following day for our trip home," Jim said.

Soon, Jim and Brigitte and sons David and Jay traveled to Houston on a house-hunting trip. "After finishing up his time with the US Marine Corps, my son Mike J. Fields commenced working on a PhD in reproductive physiology at Texas A&M University just 90 miles down the road from Houston. During our many get togethers, I talked to him about the responsibility that comes with being endowed with a strong intellect and having had the privilege of a quality education. I also tried to instill in him the importance of public service and giving something back to society. I tried to do the same thing for my sons Jay and David. Mike and I spent many interesting evenings discussing philosophy, history, politics and leadership. After Mike finished his doctorate, he spent some time at Johns Hopkins University doing bench research and later returned to the University of Florida as a professor of reproductive physiology. Mike completed his undergraduate and Master's degrees there. He has had a very successful career in research and teaching, with over 200 scientific publications, two books and many awards to his name. I don't know where he finds the time, but he also manages the family cattle farming operation. I am so very proud of Mike, both for his military and his academic contributions. I am equally proud of my son Jay who completed his B.S. in business from the University of Georgia and has had an outstanding career in business, marketing and corporate operations, nationally and internationally. Finally, I am so very proud of my third son David who received his B.S. from Oglethorpe University. He began his career in environmental science and public health and later became very successful in the insurance business. David also is a teacher and a coach," said Jim.

"We looked at several houses in Houston. Brigitte wanted lots of windows, and I wanted plenty of wall space for our pictures and paintings," Jim stated. In May 1971, they bought a large single-story home at 10722 Riverview Drive on the west side of Houston. They still live in this house at the time of this writing.

Jim's retirement date, June 1, finally arrived. He had been the chief veterinary officer for CDC and the United States Public Health Service since 1951. "I was amazed at how fast those years went by," Jim reminisced. He had been promoted all the way to the rank of O-8, with two stars, the first veterinarian in the U.S. to achieve this. "The Public Health Service hosted two retirement parties for me, one in Atlanta and one in Washington, DC. Surgeon General Jesse Leonard Steinfeld presented me with the Distinguished Service Award. The director of the National Library of Medicine, Martin Cummings, made me a lifetime fellow. It was quite overwhelming," said Jim. Jim was placed on the University of Texas payroll July 1 but did not start teaching until September.

In August, Jim, Brigitte and the Konrad Eugster family traveled by car to the World Veterinary Conference in Mexico City. Dr. Eugster had recently been hired as the head of the virology department of the Texas Veterinary Medical Diagnostic Laboratory at Texas A&M University. "Dr. William Sippel, the director of the laboratory, ragged on me for taking Konrad to Mexico just as he was starting his new job. I just told him not to worry, I would bring him back safely," Jim said. On the return trip, Konrad swerved the vehicle to avoid hitting a donkey on the road. "Everyone except Konrad was so shaken up we decided to stop early for the night. Overall, it was a memorable trip. It really helped us to get over the culture shock of our move from Atlanta to Houston!" Jim said.

By the time Jim returned to Houston, classes had already begun at the university. "I can recall being overwhelmed with things to do. I realized that the transition from CDC to university life was not going to be easy. I was used to having three secretaries and now had none. It took me about a year to get used to my new role. I had a nervous stomach for a long time," Jim recalled. Back in Atlanta, Jim's sons Jay and David had graduated from high school and were both attending Oglethorpe College.

These were times of deep reflection for Jim. He reminisced about establishing the Veterinary Public Health Division at CDC in 1947 and how it became integrated with state, federal and international programs. He recalled his early role in the polio and equine encephalitis outbreaks in Panama in 1946 and FMD in Mexico that same year. "These experiences laid the foundation for my career. They helped me to build a global program in veterinary public health," Jim said.

"I thought back on my involvement with PAHO and WHO and all the rich history that led up to these experiences. In 1945, diplomats from many countries met in San Francisco to plan the establishment of the United Nations. At that meeting, one of the topics discussed was the formation of a global health organization, which ultimately became the World Health Organization in 1948. Surgeon General Thomas Parran was the chair of the organizing committee with Dr. Gilbert Dunnahoo as his chief of staff. The organizational meeting was held in New York City. Dr. Dunnahoo asked medical leaders on SG Parran's behalf for input on how the new organization might be structured. I was asked for input from the veterinary profession. I responded with a detailed memorandum recommending that a division of veterinary public health be established in the World Health Organization that would deal with animal health issues and their effect on human health. I also relayed the sage adage of my good friend and colleague Dr. Calvin Schwabe: 'You can't have good human health without good animal health!'" said Jim.

The organizing committee must have listened to Jim. In 1948, Dr. Martin Kaplan was appointed as the first head of the WHO Veterinary Public Health Program. In 1949, Dr. Fred L. Soper, the new Director of PAHO, created the Veterinary Public Health Program (VPH) at the Pan American Sanitary Bureau. As described earlier, Dr. Kaplan invited Jim to the first meeting of the WHO/ FAO Expert Committee on Zoonotic Diseases in 1950. These interactions began a rich, longstanding collaborative relationship. They also served to anchor forever Jim's newly created field of VPH into the foundation of the WHO.

The WHO Zoonoses Panel had numerous meetings relating to animal and environmental health, culminating in a meeting in Geneva in 1966 of which Jim was the chairman. Each successive meeting underscored the role of veterinary medicine as it relates to public health. "My doctrine and mantra was and still is that all countries need to train and utilize veterinarians as part of the public health team. My role in PAHO accomplished many of the same goals that we worked to achieve at WHO. Regardless, as I thought back on it all, I was so pleased on how everything had worked out so nicely. But now it was time to move on to fresh challenges from my new base in Houston," Jim said.

"I still believe that coming to Texas after CDC was the right choice. I am overwhelmed with the many ways in which the UT School of Public Health has honored and supported my career and activities," Jim said proudly. Under the direction of president Dr. Doger Bulger, the University of Texas bestowed him with Professor Emeritus status in 1984. The faculty recognized Jim in 1984 with a University of Texas-inscribed chair that Jim has in his home to this day. In 1993, Dean Palmer Beasly created a professorship in Jim's name along with a distinguished lecture series. "My travel schedule sometimes irked the administration along the way, but it never turned into a serious issue," Jim recalled.

"I had hoped that the University of California Medical Center would support a program to carry on the work of Dr. K. F. Meyer after his death. Dr. Meyer's program at the University of California was shut down and his facilities were converted into a liver disease research laboratory," Jim said. Ironically, Dr. Palmer Beasley did much of his best work on hepatitis B and other liver diseases in collaboration with the University of California and later came to the UTSPH as dean. "We became great friends," Jim said.

In his later years, Jim read *In Search of Memory* by Eric R. Kandel. "I recall a passage where Kandel states that nothing ever comes by chance in life. You have to prepare yourself from one step to the next. You must develop your own vision and motivation for achieving your career goals. After I read that passage, I smiled, realizing that was exactly what I had done. But I couldn't have done it without the outstanding, steadfast support of some great USPHS medical officers."

CHAPTER 26:
AVIAN INFLUENZA–"THIS IS THE STEELE VIRUS!"

In 1918, children skipped rope to the rhyme:
I had a little bird,
Its name was Enza.
I opened the window,
And in-flu-enza.

In September 1918, Dr. J. S. Koen, a veterinarian from BAI, was attending the national swine breeders show in Cedar Rapids, Iowa. A high percentage of the pigs at the show were sick, many with depression, coughing, and a serous discharge from the eyes and nose. "Dr. Koen concluded that the pigs had influenza, the same disease that was killing many people in the US at the time," Jim stated. Later it was determined that many outbreaks of swine influenza H1N1 virus occurred at the same time as the 1918 pandemic outbreak of human influenza that killed approximately fifty million people worldwide, also caused by an H1N1 strain. Dr. Koen published his findings in the *Journal of the American Veterinary Medical Association.*

At the first meeting of the WHO Expert Committee on Zoonoses in Geneva, Switzerland in December 1950, the panel discussed the possibility of an animal reservoir for human influenza. "At the time, no one really believed in the idea, but the question had to be addressed nevertheless. I suspected that the pig could be a source of disease for people, but I really didn't know how to go about proving it," Jim said. The influenza virus was initially isolated from pigs in 1927 at the Iowa State Fair by infectious disease researcher Dr. Richard Shope of the Rockfeller Institutes for Medical Research in New York City.

"The disease continued to infect pigs for many years. The BAI demonstrated in one study that mucus of respiratory origin was able to transmit the disease from pig to pig, whereas filtered mucus did not. Dr. Shope was impressed with this work. I don't believe that the members of the expert committee were aware of the

BAI study at the time of our meeting in 1950. There I learned that the Czechs were doing a lot of investigation into swine influenza. Some veterinary scientists thought that these outbreaks might be hog cholera," Jim said. Louis Pasteur had done a lot of work with pigs but never successfully isolated an etiological agent. Isolation of the influenza virus from a human being was not accomplished until 1932. "This work was also conducted at the Rockefeller Institute while it was still located in New York," Jim recalled.

When the Asian flu H2N2 strain first appeared in 1957, Jim conducted challenge studies at his Montgomery, Alabama laboratory to see if pigs could be a carrier of that virus. "They developed a mild transitory illness but quickly cleared the virus. I never published these findings except in *Veterinary Public Health Notes,*" Jim said. During World War II, researchers in Quebec produced a vaccine for swine influenza strain H1N1. Jim remembered the vaccine being marketed in Kansas and Nebraska. "It created quite a stir. The vaccine did not prevent respiratory disease, so the producers stopped using it. After the arrival of the Asian flu strain, I was asked by WHO to conduct a worldwide investigation into the role that swine might play in the maintenance and transmission of influenza. I was instructed to report back to the Expert Committee on Zoonoses meeting in Geneva, 1959," said Jim.

Jim traveled with Dr. Martin Kaplan to Japan, China, Taiwan, and Southeast Asia in search of clues. "In Hong Kong, I learned about the high incidence of respiratory signs in pigs coming into slaughterhouses from Southeast Asia and elsewhere. However, I could find no confirmatory evidence of influenza," Jim said. He went to bird markets in China where they sold Peking ducks and chickens. "They sold them in groups of about twelve ducks tied together by their necks. At this time, I didn't think seriously about influenza in avian species, but I was keeping an open mind. There just wasn't much in the scientific literature to hang your hat on. I thought I might be seeing gross lesions of viral pneumonia in the Chinese abattoirs, but I couldn't get their laboratories to confirm it for me," Jim said.

Jim and Dr. Kaplan moved on to Bangkok. "We visited some of the most repulsive slaughterhouses we had ever witnessed. But we didn't see anything resembling swine influenza," Jim said. Their next stop was Ceylon. "The country had respectable veterinary services. We met with two Ceylonese veterinarians that were brothers. They described some evidence of what appeared grossly to be viral pneumonia in the slaughterhouses, but they weren't confirming lesions by histopathology or attempting to isolate an agent. The coffee industry in Ceylon had been wiped out by fungal diseases, so they converted the entire industry over to growing and harvesting tea. They also made some of the land into pasture for raising cattle," Jim said.

After a brief, uneventful stay in Saudi Arabia, Jim was off to Cairo in May, 1959. "We asked their veterinarians about influenza. Again, we received a vague response. They had done some research on fowl plague but had not considered influenza in chickens. The Muslim population shunned swine as a food source, so there were no pigs for us to examine or any data to collect. From there we moved on to Jerusalem. We discovered no evidence of influenza in animals there either," Jim reported.

Next, they made a brief stop in Greece, where they found a medium-sized swine industry. "The country was recovering from a civil war with Communist sympathizers. Their veterinarians admitted to some respiratory diseases in pigs, but sheep and goats were by far their largest animal agricultural industry. There was some pneumonia being seen in slaughter pigs but, once again, no confirmation of an influenza virus. I ate a lot of shellfish while in Greece. Then I stumbled onto a paper that described shellfish as a source of hepatitis A in Greece, so I became a little concerned. Months later, I really wasn't feeling well," Jim said.

"We arrived back in Geneva, and I presented our report to the committee. We had found no concrete evidence of influenza in swine in any of the eleven countries we visited. The whole trip was a bit anticlimactic, to say the least," Jim said. After a short trip to Yugoslavia to deliver a lecture and a quick stop back in Geneva, Jim traveled on to Madrid for the 1959 World Veterinary Conference.

After the conference, Jim traveled back to Egypt to meet with some colleagues at the University of Cairo who had been conducting research on fowl plague. "I spent considerable time in the laboratories reviewing the work of their scientists. After returning to Atlanta on or about June 1, I was feeling really weak. I couldn't swim a full lap across a pool. I looked in the mirror and thought I was jaundiced. Did I contract malaria?" Jim recalled. On the Fourth of July, Jim and Aina were invited to Dr. Langmuir's house for a party. "I remember drinking a beer and eating a hot dog. The next day I felt horrible. My mouth was unbelievably dry," Jim said.

He checked in to the Public Health Service outpatient clinic. "Admit it Jim, you're just hung over; no sympathy here! Too much Fourth of July, maybe?" the clinician joked. But he really wasn't feeling well and went straight home.

"I had no appetite, which was really unusual for me. The next morning, I woke up and looked in the mirror again. This time I was sure. I was jaundiced. I was also losing a lot of weight. Hepatitis?" Jim guessed.

Jim finally decided to check into the hospital at Fort McPherson. "They agreed with my tentative diagnosis of hepatitis and recommended that Aina and the boys get an injection of antiserum," Jim said. The hospital did a complete diagnostic workup. "Dr. Helen Casey was a virologist at CDC. She isolated two enteroviruses from my feces and an unknown virus from my blood. She placed the virus into tissue culture. She suspected a hepatitis virus. She took a second blood sample and, once again, isolated a virus. Dr. James L. Goddard was the director of CDC at the time. He asked Robert Kissling, DVM, a rabies expert and an excellent virologist, to work with the virus. He injected some chickens intravenously and they all died. He deduced that that I was infected with an avian influenza virus. Dr. Kissling asked me if I had been around any sick birds recently. I quickly recalled my visit to the poultry laboratories at the University of Cairo," Jim stated.

Based on all of the laboratory work, Jim's doctors concluded that he was likely suffering from a dual infection, hepatitis A and fowl plague. "I had lost about twenty pounds by this time. I weighed in at 210 when I was normally about 230. Dr. Telford

Work, MD, was Dr. Kissling's boss. He had quite a reputation in virology. He didn't concur with with Dr. Kissling's findings. Dr. Helen Casey and Paul Delay published a case report on the findings in the *Public Health Reports,* July, 1967," Jim stated.

Jim took off from work to convalesce for three months, from July through September of that year. When he met with friends at the APHA meeting in Atlantic City, they were shocked to see him in such poor condition. "What happened to you?" they all asked.

"I made a presentation at the meeting, but it took all the energy I could muster to get through it," Jim said.

Jim's viral isolates were finally sent to Dr. Jerry Callis, DVM at the Plum Island Animal Disease Center in New York. Dr. Robert Webster had been collaborating with Dr. Callis. Dr. Webster was interested in the possible interactions of the influenza virus between people and animals. "This was considered a very dangerous experiment at the time. Folks were concerned about creating a monster virus in the laboratory," Jim said. Dr. Callis told Dr. Webster that he could use the Plum Island lab if he wanted to test what they were now calling the *Steele virus.*

Dr. Webster did complete a study on Jim's virus at Plum Island. "He identified my isolate as an avian influenza virus, type H7N7," Jim said.

In 2003, when Dr. Webster greeted Jim at the Emerging Zoonosis Conference in Ames, Iowa, he announced, "Thanks for making me famous!"

"Through the years, I became confused and began thinking my virus had been H7N2. Dr. Webster came to the University of Texas in April 2006 to commemorate my ninety-third birthday. He was also our keynote speaker for the celebration," said Jim.

Dr. Webster began his lecture by pointing at Jim and stating bluntly, "He is carrying the Steele virus. Don't let this man out of the country. No telling what he'll bring back home with him! As far as I know, Jim Steele is the only person from whom H7N7 has ever been isolated!" Although it is not absolutely proven, the laboratory at the University of Cairo that Jim visited in 1959 was the most likely source. Dr. Webster is a world renowned virologist at St. Jude Children's Research Hospital, St. Louis, Missouri and is well known for his work on influenza. A New Zealander, he established the World Health Organization Collaborating Center on the Ecology of Influenza Viruses in Lower Animals and Birds. This is one of the world's only laboratories that researches the epidemiology of influenza as a multi-species disease.

"Was I immunosuppressed on this trip? Did the hepatitis virus make me susceptible to the fowl plague virus? Could I have carried the influenza virus for six weeks after an exposure in Cairo? I guess we will never know for sure," Jim said grinning.

At a later date, Jim shared the story with Dr. Richard Shope at a chance meeting at Princeton University. "This demonstrates how nicely you can carry a virus, Jim!" Dr. Shope said.

CHAPTER 27:
THE HANDBOOK SERIES IN ZOONOSES— CRC
AFTER CDC

"At the end of my career at CDC, I faced the realization that Aina was going to die. Some days I was almost incoherent due to the mental anguish and loss of sleep. I was living in a nightmare. I was struggling with the challenges at home and, at the same time, trying to see what the future might hold for my career. About the only thing that kept me going was my passion to carry on Dr. K. F. Meyer's work," Jim recalled. At the time, the University of California was shutting Dr. Meyer's research programs down. "K. F. just couldn't seem to bring in any new funding," Jim said. Aina died on March 8, 1969.

"When I retired from CDC in 1971, I wasn't concerned about the future of veterinary public health. I had built a sound foundation and had a cadre of bright young veterinarians like Drs. Russell Currier, Myron Schultz, Robert Huffaker, Richard Parker, George Baer, Robert Kissling, John Richardson, Paul Arnstein, John Helwig, Keith Sikes, Fred Murphy, and Peter Schantz to carry on. My sincerest apologies to anyone that I did not list here, there were so many outstanding officers," Jim said. It was time to move on to his career in academia. The next step was clear to Jim. "I was passionate about creating a comprehensive set of reference texts on the zoonotic class of diseases. I had learned about Gaylord Anderson's history of the Army Medical Corps many years earlier. This may have planted the seed in my mind for a comprehensive book series on zoonotic diseases. I remembered thinking that the world's medical libraries would not be complete until this task was done," Jim said. He knew that once he reached this goal, the allied health professions would have the desk references necessary to better understand and work with this neglected set of diseases.

"Part of my motivation, of course, was to capture K. F. Meyer's and other scientists' knowledge so that it would live on. I envisioned an encyclopedia of zoonotic diseases. But what was the best strategy for launching such an ambitious undertaking? I decided that the tables of zoonoses that I developed for so many years at CDC and the work I did for the Merck Veterinary Manual would serve as a nice starting point for a table of contents.

I often discussed the series with Dr. Meyer. He was retired but was still staying on top of his field," Jim said. Dr. Meyer responded, "Yes, Jim, this is something that you and I should do together. We have to fully document what we know about the world!" Jim hoped that in 1974, at K. F.'s ninetieth birthday party, he would announce that Dr. Meyer would be one of the lead authors in the zoonoses series. But it wasn't meant to be. Dr. Meyer died of colon cancer in April 1974, a few weeks before his ninetieth birthday celebration.

"The first hurdle was to secure funding for the project," Jim stated. Dr. Joe Mountin, retired assistant surgeon general for states relations, had died of a brain hemorrhage early in 1954. Dr. Joe Dean, Dr. Mountin's executive officer at CDC, wanted to document Dr. Mountin's contributions to public health. "I referred to these two men as my 'Joe saints' because they worked so hard to help me establish the veterinary public health program at CDC," Jim said.

Joe Dean asked Jim, "Somehow we have got to publish these papers on Dr. Mountin's work. Can you help me find some funding?"

Jim took the idea to Max and Gustav Stern at Hartz Mountain Corporation. They responded, "Just let us know how we can help you." Dr. Dean followed up with the Stern brothers. They agreed to fund the entire cost of publishing Dr. Mountin's work. "Dr. Dean and the staff at CDC were very grateful. This gave me the idea to approach Max Stern with a proposal for the series of books on zoonoses. He loved the idea, and Hartz Mountain later agreed to support our project as well. That was half the battle!" Jim said.

"The CRC Press, a scientific book publisher based in Cleveland, Ohio, made the best offer to complete the project. This company had an interesting history," Jim said. The CRC Press started as the Chemical Rubber Company, thus the acronym. Their original business supplied laboratory equipment to chemists. In 1913 the company published a manual called the *Rubber Handbook,* which was designed as an advertising publication for their products. "This manual evolved into CRC's *Handbook of Chemistry and Physics,* which became one of their best sellers and still is to this day," Jim explained. "I admired their works in chemistry, physics and other fields. It was a perfect fit for the series on zoonoses," Jim observed. The eighty-eighth edition was published in 2007 and is still referred to as the "rubber Bible."

Dr. Primo Arambulo was Jim's graduate student at the University of Texas School of Public Health in Houston, Texas. Jim and Dr. Arambulo became the nucleus of the project. "In 1976, Primo and I drove together to Ames, Iowa for the World Food Congress. We discussed our plans for the books along the way. From the Iowa meeting, we drove to Cleveland, Ohio, where the CRC Press was headquartered," Jim detailed. "The staff hosted a nice reception for us when we arrived. We quickly came to a deal. They drew up a contract that spelled out the delivery of a certain number of chapters in a specified timeframe. Primo was also working hard to finish his PhD at the time. We really had our hands full," Jim recalled.

Jim made the zoonoses series his highest-priority project. "I took a relatively low profile in my new role as a professor at the University of Texas School of Public Health. This meant taking a secondary role in soliciting grant funding and leading research projects. I served as a co-investigator on many projects but did not take on any as the primary investigator. This freed up my time to serve as editor for the CRC series. My first major task was to assemble a team of section editors and contributors. This was quite a job in itself, one that took over a year," Jim explained. The outline of the books and the participating editors and authors were as follows:

Editor-In-Chief

James H. Steele, DVM MPH, Assistant Surgeon General (Retired), US Public Health Service, Professor of

Environmental Health and Science, School of Public Health, University of Texas at Houston

Editor, Section A: Bacterial, Rickettsial, and Mycotic Diseases

Herbert Stoenner, DVM, Director, Rocky Mountain Laboratory, US Public Health Service, Hamilton, Montana
Michael Torten, DVM, PhD, Israel Institute for Biological Research, Ness-Ziona, Faculty of Medical Sciences, Tel Aviv University School of Medicine, Israel
William Kaplan, DVM MPH, Mycology Division, Center for Disease Control, Atlanta, Georgia

Editor, Section B: Viral Zoonoses

George W. Beran, DVM PhD LHD, Professor, Veterinary Microbiology and Preventive Medicine, Iowa State University, Ames, Iowa

Editor, Section C: Parasitic Zoonoses

Primo Arambulo, III DVM MPH PhD, Public Health Veterinary Consultant, PAHO & WHO, Washington, DC.

Editor, Section D: Antibiotics, Sulfonamides, and Public Health

George W. Beran, DVM PhD LHD, Professor, Veterinary Microbiology and Preventive Medicine, Iowa State University, Ames, Iowa, Associate Editor-in-Chief
Thomas H. Jukes, Professor, Department of Biophysics and Medical Physics and Department of Nutritional Sciences, University of California, Berkeley, California
Lester M. Crawford, Director, Bureau of Veterinary Medicine, Food and Drug Administration, Rockville, Maryland
Herbert L. Dupont, Professor and Director, Program in Infectious Diseases and Clinical Microbiology, University

of Texas Medical School, Houston, Texas

C. Don VanHouweling, DVM MS, Special Assistant for Agricultural Matters, Food and Drug Administration, Rockville, Maryland

The first edition was composed of two volumes on bacterial, rickettsial and mycotic zoonoses (V1 1979; V2 1980); two volumes on viral zoonoses (1981); three volumes on parasitic zoonoses (1982); and one volume entitled *Antibiotics, Sulfonamides, and Public Health* (1984). In addition to the section editors, Jim appointed an advisory board for each volume as follows:

Advisory Board, Section A: Bacterial, Rickettsial, and Mycotic Diseases (Volume I)

Pedro Acha, Director, Disease Control, Pan American Health Organization, Washington, DC

Philip Brachman, Director, Bureau of Epidemiology, Center for Disease Control, Atlanta, Georgia

Herbert Dupont, Professor and Director, Infectious Diseases, Medical School, University of Texas, Houston, Texas

John Francis, Professor, Preventive Medicine and Public Health, Veterinary School, University of Queensland, St. Lucia, Queensland, Australia

Hans-Jorgen Hansen, Director, National Veterinary Institute, Stockholm, Sweden

E. H. Kampelmacher, Deputy Director, National Institutes of Health, Bilthoven, The Netherlands

Martin Kaplan, Scientific Director (retired), World Health Organization, Geneva, Switzerland

Frank Mulhern, Administrator, Animal and Plant Health Inspection Service, U.S. Department of Agriculture, Washington, DC

E. Ryu, Director, International Laboratory for Zoonoses, Research Foundation, National University, Taipei, Taiwan

William Taylor Steele Thorp, Dean (retired), College of Veterinary Medicine, University of Minnesota, St. Paul,

Minnesota, Consultant to the Pan American Health Organization, Guayaquil, Ecuador

Advisory Board, Section A: Bacterial, Rickettsial, and Mycotic Diseases (Volume II)

Robert K. Anderson, Professor of Veterinary Public Health, Division of Epidemiology, School of Public Health, University of Minnesota, Minneapolis, Minnesota
Harvey R. Fischman, Associate Professor of Epidemiology, School of Hygiene and Public Health, Johns Hopkins University, Baltimore, Maryland
Alexander D. Langmuir, Professor of Epidemiology (retired), Medical School, Harvard University, Boston, Massachusetts
William Mitchell, Professor of Public Health, Ontario Veterinary College, University of Guelph, Guelph, Ontario
Adriano Montavani, Professor of Preventive Medicine, Veterinary Medical Faculty, University of Bologna, Bologna, Italy
Phillip A. O'Berry, Director, National Animal Disease Center, Ames, Iowa
Charles H. Pilet, Professor of Immunology, Microbiology and Infectious Disease, Ecole Nationale D'Alfort, Alfort, France
Julius Schacter, Professor of Epidemiology, George Williams Hooper Foundation, Acting Director, Karl Friedrich Meyer Laboratories, University of California, San Francisco, California
Edward A. Schilf, Assistant to the Deputy Administrator, Animal and Plant Health Inspection Service, Veterinary Services, US Department of Agriculture, Washington, DC
C. M. Singh, Director, Indian Veterinary Research Institute, Izatnagar, UP, India

Advisory Board, Section B: Viral Zoonoses (Volumes I & II)

George M. Baer, Chief, Viral Zoonoses Branch, Bureau of Laboratories, Center for Disease Control, Atlanta, Georgia

Irving Kagan, Director of Parasitology, Center for Disease
Control, US Public Health Service, Atlanta, Georgia
Adriano Mantovani, Professor of Preventive Medicine,
Faculty of Veterinary Medicine, University of Bologna,
Bologna, Italy
E. Ryu, Director, International Laboratory for Zoonoses,
Research Foundation, National University, Taipei, Taiwan
Ernest Soulsby, Professor of Parasitology, School of Vet-
erinary Medicine, Cambridge University, Cambridge,
England

"We decided that the original idea of an encyclopedic format
was not ideal. Instead, we used a more traditional chapter design
with a structured outline for each. Furthermore, we decided on
a standardized outline for subsections on each disease: Introduction; Disease Nomenclature; Etiologic Agent; Reservoir and Alternate Hosts; Distribution; Disease in Animals; Disease in Man;
General Mode of Spread; Epidemiology; Diagnosis; Prevention
and Control; Editorial Comments; Bibliography. The contributors were allowed to expand on these minimum criteria as needed.
In other words, they could add special section headings as they saw
fit," Jim explained.

Jim then tackled the grueling task of making a subject outline
for the books, listing the chapters and then deciding who would
be the best authority to actually write each chapter. "I spent a lot
of time writing letters and making phone calls to the scientists I
was recruiting. The CRC Press was quite generous in their funding support of the authors, providing roughly $25,000 US dollars
per volume. That really helped with the recruiting effort," Jim
said.

Jim was delighted by the number of outstanding scientists
around the world who responded. "Overall, there were fifty-six
contributors to the initial bacterial, rickettsial and mycotic volumes; seventy-one for the volumes on virology; sixty-two for the
volumes on parasitology and twenty-seven for the one volume on
antibiotics and sulfonamides," Jim stated. Many are surprised to
learn that Jim never received a penny for his work on the books.

"I joked with my Jewish colleagues about the fact that no one volunteered to translate the books into Hebrew. They would always laugh and reply that they could read the books in English just fine!" Jim said.

After the books were released, positive reviews began coming in from around the world. "Dr. Ed Cass, editor of the *Journal of Infectious Diseases*, wrote a very nice review. This really felt good." Jim said. The National Foundation for Infectious Diseases also published an excellent appraisal of the books. As time went on, reviews of the books made it into several foreign journals and publications. "I was quite pleased. The first printing was done only in English. Over a period of six years, the first set of eight volumes sold roughly 2,500 sets.

I asked the CRC Press who our biggest audiences were. They responded that apparently every military library in the world wanted a copy," Jim said. He learned later that the series was unofficially translated into Russian and into Farsi by Iranian scientists. Dr. Pedro Acha later wrote a one-volume book on zoonotic diseases in Spanish. "This might explain why the *CRC Series Handbook on Zoonoses* was never translated into Spanish. The CRC Series was much more extensive and would have been quite expensive to translate," Jim said.

"I saw how fast technology was changing. In the eighties, electronic media began to blossom. In 1987, I joined a project with Drs. Norman Ronald and Craig Carter at Texas A&M University to develop an infectious and parasitic disease clinical decision support and reference system now known as *Public Health Associate*. It is now available at no charge worldwide through the Veterinary Information Network headquartered in Davis, California. Much of the knowledge base in this system was adopted from the CRC series. The field of biological sciences was also changing rapidly. We decided to try to update the CRC series at a minimum every ten years. Dr. George Beran graciously accepted the editorship for the second edition for bacterial, rickettsial, chlamydial and mycotic zoonoses, which was published in 1994," Jim explained.

"As I traveled around the world, I would often see the books in offices and libraries. I received many compliments. The Brazilians explained to me how they used the series to assist in building an inventory of their endemic zoonotic diseases," Jim said.

Dr. James Gear of South Africa wrote to Jim and said, "This is probably the greatest contribution to veterinary medicine and public health ever!"

The positive reviews kept coming in from places like Australia, Japan, India, Israel and beyond. "Whenever I think about the CRC series, I get a great feeling. I am eternally indebted to all the outstanding scientists that worked so hard to make it a reality. It was such a great honor and a privilege to be the editor in chief. My only regret is that Dr. K. F. Meyer wasn't able to participate directly in the project. Regardless, it goes without saying that K. F.'s inspiration in the creation of the *CRC Handbook Series in Zoonoses* was huge," said Jim.

CHAPTER 28:
A FEW MORE DISEASES

Jim Steele and Anthrax

"My early knowledge of anthrax came from reading the descriptions written by the renown US Army Veterinary Corps officer Brigadier General Raymond Kelser. He commanded the Veterinary Corps during World War II," Jim said. General Kelser reported on anthrax in Sicily, Italy; Okinawa, Japan; and Korea during and after the war. He went on to become the dean of the School of Veterinary Medicine at the University of Pennsylvania.

The federal government was given quarantine authority to prevent the introduction of communicable diseases from foreign countries in 1944 with passage of the Public Health Service Act. "In 1947, I received a somewhat anxious phone call from Gilbert Dunnahoo, MD, the USPHS chief quarantine officer at the time. He described an outbreak of cutaneous anthrax that was occurring in textile factory workers in New York State. I dispatched Dr. Arthur Wolff, a USPHS veterinarian, to conduct the initial investigation," Jim stated. Dr. Wolff was known for his outstanding work on foodborne *Salmonella* outbreaks in Michigan. In the postwar period, coarse wool was being imported from the Mideast. The products were not inspected and often contained anthrax spores, infecting many of those working with the raw materials.

"About a year later, Dr. Dunnahoo contacted me and asked what kind of screening practice could be implemented to assure the safety of textile workers in the factories. I had knowledge of the British system of import stations where the wool was washed upon receipt. I knew of no other methods at the time," Jim explained. Jim would see his British colleagues at the World Veterinary Congress in Liverpool, England in 1949 and planned to learn more about the wool-washing technique to see if it could be implemented in the US.

"I visited the Liverpool wool-washing station. The procedure seemed to be sound, but I was concerned that it would difficult to put into practice in the US with so many ports. Then I learned that the Australians were exploring the use of irradiation to kill the latent anthrax spores," said Jim. But once again, he was concerned that this solution would be expensive and unmanageable.

"I raised the idea of anthrax vaccination for textile workers with K. F. Meyer. He responded that it would be very tricky to monitor antibody levels and to know when an individual was protected. But he did think the idea had merit," Jim said. The non-encapsulated live variant strain Sterne anthrax vaccine developed in 1937 was approved only for use in animals. The Russians reported using a filtered version of the vaccine successfully in the fifties and sixties in cattle and reported it in their scientific literature. "Dr. Max Sterne, developer of the vaccine that carried his name, told me personally that he would never recommend using this strain in people. He was afraid of inducing clinical disease with the product. The Russians reportedly vaccinated some of their soldiers with a vaccine derived from the Sterne vaccine and subsequently exposed them to live *Bacillus anthracis*. The story is told that all the guinea pigs in the same room died while the soldiers survived," Jim said.

New Hampshire was reporting several cases of cutaneous anthrax to CDC through their local health department at the time. Dr. Langmuir sent Dr. Phil Brockman, MD to investigate the human cases. "He asked me to consult with Dr. Brockman, but I stayed back in Atlanta. Dr. Brockman interviewed employees about their health histories. He learned about acute deaths in four coworkers that had been diagnosed as stroke by a physician. One of these employees was responsible for opening bales of wool at the start of the production line," Jim said.

After a consultation with Jim, Dr. Brockman decided to pursue obtaining permission from family members to exhume the bodies of the victims. "Fluorescent antibody testing for anthrax was positive, confirming the disease in these patients. I believe this incident may have stimulated the military's interest in anthrax vaccination for soldiers. Dr. Brockman soon became a consultant for Fort Detrick," Jim stated. The strain isolated in the New Hampshire cases became known as the Brockman strain.

"In the late 1950s an outbreak occurred in Philadelphia at a factory that processed animal hair that was used to upholster furniture. A secretary who worked on the factory floor died of pulmonary anthrax. The domestic quarantine program was transferred to CDC as a result of this outbreak," Jim reported. One of the first strategies that Jim recommended was to prohibit the importation of hair and wool products from areas of the world where anthrax is widespread. Fortunately, penicillin was very effective in treatment of the cutaneous form of the disease. The respiratory form is so fulminating that antibiotics are often administered too late to alter the course of the disease.

"Another outbreak of cutaneous anthrax occurred in a textile factory in Monroe, North Carolina in 1960. This case aroused so much fear in the community that they reopened an old hospital to isolate a single patient. Fortunately, she was treated and survived," Jim said. An investigation was ordered and Jim dispatched one of his best USPHS veterinary officers, Dr. John Freeman. He collected a comprehensive set of specimens from all over the factory and sent them to CDC for testing. "Anthrax spores were confirmed, even on the manager's desk. The curious and very fortunate thing about this incident was that it resulted in only one clinical case," Jim said. Dr. Freeman later became president of the AVMA.

Jim visited the Russian anthrax laboratory in Tbilisi in 1963 as head of a US exchange delegation. "My recollection of that trip is that I was basically led around by the nose. It was quite different when the Russian delegation visited the US. We showed them just about everything but the far and dark corners of Fort Detrick," Jim said. Intelligence indicated that the Russians were planning to produce anthrax weapons and were hoping to protect their soldiers on the battlefield with a vaccine. "When I asked my Russian colleagues about cattle anthrax, they said that their vaccine had totally eliminated the disease in livestock. As I moved around the country, I began to believe that they had truly achieved some real success with their vaccination programs," Jim said.

When he arrived at the Tbilisi facility, he found that they were producing enormous quantities of anthrax vaccine. "Why is production so high?" Jim asked.

"For our border friends, of course!" they responded, in an apparent reference to the Chinese.

In 1964, Jim was sent to New Guinea to investigate reports of extremely virulent strains of anthrax. "When I returned, the Department of Defense and the CIA were quite interested in hearing my findings. But I reported that I found no evidence of such strains," said Jim. In 1964, Jim attended a world conference on the movement of products of animal origin hosted in Berne, Switzerland. "By this time, the public health community was concluding that packing material of animal origin for products and souvenirs to be shipped worldwide was not a good idea," Jim explained.

Dr. David Huxsoll, the director of research at Fort Detrick, asked Jim to represent the US Army at an international congress on anthrax in Winchester, England in 1989. "Brigitte and I were invited to Max Sterne's home. I asked him if he believed we could eliminate clinical anthrax in animals with vaccination?"

He responded, "If the vaccine is used worldwide, it might be controlled, but not eliminated. The spores are ubiquitous, Jim!"

At one of the sessions, the Chinese stated that they had vaccinated over one million soldiers with the Russian modified Sterne vaccine. "Dr. Sterne spoke up and advised against this practice, as the chance for vaccine-induced anthrax was high. There was no response from the Chinese delegation," Jim said.

"I am so pleased that Max Sterne received the K. F. Meyer Gold-Headed Cane Award for his work on anthrax. To this day, I am still puzzled why the British never recognized Dr. Sterne for his work," Jim stated. Dr. Sterne painstakingly filtered many South African strains for years until he found an avirulent strain suitable for a vaccine. All animal anthrax vaccines today are still based on his strains. Jim and Max got along famously and were great friends. Jim feels strongly that he is deserving of more recognition for his contributions worldwide. The WHO never recognized the Sterne vaccine as appropriate for use in people.

"Because of my strong interest in the disease, I have maintained close contact with many anthrax investigators over the years," Jim said. Among them were Dr. Martin Hugh Jones, professor emeritus at Louisiana State University, and Colonel Sal Cirone, a veterinarian who was head of health policy at the Pentagon. His job was to conduct zoonotic disease surveillance for the US military. Anthrax was one of his highest priorities. "Dr. Phil Brockman of CDC collected soil samples from all over the world, but he had little luck in isolating the anthrax bacillus. In 1979, I had a graduate student study the coastal soils of Texas for the presence of anthrax. We found maps that outlined the routes for cattle drives in the nineteenth century. Because of this, we expected that anthrax spores would be widespread in the area. However, this turned out not to be the case. A similar study was conducted in South Africa to help explain patterns of anthrax in the hippopotamus. But once again, the organism could not readily be found in soil anywhere away from site of the buried animal," Jim said.

Jim has never endorsed the idea of anthrax vaccination for civilian or military personnel. "I hold this opinion primarily based on what I perceive as lack of risk for contracting the disease. To my knowledge, CDC never vaccinated a veterinarian or recommended that this be done even with the knowledge that veterinarians are at a high risk of exposure. A case of anthrax has never been seen in the US military. WHO and PAHO have dropped their support for human vaccination. But we must have an open mind and be prepared for unusual presentations of this disease," Jim said.

"I watched the anthrax episodes in US post offices and elsewhere after 9/11 with amazement. I was even more astounded in learning about the Fort Detrick scientist that was implicated in the distribution of the spores. Epidemiologically, nothing is absolute. You must always anticipate the unexpected. Expect outbreaks of disease with patterns that have never been seen," said Jim.

Jim Steele and the Encephalitides

In the late forties, when Jim's career was just being launched, it was already well recognized that mosquitoes were the vectors for many of the encephalitides. However, the reservoir hosts were not yet well characterized. Researchers also knew that horses were sometimes involved in the life cycle. But it was not yet recognized that horses could serve as amplifier hosts for Venezuelan equine encephalitis. "I can recall being hungry for a better understanding of the epidemiology of the encephalitides," Jim said.

"In 1951, there was a major outbreak of western equine encephalomyelitis in California. The state asked for emergency assistance from the CDC, and I immediately became involved. Interestingly, the California State budget did not pass that year, and there was no funding for mosquito control; the San Joaquin valley was thus very vulnerable," Jim said. Jim dispatched six USPHS veterinarians to provide epidemiological assistance. The CDC Division of Vector-Borne Infectious Diseases was in operation in Logan, Utah at the time. "It was later moved to Greeley, Colorado in 1967 and later on to its present location at Fort Collins. The laboratory linked songbirds into the life cycle of the disease and was using chickens as sentinels. They were even able to identify distinct strains of encephalitis virus," Jim explained.

"In 1934, the eastern equine encephalomyelitis virus was isolated from mosquitoes, and finally, in 1950, the virus was isolated from a wild bird. The disease was named 'eastern' after an outbreak on the east coast in Delaware, Maryland, Virginia and New Jersey in 1933. I became involved in an outbreak in New Jersey in 1959. I helped to establish a CDC laboratory near Atlantic City," Jim recalled. From the data generated by that facility, Jim followed horse cases all the way up the New England coast as far as the mosquito activity could be found.

"I was watching the human cases closely and observed that the attack rate was roughly one case per 1,000 population. In addition, it was affecting mostly children under fifteen and adults over fifty-five. Further epidemiological studies identified ring-necked pheasants as amplifier hosts. This had been determined during previous outbreaks. We also observed mechanical transmission from pheasant to pheasant, most likely via body fluids swapped during pecking order squabbles. This eventually led to the practice of debeaking domestic pheasants," Jim said. After this outbreak, Dr. Langmuir wanted Jim and others to establish a surveillance program for the encephalitides. This surveillance identified cases as far south as Cuba in early spring. "The cases would work their way up the eastern seaboard as it got warmer. I thought it was very interesting that the outbreaks were quite sporadic and still are today," Jim said.

"The first vaccines were developed by Jensen-Salisbury Veterinary Laboratories. They produced attenuated vaccines in the 1940s for western equine encephalitis and then for eastern equine encephalitis a little later, around 1950. Effective vaccines were eventually developed to protect pheasants against the eastern virus. When we went to Panama, the NIH made batches of a special egg embryo vaccine for us. I will never forget the golf-ball-sized swellings at the vaccination sites." Jim recalled.

Jim was involved in the Venezuelan equine encephalitis (VEE) outbreak in southern Texas that began in Mexico, April 1971. "I believe to this day that this was a manmade, accidental epidemic. Wherever animals were vaccinated in Ecuador, outbreaks would follow. Unfortunately, I was never able to confirm this. Somehow the disease leapfrogged Costa Rica and Panama and ended up in Guatemala," Jim recalled. The US Army developed an effective vaccine for VEE in Colonel Abram S. Benenson's laboratory. After Colonel Benenson left the Army, he went on to have an illustrious sixty-year medical career around the globe, eventually serving as editor in chief of the well known *Control of Communicable Disease Manual* published by the American Public Health Association from 1970 to 1995. "We were great colleagues and friends. I nominated Dr. Benenson for the K. F. Meyer Gold-Headed Cane Award from the American Veterinary Epidemiology Society, which he received in 1984," Jim said.

"The King Ranch in south Texas went direct to the White House to get the VEE vaccine approved for use in people even though it was only approved for use in animals," Jim reported. An emergency meeting on VEE was called shortly after the disease hit Texas in 1971. Jim was in Finland for meeting on arctic public health and had to return home early. "The press was waiting for me when I got off the plane in San Antonio. My advice during the meeting was simple. Employ vigorous mosquito control and vaccination programs or we will have cases as far north as Chicago!" Jim admonished. This advice turned out to be sound and ultimately gained him great respect throughout the Texas medical and veterinary communities.

"We established surveillance for VEE on the Mexican border. My old friend and colleague Dr. Robert Kokernut was at the University of Texas, School of Public Health at the time and was heavily involved in these efforts. I helped him acquire a grant from CDC to conduct the VEE surveillance. This continued all through the seventies. Dr. Kokernut was one of my more colorful colleagues, having earned DVM, MD and PhD degrees," he said. Jim first met Dr. Kokernut at the Texas Department of Health. Dr. Archie Flowers, professor of veterinary public health at Texas A&M University told Jim that Dr. Kokernut's ancestors had helped to settle West Texas in the 1800s. They reportedly had large ranch and became a major power in Texas during the twentieth century.

"I need to tell you a bit more about Dr. Kokernut. Bob came to Texas A&M for his veterinary training. He became the class president and was quite the hell-raiser," Jim mused. During World War II, Texas A&M University decided to halt the rich tradition of a bonfire the night before the Texas A&M/University of Texas football game. "Bob organized his own and was thrown out of veterinary school. He then got drafted and went off to earn a strong military record in World War II. After the war he returned to Texas and finished veterinary school. He went from there to John Hopkins University for his MD and also completed a PhD in public health," said Jim.

Dr. Kokernut later received funding from the Rockefeller Foundation and did virology research in Africa during the 1950s and 1960s. He then went to the University of Illinois to study St. Louis encephalitis virus. "I also helped fund his work in Illinois. As I neared my retirement from CDC and was interviewing around, I learned that Dr. Kokernut was in Houston at the new University of Texas School of Public Health as a professor of epidemiology. Bob arranged a press conference that made me look like one of the great CDC scientists. I really appreciated that," Jim said. Soon, Dr. Kokernut joined Texas Tech University as a professor of community medicine. "I visited him there as late as 1975, but then lost track of him. The last thing I know about Bob was that he planned to open a veterinary clinic on the Texas-Mexico border. He was a brilliant and interesting scientist. I often wonder what happened to him. I only met a few DVM/MD's in my career, including the MD that did my retirement physical at the USPHS hospital in Baltimore, Maryland. He attended veterinary school in Minnesota. And that's a true story!"

386 | ONE MAN, ONE MEDICINE, ONE HEALTH

Jim Steele and Taenia saginata

In 1948, Jim began receiving reports from Arizona about a beef tapeworm outbreak, *Taenia saginata.* "Adult beef tapeworms reside in the human intestinal tract. Cattle are infected by eating ova released from tapeworm segments. This results in cysts in the muscle. Human infection follows when eating undercooked beef, and the cycle is completed. I investigated the incident and learned that they were using effluent from sewage treatment plants to irrigate pasture. Once the hay was fed to cattle, they became infected," Jim said. Jim ordered a complete investigation and dispatched Dr. Oscar Sussman to Arizona to carry it out.

"When the US began issuing green cards for immigrant workers in the early fifties, I warned my colleagues at CDC that they would be bringing in both beef and porcine tapeworms, increasing the risk of animal infection," Jim said. At the time, he recommended that a screening program be established for immigrants. However, a screening program was never implemented. "There were outbreaks of neurocysticercosis in 1990 and 1991 in unrelated persons in New York that were ultimately tied to infected domestic workers from Latin America. This is still a problem today!" Jim stated.

Jim was called in on another beef tapeworm problem in the Texas panhandle in the late sixties. "Dr. Mike Schultz was sent to do the field investigation. We learned that ranchers weren't providing toilets for the workers, so they were resorting to defecating in the feed bins. This, of course, infected the cattle and ended up in the food chain," Jim said. As a result of this investigation, several banks halted their lines of credit to the feedlot industry. The Texas Department of Health called Jim to verify what CDC had reported. "I told them I would stake my career on this!" Jim said. The cattle industry finally accepted Jim's findings and added the necessary toilet facilities. "This, of course, solved the problem. It is all published in *Journal of the American Veterinary Medical Association* and in the CDC veterinary public health reports."

Jim still thinks about the problem of immigrant laborers and their role in these diseases. "There are more immigrants in the US than ever. I often wonder just how big the problem is," Jim said. A good friend and colleague of Jim's at CDC, Dr. Peter Schantz, a veterinarian, has devoted a large part of his career toward controlling tapeworm disease worldwide, both from a health and the economic standpoint. "*Taenia solium*, the pork tapeworm, is important as it can result in neurocysticercosis or cysts localized in the brain. I recall in the sixties reports of tennis players in Kenya dropping *Taenia saginata* tapeworm proglottids on the court as they played. I can also remember the sewage plants in Nairobi where proglottids were so numerous they appeared like clumps of floating condoms in the water. We need to continue our vigilance until this disease is totally under control in the world. Bright veterinary scientists like Peter Schantz have brought us a long way," Jim said.

CHAPTER 29:
A FEW MORE ADVENTURES

Jim Steele in Israel and Egypt

As Jim's career was just unfolding, in November 1947, the United Nations sanctioned a plan to split up what was still known as the British Mandate of Palestine into two separate states, one Jewish and the other Arabic. Jerusalem proper fell under international control. Following the Arab-Israeli War of 1948, Jerusalem was divided, with the western half becoming the state of Israel and the eastern portion annexed by Jordan. The next years were very tumultuous until the six-day war in 1967, wherein Israel captured East Jerusalem. In 1959, Jim and Dr. Martin Kaplan traveled to the World Health Organization (WHO) office in Alexandria, Egypt to discuss how to most effectively introduce the concept of veterinary public health (VPH) into the Middle East and Africa. "We were both idealists and wanted to help bring people together through improvement in public health," Jim said.

Jim's twin cousins, Myrna and Myrle, lived in Muskegon, Michigan. They were on an extended overseas vacation and had planned to meet Jim and Martin in Cairo. Instead, the twins surprised them at the airport in Alexandria, Egypt just as they were leaving. Jim quizzed the twins, "What are you doing here?"

They responded "We were looking for you, Jimmy!" From there they all flew from Cairo into East Jerusalem.

Like Egypt, Israel was interested in broadening the scope of its veterinary services to include a program in VPH. "Our agenda was to discuss control programs for bovine tuberculosis, brucellosis and rabies," Jim said.

"Martin and I made arrangements to make a quick trip to Jordan to meet with their chief veterinary officer. I can't recall his name but he had attended the University of California, Davis," Jim said. The CVO in Jordan raised an interesting question. "He stated that they had been vaccinating the Bedouins for smallpox in southern Jordan. Following this campaign there was an outbreak of horsepox. Horsepox had all but disappeared from the world scene. Could the vaccinia virus have spilled over into the horse? Jenner had described horsepox in his scientific papers in the eighteenth century. I was stunned to learn that it existed at all. I had never heard about it until that moment," Jim said.

Dr. Donald A. Henderson, chief of the WHO smallpox eradication campaign, previously deputy chief of the epidemiology branch at CDC, later asked Jim if horsepox cases were occurring during the smallpox vaccination campaign. "I spent many years contemplating the possible role of the horse in smallpox. The case reports from Jordan and elsewhere made me very curious," Jim stated. Dr. Henderson worked with the WHO on the world campaign to eradicate smallpox for more than a decade.

"Dr. Kaplan arranged for the Israeli veterinary delegation to meet us at the St. Stephens gate on the east side of Jerusalem in Jordan. All of us checked out of the hotel and traveled by bus to the gate. The cousins had their passports handed right back to them and were not allowed to pass through. Both Martin and I had WHO visas, so our paperwork was in order. It was early Sunday morning and we were stuck on the Palestinian side. Martin was pacing back and forth. We couldn't just leave the cousins behind," Jim said.

The cousins cried out, "Jimmy, why didn't you tell us about the visas?"

Jim just shrugged his shoulders and said, "I thought I did."

Finally, a guard came over and said that there was a man from the American embassy in a nearby car. Jim introduced himself and learned that the fellow was an Auburn University graduate. "Yeah, you guys beat us, Michigan State, six to three in the Orange Bowl in 1936!" Within an hour, he returned with two visas for the cousins. They shouted, "Jimmy always takes good care of us. The guards even carried our luggage!" They passed uneventfully on through the gate.

On the Israeli side, an entourage of public health and veterinary authorities greeted them with a nice reception. "After some of our recent travels in third world countries, the good, wholesome food and drinks were a welcome treat," Jim said. The meetings in Israel centered mostly on how the US and Israel could enter into joint VPH projects utilizing PL 480 funds. As discussed in chapter 12, US Public Law 480 supported governments, businesses, non-governmental organizations and educational institutions to form partnerships to eliminate hunger and to improve public health over the globe.

"Rabies was not a big problem in Israel at the time. They had implemented a robust animal control program based on our CDC model to control hydatid disease in the Canaan dogs. I was impressed with their work," Jim recalled. The Canaan dog roamed wild in Israel for thousands of years and is the Israeli analog of a coyote. "Beef tapeworm was also a problem. Wild boars carried trichinosis, but pork was only consumed by the Christian minority. Even dogs carried trichina in this part of the world," stated Jim. The Israelis wanted to market kosher chickens to the US Jim helped coordinate their request with the USDA, and this initiative was very successful. It was the end of the Eisenhower era, and relations with Israel were very good.

Jim returned to Israel to investigate hydatid disease in 1964 with his son David, who was twelve at the time. "The trip was during David's fall school term. When we returned home, the principal of the school announced that David had failed the term and would have to sit out until the beginning of the spring semester. I responded to that by enrolling both David and Jay in Lovett, a private Christian school that was highly recommended by the Episcopal Church. Both boys spent their middle and high school terms at Lovett and graduated there. It all worked out just fine!" Jim said.

Jim returned to Israel with Brigitte in 1970 to meet with Dr. A. Shimshony, the chief veterinary officer, and Dr. Rubin Katain, a veterinarian in the Ministry of Health. Israel wanted to enhance their food inspection program. Jim said, "Dr. Katain became my disciple in Israel. He strongly supported veterinary public health and set very high standards for food hygiene in the region." Jim made three more trips to Israel, in 1975, 1979 and 1984, to meet with the minister of health and veterinary colleagues. "I have always been impressed with the Israeli veterinary profession. Today, they probably have the best animal disease control programs of any countries in the Middle East."

"There were reports of a disease outbreak on the Sudan-Egyptian border in 1979 that was affecting cattle, sheep, goats, and camels. Animals were experiencing abortion, high fever and even death. At the same time, there were reports of fever, encephalitis and hemorrhagic disease in people. The outbreak progressed northward through the Nile Valley with high cattle and sheep mortality and morbidity and even reports of human deaths. I suspected Rift Valley Fever. It was soon confirmed," Jim said. At the time, Jim was evaluating veterinary services in Cyprus on a grant from the German government. The chief veterinary officer of Cyprus, Dr. K. Dorou, had asked the Germans to underwrite Jim's trip to evaluate their programs and to help build bridges between veterinary and public health services. Dr. Andreas Orphanedes, one of Jim's former graduate students from the University of Texas School of Public Health, had returned to Cyprus. "After I finished my business in Cyprus, I flew over to meet with Dr. Katain to discuss the possibility of Rift Valley Fever spilling over into Israel from Egypt," Jim recalled.

On Jim's recommendation, they established a surveillance and vaccination program on the borders along with a mosquito control program. He worked directly with Fort Detrick and the Food and Agricultural Organization (FAO) to acquire enough vaccine for Israel and other countries in the Middle East. "Eventually, there were many human deaths and tens of thousands of animal deaths due to Rift Valley Fever. Five years later, I made a follow-up trip to the Middle East and was delighted to learn that the disease had been eliminated from the region. Rift Valley Fever still raises its ugly head in the Nile Valley from time to time!"

Jim Steele in Alaska

During their excursion to the Midwest in 1947, Dr. Mountin announced, "We are branching out into Alaska, Jim." Dr. Jack Haldeman, with whom Jim had worked in Puerto Rico, was asked to kindle a public health program in Alaska. "He was coordinating this with the military and the biological warfare defense initiatives," Jim said.

Alaska would not achieve statehood until 1959, but there was already a lot of discussion about the possibility. Those in high echelons of government assumed it would happen at any time, especially with the Cold War brewing. Dr. Mountin said, "Jim, I want you to make a trip to Alaska to see how veterinary public health will fit in to the whole program."

Jim planned out the Alaska mission through the summer. "The AVMA meeting was to be held in San Francisco that year. I was already scheduled to be on the West Coast conducting investigations of the Q fever outbreaks in Los Angeles, Berkeley and Davis. This would make a good launching point for a scouting trip to Alaska," Jim said. Jim contacted Dr. Paul Brandley, a Kansas State University veterinary graduate, to see if he would like to be assigned to Alaska for one or two years. At the time, Dr. Brandley was a poultry pathologist with the USDA in Washington DC. "We had an excellent professional relationship with respect to poultry public health programs, and I also knew that Paul's knowledge of wildlife diseases was strong. He was the perfect choice for the job," Jim said.

Jim arranged to meet with Dr. Brandley in Seattle after the AVMA meeting. They decided to travel by boat up the Inland Passage. "The ship carried about 400 passengers, most of whom were on a holiday. We had nice rooms with a comfortable bed and excellent food," Jim recalled. Their first stop was the port at Ketchikan, the most sizeable southern city in Alaska. There, Jim and Paul met with government healthcare officials to discuss veterinary public health issues. Unfortunately, they learned very little.

The next stop was Wrangell, one of the oldest non-Native boroughs north of Ketchikan and an active fishing community. "There they told us about a study that incriminated scavenger birds in contaminating fish with *Salmonella* as they ate entrails discarded during the dressing process," said Jim. From there they sailed to Petersburg, a small town on the north end of Mitkof Island where Wrangell Narrows meets the Frederick Sound. "The place was very quaint, with distinctive Russian architecture. It was founded by explorers in the eighteenth century, and was named for Emperor Peter the Great. Again, there was not much public health information to glean. We moved on to Sitka and finally to Juneau, the capital, located about midway on the Alaskan panhandle. There we visited with several territorial health officials. The dialogue included enteric diseases, leptospirosis and other suspected zoonotic diseases. Interestingly, there was very little laboratory confirmation. I was already beginning to see the need for a strong veterinary public health program in Alaska," Jim said.

"The Juneau officials suggested that Anchorage would be a good place for us to gather more information. I was really interested in the incidence of rabies. Their Canadian neighbors were reporting something they called arctic dog disease, for which no etiology had been determined. They reported 100 percent mortality. Eventually it was proven to be rabies," Jim said. The Juneau newspapers soon learned about their visit. "During the interviews, we focused on public health issues and steered away from questions on biowarfare," Jim said. Soon, a cartoon appeared in the paper with one veterinarian telling another that he was "dog tired."

Upon arriving in Haines, a small village near the northern tip of the panhandle, they left the boat and took a narrow-gauge train to Skagway. The borough is one of the entry points into Canada at roughly sixty degrees latitude. They traveled back to Juneau and arranged for air travel to Anchorage on a DC-3. "I remember being pleased with the weather not being too cold, as it was August," Jim remembered. In Anchorage, they met with a variety of health officials but once again learned very little. There were reports of suspected infectious diseases, but there was little effort to confirm cases.

"We did learn that they were attempting to establish a dairy industry in the valley north of Anchorage, near Palmer. We also learned firsthand about the cost of living in Alaska. Haircuts were two dollars compared to forty cents in the States. Everything was inflated in price. Milk was being flown in from Seattle at two to three dollars a quart compared to eighty cents a gallon in the US. It certainly made sense for them to be exploring their own dairy industry," Jim said.

They drove the rental car through the Palmer region and then on up to Fairbanks in east-central Alaska. There they met with health officials, flew back to Juneau and reported their findings to the commissioner of health. "Our investigation had not confirmed any zoonotic diseases other than the *Salmonella* infections in fish. The census we did of hospitalized patients revealed that most were there for surgery. I was convinced that infectious and parasitic diseases were being routinely missed," Jim said.

After they presented their report, Jim decided to fly back to the States. Dr. Brandley stayed on to continue the investigation. "I arranged to keep him on loan from the USDA to the Public Health Service. Dr. Brandley decided to co-locate his office with those of the territorial health officials in Juneau for the next year. This worked out nicely," Jim stated.

In the meantime, Jim was recruiting for someone to establish a permanent VPH office in Alaska. Dr. Brandley told Jim about Dr. Robert Rausch, an Ohio State University veterinary graduate who had completed a PhD degree in wildlife pathology at the University of Wisconsin. "We successfully recruited him into the commissioned corps of the USPHS. He became legendary for his studies of arctic wildlife parasites and diseases. His discovery of how widespread hydatid disease was in Alaska and that rodents were an intermediate host for *Echinococcus multilocularis*, also found in foxes and wolves, was published in *Science*," Jim explained.

Later, when hydatid disease emerged in Colombia, Dr. Rausch was called in to investigate. "He identified *Echinococcus vogeli* in that outbreak. Dr. Rausch never received adequate credit for this brilliant work. He also did studies on parasites of sea mammals, seals, walrus, and sea lions. He continued his work in Alaska for at least thirty years, retiring as a captain from the Public Health

Service," Jim said. After retirement, Dr. Rausch continued his work with the University of Saskatchewan to establish a program in VPH for zoonotic parasites of the Arctic. "He later joined the University of Washington medical faculty in the eighties, where he carried on an excellent research program. His research was held in such high esteem by the Russians, he was often invited as a distinguished scientist to Siberia and Moscow after one of their own leading parasitologists died," Jim said.

In March of 1972, on a return trip from the Philippines, Jim and Brigitte stopped in Fairbanks to visit the University of Alaska and learn about Dr. Rausch's brucellosis research on Alaskan musk oxen. Dr. Rausch arranged for a special reception for Jim and Brigitte. "During the reception an Arctic hare hopped up to the window and looked in at us. Ironically, the hare was also an intermediate host for hydatid disease and might also have been carrying tularemia. Had the bunny heard about Dr. Rausch's work?" Jim said.

The local veterinarians arranged for a luncheon for Jim and Brigitte which featured a summer wear fashion show. "It was minus thirty-five degrees that night! Frostbite was very common, and when people drank too much alcohol at a party or function, they would be escorted home for their own safety," Jim said.

Alaska has carried on a strong program in VPH to this day, with many public health veterinarians on the payroll. "Alaska became a state in 1959. CDC assumed formal oversight of Dr. Rausch's work a few years later," Jim said. Unfortunately, CDC eventually shut down the research program at the University of Alaska for budgetary reasons. "I was told that their electric bill exceeded their budget for professional salaries and research. I protested, but it didn't do any good," Jim stated. Regardless, there is no question that Jim's early work in Alaska contributed much to the strong VPH programs that exist there today.

Jim Steele in Papua New Guinea

One of Jim's neighbors in Atlanta was Ralph McGill, a well known writer, anti-segregationist editor and publisher for the Atlanta *Constitution*. "Ralph had served on a troop ship bound for France in World War I in 1918 on which many soldiers died of the Spanish flu. He told me many chilling stories that I have never forgotten. In 1965, he loaned me a book entitled *New Guinea: The Last Unknown*, by Gavin Souter, published in 1963. Once I started reading it I couldn't put it down," Jim said. New Guinea is the second largest island in the world and lies north of Australia. The western portion of the island comprises Indonesian provinces, while the eastern half is the independent country of Papua New Guinea. Jim became fascinated with this region and hoped that he would be able to visit one day.

"Quite coincidentally, a health officer from Papua New Guinea, I forget his name, that I had met a year earlier in Manila contacted me shortly after I finished the book," Jim said. Jim had worked with this officer and Dr. George Beran on rabies control in the Philippines. The officer requested Jim's services through the WHO office in Manila. "They wanted me to investigate methods for biowarfare defense against rabies and other possible agents. There was real concern about an attack by the Indonesians on the western half of the island at the time," Jim explained.

"I was also interested in looking into the potential for an animal reservoir for kuru, a brain disorder that was identified in New Guinea natives in the 1950s. The disease is transmitted by cannibalistic funeral practices, and the etiology was later determined to be a prion similar to the one causing Creutzfeldt-Jakob disease," Jim stated. By 1960, veterinary pathologist Dr. William Hadlow had identified the similarities between kuru and scrapie in sheep. In 1966, Jim's friend and colleague from the National Institutes of Health, Dr. Carleton Gajdusek, brought a human brain back from Papua New Guinea. and inoculated chimpanzees. They subsequently manifested the symptoms and signs of kuru. "This pretty much proved that the disease is not genetic and steered the medical community toward prevention as a solution. For that work, Dr. Gajdusek received the Nobel Prize in Medicine in 1976. He shared the prize with Dr. Baruch Blumberg who had identified the Hepatitis B virus and developed a diagnostic test and vaccine for it. Dr. Gajdusek later served on the distinguished Nobel Prize Committee. He called Jim one day and asked, "Jim, please send me a copy of your vitae and a collection of your scientific papers. It's time to put you in for a Nobel Prize!" Jim thought, *What a nice thing for him to say!* Dr. Gajdusek died in Norway, December, 2008.

"At the time, Communist China was cozying up to Indonesia, and the British were concerned about Indonesia's overtures to Australia. In turn, the Australians were concerned about foot and mouth disease. The potential for biowarfare was being talked about in all circles of government," Jim said. The health officer had read about Jim's theories on airborne rabies and the research being done at CDC. Jim always downplayed the idea of rabies as a biowarfare agent, even though some scientists believed in the possibility that it could be delivered successfully as an aerosol. "Intelligence revealed that the dictator of Indonesia was bringing in Chinese scientists to consult on scientific issues. Australia and Papua New Guinea became concerned," Jim said. The government of Papua New Guinea wanted to know how to protect the human population from a potential attack. "They apparently decided that I was their man," said Jim.

The trip to Papua was on, and Jim was making arrangements. "I enjoyed telling Ralph McGill all about my travel plans. The McGills had our entire family over for a nice dinner at their home the night before I embarked from Atlanta to Los Angeles and on to Honolulu. Somehow, the Honolulu flight didn't have enough meals for all of the passengers so I missed out on breakfast. With only a brief layover, I then boarded a nonstop flight from Honolulu to Sydney, which was also short on food. Upon arrival in Australia, I was met by friends from the University of Sydney College of Veterinary Medicine who quickly shuttled me onto an all-night prop plane flight to Port Moresby, the largest city in Papua New Guinea, on the southeastern coast. I arrived very tired and hungry," Jim recalled. Much to his dismay, a large group greeted Jim at the airport and had a busy day planned. Fortunately, he was able to take a nap before a reception which was planned for that afternoon.

"I learned quickly how concerned the Papua New Guinea health officials were about a possible biowarfare attack," Jim said. The government team wanted Jim to see the western frontier, where they had established a *cordon sanitaire*, a French phrase which, literally translated, means 'quarantine line.' They had established a line from north to south a distance of roughly 320 kilometers long and one kilometer wide between eastern and western New Guinea to help guard against the transmission of FMD, rabies and other diseases. They had also built an array of clay cisterns filled with chlorinated water designed to mitigate a biowarfare attack.

"I flew in a small prop plane with Australian and Papua New Guinea health officials to inspect the *cordon sanitaire* from South to North all along the beautiful central range or *central cordillera*. The intensity of the sun was unbelievable," Jim recalled. Jim advised that with the *cordon* in place, an attack targeting animals would most likely be by aerosol spray. He did not believe that sick animals would walk from the west into the east. He further advised that he didn't believe rabies would be effectively transmitted by aerosol, but only through infected animals. "The Papua health officer was very disappointed to hear my analysis. I think that he hoped to become a national hero by protecting his country from biowarfare agents," Jim said. As far as Jim knew, there was no rabies on the island at the time.

"I was interviewed by a newspaper in Lae, New Guinea. The small-town press was operated by two Americans who had purchased the paper, along with some Australian veterans of World War II. Lae had become internationally recognized in July 1937, when Amelia Earhart took off from the airport there never to be seen again," Jim said. Most of the local concern about biowarfare came from the remembrance of secret programs initiated by the Japanese and Chinese in World War II. Jim perceived that the newspaper interviews were designed to assure the masses that the government's biowarfare defense was adequate.

"I toured the areas of northern New Guinea highlands where kuru was known to occur by car. During funeral ceremonies, close members of the family would eat the brain and chew on the fingers of the deceased, especially the women and children. However, for some reason the men seemed to die younger than the women," Jim said. The Australians who came in during and after World War II were the first to recognize and begin studying the disease. Jim shook the hand of a local man who wore a wide smile. "The man's smile didn't change. I was witnessing one of the classic signs of kuru, resulting from contracted facial muscles. I knew that this poor fellow probably had six to twelve months left to live," Jim said. Jim got some great photos, but unfortunately his camera malfunctioned and they were all destroyed. Cannibalism was stopped in about 1965 and the disease was eradicated.

Jim did some swimming in Wewack on the northern coast while in the highlands. "By pure chance I bumped into the son of the famous veterinarian Dr. W. Stableforth, whom I knew from the Central Veterinary Laboratory in Weybridge, England. A year later, Dr. Stableforth told me that his son had been lost at sea in the region. I knew from McGill's book that Nelson Rockefeller's son Michael had drowned off the south coast of New Guinea, in 1961," Jim said.

While in the highlands, Jim stayed at a small roadhouse inn on the north coast. "Everyone kept giving me shellfish. I ate well," he said. Jim visited a leprosarium that had been established by Germans in the late nineteenth century, when New Guinea was a German colony. Leprosy had been discovered there by missionaries. "New Guinea apparently had one of the highest incidences of leprosy in the world at the time. Over one hundred inches of rain a year created the right environment for survival of *Mycobacterium leprae* organisms outside the human body, thereby increasing the potential for exposure. I met a nurse who was working there who later came down with leprosy," Jim reported.

Jim wanted to visit the Solomon Islands and to see Kennedy Island, where John F. Kennedy swam to shore after his boat was sunk by a Japanese destroyer in World War II. "Unfortunately, I couldn't get the trip arranged. The history in the area is amazing.

General Douglas MacArthur cut off the Japanese support to New Guinea at Admiralty Island," Jim said. Jim did get to visit Samarai, New Guinea, in the far southeastern portion of the island. There he saw indigenous tree kangaroos that were plagued by a form of endemic glanders. "The farmers had tried to introduce sheep and cattle into the area but seemed to be having difficulty keeping them alive and healthy. I learned that the Mayo brothers of Mayo Clinic had attempted to establish an agricultural program in the region. The pigs I saw on the side of the road were among the healthiest I had ever seen. There was no hog cholera or any other swine diseases I could see to be concerned about," Jim said.

After Jim returned to Port Moresby, Jim learned that the Army surgeon general of Australia had traveled in to hear a report of his findings. "That was quite flattering. I was happy to report that the Aussies seemed to be doing everything right from my perspective. That night, an anti-Communist revolution erupted in Jakarta, resulting in the killing of an estimated 500,000 people with General Suharto taking over. This ignited a lively celebration in Papua New Guinea," Jim said. During the festivities, Jim witnessed a game of mud ball in which two teams of soldiers push a ball at least five feet in diameter around a meadow. The field was purposely wetted down to create muddy, difficult conditions. "The surgeon general and I must have consumed gallons of Australian beer that day. I spent most of the day urinating! The natives really knew how to throw a party. I heard that they could last two days. Our hosts barbequed an entire pig for us that night. Basically, we ate and drank until everyone passed out!" Jim recalled.

All told, Jim spent two weeks traveling around New Guinea. Afterward, he flew straight back to Sydney. "I was in awe of the beautiful coral reefs as the aircraft approached the Australian coastline," Jim said. Jim then flew directly to New Zealand for meetings with government veterinarians he had originally met at CDC, in Auckland on the north island and then in Christchurch on the south island. "The country was having problems with salmonellosis, orf, toxoplasmosis and other diseases, and they wanted my guidance. I made several presentations to groups of veterinarians. An interesting side note, I ordered rack of lamb at the hotel restaurant one evening. Curiously, when I asked that it be cooked rare, the waiter gave me a lecture about the risks of foodborne illness. It came out well done anyway!" Jim said grinning.

Pilots were flying freight planes from the US air base in Christchurch into Antarctica. Jim got to know the pilots in the bar at the hotel. "They invited me to fly a mission with them. Unfortunately, I had to get back for the American Public Health Association meeting in Chicago and couldn't accept the offer. This turned out to have been my only opportunity to see Antarctica. Instead, I spoke to the Peace Corps about a proposed rabies vaccination program at the Chicago meeting. In retrospect, this was way more important but Antarctica would have been nice," Jim said. Aina traveled with Jim to Chicago for the meeting and spent some time with her family.

Jim Steele in Ceylon, India, Pakistan, and Iran

"The Isle of Ceylon achieved independence in 1949 and became a commonwealth. The country had good relations with the United Kingdom. The name was changed to Sri Lanka in 1972. Public health officials in Ceylon and India were interested in establishing a program in veterinary public health," Jim stated. In 1959, after attending some meetings in Japan, Jim flew to Delhi, India to speak at the Pacific Science Congress. From there, he traveled to Ceylon to discuss the establishment of a research program in veterinary public health. "Ceylon had a very strong public health officer who later became the WHO regional director in Delhi. This key relationship helped me to build a program in veterinary public health in this part of the world on later trips," said Jim.

"Dr. David Semple developed a nerve-tissue-based rabies vaccine in 1911 from sheep brain, which was administered as a killed product subcutaneously in the abdominal area over a course of fourteen days. He also founded the Pasteur Institute in Kasauli, India, which was later renamed the Central Research Institute," Jim said. Jim wanted to visit the institute and another rabies center in Pune, India. "It was so hot. I was experiencing some heat stress so I decided not to make the trip. I always regretted missing the opportunity to visit this historic institute," Jim lamented.

In 1964 Jim attended a WHO/FAO meeting in Lahore, Pakistan that was focusing on public health in the Islamic states. The WHO regional headquarters was located in Alexandria, Egypt. "I brought my son David along on the trip. He was twelve at the time," Jim said. Because of Jim's busy schedule, he arranged for David to stay out in the country on a farm operated by the animal husbandry school, where he could ride horses and play with the other kids his age. But David got lonely for Dad and came back into town to stay with Jim at the hotel.

"While in Pakistan, I visited a veterinary school and a foot and mouth disease research facility. There I met Dr. Mohammad Abdullah Salam, a veterinarian and a professor of parasitology at the veterinary school. He assisted me a lot during my stay. We became good friends and colleagues," Jim reported. When

Dr. Martin Kaplan was promoted to deputy science director at WHO, Dr. Salam put Jim's name in to replace Dr. Kaplan as director of veterinary programs. "I turned it down. It just wasn't a good fit for me. Of course, they would have forced me to retire at age sixty. Ironically, Dr. Salam ended up in the position. I know that Brigitte would have loved to live in Geneva. Hopefully, she has forgiven me!" Jim said.

Jim worked very hard to get veterinarians assigned from CDC to India, attached to the WHO regional offices. "This became the foundation of the veterinary public health programs in these countries," Jim said. The Lahore meeting generated a lot of interest in VPH in the region and was focused on the Middle East. At this meeting it was decided that India would also participate in building the VPH programs.

"Before leaving Pakistan, Dr. Kaplan, Dr. Ervin Eichhorn, son David and I had a traditional desert meal in a tent, sitting on the floor in full tradition," Jim said. At the end of the meal, it was time to have tea. David stood up and said, "Can I help serve the tea?" The Pakistani minister of health stated that she didn't know that American boys were trained so well. Jim visited a veterinary school in the town of Kandy, Ceylon. "David got to spend a day working with an elephant. Afterward, I told David the story about Kipling's Elephant Boy in *The Jungle Book*," Jim said.

After the meeting in Lahore, Jim and David flew to Tehran, Iran. "Dr. Yoshiro Ozawa picked up David and me at the airport in a very small car. At the time, I believe Dr. Ozawa was in charge of FAO operations in Tehran," said Jim. He was a Japanese veterinarian who had earned his PhD in bacteriology under Dr. Henrik Stafseth at Michigan State College. "After I got into Dr. Ozawa's car, it didn't have enough power to get up the hill. Dr. Ozawa asked me to get out and walk!" Jim recalled.

In 1964, Iran was under the reign of Mohammad Reza Shah Pahlavi. The country was becoming increasingly unstable. "We were received well in Tehran. I visited several veterinary laboratory facilities. They were doing some good work on FMD," Jim said. Dr. Ervin Eichhorn, head of the veterinary section for FAO, was traveling with the FAO team. "He was very well liked and brought a lot of prestige to our group. The dean of the veterinary school in Tehran, Dr. A. Rafyi and I were friends. We would later serve together on a WHO panel," said Jim.

After visiting the laboratories, Jim decided that they would stay on a few days to see the countryside at a resort named Rasht near the Caspian Sea. At the end of the excursion, David came down with an upset stomach. Jim postponed their flight into Delhi. "I sent a telegram to Delhi with the details, but apparently it didn't get through. Unfortunately, we missed many of our appointments with public health officials there and they couldn't be rescheduled," Jim said.

Once David recovered, they took a redeye flight from Tehran to Delhi, arriving in the wee morning hours. Jim stopped in at the regional WHO office and met with CDC and NIH staff members. "I was also able to meet with the OIE regional officers in Delhi to plant the seed for a program in veterinary public health. My strategy was to help them implement a rabies control program as a pilot. I knew this would be successful and that would lead to other programs to control zoonotic diseases," Jim said. Jim heard rumors of as many as 25,000 human deaths from rabies annually in India alone. "Even if this was a greatly inflated number, it was still of major concern. They sorely needed a program in veterinary public health. The Indian program ultimately became a huge success story unto this day," Jim stated. In the late sixties, Jim sent his good friend and CDC rabies expert, Dr. Ernie Tierkel, to India to further develop their program. "Because of this assignment, Dr. Tierkel had to miss my retirement ceremony. Dr. Tierkel was then selected as my successor in the Public Health Service. He retired in 1975," Jim said.

Jim returned to India with Brigitte in 1970. They flew into Delhi, where a nice reception awaited them. This was followed by a Southeast Asia WHO regional meeting. The meeting included delegates from Mongolia, India, Taiwan, Ceylon, Nepal, Indonesia and Thailand. The Indian veterinarians wanted Jim's help to establish a control program for bovine tuberculosis. "They were estimating the incidence as high as 12 percent in their cattle herds

and didn't know what to do with the reactors. The Hindus re-
vered the animals and had established retirement farms for the
aged animals. But there were many TB reactors they couldn't find
enough pasture for them all. They were detecting reactors on pre-
mortem inspection. But at slaughter there were no lesions. The
Indians finally worked out a deal with Iraq to sell the tuberculin
reactors," Jim recalled. One of the Indian agricultural ministers
asked Jim about the possibility of approving meat from TB reactors for cooking and human consumption. "I considered this, but
I didn't think that the Minister of Agriculture would be able to
deal with this politically," Jim said.

After the meeting, the group traveled to Mukteshwar, far north
in the Kumaon Hills, at about 7,500 feet of elevation. "We stayed
at a veterinary research station where I gave lectures to graduate
students. The views of the Himalayas were breathtaking. Everyone had their own bungalows. The house man made tea each
morning. We would watch the sunrise on the mountains. It is one
of the most beautiful places we had ever been. At night it was so
very cool. We didn't want to leave because it was so hot in the rest
of the country. In the mornings, they served us sumptuous breakfasts. Because of the caste system, the graduate students were not
welcome to eat with us. This was upsetting for both of us. We figured out a way to smuggle food to the students," Jim said.

Dr. Calvin Schwabe gave lectures on parasites while Dr. Betty
Hobbs, the famed bacteriologist from England, spoke on food hygiene and the Codex Alimentarius. Others spoke on laboratory
techniques. "The audience was composed of leading veterinarians from all over Southeast Asia. It was an excellent meeting,"
Jim said.

After the meeting concluded in Mukteshwar, the WHO hosted a reception for the international participants in Delhi. "The
Indian veterinarians saw this as an excellent opportunity for me
to meet with the minister of agriculture in a private room off to
the side of the ballroom. He told me he was concerned that cattle
that tested TB positive were being slaughtered in south India and
sold to the Iraqi military for human consumption. I advised him
that this was not a problem. As long as there were no gross lesions

of TB upon slaughter, they could be passed for cooking. This was the practice in the US at the time. He responded that politically he could not support my recommendation. Of course the cow is held sacred throughout much of Hindu India. The slaughtering of cattle in those days was often prohibited," said Jim.

Some days later Jim traveled to Bombay and was driven to the capital building where he was to meet with the director of plague research in India. "They asked me to give a review of plague in the US, especially in our wildlife. For years, they thought that rodents were the only reservoir of the disease. They took out into the countryside to visit some Hindu areas where cattle were worshipped. It was a very hot day and I came down with heat exhaustion, maybe even mild heat stroke. I was examined by a doctor, treated and ordered to stay in my room at the Taj Mahal hotel for the next 48 hours.

After Jim recovered, he traveled back to Delhi to meet with the prime minister of India at the end of his visit, two weeks later. "He was a diminutive man, his head only reaching my belly height. I only had fifteen minutes with him. I spoke to him about the importance of the health of their agricultural animals and the impact on human health and to approve the utilization of the skin test reactors. I advised him not to overrule the minister of agriculture, but he replied that he'd do whatever he needed to get reelected. I counseled him that India had a significant bovine tuberculosis problem and that the public health threat from this disease should be recognized and dealt with," Jim said.

"After the meeting, we went shopping. Brigitte bought a painting of a pregnant woman in the Picasso style with sharp angles by a local artist named Rao. I named it *India's Eternal Problem*. The artist stayed quite close to me in the store. He must have thought that I could help him exhibit his art in the US. He boasted that Pan American Airlines had purchased some of his paintings. Unknowingly, the artist followed us to the airport and even tried to board our plane. He was a real nut cake for sure. Finally the authorities had to escort him away. It was quite a scene!" Jim said.

From Bombay they flew to Bangalore, one of India's most populous cities. There Jim met with a public health officer to discuss the dairy industry and bovine tuberculosis. "The typical hygiene there was terrible. Typically, the cows were kept in the back room of the home behind the family dwelling area. The dung was dried and used for fuel," Jim explained. From there they went to Madras, a port city in the southeast. Jim visited a veterinary school and examined some animals for tuberculosis. "I also visited a large clinical and research center for human tuberculosis. When I quizzed the physicians about the veterinary work on tuberculosis, I could tell that they were not impressed," Jim said.

Their next stop was Colombo, Ceylon. The movie *Bridge Over the River Kwai* was filmed there in the mid-fifties and won seven Academy Awards. Jim and Brigitte enjoyed a visit to the set of the movie. "A Dr. Singh and a colleague toured us around. They told me a story of how two public health veterinarians were murdered, but I never learned the details. They took us up to see some fortifications on a cliffside. We climbed about 2,000 feet up into the old forts and caves where we saw ancient paintings of animals, hunters, and the women they dreamed about," Jim said. Dr. Singh told Jim about Ceylon's plans to convert their highland areas for dairy production.

Jim was shown an old Ceylonese veterinary textbook on managing diseases of the elephant that dated back to 1000 AD "This was a fascinating reference book. From the knowledge I gained from that book, I later diagnosed streptococcal septicemia in an elephant in the Atlanta zoo. I advised treatment with penicillin but the animal ultimately died. The elephant is one of the few animals that can be infected by the human form of tuberculosis," Jim said.

From Ceylon, Jim and Brigitte traveled to Israel. Brigitte then flew to France to visit her father. "I returned to Atlanta just in time for a meeting of the Epidemic Intelligence Service," Jim said. While in Delhi, India on this trip, Brigitte met Dr. Calvin Schwabe. Thirty-seven years later, Jim would receive the award that bore his name from the Association of Teashers of Epidemiology and Public Health.

CHAPTER 30:
BRIGITTE'S STORY: THE TEMPERING OF STEELE

The beautiful and remarkable woman who would one day become Jim Steele's second wife was born Maria Brigitte Meyer on the Main River in Frankfort, Germany. Her younger brother, Stefan, was her only sibling. Her father and mother, Herbert and Lotte Meyer, who were Jewish, met at a costume ball at a museum of art in Munich. "My father spent four years in the German army in World War I as a communications officer," stated Brigitte. Interestingly, Dr. Meyer lived on Veterinary Strasse in Munich, where Jim Steele later lectured at the University of Munich's College of Veterinary Medicine in 1975.

"When I was only two, our family had to flee to Switzerland from the Nazis, leaving almost all of our family belongings behind in Germany," Brigitte recalled. Dr. Meyer had a legal German passport which allowed them passage into Switzerland. There they linked up with an old friend of Dr. Meyer who was a famous poet, Regina Ullnan, discovered by Rainer Maria Rilke, considered to be one of Germany's best poets of the twentieth century. Brigitte's father held a doctorate in metallurgy. "Unfortunately, foreigners, even educated ones, were unable to get a job in Switzerland," said Brigitte.

In about 1933, the Meyers moved to France, where Brigitte's mother had cousins. There, Dr. Meyer was accepted into the French Academy of Science. "This is the same academy that failed to admit Madame Marie Curie because of prejudice against women at the time," Brigitte recalled. However, as World War II loomed, anti-German sentiment was strengthening and Dr. Meyer was asked to leave the Academy of Science. The first cousin of Brigitte's mother, Gustav Rosenfelder, was successful in the fur business in Europe and the United States. Dr. Meyer was given a position in the company. But as a highly trained scientist, he found the work unfulfilling. Cousin Gustav provided visas for the family to be admitted to the US. But one of the visas was invalidated. The Vichy Government didn't want the Meyers to leave

France. General Henri Pétain was the Chief of State for Vichy France at the time.

One day while Dr. Meyer was at work, a stranger came by their house in Montmorency. Brigitte suspects that this was the beginning of their family's political harassment. In May of 1940, the German occupation began in northern France. Dr. Meyer was put in prison by the French before the invasion, and was released when he volunteered for service in the French Foreign Legion. He was soon assigned to serve in Morocco, Africa. But before he left, he came to les Sables d'Olonne, where his family was living. Dr. Meyer brought the family cat from the house in Montmorency along with him. He told Brigitte's mother that he would stay in touch with her as much as possible. He also spoke of the great uncertainty of the future. "He planned to take us all to Morocco, Africa where he was to be stationed. However, he didn't share the full plan with us until after the war," Brigitte said. After a year in Africa, he was discharged and went to occupied Paris to find his family. He learned from a Mr. Tournier, an accountant, where and under what name his family was hidden in Paris. They were living in a hotel under the assumed name, Beaulieu. The plan was to flee occupied France as soon as possible. With the help of Mr. Tournier, Dr. Meyer was reunited with his family.

"We were near Limoges when the Germans began occupying southern France in 1942. My brother, Stefan, recalls seeing the trucks and the strange uniformed men with big leather boots. My mother already knew that the Germans were present," explained Brigitte. Soldiers would come by their courtyard and make comments about their pet canaries and would notice Mrs. Meyer, who was very beautiful. There was concern that the Nazis would take her away. Mr. Tournier was the accountant for the fur business. He was a Frenchman and was very anti-Nazi. He came to Limoges with his wife and five children as he knew that the Meyers had a plan to escape from France.

For her safety, Brigitte was relocated to Cieux, where she was enrolled in St. Marguerite School, a Catholic convent. "Being Jewish, I was the only non-Catholic girl in the school. The priest was aware of my background," Brigitte said. This turned out to be the perfect cover for her. She remained in the convent until the second German occupation. The rest of the family continued to live near Limoges, in Isle. As fear mounted of another occupation from the South, the security of the convent became uncertain. Brigitte was removed from the Catholic school and came back to the hotel in Isle with the rest of her family. She then enrolled in a public school.

"One day, German tanks filled the streets. My mom went up the hill to the school and advised the teachers about the occupation, after which they dismissed all of the students. There was no heat in the hotel, and everyone was very cold, especially at night. All of the wash basins and toilets were frozen. My father would give me a drop of cognac at the bar to try to keep me warm," Brigitte stated. One of Mr. Tournier's oldest daughters would sneak milk to Brigitte's parents for her and Stefan to drink. At the time, only families with small babies were eligible for milk ration cards.

Dr. Meyer then traveled by train to the US embassy in an attempt to obtain new visas. Upon arrival, he learned that the French had closed the facility due to the second German invasion. With the help of Mr. Tournier and several strangers, they were moved to the Spanish border near Perpignan. Dr. Meyer hired a guide with some gold in his possession and arranged for them all to travel on foot from France through the Pyrenees. "We had to hide from the Germans, the Spaniards and the Pétain French during our journey. I carried the family treasure of gold coins in two hunting belts. This was the only commodity we could use for purchases at the time," Brigitte said.

Near Perpignan, they found themselves in a hotel that they discovered was full of the Gestapo, the Nazi secret police. They also soon learned that their first guide had been untruthful to them. "This forced us to escape through the window of the hotel. With the help of some new friends, my father soon found another guide that we could trust. We began a three-day walk through the Pyrenees Mountains, sleeping during the day and walking at night. We only had some bread and chocolates to eat along the way. Somehow, we lost the bread, leaving only the sweets to eat. I remember us all sleeping without blankets in the mountains.

It was December of 1942," said Brigitte. They were forced to move only at night to avoid the enemy patrolling the mountains. The gold was their only means of survival.

"My father and the new guide arranged to meet a man on the Spanish border at Figeras on a specific day and time. Fortunately, we made it to our destination right on schedule. We had to pay the guide in gold coins for helping us cross the border, as well as the man who offered his apartment for refuge," Brigitte recalled. They remained hidden there for several weeks. Brigitte and her brother were able to go outside only after dark accompanied by one of their new friends. "The Orbock family that helped us get to Spain was unknown to us at the time but we became very close. The mother in the family was a Hungarian writer. I stayed in touch with the Orbock family until the last member died in 2005," Brigitte explained.

Before the first occupation, the Meyers had changed their name to Dufour. However, in order to immigrate to America, they had to change their names back to Meyer, to conform with the names on their visas. This was accomplished by an ingenious idea of a business friend who owed money to Brigitte's father. He arranged for the family to spend a night in a Spanish jail in Figueras. They were released under the Meyer family name. The paperwork now matched the name on the last visas ever given under President Roosevelt. They could now travel legally to the US. But first, they had to get to Barcelona. Brigitte and her mother traveled in the caboose of a train for eighteen hours. Her brother traveled with the wife of the man they had met at the border. Brigitte's father followed a bit later. All of these transactions were paid for with gold coins. "I remember that my mother bought me a new dress in Madrid with the last bit of money that we had. Then we moved on to Estoril, Portugal, where we stayed a few weeks waiting for the *Nyassa* to arrive in Lisbon, Portugal. This was the ship that would take us to the United States," Brigitte stated.

The *Nyassa* was delayed, as the British were using it as a troop ship. Dr. and Mrs. Meyer were concerned that their visas would expire. When the boat finally arrived, forty-five civilians, including the Meyers, boarded. During the voyage, the captain received a

US military SOS from the Azores. "Soon we came upon about two hundred American Merchant Marines whose ship had been torpedoed by the Germans. They were brought onto our boat. Even though the *Nyassa* was a neutral Portuguese vessel, there was concern that the Germans would attack or board the boat. I remember one of the marines. He told me he was only sixteen when he joined. He had lost a leg while serving. I knew no English at the time and had never been around boys. I remember being asked to bring him a pack of Chesterfield cigarettes. 'Chesterfield' was the first English word that I learned!" Brigitte said with a smile. The marines were all hidden in the hold of the boat so as to not be seen by the German U-boats.

Two weeks later, on about April 3, 1943, the *Nyassa* arrived in Philadelphia. "The port authorities allowed the children to disembark, but the adults had to stay on board with nothing to eat. A policeman figured out that the children were hungry. He opened a barrel of olives for us to snack on while we waited. In the meantime, the US immigration staff examined all of our records," said Brigitte. They were concerned that the authorities might suspect Dr. Meyer of being a Communist sympathizer with ties to the French Academy of Science, Madame Curie and other scientists. However, their papers all appeared to be in order. The Meyer family was allowed to leave the port. From Philadelphia they traveled to New York City where Dr. Meyer's two sisters were living.

The sisters were well educated; one had earned a doctorate in music and the other, a doctorate in political science. "But jobs were scarce. Women were discriminated against in the workplace in those days," Brigitte explained. Ultimately, the Meyer family decided to live in New York City. Their home consisted of two furnished rooms facing the Hudson River with a view of the statue of Joan of Arc. Brigitte enrolled in Joan of Arc junior high school in New York City without knowing any English. "During my first years in this school, I helped teach French to my classmates upon the request of one of the teachers. The teacher knew that I had recently arrived from France.

Our family later moved to Newark, New Jersey. At the age of nineteen, I moved back to New York City. I went to work for a child psychologist who had been my first cousin's professor at Columbia University in Germany. I assisted in his practice, which focused on child psychology and family counseling, for the next twenty-five years. I stayed in New York until I married Jim," said Brigitte.

In the early sixties, Brigitte's cousin, Dr. George Baer, married a woman from Mexico by the name of Olga. "The first time I met Jim was on a trip to Mexico City to visit George and Olga. George was working on a rabies project for Jim in Mexico. The Summer Olympics were soon to be held in Mexico City, the first time ever in a Latin American country. But I only came to visit my relatives, not to attend the games," Brigitte stated. The Tlatelolco massacre occurred on October 2, 1968, just ten days before the opening of the games, during Brigitte's visit. An estimated two hundred students were killed by security forces. Among other things, they were protesting for the release of political prisoners, the abolition of the tactical police corps, and the repeal of laws that restricted free, public meetings. "A US reporter got the event on film and made it safely across the border. Another was arrested and his film destroyed by Mexican authorities. This horrific event almost caused me to leave Mexico. It was very tragic and terrifying," said Brigitte.

On the fourth day of Brigitte's visit, Dr. Baer was heading to the airport to pick up his boss, Dr. Jim Steele. He asked Brigitte to go along for the ride. When they arrived at the airport, George asked Brigitte to look for Jim. "He's a really big guy and is almost always the last one off the plane. And he always wears a big hat!" Dr. Baer said.

"I was wearing white slacks with a red, white, and blue top. Many of the people in the airport thought I was an athlete and wanted my autograph. Finally, I saw Jim with a really ugly hat. I was uncomfortable on the ride home as we all three sat in the front of the truck. As big as Jim was, it was very crowded. But once Jim started talking, I was impressed with what he had to say," Brigitte said.

Jim stayed at the Baers' home during his stay. He was there to review the progress of Dr. Baer's rabies work, but had also come to attend the Olympics. "A few days after Jim arrived, I learned that he was married, had children, and that his wife was in very poor health," Brigitte explained. Jim had some meetings to attend and afterwards he invited Brigitte to attend the Olympics. "It was no problem getting a ticket for me as so many tourists had left in the wake of the massacre. On the first day of the games, American athlete Bob Beamon long-jumped 8.90 meters and broke the world record. This record stood until 1991, when it was broken by Mike Powell, also an American. We watched the games together and enjoyed them very much. At the end of the first day, we couldn't find George's car in the parking lot. We both got soaked in a driving rain. We laughed and laughed. After dinner with the Baers one evening, we all went out for some dancing. We had a great time. Jim and I became good friends," said Brigitte.

"I was still living in New York at the time. My mother, who was an orphan at age fourteen, was an accomplished poet and pianist. Sadly, she was now suffered with Alzheimer's disease. I called and asked to Jim help me to get her into a nursing home in Atlanta," Brigitte explained. She was later moved to a home in Massachusetts and died in 1971. Jim's first wife, Aina, died in March 1969. "As you would expect, it hit Jim very hard. He had gone through so much for so many years dealing with her illness. Jim's doctor advised him to seek out companionship to help him cope with his grief. Having become good friends during our accidental meeting in Mexico, he gravitated to me for support," said Brigitte.

A few months after Aina's death, Jim and Brigitte realized that they wanted to be together and began planning for a wedding to be held on June 27, 1969. "We both realized that it was soon after Aina's passing and that some family and friends might not understand our decision. But they also knew the love they felt in their hearts. And we both believed that Aina would approve, as she would want Jim to be happy. We hope and pray that everyone can now recognize and accept this," said Brigitte.

They planned for their wedding to be held in Mexico City. "A few days after our arrival in Mexico, Jim got a bad stomach bug, *Salmonella* maybe? Fortunately, he recovered before the wedding day. He blamed the illness on dirty ice cubes," Brigitte said. Jim also didn't have his premarital blood testing paperwork in order.

With the help of the Baers, he got this taken care of just in time for the ceremony.

The ceremony was held at George and Olga Baer's home near the Cuban embassy. Olga Baer was the daughter of a Mexican general. "She arranged for a prominent justice of the peace to perform our wedding ceremony. The photographer was a very short fellow, and the pictures look like we are hanging from the ceiling. We still laugh about it today when we look at them!" Brigitte said with a smile. Unfortunately, Dr. Baer died suddenly of a heart attack on May 31, 2009 just before he was to attend his 50th veterinary school class reunion at Cornell University.

And so began an adventure that would last for several decades, forty years at the time of the writing of this biography. Back at CDC, Jim continued to serve as the assistant surgeon general for veterinary affairs for another year. "The rest of my story captures just a few of the highlights of our many years together as man and wife and as partners in the quest to promote veterinary public health and goodwill around the world," Brigitte said.

Jim and Brigitte travelled to Poznan, Warsaw, and Krakow Poland for meetings on trichinosis and leukemia in late 1969. "It was exciting to be traveling overseas with my new husband. At the time, I really had no idea how many trips we would be making together," Brigitte said. This meeting was sponsored by US Public Law 480, the global food aid program which was signed by President Eisenhower in 1954. Poland was still struggling with a Communist government. Brigitte recalled that when they were leaving Poland, they couldn't change their zlotych (Polish currency) back into American dollars. "This gave me a great opportunity to go shopping! I bought some tablecloths and amber jewelry. A special memory was provided by one of the Polish scientists, Dr. C. Gervel. He had a tablecloth that was woven by his daughter, who had won first prize in a national competition. He gave give it to us as a wedding present so that it would never get into the hands of the Communist regime," Brigitte explained.

During Brigitte's short time in Atlanta, she met many of the neighbors and made some great friends. "One of our neighbors was a professor at Georgia State University. He and his wife also enjoyed music and had two grown children so we had a lot in common. Jim's twin cousins Myrna and Myrtle would often come to visit us. On one of these stopovers, we were invited next door for a drink. The neighbor's house was nicely landscaped, with large hedges. As we were walking out of the neighbor's house, suddenly, one of the twins disappeared. We soon realized that she had fallen between two of the hedges. Everyone was laughing, especially once we knew that she was not hurt," Brigitte said smiling.

Jim was finishing up his career at CDC. "Texas wasn't even on our radar screen yet. I don't recall Jim talking much about life after CDC. I did know that he was passionate about getting to a situation that would allow him to publish the book series on zoonoses," said Brigitte.

In 1970, Jim and Brigitte were traveling to Paris to visit the Pasteur Institute. US Senator Jacobs from New York was sitting behind them on the plane, and breakfast was being served. Several salesmen and others were standing in the aisles drinking cocktails. Many other passengers did not have their seatbelts fastened. "In an instant, the plane dropped a reported 3,000 feet, effectively thrusting the unbuckled passengers up to the ceiling of the aircraft. Many were hurt, including the stewardesses, some with neck injuries. My hat landed several rows away from me. We moved around the cabin to help and calm the injured passengers," Brigitte stated. The plane was one of the first Boeing 747s in service. We turned around immediately and landed back in New York City. A new plane was quickly arranged for with a fresh crew for the trip. The scientists from the Pasteur Institute had heard about the mishap. They were planning to meet the Steeles at the airport. "The story made the headlines in the international press. I called home so that the family would not worry. Jim called CDC as well," said Brigitte.

In 1970, the Steeles traveled to Guam. "Dr. Jacob Brody met us at 5:00 A.M. at the airport and informed Jim of the busy agenda for the day. Dr. Brody was investigating Lou Gehrig's disease in the Pacific Rim. Jim was to make a presentation on rabies to the senior Navy staff. We had only gotten about three hours of sleep during the trip. There were several meetings to attend as well as a reception that followed. Jim was really exhausted. The commander of the navy base on Guam invited Jim to attend one of his staff meetings. Later they went fishing. The commander then invited us to stay in his guest quarters named after Admiral Chester William Nimitz, past Commander in Chief of the Pacific Fleet in World War II. We were treated like royalty," Brigitte recalled.

After Jim's retirement from CDC, he and Brigitte moved to Houston, Texas. He had been offered a variety of opportunities. Jim ultimately accepted a tenured professor position with the University of Texas, School of Public Health (UTSPH). "On one of our house-hunting trips, we stayed with Dr. Konrad and Kathe Eugster in College Station, Texas. Dr. Eugster was working as head of virology at the diagnostic laboratory at Texas A&M University," said Brigitte. One of Jim's colleagues at the UTSPH linked them up with a real estate agent. Jim and Brigitte found the home they wanted over one weekend on Riverview Drive in the Walnut Bend subdivision in west Houston. "We had to wait for our furniture to be shipped in from Atlanta. I remember that in 1971, the house was considered to be pretty far from the university. This was before long commutes were commonplace. While we waited, we stayed in an apartment at the UT Medical Center club," Brigitte said.

Having lived in New York City for so long, relying on taxis or buses for transportation, Brigitte thought that they could get along with one car. "When I realized that none of the Houston taxi drivers had a clue about where Walnut Bend was, we decided it was time to purchase a second car. One time, a taxi driver drove me home. I gave him a twenty-dollar bill for a five-dollar fare—he had no change. Yes, it was definitely time for that second car!" Brigitte said laughing.

In 1972, Jim and Brigitte were staying with her friend Madeleine in Paris. One morning, they wanted to go out for breakfast at one the restaurants. While they were walking to the cafe, a young man stepped out of the door of a bar for some fresh air. In French, he said, "Americans always wear shoes that are larger than their feet!" Brigitte quickly responded, also in French, "You are welcome to come over and touch his big toe if you like!" The boy was surprised at her response and they all had a nice laugh.

On the same trip to Paris in 1972, Jim wanted to take Brigitte to the *Folies Bergère*, a famous Parisian music hall that has been running since the 1890s. "This was quite a tourist attraction, but I never wanted to go there, mostly because of all the smoke," Brigitte recalled. She reluctantly agreed to go with Jim that night. After the show, they were taking a taxi back to Madeleine's apartment. Brigitte was anxious to get some rest, but Jim wanted a bowl of onion soup at one of the restaurants in the famous market known as *Les Halles*. The taxi driver barked in French, "Why don't you get out of the car and let the American do what he wants to do?"

"I realized that the driver thought I was a French prostitute!" Brigitte said with a big smile.

In 1973, Jim was invited to Samoa and Fiji to consult on veterinary public health programs. In Samoa, Jim and Brigitte stayed in a hotel that was well known in World War II by US Marines passing through. "It was one of the few places in that part of the world where a soldier could get a decent hamburger. The place had been converted into a nice guest hotel with buffet meals by the pool and dance shows every Wednesday," Brigitte said. The Samoans, as with the Tongans and Hawaiians, wore a piece of clothing called a *lavalava*. It is a long, rectangular piece of cloth that is worn like a skirt or kilt.

"Jim had two of these made made for us and decided he wanted to wear his on the night of the dance show. As he came out, the dancers were rehearsing. One of the most attractive ones came to him and showed him how to properly tie his lavalava. After the show started, Jim kept telling me how beautiful the dancer was that had helped him. He was shocked to learn that the dancer was male!" Brigitte laughed. Later, Jim was declared a Samoan chief on one of the islands. The natives game him several gifts. "Jim shared a kava drink, made from the root of a pepper plant, with one of the chiefs. This was a sign of respect and brotherhood.

After Samoa, they traveled to the Fiji Islands. "There we watched men dancing on hot rocks. It was an amazing show. We contrasted the tourist attractions on Fiji with the squalor around the King George Hospital. Many patients had to sleep outdoors, as there weren't enough beds inside the facility. We were astonished at the conditions," Brigitte said.

The Steeles had many visitors in Houston. One of their favorite places to take them was the Shamrock Hilton at the medical center. This was a members-only club that had wine to serve with the meals. "We saw some wonderful shows and entertained many guests there. We especially enjoyed it when Duke Ellington was onstage," said Brigitte. Duke Ellington died of complications of lung cancer in 1974 but continued playing music up to the very end. The Steeles were loyal fans.

One summer day in 1975, Dr. Konrad and Kathe Eugster joined the Steeles for an outing on Galveston Beach. "For several weeks, I had been telling Jim that he had a strange off-white growth on his back. I mentioned it again this day on the beach. Jim ignored me. About then, Konrad took a cigarette and lit the 'growth' on Jim's back. It was a tick! This was my introduction to ectoparasites!" said Brigitte.

In 1977, Jim was invited to be a visiting professor two months at the University of Ibaden, College of Veterinary Medicine in Nigeria. "Jim told his students that if they wanted to pass his course, they must beat him in a game of tennis. They loved it! I remember that the heat in the classrooms was almost unbearable," Brigitte said. The Rockefellers had built some nice guest houses on campus. The Steeles were staying in a one-room apartment. "We were happy as long as the water was running and the air conditioning was working. The water wasn't for drinking, so we drank Dutch beer instead. We were told it was 9 percent alcohol, so I had to be careful. We had no other choice," she said. Brigitte spent her spare time observing the people and learning the culture of Nigeria. There were many artists on campus who sold unique gifts. Towards the end of their stay, Brigitte met a talented painter. "At first I thought we might sponsor him to come to the US. However, I later became suspicious that he was on drugs and decided against it. I did purchase three of his paintings done on cotton. Canvas was apparently too expensive. Many of the Nigerians wore cotton clothing called blue cloth, all with original designs created by hand. I bought some of these clothes for myself," Brigitte explained.

"Near the end of our stay, we received many gifts. One was a bust of the *Mother of Benin,* which is tied to a story that dates back to a civil war in Nigeria in the fifteenth century. The man presenting the gift was the director of mental health for Nigeria. Benin is a lovely city that we visited. Upon seeing the bust, I asked if I could pay for it. He told me no, but that he would come to Texas, knock on our door and ask for $100. We never heard from him. But during the Christmas season in 2003, a large poinsettia arrived with no name of the sender. The following day a bouquet of roses arrived once again with no name. I wondered if this could be from the professor in Nigeria. I was thinking, *Who else could it be?* As it turned out, it was from my loving husband, Jim. We had a long laugh over it. Right before we left Nigeria, the dean of the University of Ibaden and his wife gave us both native outfits. Of course, I wore mine to the airport. We ended up waiting twelve hours for our plane," said Brigitte.

Back home in Houston in 1980, Jim was still able to walk without any difficulty. "We would often take long walks with our schnauzer, Happy. Happy was given to us in 1978 by Jim's cousin Dr. Bill Thorp, who was living in Ecuador at the time," said Brigitte. According to Cousin Bill, Happy's sire was a champion. Sometimes during their walks in Houston, a stray dog would come after their other dog, Indy. "I would carry Indy in my arms so that nothing would happen to her. We really miss the simple pleasures of walking a dog in our neighborhood," Brigitte stated. All in all, the Steeles have had five schnauzers born in their house. "They all brought so much joy into our lives. But once the last one died of cancer, we decided that we just couldn't go through the pain anymore. There would be no more dogs in the Steele household," Brigitte lamented.

One day in June of 1984, Jim and Brigitte left Houston bound for son David Steele's home in Lilburn, Georgia to attend their grandson Taylor's baptism. David and his former wife, Janis, also have a daughter, Ashley, who is three years older than Taylor. They flew from Houston to Atlanta and rented a car for the road trip to Lilburn. Upon arrival, Jim was walking up the stairs at David's home and suddenly stopped. "David, I need help!" Jim shouted.

"David noticed that his dad was bleeding from the mouth. He immediately called 911. An ambulance came within minutes. Due to the emergency, the baptism ceremony was cancelled," Brigitte said.

After a short stay at the local hospital in Lilburn, Jim requested to be transferred to the Emory University Hospital, where he knew some of the physicians on staff. "They could have performed surgery, but Jim's doctor wanted to take a more conservative approach. They treated Jim in the hospital for two weeks and he was released. He was diagnosed with stomach bleeding related to long term aspirin use along with an anti-inflammatory drug to ease his foot pain. To his knowledge, Jim has had no problem since. I thank the doctors and all our friends for helping us get through this crisis," Brigitte said.

In his role as a PAHO consultant, Jim was invited to the Ministerial Meeting of Health and Agriculture in Brasilia, Brazil in 1985. "One day while walking on the beach enjoying the cool, blue water, Jim told me that his foot was hurting and he wanted to return to the hotel. When we got back to the room and took his shoe off, we found a roll of camera film under his toe in the shoe. Why didn't he feel it immediately? Was this another early sign of Jim's developing peripheral neuropathy?" Brigitte asked.

On the same trip, Jim and Brigitte took an excursion to see the magnificent Iguassu Falls in the southwest on the Argentine border. They stayed for several days in the oldest hotel in the town. "We enjoyed walking around sightseeing, and even took a helicopter ride over the falls and rainforest on the last day. We couldn't get over the greenness and density of the forest in the area. Our room at the hotel was very nice, with big, comfortable beds," said Brigitte. But one evening, suddenly there was a huge crash in the room. Jim awoke and found himself on the floor, yet still in the middle of the bed. "The log supports under the bed had evidently given way under Jim's weight. Once we saw that we were both unhurt, we had a grand laugh!" Brigitte said. The hotel management fixed the bed the next day.

In 1988, Jim was invited by Dr. Abraham Horwitz to attend a Pan American Health Organization (PAHO) to chair a Scientific Advisory Meeting in Buenos Aires, Argentina. Dr. Horwitz was director of PAHO at the time. "I had Jim's beige suit cleaned after our arrival in Buenos Aires. He looked dapper for the closing ceremony of the meeting that evening. Later on the same day, Jim became ill. He felt so bad, he asked me to tell Dr. Acha that he could not make it to the closing ceremony. Later we learned that the dry cleaning service at the hotel was leaving high levels of chemical residues in the clothes. This was making some of the customers sick. Fortunately, Jim was feeling much better in a couple of days. You never know what you will have to deal with!" Brigitte exclaimed.

Jim and Brigitte returned to Peru in 1988 for a visit. Jim was to receive the PAHO Presidential Award that year. In addition, they were scheduled to visit Dr. Aurelio Malaga, a veterinarian of Peru who had graduated from the Royal School of Veterinary Studies in Edinburgh, Scotland. "He was a friend and colleague of Jim's for for many years," Brigitte said. Upon arrival at the airport, the Steeles had a long wait. The airport staff was on silent strike. "During the delay, I met an elegant lady who was there to buy some horses. When I told her about Jim and Dr. Malaga, she invited us to come with her to see some horses. When we arrived at the farm, the owner asked Dr. Malaga if he would like to ride one of the horses. He quickly agreed. We were both impressed that at eighty he still had the confidence and stamina to ride a horse. We had a nice lunch at the farm. It was a wonderful day," said Brigitte. Later, Brigitte learned that the lady ended up marrying the man who showed them the horses. "I was so happy that I reached out to her!" Brigitte said.

In 1988, Jim was asked to provide an opinion on Agent Orange and its potential detrimental effects on Vietnam veterans. He was scheduled to meet with Mrs. Virginia Knauer, the White House consumer advocate. She had occupied this post for Presidents Nixon, Ford and Reagan. "I came along with Jim this time. After their meeting, Mrs. Knauer introduced us to a number of her White House staff members, which ran us quite late. We had borrowed a car from Dr. Leon Jacobs, who lived in Washington, DC. When we arrived back at Dr. Jacobs's car, it was covered with parking tickets," said Brigitte.

Jim was scheduled for a court hearing two days later. He arrived, walking with a cane and leading their schnauzer, Happy. The judge asked Jim, "Do you need that dog to get around?" Jim replied, "Why, of course, your honor!" The total on all the tickets was $240. Jim told the judge that Mrs. Knauer at the White House had kept him late that day. The judge asked him once again if the dog was truly necessary for his well being. "Absolutely sir!" Jim stated. "With that, the judge reduced his fine to forty dollars. Happy saved the day!" Brigitte reported.

In June, 1989, Jim had just attended the wedding of Dr. Konrad Eugster's daughter in College Station. "Everyone was saying that Jim looked exhausted and I agreed. After we got back to Houston, he continued to complain about being tired. About two days later, Jim began complaining of back and armpit pain. We were scheduled to travel to Stockholm the following Monday for an international meeting on food hygiene. When Jim made the statement that he didn't want to go on the trip, I told him to call his doctor. This wasn't like him. When Jim explained his symptoms to the doctor, he told him he was likely having a heart attack and to get to the hospital immediately. Chris Eugster was at our home that day so he drove Jim to the hospital. "Upon arrival, they asked Jim when he had his back surgery and he told them he was having a heart attack!" said Brigitte. Jim had an angiogram which revealed that the anterior descending artery of the left ventricle was blocked. They performed an angioplasty which cleared the blockage. Jim was in the hospital for about a week. "His doctor told him to go home and rest for a couple months. In August, we went to Maine and stayed at a nice resort. Jim continued to improve. We went from there to Dr. Ernie Tierkel's wedding at Dartmouth, Vermont. After that, we came home and Jim did very well. He hasn't had another episode since, thank God!" said Brigitte.

In 1993, after the Berlin Wall had been torn down, Jim was asked by Dr. Dieter Grossklauss to speak at the famous Reichstag Building in Berlin. The building opened in 1894 and housed the parliament, or *Reichstag,* of the German Empire. The building was severely damaged by fire in 1933. The fire was related to an event in which Hitler was trying to flush Communism out of Germany. It was restored from 1961 to 1964 and was then used only for meetings and exhibitions. Dr. Grossklauss was the chief veterinary officer and surgeon general for veterinary affairs for Germany and had escaped East Germany during World War II. The mayor of Berlin gave a speech that day at the Reichstag to help dedicate a new research center. Jim gave a response to the mayor's speech. "Jim spoke rather boldly about Germany under Hitler's reign. He told of the tragic loss of so much scientific and artistic talent and the horror of the Holocaust and the gypsies in the camps. At the end of Jim's response, all of the guests just filed out of the room in silence. It was very interesting," Brigitte said.

Jim and Brigitte attended the World Veterinary Congress in Rio de Janeiro, Brazil in 1991. Jim was presiding over the American Veterinary Academy on Disaster Medicine meeting with Dr. Craig Carter, an epidemiologist from the diagnostic laboratory at Texas A&M University. Very late one night toward the end of the meeting, Brigitte heard a knock on their hotel room door. "Craig had just proposed to his fiancé, Ronda, on their balcony with the Corcovado shining down in the distance. We joined them in their room and shared a bottle of Champagne in celebration," said Brigitte.

"In 1994, we attended Craig and Ronda's wedding in Bryan, Texas, acting as Craig's surrogate parents. His biological parents had passed on many years prior. On the way up from Houston for the ceremony, a tornado crossed the path of our car on highway 290, delaying our arrival. When we walked into the wedding chapel, the ceremony was beginning. Craig and Ronda were both dressed in white. I thought to myself, what a contrast it was from the black clouds that almost swept us away on the highway only minutes before. They both looked so glorious, all in white!" Brigitte recalled.

One evening in the early nineties, Brigitte and Jim decided to take a walk after dark. Jim's legs were really beginning to become problematic, and he took every opportunity to savor his waning ability to walk. "We were having a nice stroll, and suddenly, Jim just fell to the ground. Having been an athlete in his younger days, he knew how to fall without hurting himself. I was thinking, *What do we do now? How will I get him up?* There was no one around. Jim began crawling toward a tree. When he reached it, he slowly pulled himself up to his feet using the strength in his arms. I could only support him with words and encouragement. I was powerless to assist him physically. To this day, Jim still exercises with his trainer three times a week to maintain his strength, especially in his upper body. He wants to try to be ready for all possible situations," Brigitte stated.

In 1993, Jim was invited to Warsaw, Poland to receive the Rector's Medal at the University of Poznan. Brigitte accompanied him to this event. Jim had spent some time in Poland in 1957, as an invited speaker for the World Health Organization (WHO) in Warsaw, and again in 1972, as a PAHO consultant to evaluate their research program (see chapter 19). "I knew that the Poles liked US currency and had some novel means of obtaining it. One day, Jim and I were eating lunch at one of the hotels. Our waiter knew that we were Americans. He came to our table with a basket and offered us some bread. When he pulled back the napkin, we were surprised to see several boxes of caviar that he was trying to sell. We were told that he was working with Russian truckers who all wanted US dollars to buy western clothing. In Warsaw, you could get anything you wanted with American dollars!" Brigitte said.

In 1998, Jim had a busy schedule. "He received the Alumni Medal of Merit award from Harvard; was an invited OIE lecturer in Paris, France; and spoke on food irradiation in Berlin," Brigitte recalled. In June of that year, Jim and Brigitte took a cruise with Holland America Line. "We departed from Copenhagen and sailed for the Norwegian coast. We had a nice large cabin designed for handicapped passengers. Bergen was one of our first stops. We were able to leave the boat and enjoy the restaurants and surroundings," said Brigitte. There was a large group of physicians and nurses on the cruise, including retired surgeon general Everett Koop, an old friend and colleague of Jim's. "He asked Jim and me to join him for dinner and also to attend a birthday party for his wife. Of course, Jim and Dr. Koop talked public health the whole evening!" Brigitte said, laughing.

The boat was very large, and Brigitte took long, enjoyable walks. One day, Brigitte adventured through a poorly lit, glassed-in tennis court. Suddenly, Brigitte tripped over the net. She called out in vain for help and then crashed to the ground. "I realized immediately that I could not get up. A nurse was summoned, and she carried me to a chair. Jim and Dr. Koop were quickly called to the scene. They both feared that I had broken my ankle," Brigitte recalled. Brigitte was taken to the first aid, station where a temporary cast was applied to her ankle.

There was some discussion of airlifting Brigitte to Narvik, Norway by helicopter, but this did not occur. On the third day after the accident, the boat finally came ashore. "An ambulance took me to the university hospital at Tromso. This is the northernmost hospital in the Europe at seventy degrees latitude. There they diagnosed three broken bones in my foot. Corrective surgery was performed three days later. Jim was allowed to stay in my room day and night. The staff even fed Jim three meals a day at no charge!" said Brigitte.

Brigitte mentioned to Jim how handsome the doctors were, and he replied, "Have you seen the nurses?" Jim enjoyed swimming every day in their therapeutic pools at the hospital with the help of the son of one of the doctors.

Brigitte stayed in the hospital for two weeks with Jim right by her side. Then she was transferred to a rehabilitation clinic that was operated by the Seventh Day Adventist Church. "Even though this religion does not allow coffee consumption by their members, they graciously served us instant coffee every day. I remained in the rehab clinic for four weeks. They took such good care of both of us. At the high latitude in the summer months, the midnight sun was present. We still talk about the beautiful gold light on the mainland and the water from the window of the rehabilitation hospital. On the last evening of my stay, we looked out the window and saw a large, new ship. We later learned that we had witnessed the maiden voyage of the Queen Mary to Norway. Even though

I broke three bones in my ankle and had experienced a lot of pain, this was offset by the total compassion of the medical staff and the great care we both received. Overall, it was a very positive experience," Brigitte said.

On the occasion of Jim's ninetieth birthday celebration in 2003, Cousin Tracy Cadell and her husband, Ian, came to Jim and Brigitte's house in Houston, Texas to look at some photographs. It was their first visit to Houston. Later on Saturday night, Jim and Brigitte were driving them back to their hotel. Suddenly, a car started bumping into the backside of their Lexus SUV. "I could make out two men in the vehicle even in the dark. The traffic was bumper-to-bumper at the time, and I was driving. Whenever I changed lanes, the vehicle behind us did the same," Brigitte recalled.

She made an abrupt right turn and suddenly, there was a policeman near the corner. "The officer immediately saw what was going on, pulled their vehicle over, apprehended the two men and put them in handcuffs. It took about two hours for the backup police cars to respond to the scene. The officers told us that they saw we were in trouble, but were unable to get to us because of the traffic. After filing all the reports, we finally got Ian and Tracy back to their hotel at 4:00 A.M.," Brigitte said.

When Ian and Brigitte got out of the car, Ian exclaimed, "Now I know I am in Texas!"

Brigitte's French friend, Claire, lived near the Steeles in Houston. In 2004, Claire invited her father, who was living in France, to visit her in Texas. "This was his first time to the US, and he wanted to visit a large cattle ranch. Jim made the arrangements. We all drove up to the ranch with Claire's two children," said Brigitte. On arrival, they were asked to sit and wait in a room. Brigitte saw two men talking to each other, and she became curious. "Are you German?" she asked.

Mr. Klaus Kirkel, the owner of the ranch, replied, "Well, yes!" They had a wonderful tour.

"We then drove over to New Braunfels, an old Texas German community. The carefully painted bed-and-breakfast homes reminded me of a village in France. Claire and her father were very surprised to see this in Texas and commented on the stark contrast among Houston, the ranch and New Braunfels old homes," said Brigitte.

In July of 2007, Jim and Brigitte traveled to Mexico City on Air Mexicana to attend the wedding of George and Olga Baer's youngest daughter, Isabella. "Of course, we were married in the Baers' home. This was such an exciting event for us. For some reason, Jim couldn't get comfortable on the plane, even though we were in first class seating. They moved Jim to the first row of tourist class so he could stretch out a little more. Of course, he was upset, as now he was not eligible for first class service, including complimentary dinner and wine!" Brigitte said.

Dr. Baer met them at the airport in Mexico City, bringing Jim a wheelchair. By this time, Jim's peripheral neuropathy had progressed and he could not walk very far. They waited at the airport until other guests arrived so that they could all travel back to the Baer's home together. "The wedding was a magnificent affair. There were about approximately 150 guests. The event was hosted at the Baers' recently renovated sixteenth century hacienda. The occasion lasted two days, with many bands and performers. There were several opera singers, one from Vienna, who performed," Brigitte said. After the wedding, Jim and Brigitte stayed a few days and enjoyed the beautiful grounds, including a 300-year-old tree surrounded by beautiful flowers. "Olga prepared a nice dish of hot peppers and vegetables. Jim liked it so well he ate three servings. In the middle of the night, Jim's digestive tract protested violently. But after two more days of rest in the splendid hacienda, he fully recovered," Brigitte said with a smile.

There have been so many good times shared by the Steeles. But for Brigitte, the worst times have been when Jim has gotten ill. "I worry continually about his well being. I know he is tough, but I still worry. He keeps bouncing back, much to everyone's delight," said Brigitte. She has been a constant source of energy, love, and support. She has been there for whatever Jim dreams about, pursues and accomplishes. Over four decades, they have been an extraordinary team. Because of their collective efforts, talent and dedication, the world is a better place.

We wish them many more adventurous years together!

CHAPTER 31:
ONE MEDICINE, ONE HEALTH—COMMENTARY
BY DR. JAMES STEELE

"Human and animal health are inextricably linked. They always have been. They always will be. We are seeing a powerful resurgence of this truth, re the global One Health Initiative being forged by great leaders like Laura Kahn, MD, Bruce Kaplan, DVM, Thomas Monath, MD, Roger Mahr, DVM and many others. Dr. William Foege, former director of CDC, professor at Emory School of Public Health and now a consultant to the Bill and Melinda Gates Foundation, often quotes Dr. Calvin Schwabe's dictum that we cannot have good public health unless we have good animal health. We can also invert that and state that we cannot have good animal health unless we have good public health. In the United States, the veterinary medical profession has been a vital proponent in the elimination of animal health diseases that have had serious public health ramifications. Bovine tuberculosis and brucellosis are excellent examples. In recent years, advances in rabies immunization programs have nearly eliminated the disease in pets in the US.

"Looking beyond, there is a sizable list of parasitic diseases, including tapeworms, which have been brought under control in the United States. But some of these are being reintroduced by immigrants from Mexico and Central and South America, who do not know they are carrying the infestation. This rekindles old problems that can affect society in the United States. It is becoming increasingly apparent that we have to work harder to share our knowledge with the developing world of the Americas as well as Africa and Asia. Many of these countries are facing the problems that the United States eliminated in the past century through good hygiene.

"As we move into the twenty-first century, the technology for controlling diseases is vastly improved. Methods that have been proven effective in the United States can and must be used worldwide. We need to work diligently toward disseminating our knowledge and technologies throughout the globe. Many challenges still exist for controlling diseases like bovine tuberculosis. There is a dire need for vaccines to prevent tuberculosis in animals. However, effective products are still not available. A nice summary of global zoonoses is presented in a table at the end of the *Merck Veterinary Manual* zoonosis section, 2005 edition. I enjoyed fifty years as a contributing editor of this section.

"All one has to do is look at history in Europe over the past fifty years. After World War II, tuberculosis was a major problem in Central Europe, especially in Germany and Eastern Europe; problems remain even in Western Europe. In Europe, there has been a certain degree of over-confidence in the BCG vaccine. Studies in South Africa demonstrated that the vaccine increases the severity of the disease and causes false positive caudal fold skin tests. Both findings diminish the usefulness of the vaccine in my opinion.

"The World Health Organization, the Food and Agricultural Organization, the USDA and animal health consultants have all discouraged the use of BCG vaccines to control bovine tuberculosis. The test-and-cull system has proven to be the most successful thus far. Maybe a good vaccine will be developed utilizing molecular genetics. Unfortunately, we have lived with that hope for 100 years. Regardless, our neighbors in Mexico, Central America and South America have the opportunity to further their own disease control by employing the proven techniques used in the United States and Europe. They need to continue to collaborate with the Pan American Health Organization's veterinary public health programs.

"The control of brucellosis in the developing world is a larger problem than bovine tuberculosis. Some years ago, Dr. George Baer described the human disease in Mexico and said that practically all rural people who had reached the age of forty had evidence of past infection with brucellosis. This same can be said for the countries of Latin America where goats have a high prevalence of *Brucella melitensis* infection. To control goat brucellosis will be a difficult task; it is critical that the governments face up to the issue.

"The new RB51 rough strain vaccine developed in the United States is showing promise. This vaccine was researched for at least fifty years before the USDA veterinary scientists were able to produce an effective vaccine for cattle. This vaccine has not been successful in goats and sheep. The control of brucellosis has been given little attention where it is widespread in North Africa. The Middle East and Asia also have an extensive brucellosis problem. Our young scientists need to continue to be a resource for these countries.

"The World Health Organization, through its consultancies and expert committee on rabies, has done a fine job of communicating the importance of canine rabies vaccination programs throughout the world. We can say with some degree of pride that the technology developed by veterinarians at the Communicable Disease Center and carried to other parts of the world by authorities such as the late Dr. Ernest Tierkel, Dr. George Baer, Dr. Keith Sikes, Dr. Charles Rupprecht and their associates have made a great contribution to the world scene. We can see the light at the end of the tunnel for worldwide control of canine rabies. New rabies vaccines have been developed in the Americas and Europe, providing more methods for disease control.

"In the realm of parasitology, there is a great interest in the control of trichinosis. This has been a topic of prominent scientific congresses conducted every few years. I am happy to see that the results are favorable worldwide today. There has been a drastic reduction of trichinosis in North America and Europe. Unfortunately, problems have arisen in connection with the disease in wild animals, especially those found in the arctic, including the polar bear, fox, wolf and even marine mammals.

"*Taenia saginata* and *T. solium* are receiving more attention in the areas of disease control and hygiene. In the Americas, the problem has been carried from one country to another by human carriers and spread to animals. New foci have been established in North America. There have been recent WHO and FAO meetings advocating plans for a worldwide control program. In my way of thinking, the control of *Taenia saginata* is a measurement of good hygiene and good waste control in any country where it is present.

"Shortly after I came to CDC in the late forties, there was an outbreak of leptospirosis in Georgia in children. The infection was traced back to a small pond that they were swimming in. Mildred Galton quickly linked this to infected livestock that had access to the pond. We followed other outbreaks of leptospirosis in North Carolina, Louisiana and Iowa. I came to recognize that leptospirosis was a problem that often emerged in association with natural disasters around the world. Dr. Tom Murnane, an Army Veterinary Corps officer, came to me in in the sixties to query me about which diseases he might encounter in his soldiers and military working dogs in Vietnam. I told him that I had learned from British veterinarians and scientists that leptospirosis was a major problem there and is not uncommon in war zones.

Dr. Richard Spiegel became an expert in the epidemiology of leptospirosis before he joined CDC. He investigated leptospirosis in natives in the Ecuadorian interior that was related to their drinking water. He also investigated outbreaks of leptospirosis associated with flooding in Nicaragua following a hurricane. Unfortunately, he succumbed to cancer of the thyroid at age fifty, just after being appointed to a position with the Bill and Melinda Gates Foundation to promote vaccination programs in developing countries. Leptospirosis continues to be a widespread problem throughout the world. It is one of the major zoonotic problems, and much work remains to develop effective prevention and control programs. I implore some of you bright young scientists to approach this insidious disease head on.

"The veterinary public health programs of CDC have been instrumental in the globalization of zoonotic disease control, to include diseases such as rabies, bovine tuberculosis, trichinosis, taeniasis and more. Many of the veterinary officers who served on the WHO Expert Committees on Zoonoses have provided personnel to carry out detailed missions for WHO. The CDC program has been supportive of PAHO veterinary activities, and has assigned veterinary officers to Mexico, Panama, Peru, Argentina and, most recently, Brazil, for foot and mouth disease control. Surgeon

General (Ret.) Richard Carmona has been an active supporter of the globalization of public health. Below, is an excerpt from a speech he delivered on June 8, 2005 in Philadelphia at the Commissioned Officers Association annual meeting:

> The emerging diseases increased in the latter part of the twentieth century. Infectious disease scientists have found that AIDS is a disease that makes people more susceptible to zoonotic infections. People with Acquired Immune Deficiency Syndrome are much more susceptible in general to zoonotic diseases including bovine tuberculosis and related mycobacterial infections as well as toxoplasmosis, cryptosporidiosis, foodborne *Salmonella* and enteric infections including *Campylobacter, Listeria* and *Yersinia.* It is possible that other zoonotic diseases that are dormant or infrequent may emerge in individuals with AIDS/HIV or immune compromised conditions. Related latent or nonpathogenic viral diseases have been described in tropical cats of Africa, including lions as well as domesticated cats. In Australia and Malaysia new diseases have been reported in horses and swine that also affect humans. They are caused by the morbilliviruses–the measles-like viruses that cause canine distemper and rinderpest. Another virus that killed the wild felids in the Cairo Zoo has not been identified. Some of the emerging viral diseases that have a rodent or unknown animal hosts have caused fatal, devastating diseases in humans in Africa and South America, namely Lassa Fever and South American Hemorrhagic diseases in Argentina and Bolivia. In Africa, Ebola Fever and Marburg, the latter a monkey disease, caused disease in medical personnel, handlers and people who are only remotely connected. One that surprised me many years ago was the death of workers in Middle East abattoirs caused by Crimean Hemorrhagic Fever carried by ectoparasites. One example of developing diseases or emerging diseases or relatively unknown diseases is SARS, a disease that erupted a few years ago in China and was carried to many parts of

the world. Recently there has been information that bats may be a reservoir of the coronavirus that causes SARS. Even though SARS may have been an occasional emerging disease that disappeared as rapidly as it appeared, there may have been other infections from bats that have been around this world some millions of years.

"Influenza has recently been given notable attention. Where do we stand with these viruses? Are wild birds the true reservoirs? Are they responsible for infecting our domestic flocks? This is all quite bewildering but presents exciting challenges at the same time.

"Going beyond infectious diseases, there is a new disease-causing agent known as the prion. Prions are proteins that elicit disease without any DNA or RNA involvement. This is puzzling, especially when we read that saliva may be a portal of exit for transmission. Immediately, veterinarians think of rabies being carried by saliva. Is it possible that something that prions in the brain are secreted through nerve fibers that innervate the salivary gland? Prions are of great concern—or, rather, continuous concern. These are new types of diseases to which our associates in chemistry, physics, and physiology may offer clues as well as to other neurological diseases. Effective prevention is afforded by preventing the introduction of animal parts in feed. There are reports that saliva on vegetation may transmit prion-related disease among members of the deer family. This reminds me of the report that I heard in South Africa many years ago about transmission of anthrax by vegetation. At the time, I couldn't quite comprehend it. It is hard for me to accept that animals browsing on vegetation contaminated with *Bacillus anthracis* can become infected.

"Prion disease in humans and animals can be caused by the ingestion of contaminated food. In humans, a spontaneous disease called CJD, or Creutzfeldt-Jakob disease, is also observed worldwide in elderly people. There are also suspected spontaneous neurological disease cases with a similar pattern in elderly animals. I leave you with an interesting question: Is there such a disease as CJD in aged animals?

"One subject I want to approach is humaneness. It is very important that we abide by sensible, humane policies as applied to animals. However, humaneness can be carried to such an extreme that it actually limits our ability to protect our pets, our farm animals that produce food, and our precious wildlife. Periodically we read about animal overpopulation in different areas. Society calls for conservative measures for population control that applies to pets, wild animals and domestic animals. Many species of animal are disease carriers and can be destructive of the ecology and the environment. So I say that all veterinarians, especially those in public health, have a responsibility to help to develop balanced humane regulations and public guidance.

"In the United States, 80 to 90 percent of veterinarians treat pets for various diseases. It is very important that clinical veterinarians have a broad, basic knowledge of public health issues and be alert for new public health issues that can be resolved with new antibiotics, new procedures and tender loving care. The 70,000 or more veterinarians in the United States are an important resource in public health, through the recognition and control of zoonotic diseases. Their voices must be heard!

"Something that I believe is very important is that basic veterinary science must be able to hold its own with all of medical science. A full integration of the veterinary and medical sciences needs to occur, in line with the growing philosophy of *One Medicine, One Health, One World.* Most research seen in our medical publications is based on support from the National Institutes of Health of the United States Public Health Service. At the AVMA meeting in July 2000, Senator Hatch of Utah spoke highly of the public health activities in the field of veterinary medicine. He even went on to say that there may be an NIH Veterinary Science Institute in the future. It behooves us all to remember that the agricultural interest in public health is an important issue to the American public. Animal health is so very important in communities worldwide in helping the world to provide for public health. Public health should be guided, not by economic interests, but by the interests of all society. I go back to my earlier statement that animal health and public health are of major interest to all parties, and we must have good animal health to have good public health. Good public health is also necessary for good animal health.

"As we look to the future, we have to have open minds and remember that anything can occur in biology. I would like to quote my old dean from Michigan State College, Dr. Ward Giltner, who said that the only thing about biology we can accept that remains a firm truth is that there is always new information that provides exceptions. Looking at it broadly, all infectious things in nature, including prions, which we can't say are truly infectious, are always looking for new hosts. I like to say they are seeking social security, as most of the world is!

"Almost forty years after my retirement from CDC, it is a great pleasure to reflect on all the public health service officers and other veterinarians and scientists, both women and men, who are the champions for veterinary public health internationally. Individuals like Dr. Michael Cates, who became chief of the US Army Veterinary Corps and commander of the Center for Health Promotion and Preventive Medicine, and Dr. William Stokes, one of my successors as chief veterinary officer for the USPHS all make me so very proud. I want to salute Dr. Lonnie King for his outstanding leadership in expanding our understanding of zoonotic diseases through his key role at CDC as the first director of the National Center for Zoonotic, Vector-borne, and Enteric Diseases.

"In closing, I encourage all of you bright young people to move forward into the new challenges for public health in the twenty-first century. I wish I could continue to be a part of it, but it seems time has a way of saying:

You have been here–you have enjoyed it—it's time for the next generation!

"On the grand occasion of the publication of my biography, and for the recognition of well over sixty years of my involvement in public health, I am elated to say to the audience, especially teachers of public health science–carry on!"

APPENDIX 1

A. L. Ritterson, Ph.D

Rochester, NY 14642   University of Rochester Medical Center

VALENTINE'S DAY: IS LOVE REALLY A ZOONOSIS?

To the Editor: Valentine's Day is a celebration of love dating back to the third century A.D., when the Christian festival of St. Valentine, celebrated on the 14th of February, was fortuitously merged with the pagan ritual of Lupercalia, traditionally celebrated on February 15th. Legend has it that St. Valentine was known as a benefactor of troubled lovers. Lupercalia was an ancient Roman ceremony with the unromantic goals of ensuring fertility, purifying women, and expiating evil, symbolized by the wolf. All this was accomplished by sacrificing goats and a dog; after that young men, the Luperci, dressed only in goat-skin bikinis, ran among the audience light-heartedly flogging the citizens with thongs made from the same skins. The modern practice of towel snapping clearly derives from the pagan rite, probably with little change in intent.

Since that early time, poets and philosophers have led us all to accept the idea that love is a sickness. But was it always? Certainly not! As Ambrose Bierce observed, the "disease, like caries and other ailments, is prevalent only among civilized races." St. Valentine's Day celebrates the time of transition, from primitive to cultured. But what was the nature of the original malady that is now tradition-fixed and only expressed psychosomatically? For nearly 2000 years, poets and lyricists have faithfully recorded its clinic symptoms: weakness, aching, malaise, insomnia, recurrent depression, a rise in evening temperature and sometimes, even heart-break. Any second-year medical student worthy of a learner's caduceus would tell you that these symptoms are characteristic of brucellosis. History tells the rest. *Brucella melitensis* is an infection of goats transmissible to human beings by contact, as in the Lupercalian rite of flogging with skins of freshly killed animals. Indeed, the etiologic agent was finally discovered in goats on the

Mediterranean island of Malta late in the 19th century. Obviously, the heathens had perpetuated a zoonosis and innocently elevated it to epidemic status by their well-intentioned custom. With the Christianization of Lupercalia, the whole thing got mixed together and entered our folklore and consciousness. Even the now widely popular belly dance symbolizes the undulant character of the love-linked infection.

Oh, how chancy life is! Just imagine what our literature, lyrics, and even love itself would be if those old goats had had anthrax!

The New England Journal of Medicine, circa 1984

APPENDIX 2

Live Begins at Eighty

I have good news for you. The first 80 years of life are the hardest and the second 80 are a succession of birthday parties. Once you reach 80, everyone wants to carry your luggage and help you up the steps. If you forget your telephone number, how many grandchildren you have, or promises to be three places at one time, they just look at you and smile because you are 80. Being 80 is a lot better than being 70. At 70 people are mad at you for everything. At 80 you have a perfect excuse no matter what you do. If you act foolishly, it's your second childhood. Everybody is looking for symptoms of softening of the brain. Being 70 is no fun at all. At that age they expect you to retire to a house in Florida and complain about your arthritis (they used to call it lumbago) and understand them (actually your hearing is about 50% gone). If you survive until you are 80, everybody is surprised that you are still alive. They treat you with respect just for having lived so long. Actually they seem surprised that you can walk and talk sensibly. So please, folks, try to make it to 80. It's the best time of life. People forgive you for anything. If you ask me, life begins at 80.

By Frank Laubach
Education, Summer 2000

Jim Steele's comment–

The 80's were great—friends, colleagues, and even relatives, say nice words. The parties, lectures, and honors make it the greatest. But the question that I have at 90: *What happened?* Where did the 80's go? Anyway, the 90's are worthwhile. On to a hundred – CHARGE!

APPENDIX 3

In celebration of Jim Steele's 90th Birthday
Annual James H. Steele Lecture
University of Texas School of Public Health
Houston, Texas
April 3, 2003

The Greatest Gift
By Bill Foege

Some years ago Jim asked me if I would be here on his 90th birthday and I readily agreed. Every year he would contact me to be sure it was on my calendar. Today I find that his real concern was whether I would make it this long!

But why are we here?

Russ Alexander explained it to me. He used to work across the hall from Jim and there was a time when he describes Jim as having gone from his usual Michigan-State-bear-hug-self to being more like a large weak kitten. Jim's blood was sent to various people who were in the early stages of identifying hepatitis antigens. The tests were negative. A blood specimen made it to the Plum Island laboratory. They immediately sent word to CDC that they had identified Fowl Plague, an agent that should not be in this country. They ordered the CDC to immediately euthanize the animal that this specimen came from.

Despite his weakness, no one had the nerve to do that. And so this violation of orders explains why we are celebrating a 90th birthday!

My objective is simple. I want to celebrate life, by celebrating a life, and to celebrate the complexity, excitement and the never-ending surprises of this world.

But first...lets look back. What was 1913 like?

There were new products, other than Jim of course. The include:

- Life Savers,
- Puffed Rice and Puffed Wheat,
- The first US Crossword puzzle,
- Camel cigarettes were introduced,
- It is no big surprise that the American Cancer Society was also founded.

But there were other things of note.

- The first buffalo nickel was introduced,
- Grand Central Station opened,
- Parcel Post was inaugurated,
- The Rice Hotel opened in Houston,
- The London Daily Mail offered 10,000 pounds for a flight across the Atlantic. It was seen as a publicity stunt,
- And the income tax was introduced in the US.

As a harbinger of Jim's involvement in global health...

- The Rockefeller Foundation was created,
- Albert Schweitzer founded a hospital in French Equatorial Africa,
- Goldberger studied the problem of Pellagra,
- The Russians showed that cholesterol causes arteriosclerosis in rabbits.

And at the age of 1, Jim found himself living in the First World War.

Fast-forward 90 years. To Jim it feels like it actually was fast forwarded because it has been said that inside every older person there is a younger person wondering what happened. The MacArthur Foundation funded a study on predictors of successful aging. Those predictors included such things as continuous education, empathy, a rich social network, purpose in life, optimism...traits we recognize in Jim. But I want to take a slightly different look.

Norman Cousins asked a question, in the Saturday Review, at the time of the counties bicentennial. The question was, "Whatever is the greatest gift this country has given the world?" His answer was that the greatest gift was the demonstration that it is possible to plan a rational future. It is a lesson we have to relearn on a continuous basis.

In health, the greatest gift we can leave is to contribute to a rational health future. And so we gather to celebrate a life dedicated to this greatest gift...a rational health future.

There are tools involved in this rational health future. Tools that change everything. We think of:

- The day Edward Jenner did the first vaccination.
- The day in 1955 when Jonas Salk announced that polio vaccine protected children.
- The development of antibiotics.
- The discovery of how iodine and Vitamin A Save brains and ives.

In Jim's lifetime the tools have changed completely. But it is not just tools that help build that rational future. It is also people. Tens of thousands of us deliver, using the tools. But a handful of people provide the vision, the leadership, the ideas, and the passion. We think of:

- Jenner
- Semmelweiss
- Pasteur
- Langmuir
- Salk
- Steele. Yes Jim Steele who made the point at CDC, PAH, WHO, indeed everywhere, that you cannot consider the health of people in the absence of considering the health of animals. The two are inseparable.

The integration is part of the greatest gift? It is not a gift of a day or a year or 90 years. But rather, it is a gift that will travel forever. As long as people gather to plan for the collective health, his contributions both known and unknown will continue to influence the debate.

It is 138 years since Lincoln died. There is none of his DNA in our human gene pool. Absolutely none. Yet not a day goes by that we don't recall the importance of his life among us. Why? Because he left the social equivalent of DNA. His social DNA will flow until the end of the human story. As will the social DNA of Jim Steele. What a thought. His social- public health DNA will enter the lives of billions of people now and in the future.

What are some of the ingredients of this greatest gift? I start with caution when students ask advice about their careers. I tell them that we all fall into the trap of somehow justifying our own actions and career track...by recommending it. But there are a few careers that are not only good examples but also metaphors for life well lived. What are some of the attributes and ingredients of the life of Jim Steele that are an inspiration to the rest of us?

1. Longevity – I suppose most would start with the great example of remaining active at at 90. But, life expectancy is made up of two parts.

- Years lived, and 90 puts Jim in an elite group...
- And the function of those years. What can be accomplished in each year? And that is more amazing than the number 90. In terms of functional life expectancy, that is what one can do in a lifetime, Jim's 90 years represent a thousand years lived by the greats of the past. His exposure to new cultures, new ideas, and new people annually exceeded what Marco Polo was able to do in a lifetime. So his functional life expectancy in terms of exposure to the world was 40 or 50 times that of Marco Polo. In terms of knowledge exposure he was exposed to as much knowledge every 3 or 4 years as Aristotle was in a lifetime, so Jim has lived 10 or 20 Aristotelian lifetimes.

2. Generalist – Professor Pelican from Yale has said that good scholarship can usually be traced to the place of training, mentors etc. But great scholarship can often be traced to how much a person knows outside their field. We think of Jim as a generalist interested in everything.

I mentioned Schweitzer starting his hospital the year Jim was born. Schweitzer developed his philosophy of "Reverence of Life" as the result of concluding that the study of ethic, at that time, was flawed because it dealt only with humans. He said that ethics should include people, animals, insects, plants and the entire environment because they are all connected. He was a precursor to the environmentalists of today.

What is the value of being a generalist? The absolute conviction that everything affects everything. There are no isolated events.

Jim took this to a new level in public health by showing that health must be seen in the most inclusive way.

It has been said that the real definition of genius is to see one's field whole. Does that not describe Jim Steele, the generalist?

3. Specialist – I tell students that the ideal is to be a generalist and a specialist simultaneously. Jim was mor ethan a specialist in the diseases of the animal kingdom or in the realm of public health. He could integrate that knowledge.

Ernie Boyer once wrote a report for Carnegie on the university of the future. He wrote that in the future tenure should be based on four items. They would be the scholarship of new knowledge development, the scholarship of knowledge integration, the scholarship of knowledge transmission and the scholarship of knowledge application. What are the implications of that approach? It means that Jim was already a future university before he even came to this university.

4. Globalist – Gandhi said we should seek interdependence with the same zeal used to seek self-reliance. Einstein told us that nationalism is an infantile disease. He called it the measles of mankind. Polybius told us over 2000 years ago – It may have been possible for things to have happened in isolation in the past but from now on we must see the world as an organic whole. We don't actually have a choice but most don't recognize that. Jim is a globalist because he has always recognized the truth of our interdependence.

5. Futurist – There are two types of futurists. There are those who predict the future and those who change the future. We need to be both. We can no longer live in a single time zone or a single time period.

Our quest must be a relentless search for what might be best in the long run, 200, 500, a thousand years in the future. In Amistad there was that great moment when the leader of the slaves reflected on his ancestors and said, "At this point I am the only reason they ever existed." In 1000 years people will feel they are the only reason we ever existed. The question will be "How did we do as futurists?"

6. Another ingredient – Openness – Certainty is the Achilles heel of both science and religion. As Chris Rock has said, just when we think we understand the rules, just when we have certainty you find, "The best rapper is white, the best golfer is black, the Swiss hold the Americas Cup, the tallest player in the NBA is Chinese, lemonade is made from artificial flavors while furniture polish is made from real lemons, France is accusing the US of arrogance, and Germany doesn't want to go to war."

One wonders at the absolute certainty of people in every age. I blush over my certainty in arguments 10 and 20 years ago. The crusades were based on certainty. In the 16th century, we find people willing to make beliefs on baptism a capital offense…and then follow through on that idea to actually kill people. Certainty in religion can be dangerous but the same is true in science.

Richard Feynmann spoke at the University of Washington in 1963 and said that science is based on the understanding of uncertainty. He said some things are more certain than others but we must have a mindset that is always out to prove even the most certain things wrong, and if we succeed, to accept that knowledge.

It surprises us to find that such certainty characterizes our age. The attack on 9/11 is an example…it is based on the certainty of a belief of a group. But we hear the same certainty in our daily news from American leaders.

In contrast, Jim brings openness. He has a willingness to consider new information. And he has an eagerness to know what is coming next, what is over the horizon. He has the insatiable curiosity of Benjamin Franklin.

I attended my first Epidemic Intelligence Service conference 41 years ago. It has become the custom to have Jim attend to ask questions, to put a presentation in historical perspective, to suggest a new line of inquiry.

7. Moralist – We have much to learn from the past. Roger Bacon told us 7 centuries ago that science lacks a moral compass. Then 500 years ago the great French physician and humorist, Rabelais, uses in one of his books what Will Durant called ten words that challenge our time. He said, "Science without conscience is but the ruin of the soul."

Jim has consistently brought conscience, morals, and ethics to his pursuit of science, asking, "What is the right thing to do."

But now the list of ingredients gets too long for the allotted time. Should I mention his tenacity? Mae West once described a man as so tenacious that the only way to get rid of him was to marry him. Jim brings that kind of tenacity to every problem.

Should I expound on his role as a teacher? There is not need. Simply look around you at the crowd of students and younger colleagues adopted from every corner of the world. If you could have heard the tribute session this morning you would have seen lives intertwined, careers determined by his words, you would have heard the epidemiology of inspiration. So you now see that when you were teaching your students you were actually teaching your students' students.

Should I dwell on kindness? It is only kindness that makes sense over 90 years.

Should I mention the strong obligation to use science in the service of humanity? Or is it all too obvious?

There is one final attribute that I do want to work into the time we have.

8. Jim as Optimist – Fatalists simply don't go to Cuba at age 89. Jim has what Harlan Cleveland has said characterizes public health workers, "Unwarranted optimism.""

Rabelais, in his satire of Gargantua, describes, "A certainty gaiety of spirit preserved in contempt of the accidents of life."

On my father's 90th birthday I quoted from a study made of people at age 100 who said their best decade had been the 90's.

And so our tribute to a long life well lived as generalist, specialist, globalist, futurist, moralist, optimist and gift giver...is mixed with gratitude, gratefulness and the anticipation of the next decade being the best ever.

On behalf of countless generations, yet unborn, we say:

Thank you Jim for this greatest gift...

Jim Steele's favorite poem:

The Deacon's Masterpiece or The Wonderful "One-Hoss Shay" A Logical Story
By Oliver Wendell Holmes

Have you heard of the wonderful one-hoss-shay,
That was built in such a logical way
It ran a hundred years to a day,
And then, of a sudden, it—ah, but stay
I'll tell you what happened without delay
Scaring the parson into fits
Frightening people out of their wits, –
Have you ever heard of that, I say?

Seventeen hundred and fifty-five,
Georgius Secundus was then alive, –
Snuffy old drone from the German hive;
That was the year when Lisbon-town
Saw the earth open and gulp her down
And Braddock's army was done so brown,
Left without a scalp to its crown.
It was on the terrible Earthquake-day
That the Deacon finished the one-hoss-shay.

Now in building of chaises, I tell you what,
There is always somewhere a weakest spot,
In hub, tire, felloe, in spring or thill,
In panel, or crossbar, or floor, or sill,
In screw, bolt, thoroughbrace, lurking still
Find it somewhere you must and will
Above or below, or within or without
And that's the reason, beyond a doubt
A chaise breaks down, but does n't wear out.

But the Deacon swore (as Deacons do,
With an "I dew vum," or and "I tell yeou")
He would build one shay to beat the taown
'n' the keounty 'n' all the kentry raoun';
It should be so built that it could n't break daown;
"Fur," said the Deacon, "t's mighty plain
That the weakes' place mus' stan' the strain;
"n" the way t' fix it, uz I maintain, Is only jest
T' make that place uz strong uz the rest."

So the Deacon inquired of the village folk
Where he could find the strongest oak,
That could n't be split nor bent nor broke,
That was for spokes and floor and sills'
He sent for lancewood to make the thills;
The crossbars were ash, from the straightest trees,
Theplanels of white-wood, that cuts like cheese,
But lasts like iron for things like these;
The hubs of logs from the "Settler's ellum"
Last of its timber, they could n't sell 'em.

Never an axe had seen their chips,
And the wedges flew from between their lips
Their blunt ends frizzled like celery-tips;
Step and prop-iron, bolt and screw,
Spring, tire, axle, and linchpin too.
Steel of the finest, bright and blue;
Thoroughbrace bison-skin, thick and wide;
Boot, top, dasher, from tough old hide
Found in the pit when the tanner died.
That was the way he "put her through."
"There!" said the Deacon, "naow she 'll dew!"

Do! I tell you, I rather guess
She was a wonder, and nothing less!
Colts grew horses, beards turned gray,
Deacon and deaconess dropped away,
Children and grandchildren–where are they?
But here stood the stout old one-hoss-shay
As fresh as on Lisbon-earthquake day!

Eighteen Hundred–it came and found
The Deacon's masterpiece strong and sound.
Eighteen hundred increased by ten;
"Hahnsum kerridge" they called it then.
Eighteen hundred and twenty came;
Running as usual; much the same.
Thirty and forty at last arrive,
And then come fifty, and FIFTY-FIVE.

Little of all we value here
Wakes on the morn of its hundredth year
Without both feeling and looking queer.
In fact, there's nothing that keeps its youth,
So far as I know, but a tree and truth.
(This is a moral that runs at large;
Take it. You're welcome. No extra charge.)

First of November, the Earthquake-day,
There are traces of age in the one-hoss-shay,
A general flavor of mild decay,
But nothing local as one may say.
There couldn't be, for the Deacon's art
Had made it so like in every part

That there wasn't a chance for one to start.
For the wheels were just as strong as the hills,
And the floor was just as strong as the sills,
And the panels just as strong as the floor,
And the whipple-tree neither less nor more,
And the back crossbar as strong as the fore,
And spring an axle and hub encore.
And yet, as a whole, it is past a doubt
In another hour it will be worn out!

First of November, 'Fifty-five!
This morning the parson takes a drive.
Now, small boys, get out of the way!
Here comes the wonderful one-hoss-shay,
Drawn by a rat-tailed, ewe-necked bay.
"Huddup!" said the parson. – Off went they.

The parson was working his Sunday's text –
Had got to fifthly, and stopped perplexed

At what the–Moses–was coming next.
All at once the horse stood still,
Close by the meet'n'house on the hill.
First a shiver, and then a thrill,
Then something decidedly like a spill,
And the parson was sitting upon a rock,
At half past nine by the meet'n'house clock,
Just the hour of the Earchquake shock!
What do you think the parson found,
When he got up and started around?
The poor old chaise in a heap or mound.
As if it had been to the mill and ground!
You see, of course, if you're not a dunce,
How it went to pieces all at once,
All at once, and nothing first,
Just as bubbles do when they burst.

End of the wonderful one-hoss-shay.
Logic is logic. That's all I say.

APPENDIX 5

James H. Steele Chronology

- 1913 – Born in Chicago, April 3, James Harlan Steele
- 1918 – Influenza pandemic
- 1919 – Started attending school
- 1926 - Hamilton Elementary; this was the first class in which all students went on to high school
- 1930 – Graduated Lakeview High School
- 1930-37 – Employed as insurance clerk
- 1937 – Mother died; went to Michigan State U.
- 1938-41 – Michigan Department of Agriculture, brucellosis testing laboratory
- 1938 – Entered veterinary medical program
- 1940 – Graduate student, Michigan State Health Department laboratory—prepared vaccines/diagnostic tests
- 1941 – Graduated from Michigan State veterinary school, married Aina Oberg
- 1941 – Received USPHS fellowship, Harvard University; started in September
- 1941 – Aina diagnosed with tuberculosis, in sanitariums until March 1949
- 1942 – Graduated with MPH from Harvard; went to work for Ohio Health Department as a public health intern
- 1943 – Commissioned in USPHS as a sanitarian (Chicago, Puerto Rico, Caribbean basin)
- 1944 – First child born, Michael J. Steele Fields
- 1945 – Awarded US Military Forces Service and Victory Medals.
- 1945 – Pan American Health Organization consultant (to present)
- 1945 – Initiated veterinary public health (VPH) program at USPHS
- 1947 - VPH program approved

- 1946 – Investigation of encephalitis and polio in Panama for the Pan American Sanitary Bureau
- 1945 – VPH survey of Haiti and Dominican Republic for the Pan American Sanitary Bureau
- 1946 – Established the first public health ection in the AVMA
- 1947 – Organized the Conference of Public Health Veterinarians, APHA Affiliate
- 1947 – VPH becomes a division of CDC
- 1947 – Veterinary Medical Officer category approved
- 1947 – Named chief, Veterinary Public Health Division, CDC (first in any world government)
- 1947 – Investigation of foot and mouth disease outbreak in Mexico
- 1948 – Attended second Inter-American Brucellosis Conference, Buenos Aires, Argentina
- 1949 – Delegate to World Veterinary Congress, London, England
- 1950 – Organized first CDC Conference on Veterinary Public Health
- 1950 – Founder of the American Board of Veterinary Public Health (later ACVPM)
- 1950 – World Health Organization consultant (to present)
- 1950 – James H. Steele, Jr. born
- 1950 – Became chief veterinary officer and advisor to surgeon general at CDC
- 1950 – *APHA Handbook of Control of Communicable Diseases*, editorial board until present
- 1950 – Consultant, WHO/FAO expert committee on zoonoses, Geneva, Switzerland
- 1951 – Invited speaker, Pan American Veterinary Congress, Lima, Peru
- 1952 – Received Carlos Finlay Medal, Cuba and invited speaker on rabies, Pan American Public Health Congress, Havana, Cuba
- 1952 – David A. J. Steele born

- 1952 – Founder, with Jessie Irons, Southwest Conference of Diseases in Nature
- 1953 – Invited speaker on milk hygiene, World Veterinary Congress, Stockholm, Sweden
- 1955 – Founding member, International Trichinosis Conference
- 1955 – Michigan State University Alumni Award for Distinguished Service
- 1955 – WHO European veterinary public health study group, Geneva, Switzerland
- 1957 – Consultant to establish CEPANZO, the PAHO zoonoses center in Argentina
- 1957 – Invited speaker, WHO European VPH Seminar, Warsaw, Poland
- 1958 – Michigan State University Alumni Award
- 1958 – WHO Expert Committee on Zoonoses and Viral Diseases, Stockholm, Sweden
- 1958 – Consultant to PAHO zoonoses center, Honduras, Costa Rica, Peru, Brazil
- 1959 – Consultant, WHO VPH seminar, Tokyo, Japan
- 1959 – Survey of VPH problems and animal influenza, Southwest Asia
- 1959 – Survey of VPH problems and animal influenza, Middle East
- 1959 – Survey of VPH problems and animal influenza, Alexandria, Egypt
- 1959 – Invited speaker on veterinary epidemiology, World Veterinary Congress, Madrid, Spain
- 1959 – Investigation of public health problems at WHO, Geneva, Switzerland
- 1960 – Michigan State University Veterinary Medicine Award
- 1960 – WHO consultant and visiting lecturer, University of Zagreb, Zagreb, Yugoslavia
- 1960 – WHO consultant to Southern Africa and Congo
- 1960 – Invited speaker, VPH seminar, Nairobi, Africa

- 1960 – Food and Agriculture Organization of the United Nations, consultant until 1982
- 1961 – Consultant, Commission for Technical Cooperation, Africa
- 1963 – USPHS Meritorious Service Medal
- 1963 – Chief of USPHS scientific exchange on veterinary medicine and public health, Russia
- 1963 – Invited speaker on leucosis, World Veterinary Congress, Hanover, Germany
- 1963 – Invited speaker, International Congress of Tropical Medicine, Rio de Janeiro, Brazil
- 1964 – Founder and president of the American Veterinary Epidemiology Society, president 1964 - 1990
- 1964 – US delegate, International quarantine conference, Berne, Switzerland
- 1964 – Invited speaker, WHO VPH conference, Lahore, Pakistan and Tehran, Iran
- 1964 – Honorary member, Philippines Veterinary Medical Association 1964 – Invited speaker at WHO regional diarrhea symposium, Manila, Philippines
- 1965 – Consultant to WHO, evaluation of bioterrorism problems in New Guinea and Papua
- 1965 – Vice president of the American Association of World Health (until 1985)
- 1965 –Delta Omega Lecture, Yale University
- 1965 – Fellow, AAAS
- 1966 – Chairman, FAO/WHO Expert Committee on Zoonoses, Geneva, Switzerland
- 1966 – American Veterinary Epidemiology Society, Karl F. Meyer Gold-Headed Cane Award
- 1967 – World Bank, Inter-American Bank, Agency for International Development, until 1983
- 1967 – Invited speaker, PAHO conference, Buenos Aires, Argentina
- 1967 – Chairman, VPH section, World Veterinary Congress, Paris, France

- 1968 – Consultant to evaluate PL 480 malaria project at USPHS projects in Ceylon
- 1968 – Invited speaker on toxoplasmosis, Pacific Science Congress, Tokyo, Japan
- 1968 – Consultant, CEPANZO advisory group, Buenos Aires, Argentina
- 1968 – Named assistant surgeon general for veterinary affairs
- 1969 – Named honorary member in absentia, International Congress of Tropical Medicine, Tehran, Iran
- 1969 – President's Commission on Consumer Affairs under Virginia Knauer, White House, until 1989
- 1969 – Aina, Jim's first wife, died of tuberculosis in Atlanta, Georgia on March 8.
- 1969 – Chairman, PAHO to evaluate foot and mouth disease, Rio de Janeiro, Brazil
- 1970 – Consultant, WHO Western Pacific PH Seminar, Manila, Philippines
- 1970 – Consultant, WHO Southeast Asia regional office and Mukteswar, New Delhi, India
- 1970 – Lecturer, Universities in India and Ceylon
- 1970 – Chairman, PAHO to evaluate zoonoses program, Buenos Aires, Argentina
- 1971 – PAHO meeting of the ministers of health and agriculture, Lima, Peru
- 1971 – Distinguished Service Award, USPHS (retirement, May 31, 1971)
- 1971 – Joined University of Texas School of Public Health as professor of environmental science
- 1971 – Invited speaker on rabies, Arctic Science Congress, Oulu, Finland
- 1971 – Invited speaker, World Veterinary Congress, Mexico City, Mexico
- 1971 - Founder and president, World Veterinary Epidemiology Society, Mexico City, Mexico
- 1971 – Bronfman Award, APHA

- 1972 – Government consultant, established a national VPH program, consultant on rabies control and zoonoses, Philippines
- 1972 – Consultant, CDC for evaluation of trichinosis research, Poland
- 1972 – Invited speaker on environmental health, European Veterinary Congress, Wiesbaden, Germany
- 1972 – Centennial Award, APHA
- 1973 – Consultant to WHO, bovine tuberculosis, zoonoses, VPH problems in Samoa and Fiji
- 1973 – Michigan State University School of Veterinary Medicine Alumni Award
- 1974 – Consultant to WHO, socioeconomic consequences of zoonoses, Geneva, Switzerland
- 1974 – Invited speaker, Canadian tropical medicine meeting, Montreal, Canada
- 1974 – Honorary member, Canadian Public Health Association, Ottawa, Canada
- 1975 – Invited speaker, World Veterinary Congress, Thessalonica, Greece
- 1975 – James H. Steele Award established
- 1975 – FAO consultant to Cyprus
- 1975 – Honorary member, CDC Epidemiology Intelligence Service
- 1975 – Honorary Diploma and Life Honorary Member, WVA, Thessalonica, Greece
- 1976 – Editorin chief, *CRC Zoonosis Series*, eight volumes
- 1976 – Honored guest, German federal health services centennial, Berlin, Germany
- 1976 – Consultant, CDC, trichinosis research program in Poland
- 1977 – University visiting professor, Texas A&M University
- 1977 – Consultant to WHO, Israeli ministry of health
- 1977 – Consultant and lecturer to WHO, International Congress on Hydatid Disease, Athens Greece
- 1977 – Honorary member, Hellenic Veterinary Medical Society

- 1978 – Trustee, National Foundation for Infectious Diseases
- 1978 – University visiting professor, University of Ontario
- 1978 – University visiting professor, University of Ibadan, Nigeria
- 1978 – Honorary Fellow, Military Surgeons
- 1979 – Consultant, Cyprus
- 1979 – Consultant, Israel
- 1979 – Consultant, confinement of Rift Valley fever, Egypt
- 1979 – Honorary member, World Veterinary Congress, Moscow, USSR
- 1980 – Visiting professor, University of Montreal, Quebec
- 1980 – Chairman, WHO/WFVFH *Salmonella* control conference, Bilthoven, Netherlands
- 1980 – PAHO scientific advisory committee, Buenos Aires, Argentina
- 1980 – Consultant, American Council on Science and Health (to the present)
- 1981 – Invited speaker, World Veterinary Food Hygiene Congress, Dublin, Ireland
- 1981 – Honorary fellow, American Academy of Veterinary Toxicology
- 1981 - Fellow, American College of Epidemiology
- 1982 – Consultant, PAHO/CEPANZO, Buenos Aires, Argentina
- 1982 – Consultant to WHO/FAO, Food-borne Disease and Zoonoses Center, West Berlin, Germany
- 1983 – James Law Lecture Award, New York Veterinary College
- 1983 – Honorary Award of the Surgeon General, USPHS, seventieth birthday
- 1983 – Honorary Diplomate, American College of Veterinary Preventive Medicine
- 1983 – Invited speaker, food irradiation, World Veterinary Congress, Perth, Australia
- 1983 – Visiting professor, University of Pretoria, Onderstepoort, Madunsa, Witswaterand, Cape Town, South Africa

- 1983 – American Society of Tropical Medicine (to the present)
- 1984 – Consultant to WHO, Israel
- 1984 – AVMA International Veterinary Prize
- 1984 – APHA forty-year service award
- 1984 – University of Pennsylvania School of Veterinary Medicine Centennial Year Award
- 1985 – Delegate, World Veterinary Food Hygiene Congress, Budapest, Hungary
- 1985 – Consultant to PAHO, ministerial meeting of health and agriculture, Brasilia, Brazil
- 1986 – Invited speaker, Second World Congress on Foodborne Infections, Berlin, West Germany
- 1986 – Invited speaker for retirement of Dan Kampelmacher, National Institute of Health and the Environment, Bilthoven, Netherlands
- 1986 – National Academy of Practitioners, distinguished practitioner, Washington, DC
- 1987 – AVMA Public Health Council Recognition Award, Chicago, Illinois
- 1987 – American Society of Tropical Veterinary Medicine, Founder's Award
- 1987 – Invited speaker, World Veterinary Congress, Montreal, Canada
- 1987 – Consultant to Dieter Grossklaus, German Federal Health Service, Dahlem, Berlin, Germany
- 1988 – Establishment. of James H. Steele Chair of Public Health, UTSPH, Houston, Tx
- 1988 – Distinguished Service Award, CDC Epidemiology Program
- 1988 – Presidential Award, PAHO, Lima, Peru
- 1988 – AMVA Conference of Public Health Veterinarians Founder's Award
- 1988 – Establishment of the James H. Steele Symposium, APHA
- 1988 – Honorary Diploma, Contributions to WHO and International Health, Berlin, Germany

- 1988 – Consultant, German Federal Health Service, Dahlem, Berlin, Germany
- 1988 – Invited speaker, National Academy of Science Anthrax Symposium, Washington, DC, and Harvard University
- 1989 – Invited speaker, International Anthrax Symposium, Winchester, England
- 1991 – Member, US delegation, OIE/GATT meeting, Paris, France
- 1991 – Consultant, German Federal Health Service, Berlin, Germany
- 1991 – Invited speaker, World Veterinary Congress, Rio de Janeiro, Brazil
- 1992 – Member, US delegation, OIE/GATT meeting, Paris, France
- 1992 – Visiting professor, Humboldt University, Berlin, Germany
- 1992 – German Health Service dedication of VPH Research Center, Berlin, Germany
- 1992 – Invited speaker, Third World Congress on Food-borne Infections, Berlin, Germany
- 1992 – Meeting to update European media on food irradiation at Marseilles, France
- 1992 – Invited speaker, international symposium on *Salmonella* and salmonellosis, Saint-Brieuc, France
- 1993 – AVMA Public Service Award
- 1993 – Member, US delegation, OIE, Paris, France
- 1993 – Rector's Medal, University of Poznan, Poland
- 1993 – German Federal Health Award for Meritorious Services, Berlin, Germany
- 1993 – Eightieth birthday honors, German Federal Health Services, Berlin, Germany
- 1993 – USPHS Officer's Plaque
- 1993 – First James H. Steele Lecture, Robert Wood Johnson Foundation, UTSPH
- 1993 – U. S. Army Medallion
- 1994 – Presidential Award, ACVPM

- 1996 – Guest lecturer, OIE, Paris, France
- 1996 – Founder's Award, Tuskegee College of Veterinary Medicine
- 1996 – Member US delegation, OIE, Paris, France
- 1998 – Alumni Award of Merit, Harvard School of Public Health
- 1998 – Guest lecturer, OIE, Paris, France
- 1998 – Lecturer on food irradiation, World Food-borne Disease Congress, Berlin, Germany
- 1999 – Lecturer, Polish-American collaboration on zoonotic parasitic diseases, San Antonio, TX
- 2000 – Wrote history of veterinary public health program in PAHO.
- 2000 – Received Campanero Award from PAHO for US/Mexico border health services in El Paso, Texas
- 2000 – Invited speaker, History of public health and public health service, AVMA, Salt Lake City, UT
- 2000 – Invited speaker, fiftieth anniversary of the Southwest Conference on Diseases In Nature, San Antonio, TX
- 2000 – Lecturer, German Institute of Veterinary Public Health, for seventieth birthday of Dieter Grossklaus, Berlin, Germany
- 2000 – Consumer Medal, European Congress of Parasitology, University of Poznan, Poland
- 2001 – Lecturer, Pan American Veterinary Congress, 50th Anniversary of PAHO, Panama City, Panama
- 2001 – AVMA, spoke on the history of VPH in the USPHS, Boston, MA
- 2002 – Chaired seminar on food irradiation at World Veterinary Congress, Tunis, Tunisia
- 2003 – AVMA, animal health expert panel, question and answer session with George Beran, Philadelphia, PA
- 2005 – AVMA, spoke on bovine tuberculosis and public health implications, Minneapolis, MN
- 2005 – Co-authored biography of Dr. Henrik Stafseth with Ole Stalheim

- 2005 – Co-authored book on *Mycobacterium bovis* infection in animals and humans with Dr. Charles Thoen.
- 2005 – Received the Surgeon General's Medallion (only veterinarian to ever receive this)
- 2006 – Received PAHO Abraham Horwitz Award for leadership in Inter-American Health
- 2007 – One Medicine, One Health, One World at AVMA in Washington, D.C. presented by Craig Carter, DVM
- 2008 – World Veterinary Conference in Vancouver British Columbia presented paper on Veterinary public health: Past success, new opportunities
- 2008 – Lecture series, Iowa State University

BIBLIOGRAPHY

Baer, George M. *The Natural History of Rabies,* New York Academic Press, 1975.

Barry, John M. *The Great Influenza,* Penguin Books, New York, 2005.

Belotto, Albino; Held, Joe R., Fernandes, Daniela et al. Veterinary Public Health Activities in the Pan American Health Organization over the past 58 Years: 1949-2007, *Veterinary Italiana,* 2007.

Billings, Frank S. *The Relation of Animal Diseases to the Public Health,* Appleton and Company, New York, 1884.

Cordero del Campillo, Miguel. On the History of Veterinary Knowledge in the Old and New Worlds, *Argos,* 2004.

Dehaven, Ron W. Can Our Food Production System Meet Demand in a Changing Global Society? Journal of the American Veterinary Medical Association, 2008.

Delay, Paul D et al. Comparative Study of Fowl Plague Virus and a Virus Isolated from Man, *Public Health Reports,* 1967.

Dunlop, Robert H; Williams David J. Veterinary Medicine: An Illustrated History. , Mosby, 1996.

Fleming, George. Rabies and Hydrophobia, Chapman and Hall, 1872.

Gipson, Fred. *The Cow Killers,* University of Texas Press, Austin, TX, 1956.

Henderson, Donald A. Smallpox Eradication: A Saga of Triumph and Betrayal, *Infectious Diseases in Clinical Practice,* 1999.

Joint WHO/FAO Expert Committee on Zoonoses, First Report, published jointly by FAO and WHO, Geneva, Switzerland, 1950.

Joint WHO/FAO Expert Committee on Zoonoses, Second Report, published jointly by FAO and WHO, Geneva, Switzerland, 1959.

Joint WHO/FAO Expert Committee on Zoonoses, Third Report, published jointly by FAO and WHO, Geneva, Switzerland, 1967.

King, Lonnie J et al. Executive Summary of the AVMA One Health Initiative Task Force Report, *Journal of the American Veterinary Medical Association,* 2008.

Law, James. Reports on Diseases of Domestic Animals, *American Veterinary Review,* 1880.

Murnane, Tom G. Historic and Future Perspectives of the American College of Veterinary Preventive Medicine, *Journal of the American Veterinary Medical Association,* Volume 217, 2000.

Myers, J. Arthur; Steele, James H. *Bovine Tuberculosis: Control in Man and Animals,* Warren H. Green, Inc, St. Louis, MO 1969.

Pappaioanou, Marguerite et al. Veterinarians and Public Health: The Epidemic Intelligence Service of the Centers for Disease Control and Prevention, 1951-2002, *Journal of Veterinary Medical Education,* Volume 30, 2003.

Salmonella outbreak is documented in the *Seventy-second Annual Report of the Commissioner of the Michigan Department of Health* (1944), and in the *Annals of the New York Academy of Sciences* (1956).

Sasselov, Dimitar et al. Harvard Origins of Life Initiative, White Paper to the Harvard Task Force on Science and Technology, December 2004.

Schwabe, Calvin W. *Cattle, Priests and Progress in Medicine,* University of Minnesota Press, Minneapolis, MN, 1978.

Schwabe, Calvin W. *Veterinary Medicine and Human Health,* Baltimore: Williams and Wilkins, 1984.

Stalheim, Ole H. V.; Steele, James H. *Henrik Joakim Stafseth and Public Health Veterinarians,* Ole H. Stalheim, 2005.

Stalheim, Ole H. V. *The Winning of Animal Health,* Iowa State University Press, 1994.

Steele, James H. Over 200 personal interviews, mostly conducted at his home in Houston, Texas, with occasional sessions in College Station, Kentucky, and around the country at meetings; review of correspondence and communications, 1990-2009.

Steele, James H. Veterinary Survey in Mexico, Central America and Colombia: A Summary, *Bulletin of the Pan American Sanitary Bureau,* 1946.

Steele, James H; Habel Karl. Observations on an Outbreak of Encephalomyelitis in Panama, *Journal of the American Veterinary Medical Association,* 1947.

Steele, James H. International Control of Rabies, *Bulletin of the Pan American Sanitary Bureau,* 1950.

Steele, James H. Secretary's Report of the First Meeting of the Council to Organize an American Academy of Veterinary Public Health, 1949.

Steele, James H. Animal Diseases of Interest to Human Health, *The Merck Report,* 1955.

Steele, James H. Diseases Transmitted by Pets and Domestic Animals, *Consultant,* 1963.

Steele, James H. The Socioeconomic Responsibilities of Veterinary Medicine, *Public Health Reports,* 1964.

Steele, James H. A Bookshelf on Veterinary Public Health, *American Journal of Public Health,* 1973.

Steele, James H. The Epidemiology and Control of Rabies, *Scandinavian Journal of Infectious Diseases,* 1973.

Steele, James H; Arambulo, Primo V; Beran, George W. The Epidemiology of Zoonoses in the Philippines, *Archives of Environmental Health,* 1973.

Steele, James H. The Development of Disease Surveillance: Its Uses in Disease Control that Relate to Public and Animal Health, *Animal Disease Monitoring,* 1975.

Steele, James H. Veterinary Public Health in the United States, 1776 to 1976, *Journal of the American Veterinary Medical Association*, 1976.

Steele, James H. The Zoonoses in the South Pacific and their Public Health Significance, 1977.

Steele, James H. Veterinary Public Health: Early History and Recent World Developments, *Journal of the American Veterinary Medical Association, 1978*

Steele, James H., ed. *CRC Handbook Series on Zoonoses,* Boca Raton, FL: CRC Press, 1980.

Steele, James H. Population Trends: A Historical Review and Projection as to its Effects on Veterinary Medicine and Science, presented to the 20th Anniversary of the American Veterinary Epidemiology Society, 1983.

Steele, James H. The Zoonoses, *International Journal of Zoonoses, 1985.*

Steele, James H. Pesticides and Food Safety: Perception vs. Reality, *Proceedings of the 93rd Meeting of the US Animal Health Association, 1989.*

Steele, James H. Radiation Processing of Food, *Journal of the American Veterinary Medical Association,* 1992.

Steele, James H. History of Veterinary Public Health in the United States of America, *Review of Science and Technology, Office of International Epizootics,* 1991.

Steele, James H. It's Time for Food Irradiation, *Journal of Public Health Policy,* 1993.

Steele, James H; and Schultz, Myron G. Veterinary Public Health and Alexander D. Langmuir, *American Journal of Epidemiology,* 1996.

Steele, James H. The 50th Anniversary of the Veterinary Medical Corps Officers of the US Public Health Service, *Journal of the American Veterinary Medical Association,* 1998.

Steele, James H. Food Irradiation: A Public Health Measure Long Overdue, *21st Century Science and Technology,* 1999.

Steele, James H. Polish and American Collaboration on Zoonotic Parasitic Studies, 1960-1967, *Military Medicine,* 2000.

Steele, James H. Food Irradiation: A Public Health Challenge for the 21st Century, Clinical Infectious Diseases, 2001.

Steele, James H. Veterinary Public Health: Past Success, New Opportunities, keynote address at a Symposium Honoring the Legacy of Dr. James H. Steele, St. Louis, MO at the Conference of Research Workers in Animal Diseases, December 4, 2005.

Steele, James H. A Personal History of Veterinary Public Health in the Pan American Health Organization, Veterinary Italiana, 2007.

Steele, James H. Veterinary Public Health: Past Success, New Opportunities, Preventive Veterinary Medicine, 2008.

Thacker, Stephen B et al. Epidemic Intelligence Service of the Centers for Disease Control and Prevention: 50 Years of Training and Service in Applied Epidemiology, American Journal of Epidemiology, Volume 154, 2001.

The Last Two Million Years, The Reader's Digest Association, London, 1981.

Tierkel, Ernest. Oral History Interview with James Steele, DVM, 1971, donated to the National Library of Medicine, 1988.

Turnbull, Peter C. B. Anthrax vaccines: past, present and future, Vaccine 1991 Volume 9 Pages 533-539

Webster, Leslie Tillotson, Rabies, New York, Macmillan, 1942.

West, Geoffrey P. Rabies in Animals and Man, Newton Abbot, David and Charles, 1972.

Williams, Ralph C. The United States Public Health Service, 1798-1950, Commissioned Officers Association, 1951.

Made in the USA